THE WELSH CUP
1877-2019

THE COMPLETE RESULTS

Statistics sourced from the

Welsh Football Data Archive

FOREWORD

We are indebted to Dave Collins and Mel Thomas who act for the Welsh Football Data Archive which provided the bulk of the information contained within this book.

In addition, special thanks go to Mick Blakeman, who helped greatly with a number of queries and anomalies which inevitably arose during the final edit of the text.

British Library Cataloguing in Publication Data
A catalogue record for this book is available from the British Library

ISBN 978-1-86223-416-1

Copyright © 2019, SOCCER BOOKS LIMITED. (01472 696226)
72 St. Peter's Avenue, Cleethorpes, N.E. Lincolnshire, DN35 8HU, England

www.soccer-books.co.uk

All rights are reserved. No part of this publication may be reproduced, stored in a retrieval system or transmitted, in any form or by any means, electronic, mechanical, photocopying, recording, or otherwise, without the prior written permission of Soccer Books Limited.

Printed by 4Edge Ltd.

THE WELSH CUP – BRIEF HISTORY

The Football Association of Wales was founded in 1876 and, for the first 110 years of its existence, was based in the north of the country at Ruabon near Wrexham, before moving down to it's present location in Cardiff.

The Welsh Cup itself is one of the oldest competitions in world football with the very first-ever match being played on the 13th October 1877, a game between The Druids and Newtown which ended in a 1-1 draw.

Over the 140-year history of the competition and particularly in the earlier years, clubs were frequently unable to replay drawn matches or indeed to fulfil some fixtures at all because of the difficulty and costs of travelling. On occasion this led to winning teams withdrawing from the competition teams who had lost earlier rounds were reinstated. Information about this has been included where possible. In addition, many teams who won replays received byes in the following round to ensure that the competition could continue without delays caused by the difficulty of arranging further fixtures.

Between 1877 and 1995 all Welsh clubs were invited to participate (including those which played in various English Leagues) and, in addition, a number of English clubs (mostly from area bordering Wales) were also allowed to play. On rare occasions, this led to two English teams facing each other in the Welsh Cup Final!

However, between 1996 to 2011, participation was limited to clubs playing in Welsh Leagues which, in effect, excluded Cardiff City FC, Swansea City FC, Newport County FC, Wrexham FC, Colwyn Bay FC and Merthyr Tydfil Town FC completely.

In 2011, the six clubs mentioned above were again invited to compete in the competition but only Wrexham FC and Merthyr Tydfil Town FC accepted the invitation. The final change in the eligibility of clubs which could participate took place in 2012 when UEFA ruled that only clubs within the Football Association of Wales League Pyramid would be able to qualify for European competitions via the Welsh qualification criteria. This, effectively, seems to have excluded the so-called 'exiles' from further participation in the Welsh Cup.

1877/78 Welsh Cup

First Round

Druids FC Ruabon	1-1	Newtown
Bangor	1-0	Carnarvon
Oswestry	12-0	Chirk
Gwersyllt Foresters	0-0	Northwich Victoria
Corwen	0-0	Bala
Newtown White Stars	1-0	Ruabon
Wrexham	3-1	Civil Service Wrexham
Swansea	v	Aberystwyth (w/o)
Rhosllanerchrugog	bye	
23rd RWF Newtown (withdrew)	v	Llangollen (w/o)

First Round Replays

Newtown	0-4	Druids FC Ruabon
Northwich Victoria	1-4, 0-4 or 1-2	Gwersyllt Foresters

Goals were disputed by both sides!

Bala	0-0	Corwen

First Round Second Replay

Corwen	1-0	Bala

Second Round

Bangor	7-0	Corwen
Druids FC Ruabon	3-0	Rhosllanerchrugog
Gwersyllt Foresters	2-1	Llangollen
Wrexham	1-1	Oswestry
Aberystwyth (withdrew)	v	Newtown White Star (w/o)

Match result not found

Second Round Replay

Oswestry	0-2	Wrexham

Third Round

Wrexham	8-0	Gwersyllt Foresters
Druids FC Ruabon	1-1	Newtown White Star
Bangor	bye	

Third Round Replay

Newtown White Star	1-1	Druids FC Ruabon

Third Round Second Replay

Druids FC Ruabon	3-0	Newtown White Star

Semi-finals

Bangor	0-0	Druids FC Ruabon

Played at the Racecourse

Wrexham	bye	

Semi-final Replay

Druids FC Ruabon	1-0 (aet)	Bangor

Played at Rhyl

1878 WELSH CUP FINAL

30th March 1878 at Acton Park, Wrexham

Wrexham	1-0	Druids

Jas Davies

Wrexham: E Phennah, C Murless, T W Davies, A Davies, E A Cross, E Evans snr, C Edwards, J Davies, John Price, E Evans jnr, H Loxham

Druids: B Roberts, J Powell, L Kenrick, H Morris, W Williams, C F Ketley, E Bowen, Dr D Grey, G F Thomson, J Jones, J Vaughan

Referee: J W Thomas (Stoke)

Attendance: 1,500

1878/79 Welsh Cup

First Round

Carnarvon	0-1	Bangor
Friars School Bangor	1-0	Rhyl
Newtown White Star	4-1	Aberystwyth
Rhosllanerchrugog	1-1	Gwersyllt Rangers
Chirk	1-0	Ruabon
Llangollen	8-1	Mold
Druids FC Ruabon (withdrew)	v	Civil Service Wrexham (w/o)
Corwen	0-2	Wrexham
Oswestry	bye	

First Round Replay

Gwersyllt Rangers	0-3	Rhosllanerchrugog

Second Round

Rhosllanerchrugog (withdrew)		Bangor (w/o)
Chirk	1-0	Trinity Shrewsbury
Llangollen	0-1	Newtown White Star
Friars School Bangor	1-3	Wrexham
Oswestry	6-0	Civil Service Wrexham
Newtown	bye	

Third Round

Newtown	3-1	Chirk
Bangor	2-2	Newtown White Star
Wrexham	bye	

Third Round Replay

Newtown White Star	3-1	Bangor

Bangor left the field before the end of the game and were deemed to have scratched.

Semi-finals

Newtown White Star	1-1	Newtown
Wrexham	2-0	Oswestry

Semi-final Replay

Newtown	1-3	Newtown White Star

1879 WELSH CUP FINAL

29th March 1879 at the Cricket Field, Oswestry

Newtown White Star   1-0   Wrexham
E Rees

Newtown White Stars: G Mumford, J Davies, T Jones, E H Morgan, T Pryce, W Andrew, G Woosnam, E Gittins (capt), G Thomas, S Davies, E Rees

Wrexham: J Davies, C Murless, T W Davies, F Owen, C Edwards, E A Cross, T Boden, J W Lloyd, J Price, E Evans, H Loxham

Referee: A E Daniel (Birmingham)

Attendance: 2,500

1879/80 Welsh Cup

First Round

Wrexham	1-1	Northwich Victoria
Civil Service Wrexham	1-1	Gwersyllt Foresters
Wrexham Albion	2-1	Wrexham Grosvenor
Newtown White Star	3-0	Dolgellau
Corwen	7-3	Bala
Newtown Excelsior	6-0	All Saints (Salop)
Aberystwyth	1-0	Oswestry
Ruthin	4-0	Llangollen
Mold (withdrew)	v	Druids FC Ruabon (w/o)
23rd RWF (withdrew)	v	Rhyl (w/o)

First Round Replays

Northwich Victoria	0-1	Wrexham
Gwersyllt Foresters	—	Civil Service Wrexham

The result of this replay is not recorded, but was a draw.

First Round Second Replay

Civil Service Wrexham	1-2	Gwersyllt Foresters

Second Round

Rhyl	1-1	Aberystwyth
Newtown Excelsior	1-0	Wrexham Albion
Druids FC Ruabon	1-0	Wrexham
Newtown White Star	2-0	Gwersyllt Foresters
Ruthin	3-0	Corwen

Second Round Replay

Aberystwyth	0-0	Rhyl

Played at Dolgellau

Second Round Second Replay

Rhyl	0-3	Aberystwyth

Played at Dolgellau

Third Round

Druids FC Ruabon	6-0	Aberystwyth
Newtown Excelsior	1-1	Ruthin

Both matches played at the Rhosddu Recreation Ground

Newtown White Star   bye

Third Round Replay

Newtown Excelsior	2-4	Ruthin

Played at the Racecourse, Wrexham

Semi-finals

Druids FC Ruabon	3-1	Newtown White Star

Played at Oswestry

Ruthin   bye

1880 WELSH CUP FINAL

13th March 1880 at the Racecourse, Wrexham

Druids	2-1	Ruthin
Vaughan, John Jones		Goodwin

Druids: B Roberts, J Powell, Llewelyn Kenrick, W Williams, E Bowen, Dennis Heywood, John Jones, K Cross, C F Ketley, Jack Jones, J Vaughan

Ruthin: H Parry, J Roberts, J Halley, R Maddocks, P Mostyn, R Williams, W P Owen, W H Roberts (capt), A Lloyd, U Goodwin, G H Simon

Referee: Mr Brooks (Wolverhampton)

Attendance: 4,000

1880/81 Welsh Cup

First Round

Shrewsbury Engineers	0-1	Newtown White Star

A protest was lodged that the referee was ineligible to take charge so a rematch was ordered:

Shrewsbury Engineers	0-0	Newtown White Star
Llanidloes	5-0	Oswestry
Dolgellau Idris	0-1	Ruthin
Druids	3-1	Llangollen
Northwich Victoria	3-0	Wrexham Grosvenor
Mold	0-1 or 0-2	Wrexham

One of the goals was disputed.

Civil Service Wrexham	3-1	Gwersyllt Foresters
Chirk	bye	Llangollen

First Round Replay

Newtown White Star	1-0	Shrewsbury Engineers

Second Round

Ruthin	1-1	Druids

Ruthin then withdrew

Newtown White Star	2-1	Wrexham

Played at Rhosddu Recreation ground

Llanidloes	1-0	Civil Service Wrexham
Northwich Victoria	2-1	Chirk

Semi-finals

Druids 3-0 Northwich Victoria
Played at the Racecourse, Wrexham
Newtown White Star 2-0 Llanidloes
Played at Rhosddu Recreation ground

1881 WELSH CUP FINAL

26th March 1881 at the Racecourse, Wrexham

Druids 2-0 Newtown White Star

Vaughan, Cross

Druids: B Roberts, J Powell, A Powell, W Williams, E Bowen, D Heywood, J W Lloyd, C F Ketley, K Cross, J Jones, J Vaughan

White Stars: H Hibbott, T Jones, D Owen, A Andrew, E H Morgan, W Andrew, E Gittins (capt.), D Williams, E Rees, Williams, Woosnam

Referee: C Crump (Wolverhampton)

Attendance: 4,000

1881/82 Welsh Cup

First Round

Hartford St Johns	1-3	Gwersyllt Foresters
Holywell	0-3	Northwich Victoria A
Wrexham Athletic	4-1	Rhyl
Equitable (Coedpoeth)	3-4	Flint Amateurs (Mold)
Wrexham Athletic (Wrexham)	2-1	Hare & Hounds
Northwich Victoria B (w/o)	v	Ruthin (withdrew)
Dolgellau Idris	0-6	Druids A
Aberystwyth	2-1	Druids B
Shrewsbury Castle Blues	1-0	Welshpool Warriors
Chirk	4-3	Oswestry White Stars
Berwyn Rangers	4-0	Oswestry

Second Round

Wrexham A	2-0	Coedpoeth
Played at Coedpoeth		
Northwich Victoria	7-0	Mold
Gwersyllt Foresters	bye	
Wrexham B	0-5	Druids
Ruthin	11-0	Rhostyllen
Aberystwyth	3-1	Shrewsbury Castle Blues
Oswestry White Stars	2-1	Chirk

A replay was ordered following a protest by Chirk

Second Round Replay

Chirk 2-1 Oswestry White Stars

Third Round

Druids 0-0 Ruthin
Played at the Racecourse
Chirk 2-1 Aberystwyth
Played at Newtown.
Wrexham A 0-0 Northwich Victoria
Played at the Racecourse, Wrexham. The match was subsequently declared void.

Third Round Replay

Ruthin 1-2 Druids
Played at the Racecourse
Northwich Victoria 5-1 Wrexham A
Played at Wynnstay Park.

Semi-finals

Chirk 2-2 Northwich Victoria
Played at the Racecourse, Wrexham.
Druids bye

Semi-final Replay

Northwich Victoria 5-1 Chirk
Played at the Racecourse, Wrexham.

1882 WELSH CUP FINAL

8th April 1882 at the Racecourse, Wrexham

Druids 5-0 Northwich Victoria

Ketley 2, Bowen 2, Own goal

Druids: B Roberts, J Powell, A Powell, W Williams, E Roberts, D Heywood, E Bowen, C Ketley, J P Davies, Jack Jones, J Vaughan

Northwich Victoria: J Hitchens, F W Hughes, E Butterworth, A F Russell, W Hughes, B Dobell, A Atherton, W Spruce, G Vernon, E Turnbull, G Plant

Referee: Mr Hindle (Darwen)

Attendance: 2,000

1882/83 Welsh Cup

First Round

Rhyl (w/o)	v	Corwen

Corwen failed to appear on the date fixed for the tie

Dolgellau Idris	6-1	Holywell Rovers
Played at Corwen.		
Denbigh	3-3	Ruthin
Aberystwyth	bye	
Hartford	9-0	Crown FC Wrexham
Hare & Hounds FC Wrexham	1-1	Coedpoeth
Wrexham	4-1	Davenham
Hope	1-10	Northwich Victoria
Played at Caergwrle		
Trefonen	0-1	Oswestry White Stars
Played at Oswestry		
Chirk	2-3	Druids
Black Park 0-5	0-5	Berwyn Rangers
Dolgellau Mountaineers	bye	

First Round Replay

Coedpoeth	2-2	Hare & Hounds FC

Both clubs progressed to the next round

Second Round

Aberystwyth	2-0	Dolgellau Idris

A protest by Idris following the game was rejected.

Ruthin	bye	
Rhyl	3-2	Hartford
Hare & Hounds Wrexham	1-5	Northwich Victoria
Druids	12-1	Dolgellau Mountaineers
Berwyn Rangers	5-2	Oswestry White Stars

Third Round

Northwich Victoria	1-1	Berwyn Rangers
Wrexham	4-2	Ruthin

Played at Rhosddu recreation ground

Aberystwyth	1-4	Druids
Rhyl	bye	

Third Round Replay

Berwyn Rangers	1-1	Northwich Victoria

Both clubs progressed to the next round.

Fourth Round

Wrexham	5-2	Rhyl

Played at Rhosddu recreation ground

Berwyn Rangers	2-5	Druids
Northwich Victoria	bye	

Semi-finals

Druids	3-0	Northwich Victoria
Wrexham	bye	

1883 WELSH CUP FINAL

21st April 1883 at the Racecourse, Wrexham

Wrexham	1-0	Druids

W Roberts

Wrexham: J Trainer, G Thomas, W Davies, T Burke, E Griffiths, H Edwards, R Davies, W Roberts, M Davies, J Davies, J Jones

Druids: H Adams, J Powell (capt), A Powell, E Bowen, R Roberts, W Williams, J W Lloyd, J Doughty, C F Ketley, Jack Jones, J Vaughan

Referee: W H Holt (Shrewsbury)

Attendance: 2,000

1883/84 Welsh Cup

First Round

Oswestry White Stars	2-2	Chirk
Trefonen	5-2	Black Park

Played at Woodhill, Oswestry

Corwen	0-6	Wrexham
Coedpoeth	0-9	Druids
Gwersyllt Foresters	6-5	Hare & Hounds FC Wrexham
Rhostyllen Victoria	1-1	Crown FC Wrexham

Northwich Victoria (withdrew due to distance) v Rhyl (w/o)

Davenham	16-0	Holywell Rovers
Hartford	bye	
Berwyn Rangers	3-1	Ruthin
Denbigh	5-2	Ellesmere
Hope Wanderers	bye	

First Round Replays

Chirk	1-4	Oswestry White Stars
Crown FC Wrexham	1-1	Rhostyllen Victoria

Both clubs progressed to the next round.

Second Round

Trefonen	0-4	Oswestry White Stars

Played at Woodhill, Oswestry

Wrexham	2-0	Rhostyllen Victoria
Druids	7-1	Gwersyllt Foresters
Crown FC Wrexham	bye	
Hartford	2-3	Rhyl
Davenham	bye	
Denbigh	5-2	Hope Wanderers

Third Round

Oswestry White Stars	bye	
Berwyn Rangers	5-1	Denbigh
Wrexham	5-1	Crown FC Wrexham
Rhyl	3-1	Davenham
Denbigh	1-5	Berwyn Rangers

Played at Llangollen

Fourth Round

Druids	3-1	Wrexham
Oswestry White Stars	bye	
Berwyn Rangers	bye	

Semi-finals

Oswestry White Stars	2-1	Berwyn Rangers
Druids	4-1	Rhyl

1884 WELSH CUP FINAL

5th April 1884 at the Racecourse, Wrexham

Oswestry White Stars	0-0	Druids

Oswestry White Stars: R T Gough, J H Williams, S Powell, W T Foulkes, M Evans, S Smith, J Evans, E G Shaw, W H Davies, G Farmer, J Roach

Druids: B Roberts, R Jones, A Powell, E Bowen, R Davies, R Roberts, J Doughty, T Jones, W Davies, R A Jones, W Williams

Referee: T Sloan (Liverpool)

Attendance: 2,000

1884 WELSH CUP FINAL REPLAY

14th April 1884 at the Racecourse, Wrexham

Oswestry White Stars 1-0 Druids

J Evans

Druids: B Roberts, R Jones, A Powell, E Bowen, R Davies, R Roberts, J Doughty, T Jones, W Davies, R A Jones, W Williams

Oswestry White Stars: R T Gough, J H Williams, S Powell, W T Foulkes, M Evans, S Smith, J Evans, E G Shaw, W H Davies, G Farmer, J Roach

Referee: G Tagg (Wrexham)

Attendance: 3,000

1884/85 Welsh Cup

First Round

Northwich Victoria	3-0	Crewe Alexandra
Davenham	bye	
Rhyl	1-1	Bangor
Carnarvon Athletic	bye	
Trefonen	1-2	Newtown
Shrewsbury Castle Blues	8-1	Ellesmere
Welshpool	0-8	Oswestry White Stars
Wrexham Olympic	1-1	Druids
Played at Oswestry		
Rhostyllen Victoria	0-5	Crown Wrexham
Chirk	11-0	Gwersyllt

First Round Replays

Bangor	1-1	Rhyl

A replay was ordered after Rhyl protested about the eligibility of some of Bangor's players.

Druids	2-1	Wrexham Olympic
Played at Oswestry		

First Round Second Replay

Rhyl	0-1	Bangor

Second Round

Northwich Victoria	4-1	Davenham
Carnarvon Athletic	5-2	Bangor
Shrewsbury Castle Blues	1-2	Newtown
Oswestry White Stars	bye	
Rhostyllen Victoria	0-0	Chirk
Druids	bye	

Second Round Replay

Chirk	4-0	Rhostyllen Victoria

Third Round

Northwich Victoria	bye	
Carnarvon Athletic	bye	
Newtown	1-1	Oswestry White Stars
Druids	2-0	Chirk

Third Round Replay

Oswestry White Stars 1-0 Newtown

Newtown disputed the goal and walked off before the end of the game.

Semi-finals

Druids	3-1	Carnarvon Athletic
Played at the Racecourse, Wrexham		
Oswestry White Stars	2-1	Northwich Victoria
Played at Crewe		

1885 WELSH CUP FINAL

7th March 1885 at the Racecourse, Wrexham

Druids 1-1 Oswestry White Stars

Powell *Topham*

Druids: J Jones, W H M Jones, R Jones, J Davies, W Williams, R Davies, E Bowen, R Doughty, A Powell, R A Jones, T Jones

Oswestry White Stars: R T Gough, J H Williams, S Powell, W T Foulkes, A Roberts, M Evans, J E Davies, J Evans, R Topham, G Farmer, J Roach

Referee: T Sloan (Liverpool)

Attendance: 2,000

1885 WELSH CUP FINAL REPLAY

14th April 1884 at the Racecourse, Wrexham

Druids 3-1 Oswestry White Stars

After extra time. 1-1 at full time

Bowen, Powell, Unknown scorer *J Evans*

Druids: J Jones, W H M Jones, R Jones, J Davies, W Williams, R Davies, E Bowen, R Doughty, A Powell, J Doughty, R A Jones

Oswestry White Stars: R T Gough, J H Williams, S Powell, W T Foulkes, A Roberts, M Evans, J E Davies, J Evans, R Topham, G Farmer, J Roach

Referee: T Sloan (Liverpool)

Attendance: 2,000

1885/86 Welsh Cup

First Round

Berwyn Rangers	2-1	Rhostyllen

A replay was ordered following a protest regarding the roping off of the ground.

Druids	5-1	Chirk
Wrexham Olympic	1-5	Ellesmere

Shrewsbury Castle Blues	6-0	Trefonen
Oswestry	1-2	Newtown
Welshpool	5-2	Vyrnwy United
Llanfyllin	8-0	Wem White Stars
Chester	0-3	Crewe Britannia
Davenham	0-2	Northwich Victoria
Crewe Alexandra	7-1	Hartford
Portmadoc	2-1	Carnarvon
Rhyl	1-4	Bangor

First Round Replay

Rhostyllen	2-1	Berwyn Rangers

Second Round

Druids	7-1	Ellesmere
Rhostyllen	bye	
Welshpool	0-0	Newtown
Shrewsbury Castle Blues	3-0	Llanfyllin
Played at Llanfyllin		
Crewe Alexandra	5-1	Crewe Britannia
Northwich Victoria	bye	
Bangor	4-0	Portmadoc

Second Round Replay

Newtown	4-0	Welshpool

Third Round

Rhostyllen	0-0	Druids
Shrewsbury Castle Blues	1-1	Newtown
Crewe Alexandra	1-1	Northwich Victoria
Bangor	bye	

Third Round Replays

Druids	5-1	Rhostyllen
Newtown	2-0	Shrewsbury Castle Blues
Northwich Victoria	1-1	Crewe Alexandra

Third Round Second Replay

Crewe Alexandra	2-1	Northwich Victoria

Semi-finals

Bangor	0-0	Newtown
Druids	3-0	Crewe Alexandra
Played at the Racecourse, Wrexham		

Semi-final Replay

Bangor	0-0	Newtown
Played at Chester		

Semi-final Second Replay

Bangor	0-1	Newtown
Played at the Racecourse, Wrexham		

1886 WELSH CUP FINAL

3rd April 1886 at the Racecourse, Wrexham

Druids	4-0	Newtown

Vaughan 2, Bowen, J Doughty

Druids: G H Williams, A Powell, W H M Jones, W Williams, E Moulden, J Davies, W Owen, E Bowen, J Doughty, R Doughty, J Vaughan

Newtown: A Townsend, J W H Lloyd, H Owen, W Gentle, J Andrew, A Jones, J W Lloyd, W Owen, H Hibbott, J Chapman, D Andrew

Referee: T Sloan (Liverpool)

Attendance: 3,000

1886/87 Welsh Cup

First Round

Over Wanderers	0-3	Northwich Victoria
Chester	4-2	Hartford St Johns
Davenham (w/o)	v	Crewe Alexandra (withdrew)
Carnarvon Wanderers	3-1	Portmadoc
Llandudno Gloddaeth	8-0	Rhyl
Bangor	bye	
Oswestry	4-0	Oswestry Cambrians
Llanfyllin	v	Aberystwyth Town

Aberystwyth Town were drawn to play Llanfyllin in the First Round. This was stated in a meeting of the Town club held during September with the match due to take place at Llanfyllin on Saturday 16th October 1886. However, the match was not played. The 23rd October 1886 edition of the Aberystwyth Observer contained the following report which explains that Aberystwyth probably scratched to Llanfyllin.

"Saturday, October the 16th, 1886, will be a day long remembered in the history of North Cardiganshire, and Abersytwyth in particular. A storm of peculiar violence, accompanied by excessively heavy rains, raged the whole of Friday, but as the day advanced and evening and night drew on the wind increased in power and violence, so that it became dangerous for parties to be abroad."

The report later stated that no trains ran on the Saturday, so we can only assume that the team were unable to travel and therefore scratched. Later issues of the Observer have Aber Town playing regularly but there was no mention of any match with Llanfyllin.

Wem White Stars	0-10	Shrewsbury
Newtown	14-0	Welshpool
Vyrnwy United	bye	
Chirk	10-1	Wrexham Excelsior
Ellesmere	0-7	Wrexham Olympic
Rhostyllen	1-4	Druids

Second Round

Davenham	0-0	Chester
Northwich Victoria	bye	
Llandudno FC	2-7	Bangor
Carnarvon Wanderers	bye	
Vyrnwy United	1-7	Llanfyllin
Shrewsbury	0-1	Newtown
Oswestry	bye	
Druids	0-1	Chirk
Wrexham Olympic	bye	

Second Round Replay

Chester	1-2	Davenham

Third Round

Northwich Victoria	1-1	Davenham
Carnarvon Wanderers	2-7	Bangor
Oswestry	1-1	Newtown
Wrexham Olympic	1-8	Chirk

Third Round Replays

Davenham	1-0	Northwich Victoria
Newtown	1-2 (aet)	Oswestry

Fourth Round

Davenham	bye	
Bangor	bye	
Chirk	bye	
Llanfyllin	0-2	Oswestry

Semi-finals

Chirk	2-2	Bangor
Played at the Racecourse		
Davenham	2-1	Oswestry
Played at Crewe		

Semi-final Replay

Bangor	0-2	Chirk
Played at the Racecourse, Wrexham		

1887 WELSH CUP FINAL

16th April 1887 at Nantwich Road, Crewe

Chirk	2-1	Davenham
W Owen 2		Holland

Chirk: E Povey, T Wynne, 'Di' Jones, H Owen, J Owen, J Jones, W Owen, P Griffiths, T Williams, G Owen, G Griffiths

Davenham: F Leather, H Goulding, R Riley, D Dalton, A Pye, G Vernon, H Holland, W Rowbottom, R Leather, H Cross, L Stringer

Referee: W H Jope (Wednesbury)

Attendance: 1,500

1887/88 Welsh Cup

First Round

Vale of Llangollen	5-0	Wrexham Excelsior
Wrexham Olympic	4-0	Alyn White Stars
Druids	3-0	Rhostyllen Victoria
Chirk	bye	
Shrewsbury Town	0-2	Oswestry
Newtown	9-0	Wem White Stars
Ellesmere	0-8	Welshpool

Welshpool were dismissed from the competition following a protest and Ellesmere progressed.

Llanfyllin	bye	
Davenham	2-0	Chester St Oswalds
Crewe Alexandra	2-3	Northwich Victoria
Over Wanderers	bye	
Bangor	3-1	Llandudno FC
Portmadoc	3-1	Corwen
Mold	0-1	Ruthin

Second Round

Wrexham Olympic	4-1	Vale of Llangollen

Vale protested the result due to a late start and the fact that ground was not enclosed. This was sustained and a replay was ordered. Wrexham refused to appear so Vale progressed to the next round.

Druids	1-2	Chirk
Oswestry	6-0	Ellesmere
Newtown	Not known	Llanfyllin

The result is not recorded but Newtown progressed.

Northwich Victoria	3-0	Over Wanderers
Davenham	bye	
Bangor	1-2	Mold
Portmadoc	bye	

Third Round

Chirk	3-1	Vale of Llangollen
Newtown	3-1	Oswestry
Northwich Victoria	2-0	Davenham
Mold (w/o)	v	Portmadoc (withdrew)

Semi-finals

Mold	0-2	Newtown
Played at Oswestry		
Chirk	5-0	Northwich Victoria
Played at Chester		

1888 WELSH CUP FINAL

5th May 1888 at the Chester Road, Wrexham

Chirk	5-0	Newtown

W Owen 2, G Owen, Davies, G Griffiths

Chirk: E Povey, T Wynne, 'Di' Jones, J Jones, Wise, P Griffiths, W Owen, J Davies, T Williams, G Owen, G Griffiths

Newtown: H Hibbott, J W H Lloyd, H Owen, T Davies, N Gentle, R Jones, W Owen, C Davies, D Andrew, Tom Worthington, J Chapman

Referee: Mr Darley (Blackburn)   **Att**: 3,000

1888/89 Welsh Cup

First Round

Holywell	2-4	Ruthin
St Asaph	0-7	Bangor
Mold	3-0	Portmadoc
Played at Corwen		
Builth	1-8	Chirk
Played at Knighton		
Oswestry	1-0	Newtown Royal Welsh Warehouse
Llangollen Rovers	5-4	Alyn White Stars
Druids	2-2	Wrexham
Rhostyllen Victoria	8-1	Corwen
Vale of Llangollen	bye	
Nantwich (w/o)	v	Crewe Alexandra (withdrew)
Over Wanderers	1-2	Northwich Victoria
Chester St Oswalds	5-1	Crewe Athletic
Davenham	bye	

First Round Replay

Wrexham	2-1	Druids

Second Round

Ruthin	9-0	Mold

A protest by Mold about poor light during the game was upheld and a replay was ordered.

Bangor	bye	
Chirk (w/o)	v	Oswestry (withdrew)
Wrexham	4-1	Alyn White Stars

Alyn protested that Wrexham had fielded an ineligible player and a replay was ordered.

Rhostyllen Victoria	3-3	Vale of Llangollen
Davenham	2-2	Nantwich
Northwich Victoria	2-1	Chester St Oswalds

Second Round Replays

Ruthin	3-0	Mold
Played at St Asaph		
Wrexham	3-0	Alyn White Stars
Vale of Llangollen	1-2	Rhostyllen Victoria
Nantwich	3-2	Davenham

The match was abandoned due to poor light when the scoreline was 3-2.

Second Round Second Replay

Davenham	5-1	Nantwich

Third Round

Ruthin	1-4	Bangor
Wrexham	1-0	Rhostyllen Victoria

Rhostyllen lodged a protest and a replay was ordered.

Chirk	bye	
Davenham	0-0	Northwich Victoria

Third Round Replays

Wrexham	4-0	Rhostyllen Victoria
Northwich Victoria	4-3	Davenham

Semi-finals

Wrexham	2-3	Bangor
Played at Chester		
Chirk	1-1	Northwich Victoria
Played at Chester		

Semi-final Replay

Chirk	2-3	Northwich Victoria
Played at Chester		

1889 WELSH CUP FINAL

22nd April 1889 at the Racecourse, Wrexham

Bangor	2-1	Northwich Victoria
Hughes, Roberts		Leather

Bangor: M Hewitt, S Willman, J S Jones, D C Davies, E P W Hughes, P Lerry, R Jones, D Lewis, W Lewis, R O Roberts, D Jones

Northwich Victoria: Fallows, Maddock, Cross, Hankey, Whitlow, D Dalton, W Rowbottom, R Leather, Lever, Pickering, Upton

Referee: Mr Mitchell (Blackburn)

Attendance: 4,000

1889/90 Welsh Cup

First Round

Rhyl	4-6	Bangor
Gloddaeth Llandudno FC	10-0	St Asaph
Colwyn Bay	15-0	St Asaph Wanderers
Portmadoc	bye	
Newtown	1-0	Builth
Shrewsbury Town	15-0	Aberdare
Rhostyllen Victoria	8-1	Vale of Llangollen
Rhosllanerchrugog	1-2	Overton
Played at Johnstown		
Druids	4-0	Wynnstay
Chirk	1-0	Oswestry
Wrexham (w/o)	v	Nantwich

Nantwich withdrew due to the distance to be travelled.

Over Wanderers	4-3	Mold Alexandra
Hartford & Davenham Utd	2-0	Northwich Victoria
Crewe Alexandra Reserves	bye	

Second Round

Bangor	4-0	Gloddaeth Llandudno FC
Portmadoc	1-0	Colwyn Bay
Newtown	1-0	Builth
Shrewsbury Town	bye	
Newtown	bye	
Rhostyllen Victoria	3-0	Overton
Druids	1-3	Chirk
Westminster Rovers	1-1	Wrexham
Crewe Alexandra Res.	5-0	Hartford & Davenham Utd

A protest regarding Crewe's professionalism was upheld and Hartford & Davenham United progressed.

Second Round Replay

Wrexham	1-1	Westminster Rovers

Second Round Second Replay

Westminster Rovers	0-1	Wrexham

Third Round

Bangor	9-0	Portmadoc
Newtown	4-0	Shrewsbury Town
Chirk	7-1	Rhostyllen
Wrexham	2-1	Hartford & Davenham Utd

Semi-finals

Wrexham	3-1	Bangor
Played at Chester		
Chirk	3-2	Newtown
Played at Oswestry		

1890 WELSH CUP FINAL

19th April 1890 at the Racecourse, Wrexham

Chirk	1-0	Wrexham

Morris

Chirk: E Povey, E Roberts, P Griffiths, J Jones, J Mates, J Rogers, J Davies, J Butler, W Owen, H Morris, G Griffiths

Wrexham: R E Turner, F T Evans, J Ollerhead, E Davies, A Hayes, W J Hughes, O Davies, R Davies, J Wilding, W H Turner, A Lea

Referee: W H Jope (Wednesbury)

Attendance: 3,500

1890/91 Welsh Cup

First Round

Mold	3-2	Holywell
Carnarvon	3-4	Rhyl
Bangor	7-4	Colwyn Bay

A replay was ordered following a protest by Colwyn Bay.

St Asaph	3-2	Bangor Athletic
Buckley (withdrew)	v	Northwich Victoria (w/o)
Brymbo Institute	2-2	Gresford
Westminster Rovers (w/o)	v	Nantwich (withdrew)
Crewe Alexandra (withdrew)	v	Wrexham (w/o)
Chirk	2-1	Druids
Wrexham Hibernians	2-2	Overton
Corwen	0-2	Rhosllanerchrugog
Oswestry	4-3	Rhayader

Shrewsbury Town, Wellington St George and Builth all received byes

First Round Replays

Colwyn Bay	1-3	Bangor
Gresford	2-1	Brymbo Institute
Overton	2-3	Wrexham Hibernians

Second Round

St Asaph (withdrew)	v	Rhyl (w/o)
Bangor	4-1	Mold

Bangor were disqualified following a protest by Mold about the width of the ground.

Northwich Victoria (withdrew)		v
Wrexham (w/o)		
Gresford	3-4	Westminster Rovers
Rhosllanerchrugog	2-1	Chirk
Wrexham Hibernians	3-5	Rhostyllen Victoria
Oswestry	1-0	Wellington St George
Shrewsbury Town	4-1	Builth

Third Round

Rhyl	2-2	Mold
Westminster Rovers	0-1	Wrexham
Rhostyllen Victoria	1-2	Chirk
Shrewsbury Town	6-0	Oswestry

Third Round Replay

Mold	3-2 (aet)	Rhyl

Semi-finals

Wrexham	4-3	Chirk
Played at Shrewsbury		
Shrewsbury Town	5-0	Mold
Played at the Racecourse, Wrexham		

1891 WELSH CUP FINAL

31st March 1891 at the Cricket Field, Oswestry

Shrewsbury Town	5-2	Wrexham

Holloway, Ellis, Green, A Davies 2   W Roberts, W Turner

Shrewsbury Town: Rogers, W Steadman, J C Davies, F M Aston, H Pearson, H Rowlands, H Holloway, 'Alty' Davies, G Green, A Ellis, T Cosson

Wrexham: R E Turner, R Roberts, A E Ellis, J Owen, A Hayes, E Williams, O Davies, W Roberts, W H Turner, J Turner, A Lea

Referee: W H Jope (Wednesbury)

Attendance: 3,000   (Attendance was reported as betwen 4,000 and 5,000 in another report)

1891/92 Welsh Cup

First Round

Saltney	0-5	Crewe Alexandra Hornets
Nantwich	bye	
Portmadoc	1-4	Bangor
Wrexham	2-1	Rhostyllen Victoria
Brymbo Institute	3-4	Westminster Rovers

A replay was ordered following a protest by Brymbo.

Gresford	bye	
Druids	4-2	Ruabon
Rhosllanerchrugog	6-1	Llangollen Rovers
Chirk	v	Oswestry (withdrew)
Ellesmere Volunteers	bye	
Newtown	6-1	Rhayader
Builth	bye	
Wellington St George	2-3	Shrewsbury Town
Cardiff	bye	

First Round Replay

Westminster Rovers	4-1	Brymbo Institute

Second Round

Crewe Alexandra Hornets	v	Nantwich (withdrew)
Denbigh	0-0	Bangor
Wrexham	8-1	Wrexham Victoria
Gresford	1-6	Westminster Rovers
Rhosllanerchrugog	2-1	Druids
Chirk	9-0	Ellesmere Volunteers
Newtown	6-1	Builth
Shrewsbury Town (w/o)	v	Cardiff (withdrew)

Second Round Replay

Bangor	2-2	Denbigh

Second Round Second Replay

Denbigh	1-3	Bangor

Third Round

Bangor	0-1	Chirk
Crewe Alexandra Hornets	–	Westminster Rovers

The result of this game has not been found. Historians at current Crewe Alexandra club can find no record either but Westminster Rovers progressed to the next round.

Wrexham	3-1	Rhosllanerchrugog
Shrewsbury Town	5-1	Newtown

Semi-finals

Chirk	0-0	Wrexham

Played at Shrewsbury

Westminster Rovers	0-4	Shrewsbury Town

A protest relating to the state of the ground was upheld and a replay was ordered.

Semi-final Replays

Wrexham	1-2	Chirk

Played at the Racecourse, Wrexham

Shrewsbury Town	1-3	Westminster Rovers

1892 WELSH CUP FINAL

18th April 1892 at the Racecourse, Wrexham

Chirk	2-1	Westminster Rovers
G Owen, James		Wilding

Chirk: E Povey, G O Postle, W P Jones, R C Jones, J Mates, E Morris, W Owen, E James, J Butler, G Owen, W Egan

Westminster Rovers: Williams, C Jones, J Jones, E Samuels, J Wilding, W Fisher, G Samuels, James Jones, G Jones, J Powell, E Davies

Referee: W Cotton (Rhostyllen)

Attendance: 4,500

1892/93 Welsh Cup

First Round

Flint	0-2	Llandudno Swifts
Carnarvon Ironopolis	2-7	Bangor
Holywell (w/o)	v	Portmadoc (withdrew)
Denbigh (withdrew)	v	Rhostyllen Victoria (w/o)
Brymbo Institute	2-2	Druids
Rhosllanerchrugog	bye	
Whitchurch (withdrew)	v	Llanidloes (w/o)
Ellesmere	0-5	Newtown
Nantwich	bye	
Wellington Town	1-2	Wellington St George
Ironbridge (withdrew)	v	Cardiff (w/o)
Chirk	bye	
Wrexham	bye	
Shrewsbury	bye	
Westminster Rovers	bye	

First Round Replays

Druids	11-1	Brymbo Institute

Second Round

Llandudno Swifts	2-0	Bangor
Holywell	bye	
Rhostyllen Victoria	2-2	Rhosllanrchrugog
Druids	bye	
Newtown	3-0	Llanidloes
Nantwich	bye	
Wellington St George	v	Cardiff (withdrew)

Second Round Replay

Rhosllanerchrugog	1-1	Rhostyllen Victoria

Second Round Second Replay

Rhostyllen Victoria	2-3	Rhosllanerchrugog

Third Round

Llandudno Swifts	v	Holywell (failed to appear)
Rhosllanerchrugog	2-4	Druids
Newtown	bye	
Wellington St George	bye	

Fourth Round

Llandudno Swifts	4-0	Shrewsbury Town
Druids	1-0	Westminster Rovers
Wrexham	2-1 (aet)	Newtown

The score at full-time was 1-1.

Chirk	9-0	Wellington St George

Semi-finals

Wrexham	2-1	Llandudno Swifts

Played at Flint

Chirk	6-1	Druids

Played at the Racecourse, Wrexham

1893 WELSH CUP FINAL

3rd April 1893 at the Cricket Field, Oswestry

Wrexham	2-1	Chirk
Pritchard, Unknown scorer		*G Owen*

Wrexham: S Jones, L Edwards, A E Ellis, E Samuels, A Lea, A Hughes, S Pritchard, E Williams, J Hughes, Robert Davies, Joseph Turner

Chirk: E Morris, G O Postle, Grainger, M Roberts, J Mates, G Williams, W H Meredith, W Owen, J Butler, E James, G Owen

Referee: Mr Roberts (Birkenhead)

Attendance: 5,000

1893/94 Welsh Cup

First Round

Bangor	1-2	Flint
Holywell	1-2	Portmadoc
Rhosllanerchrugog	5-3	Brymbo Institute
Rhostyllen Victoria	0-3	Westminster Rovers
Newtown	5-0	Whitchurch
Oswestry United	bye	
Aberystwyth	bye	
Llanidloes	bye	
Mountain Ash	0-4	Cardiff
Market Drayton	2-1	Ironbridge

Market Drayton were subsequently disqualified for fielding an ineligible player following a protest by Ironbridge.

Shrewsbury Town	6-1	Wellington St George
Welliington Town	bye	
Wrexham	bye	
Chirk	bye	
Druids	bye	
Llandudno Swifts	bye	

Second Round

Portmadoc (withdrew)	v	Flint (w/o)
Westminster Rovers	3-2	Brymbo Institute
Newtown	4-1	Llanidloes
Oswestry United	7-2	Aberystwyth
Shrewsbury Town (w/o)	v	Wellington Town (withdrew)
Ironbridge	4-1	Cardiff

Third Round

Flint	bye	
Westminster Rovers	bye	
Oswestry United	2-2 (aet)	Newtown
Shrewsbury Town	4-1	Ironbridge FC

Third Round Replay

Newtown	0-2	Oswestry United

Fourth Round

Wrexham	6-0	Flint
Druids	3-4	Westminster Rovers
Chirk	3-2	Llandudno Swifts
Oswestry United	2-0	Shrewsbury Town

Semi-finals

Chirk	2-1	Oswestry United

Played at the Racecourse, Wrexham

Wrexham	3-5	Westminster Rovers

Played at the Racecourse, Wrexham

1894 WELSH CUP FINAL

25th March 1894 at Wynnstay Park, Ruabon

Chirk	2-0	Westminster Rovers
Lockley, James		

Chirk: J Morgan, E Powell, J Williams, G Williams, J Mates, H Morgan, W H Meredith, W Owen, H Roberts, E James, A Lockley

Westminster Rovers: Cafferty, C Jones, J Randles, W Ellis, J Wilding, W Fisher, J Pountney, J Powell, H Trainer, J Lewis, A Roberts

Referee: Mr Roberts (Birkenhead)

Attendance: 3,000

1894/95 Welsh Cup

First Round

Llandudno Swifts	1-0	Flint
Rhostyllen Villa	1-4	Brymbo Institute
Mold Alyn Stars	0-21	Shrewsbury Town
Druids	5-3	Mold Red Stars
Rhosllanerchrugog	4-4	Wellington Town

Wellington Town withdrew from the competition.

Market Drayton (w/o)	v	Whitchurch (withdrew)
Wrockwardine Wood	2-1	Ironbridge
Wellington St George	3-8 (aet)	Aberystwyth

The scoreline at full-time was 3-3.

Newtown	4-0	Llanidloes
Aberdare	0-2	Swansea
Knighton	10-1	New Tredegar
Barry District	1-0	Cardiff

Bangor, Carnarvon Ironopolis, Portmadoc, Chirk, Wrexham, Oswestry United and Westminster Rovers all received byes.

Second Round

Llandudno Swifts	3-2 (aet)	Carnarvon Ironopolis
Portmadoc	2-4	Bangor
Brymbo Institute	4-1	Rhosllanerchrugog
Druids	4-0	Shrewsbury Town
Newtown (w/o)	v	Market Drayton (withdrew)
Aberystwyth	4-3 (aet)	Wrockwardine Wood
Swansea	2-1	Knighton

A replay was ordered following a protest by Knighton about the size of the pitch.

Barry District bye

Second Round Replay

Knighton	6-1	Swansea

Third Round

Bangor	1-1	Llandudno Swifts
Brymbo Institute	1-0	Druids
Newtown	5-0	Aberystwyth
Barry District	1-2	Knighton

Third Round Replay

Llandudno Swifts	0-1	Bangor

Fourth Round

Oswestry United	1-0	Wrexham

A replay was ordered following a protest by Wrexham

Brymbo Institute	1-0	Bangor
Newtown	1-0	Westminster Rovers
Chirk	7-0	Knighton

Fourth Round Replay

Wrexham	2-1 (aet)	Oswestry United

The scoreline after full-time was 1-1

Semi-finals

Chirk	0-4	Newtown

Played at Shrewsbury

Brymbo Institute	0-4	Wrexham

Played at Stansty Park, Wrexham

1895 WELSH CUP FINAL

15th April 1895 at Welshpool

Newtown	3-2	Wrexham

W Pryce-Jones 2, unknown   Harrison, Lewis

Newtown: R Goodwin, A Townsend, J Harper, H Tucker, T Chapman, T Worthington, W E Pryce-Jones (capt), E Morgan, H F Mytton, H Parry, A W Pryce-Jones

Wrexham: W Ball, A E Ellis, E Samuels, H Beeston, A Lea, A Hayes, B Lewis, T Owen, H Trainer, R Davies, W C Harrison

Referee: Mr Brodie (Wolverhampton)

Attendance: 5,000

1895/96 Welsh Cup

First Round

Llandudno Swifts	2-3 (aet)	Bangor

The scoreline after 90 minutes was 2-2.

Flint	0-1	Westminster Rovers
Mold Red Stars	1-3	Carnarvon Ironopolis
Wrockwardine Wood	2-0	Rhostyllen Victoria
Rhos	0-3	Wellington St.George
Market Drayton	2-2	Wellington Town
Ironbridge	2-1	Druids

Ironbridge were subsequently disqualified for fielding unregistered players.

Oswestry United	3-0	Llanidloes
Aberystwyth Town	bye	
Whitchurch	bye	
Portmadoc	bye	
Builth	1-2	Rhayader
Rogerstone	0-4	Hereford
Cardiff	v	Aberdare (w/o)

Cardiff withdrew due to a league commitment

Wrexham	bye
Brymbo	bye
Newtown	bye
Chirk	bye

First Round Replay

Wellington Town	3-1	Market Drayton

Second Round

Westminster Rovers	v	Carnarvon Ironopolis

Carnarvon Ironopolis withdrew due to distance.

Bangor	bye	
Druids	7-0	Wrockwardine Wood
Wellington St George	4-2	Wellington Town

A replay was ordered following a protest regarding the pitch being roped off.

Oswestry Utd (w/o)	v	Portmadoc (withdrew)
Whitchurch	3-4	Aberystwyth Town
Hereford	v	Rhayader (withdrew)
Aberdare	bye	

Second Round Replay

Wellington Town	2-6	Wellington St George

Third Round

Bangor	1-1	Westminster Rovers
Druids	2-2	Wellington St George
Oswestry United	3-4	Aberystwyth Town
Aberdare	2-4	Hereford

Third Round Replays

Westminster Rovers	1-3	Bangor
Wellington St George	3-0	Druids

A replay was ordered following a protest by Druids that the game was not played at Wellington's usual ground.

Third Round Second Replay

Druids	0-1	Wellington St George

Played at Shrewsbury

Fourth Round

Brymbo	2-3	Aberystwyth Town
Wrexham	4-0	Chirk
Hereford	0-0	Newtown
Bangor	1-1	Wellington St George

Fourth Round Replays

Newtown	3-1	Hereford
Wellington St George	4-0	Bangor

Semi-finals

Newtown	1-1	Bangor

Played at the Racecourse, Wrexham

Wrexham	1-0	Aberystwyth Town

Played at Welshpool

Semi-final Replay

Bangor	3-0	Newtown

Played at the Racecourse, Wrexham

1896 WELSH CUP FINAL

6th April 1896 at the Council Field, Llandudno

Bangor FC	3-1	Wrexham

Thomas, Jones, J Roberts   *Pugh*

Bangor: W Arridge, R Roberts, D H Williams, W H Jones, T Buckland, S Roberts, Walter Lewis, R Owen, C Jones, J Roberts, T Thomas

Wrexham: W Ball, E Samuels, A E Ellis, F Stokes, E Robinson, J P Rogers, D H Pugh, T Owen, J Hughes, W C Harrison, A Williams

Referee: T Gough (Oswestry)

Attendance: 7,000

1896/97 Welsh Cup

First Round

Rhyl Athletic	3-2	Carnarvon Ironopolis
Holywell	2-1	Llandudno Swifts
Portmadoc (withdrew)	v	Flint (w/o)
Chirk	4-2	Druids
Rhostyllen Victoria	2-0	Westminster Rovers
Rhosllanerchrugog (withdrew)	v	Brymbo Institute (w/o)
Llanidloes	0-1 (aet)	Oswestry United
Towyn Rovers	1-6	Welshpool United
Wellington Town	1-0	Wrockwardine Wood
Ironbridge	5-2	Market Drayton
Rogerstone	5-0	Swansea Association
Knighton	7-1	Aberdare
Builth	2-2	Rhayader

Builth subsequently withdrew from the competition.

Wrexham	bye	
Bangor	bye	
Newtown	bye	
Aberystwyth Town	bye	

Second Round

Rhyl Athletic	2-2	Holywell

Rhyl subsequently withdrew from the competition.

Flint	bye	
Druids	8-0	Rhostyllen
Brymbo Institute	bye	
Oswestry United	3-0	Ironbridge
Wellington Town	1-2	Welshpool United
Knighton	2-1	Rhayader
Rogerstone	bye	

Third Round

Holywell	2-3	Flint
Druids	3-1	Brymbo
Oswestry United	2-0	Welshpool United
Knighton	7-2	Rogerstone

Fourth Round

Flint	1-1	Knighton
Druids	1-3	Oswestry United
Bangor	1-1	Wrexham
Newtown	3-0	Aberystwyth Town

Fourth Round Replays

Knighton	3-2	Flint
Wrexham	6-0	Bangor

Semi-finals

Wrexham	3-2	Oswestry United

Played at Chirk

Newtown	1-0	Knighton

Played at Shrewsbury

1897 WELSH CUP FINAL

19th April 1897 at the Cricket Field, Oswestry

Wrexham	2-0	Newtown

Williams, Robinson

Wrexham: D Jardine, J Jones, A E Ellis, J Taylor, E Robinson, F Stokes, D H Pugh, W C Harrison, T C Davies, B Lewis, A Williams

Newtown: A Edwards, E Rees, C Parry, H Tucker, W Parry, E Davies W E Pryce-Jones, E Morgan, J Miller, J P Sweetenham, A Sweetenham

Referee: H Jones (Bangor)

Attendance: 6,000

1897/98 Welsh Cup

First Round

Rhyl Amateurs (withdrew)	v	Holywell (w/o)
Carnarvon Ironopolis	8-0	Portmadoc
Bangor	1-0	Llandudno Swifts
Rhyl Town	bye	
Mold	2-5	Caergwrle Wanderers
Druids	3-1	Buckley Town
Brymbo	0-3	Chirk
Flint	bye	
Market Drayton	2-0	Wrockwardine Wood
Wellington Town	3-1	Ironbridge
Newport	5-0	Welshpool
Wem	bye	
Swansea Association	6-0	Aberdare

Aberdare protested the result and were awarded the tie.

Aberystwyth Town	7-0	Llanidloes
Towyn Rovers	bye	
Builth	bye	
Wrexham	bye	
Newtown	bye	
Oswestry United	bye	
Knighton	bye	

Second Round

Holywell	3-3	Carnarvon Ironopolis
Rhyl Town	4-1	Bangor
Flint	2-1	Caergwrle Wanderers
Chirk	0-1	Druids
Wellington Town (w/o)	v	Market Drayton (withdrew)
Wem	2-0	Newport
Builth	6-0	Towyn Rovers
Aberdare	1-3	Aberystwyth Town

Second Round Replay

Carnarvon Ironopolis	3-0	Holywell

Third Round

Carnarvon Ironopolis	3-1	Rhyl Town
Druids	6-0	Flint
Wem	1-5	Wellington Town
Aberystwyth Town	7-0	Builth

Fourth Round

Oswestry United	2-1	Newtown
Wrexham	2-1	Rhyl Town
Knighton	0-2	Druids
Aberystwyth Town	1-2	Wellington Town

Semi-finals

Wellington Town	0-0	Druids
Played at Oswestry		
Wrexham	2-1	Newtown
Played at Welshpool		

Semi-final Replay

Druids	1-0	Wellington Town
Played at Oswestry		

1898 WELSH CUP FINAL

10th April 1898 at the Cricket Field, Oswestry

Druids	1-1	Wrexham
Vaughan		Williams

Druids: W Edwards, C Thomas, A Hughes, G Richards, J Price, T Davies, James Vaughan, W Butler, T Owen, Jones, J Davies

Wrexham: Jardine, J Jones, H Blew, J Taylor, E Robinson, J P Rogers, F C Kelly, A Williams, H Grainger, Mitchell, Challoner

Referee: R T Gough (Oswestry)

Attendance: 4,500

1898 WELSH CUP FINAL REPLAY

30th April 1898 at the Cricket Field, Oswestry

Druids	2-1	Wrexham
Unknown scorer, Vaughan		Harrison

Druids: W Edwards, C Thomas, A Hughes, G Richards, J Price, T Davies, James Vaughan, W Butler, T Owen, Jones, J Davies

Wrexham: Jardine, J Jones, H Blew, J Taylor, E Robinson, J P Rogers, F C Kelly, A Williams, H Grainger, Mitchell, Challoner

Referee: R T Gough (Oswestry)

Attendance: 1,500

1898/99 Welsh Cup

First Round

Portmadoc	2-5	Bangor
Holywell	0-3	Carnarvon Ironopolis
Rhyl United	3-2	Llandudno Swifts
Chirk	7-0	Rhos Eagle Wanderers
Oswestry United	13-0	Llanidloes
Newport	1-0	Aberystwyth Town
Ironbridge	6-2	Knighton
Wem	3-1	Welshpool United
Barry Dock	4-1	Builth
Blaina Town	1-7	Aberdare
Rogerstone	v	Rhayader (withdrew)

Brecon, Flint, Buckley Victoria, Caergwrle Wanderers, Mold Town, Druids, Wrexham, Newtown and Wellington Town all received byes.

Second Round

Bangor	3-1	Carnarvon Ironopolis
Rhyl United	2-0	Flint
Mold Town	0-5	Chirk
Caergwrle Wanderers	1-2	Buckley Victoria
Oswestry United	6-1	Ironbridge

Newport (w/o) v Wem (withdrew)
Brecon (withdrew) v Rogerstone (w/o)
Barry Dock 3-2 Aberdare

Third Round

Bangor 1-1 Rhyl United
Rhyl were disqualified after fielding an ineligible player.
Buckley Victoria 1-2 Chirk
Newport 1-4 Oswestry United
Barry Dock 2-1 Rogerstone

Fourth Round

Newtown (w/o) v Wellington Town (withdrew)
Oswestry 2-2 Chirk
Wrexham 7-1 Barry Dock
Druids 5-2 Bangor

Fourth Round Replay

Chirk 2-1 (aet) Oswestry

Semi-finals

Wrexham 1-0 Chirk
Played at Wynnstay Park, Ruabon
Druids 4-0 Newtown
Played at Oswestry

1899 WELSH CUP FINAL

11th April 1899 at the Hand Field, Chirk

Druids 2-2 Wrexham
Vaughan 2 *Robinson, Kelly*

Druids: S Jones, C Thomas, A Hughes, G Richards, J Price, T Davies, James Vaughan, W Butler, J Davies, R Jones, Pugh

Wrexham: Jardine, Povah, H Blew, J P Rogers, E Robinson, W C Harrison, F C Kelly, A Williams, H Grainger, B Lewis, Challoner

Referee: R Roberts (Crewe)

Attendance: 4,000

1899 WELSH CUP FINAL REPLAY

15th April 1899 at the Hand Field, Chirk

Druids 1-0 Wrexham
Pugh

Druids: S Jones, C Thomas, A Hughes, G Richards, J Price, T Davies, James Vaughan, W Butler, J Davies, R Jones, Pugh

Wrexham: Jardine, Povah, H Blew, J P Rogers, E Robinson, W C Harrison, F C Kelly, A Williams, H Grainger, Mitchell, Challoner

Referee: R Roberts (Crewe)

Attendance: 3,500

1899/1900 Welsh Cup

First Round

Ironbridge (w/o) v Wem (withdrew)
Aberdare 2-0 Barry Dock
Portmadoc, Carnarvon Ironopolis, Rhyl United, Buckley Victoria, Flint, Welshpool, Towyn, Newport, Rhayader, Knighton, Builth, Llandrindod Wells, Rogerstone, Druids, Chirk, Newtown, Wrexham, Llandudno Swifts, Bangor, Oswestry United, Aberystwyth Town all received byes.

Second Round

Carnarvon Ironopolis 5-0 Portmadoc
Rhyl United bye
Buckley Victoria 3-1 Flint
Welshpool 5-0 Towyn
Newport v Ironbridge
The tie was awarded to Newport.
Rhayader 2-1 Knighton
Builth 0-1 Llandrindod Wells
The match was abandoned but the scoreline at the time was allowed to stand.
Rogerstone 0-2 Aberdare

Third Round

Newtown 6-1 Llandudno Swifts
Oswestry United (w/o) v Wrexham (withdrew)
Bangor (w/o) v Llandrindod Wells
(withdrew)
Rhayader 0-1 Aberystwyth Town
Druids 2-0 Chirk
Buckley Victoria (w/o) v Newport (withdrew)
Carnarvon Ironopolis 4-2 Welshpool
Rhyl United 2-1 Aberdare

Fourth Round

Oswestry United 1-1 Rhyl United
Rhyl were disqualified from the competition following a protest that they had fielded an ineligible player.
Aberystwyth Town 1-0 Newtown
Bangor 0-4 Druids
Carnarvon Ironopolis 2-1 Buckley Victoria

Semi-finals

Aberystwyth Town 1-0 Carnarvon Ironopolis
Played at Oswestry
Druids 2-0 Oswestry United
Played at Chirk

Semi-Final Replay

Aberystwyth Town 2-0 Carnarvon Ironopolis
Played at Towyn

1900 WELSH CUP FINAL

16th April 1900 at the Cunnings, Newtown

Aberystwyth Town   3-0   Druids

Green, James, Storey

Aberystwyth Town: L R Roose, C Parry, G Evans, W R Jones, J H Edwards, D M Evans, Whelan, J Evans, A W Green, Storey, E James

Druids: T Pryce, C Thomas, A Hughes, Tom Davies, J Price, A Potts, Spencer, W Butler, J Davies, W Davies, R Jones

Referee: R T Gough (Oswestry)

Attendance: 3,000

1900/01 Welsh Cup

First Round

None was played

Second Round

Portmadoc	bye	Portmadoc
Llandudno (w/o)	v	Buckley Victoria (withdrew)
Royal Welsh Warehouse Newtown	2-1	Welshpool
Knighton	2-4	Llandrindod Wells
Rogerstone	1-1	Barry Unionists
Broughton	bye	
Towyn	bye	
Aberdare	bye	

Second Round Replay

Barry Unionists	0-2	Rogerstone

Third Round

Aberystwyth Town	1-2	Aberdare
Chirk (w/o)	v	Llandudno FC (withdrew)
Rhyl United	5-1	Rogerstone
Portmadoc	0-3	Druids
RWW Newtown	2-2	Bangor

A Newtown protest regarding the width of the Bangor playing field was upheld and a replay was ordered at Wrexham. RWW Newtown subsequently withdrew.

Broughton United	2-1	Carnarvon Ironopolis
Llandrindod Wells	v	Flint (withdrew)
Oswestry United (w/o)	v	Towyn Rovers (withdrew)

Fourth Round

Druids	4-1	Bangor
Llandrindod Wells	2-3	Rhyl
Oswestry United	4-1	Aberdare
Chirk	4-0	Broughton

Semi-finals

Oswestry United	1-1	Rhyl

Played at the Racecourse, Wrexham

Druids	2-1	Chirk

Played at Oswestry

Semi-Final Replay

Rhyl	0-1	Oswestry United

Played at the Racecourse, Wrexham

1901 WELSH CUP FINAL

8th April 1901 at the Racecourse, Wrexham

Oswestry United   1-0   Druids

Roose (own goal)

Oswestry United: J Tracey Morgan, J Edwards, H Jones, G Richards, Butterton, Jarman, Hodnett, M Watkins, Storey, H Goodrich, T D Parry

Druids: L R Roose, C Thomas, A Hughes, T Davies, J Price, J Hughes, F C Kelly, W Butler, L Davies, Spencer, W Davies, E Williams

Referee: R Roberts (Crewe)

Attendance: 5,000

1901/02 Welsh Cup

First Round

Porth	3-0	Barry Unionists Athletic

A replay at Barry was ordered following a protest about the size of Porth's ground.

Aberaman	2-1	Rogerstone

A protest by Rogerstone was dismissed.
All other clubs received byes

First Round Replay

Barry Unionists Athletic	0-1	Porth

Second Round

Portmadoc	bye	
Carnarvon Ironopolis	bye	
Chester (withdrew)	v	Broughton United (w/o)
Wellington Town	bye	
Welshpool	bye	
Towyn Rovers	0-1	Aberystwyth Town

Third Round

Chirk	1-1	Royal Welsh Warehouse Newtown
Rhyl	7-0	Llandrindod Wells

The match was abandoned after 58 minutes but the result was allowed to stand.

Portmadoc	2-2	Aberystwyth Town
Aberaman	2-0	Bangor
Wellington Town	3-1	Oswestry United
Carnarvon Ironopolis (w/o)	v	Aberdare (withdrew)
Broughton United	0-2	Welshpool
Druids	0-2	Wrexham

Third Round Replays

RWW Newtown	6-1	Chirk
Aberystwyth Town	1-1	Portmadoc

Third Round Second Replay

Portmadoc	2-1	Aberystwyth Town

Fourth Round

RWW Newtown	1-1	Wrexham
Rhyl	2-3	Wellington Town
Carnarvon Ironopolis	5-1	Portmadoc
Aberaman	1-2	Welshpool

Fourth Round Replay

Wrexham	1-1	RWW Newtown

Fourth Round Second Replay

RWW Newtown	1-5	Wrexham

Semi-finals

Welshpool	0-2	Wellington Town
Played at Oswestry		
Carnarvon Ironopolis	1-3	Wrexham
Played at Rhyl		

1902 WELSH CUP FINAL

31st March 1902 at the Racecourse, Wrexham

Wellington Town	1-0	Wrexham

G Evans

Wellington Town: J Foulke, G Davies, T Poole, W Jones, Dodd, G Owen, Worthington, G Evans, Duckers, T Jones, Mooney

Wrexham: R O Evans, D Davies, H Blew, H Grainger, E Robinson, L Davies, R Hughes, T Gordon, Pountney, L Griffiths, J Owens

Referee: R T Gough (Oswestry)

Attendance: 6,000

1902/03 Welsh Cup

First Round

Aberdare (withdrew)	v	Aberaman (w/o)
Treharris	bye	
Barry United	7-0	Caerphilly
Rogerstone	2-2	Porth

First Round Replay

Porth	3-1	Rogerstone

Second Round

Portmadoc	bye	
Rhyl Athletic	0-14	Rhyl United
Oswestry United	bye	
Royal Welsh Warehouse Newtown	bye	
Towyn	2-3	Aberystwyth Town
Knighton	1-1	Llandrindod Wells
Treharris	0-6	Aberaman
Played at Aberaman		
Porth	2-3	Barry United

Second Round Replay

Llandrindod Wells	1-1	Knighton

Second Round Second Replay

Knighton	0-0	Llandrindod Wells

Second Round Third Replay

Llandrindod Wells	5-2	Knighton

Third Round

Chester	0-2	Wrexham
Welshpool	2-4	RWW Newtown
Bangor	3-3	Portmadoc
Wellington Town	10-0	Llandrindod Wells
Druids	2-2	Chirk
Oswestry United	1-1	Aberystwyth Town
Carnarvon Ironopolis	2-3	Rhyl United
Porth	0-2	Aberaman

Third Round Replays

Portmadoc	0-4	Bangor
Chirk	1-1	Druids
Aberystwyth Town	0-2	Oswestry United

Third Round Second Replay

Druids	3-0	Chirk

Fourth Round

Wrexham	9-0	RWW Newtown

The match was not played on the originally planned date due to an outbreak of smallpox in Newtown.

Rhyl United	1-4	Druids
Oswestry United	0-1	Wellington Town
Bangor	1-4	Aberaman

Semi-finals

Druids	2-3	Aberaman
Played at Shrewsbury		
Wellington Town	0-4	Wrexham
Played at Oswestry		

1903 WELSH CUP FINAL

13th April 1903 at the Racecourse, Wrexham

Wrexham	8-0	Aberaman

W Davies 2, Gordon 2, Griffiths 2, Owens 2

Wrexham: R O Evans, D Davies, H Blew, J Cane, E Robinson, L Davies, H Grainger, T Gordon, W Davies, L Griffiths, J Owens

Aberaman: Eggington, H Jones, W Boulton, R Rooke, W J Jones, S Jones, W Bowell, J Rooke, C Grimmel, T D Jones, R Praddy

Referee: R T Gough (Oswestry)

Attendance: 5,500

1903/04 Welsh Cup

First Round
All clubs were awarded byes

Second Round
Knighton	1-1	Llandrindod Wells
Porth	2-3	Aberdare
Rogerstone	5-3	Ebbw Vale

Second Round Replay
Llandrindod Wells	1-3	Knighton

Third Round
Colwyn Bay	3-1	Llandudno FC

The game was stopped after 87 minutes due to poor light but the score was allowed to stand.

Bangor	6-1	Rhyl
Broughton United	2-0	Wrexham
Druids	1-0	Chester
Welshpool	1-3	Chirk
Machynlleth	1-3	Oswestry United
Knighton (w/o)	v	Wellington Town (withdrew)
Rogerstone	0-0	Aberdare

Rogerstone walked off the pitch after 35 minutes and a replay was ordered.

Third Round Replay
Aberdare	4-0	Rogerstone

Fourth Round
Druids	4-2	Broughton United
Colwyn Bay	1-2	Knighton
Oswestry United	2-1	Bangor
Chirk	1-3	Aberdare

Semi-finals
Aberdare	2-0	Oswestry United

Played at Hereford

Druids	7-0	Knighton

Played at Oswestry

1904 WELSH CUP FINAL

4th April 1904 at the Racecourse, Wrexham

Druids	3-2	Aberdare

Evans, Potts, E Williams — Parker, Price

Druids: J Tracey Morgan, J E Williams, L Davies, W Davies, A Potts, T Davies, A Davies, T Read, R Evans, E Williams, W Jones

Aberdare: Seward, W Golding, A Davies, S Parker, W Wedlock, H Price, W Bowell, P Lloyd, T D Jones, Woollacott, W Read

Referee: J Lewis (Blackburn)

Attendance: 6,500

1904/05 Welsh Cup

First Round
Welshpool	2-2	Aberystwyth Town
Ebbw Vale	1-0	Treharris
Rogerstone	3-2	Hafod

First Round Replay
Aberystwyth Town	2-0	Welshpool

Second Round
Aberystwyth Town (w/o)	v	Newtown (withdrew)
Ebbw Vale	2-2	Rogerstone

All other clubs were awarded byes

Second Round Replay
Rogerstone	2-1	Ebbw Vale

Third Round
Rhyl	3-1	Colwyn Bay
Llandudno FC	2-4	Bangor
Wrexham	2-0	Chester
Druids	4-0	Broughton United
Wellington Town	4-1	Aberystwyth Town
Chirk	1-2	Oswestry United
Knighton	1-0	Llandrindod Wells
Aberdare	2-0	Rogerstone

Fourth Round
Rhyl	1-0	Bangor
Druids	0-2	Oswestry United
Wrexham	3-0	Wellington Town
Aberdare	8-0	Knighton

Semi-finals
Rhyl	1-3	Aberdare

Played at Oswestry

Wrexham	1-0	Oswestry

Played at Chirk

1905 WELSH CUP FINAL

24th April 1905 at the Racecourse, Wrexham

Wrexham	3-0	Aberdare

Griffiths, Davies, Owens

Wrexham: J Tracey Morgan, L Davies, H Blew, E Hughes, E Robinson, Hesketh, R Hughes, L Griffiths, W Davies, T Gordon, J Owens

Aberdare: Seward, W Golding, L Grant, S Parker, W Wedlock, E N Shenton, McKiernan, W Ingham, M I Jones, G Brown, T D Jones

Referee: J Lewis (Blackburn)

Attendance: 6,191

1905/06 Welsh Cup

Preliminary Round

Llanbradach	4-1	Rogerstone

First Round

Treharris	3-2	Llanbradach
Newport	0-2	Hafod

Second Round

No record of any Second Round matches has been found so it is possible that none were played.

Third Round

Aberystwyth (withdrew)	v	Welshpool (w/o)
Hafod	0-5	Treharris

Fourth Round

Wrexham	3-0	Druids
Oswestry United	6-0	Welshpool
Chirk (w/o)	v	Colwyn Bay (withdrew)
Broughton United (w/o)	v	Bangor (withdrew)
Rhyl (w/o)	v	Chester (withdrew)
Wellington Town (w/o)	v	Llandrindod Wells (withdrew)
Whitchurch	1-1	Shrewsbury Town
Treharris	6-4	Aberdare

Fourth Round Replay

Whitchurch	0-0	Shrewsbury Town

Played at Whitchurch

Fourth Round Second Replay

Whitchurch	1-0	Shrewsbury Town

Fifth Round

Wrexham	3-1	Broughton United
Wellington Town	3-2	Rhyl
Chirk	0-1	Oswestry United
Treharris	2-2	Whitchurch

Fifth Round Replay

Whitchurch	1-0	Treharris

Semi-finals

Wellington Town	2-2	Oswestry United

Played at Chirk

Wrexham,	1-2	Whitchurch

Played at Oswestry

Semi-Final Replay

Wellington Town	1-0	Oswestry United

Played at Chirk

1906 WELSH CUP FINAL

16th April 1906 at the Racecourse, Wrexham

Wellington Town	3-2	Whitchurch
Scarratt 2, W Davies		*Foster, Evans*

Wellington Town: Bayliss, G Davies, Griffiths, Mason, Williams, W Davies, Paddock, Scarratt, J Newbound, W Thomas, W Jones

Whitchurch: Latham, G Lindop, Billington, J Mitchell, W Jones, Pendlebury, A Davies, Joe W Foster, Challoner, Jack Foster, Evans

Referee: R T Gough (Oswestry)

Attendance: 4,000

1906/07 Welsh Cup

First Round

Llanbradach	2-3	Ton Pentre
Cardiff Corinthians	3-2	Barry District

A replay to be held at Cardiff Corinthians was ordered following a protest.

First Round Replay

Cardiff Corinthians	1-3	Barry District

Second Round

Rhyl	bye	
Tranmere Rovers	bye	
Wrexham Victoria	2-0	Druids
Welshpool (w/o)	v	Aberystwyth Town (withdrew)
Llandrindod Wells	bye	
Abergavenny	0-1	Pontlottyn
Ton Pentre	5-2	Barry District
Milford Haven United	bye	

Third Round

Chester	4-0	Bangor
Rhyl	2-0	Tranmere Rovers
Wrexham	2-0	Wrexham Victoria
Whitchurch	1-0	Chirk
Oswestry United	3-1	Wellington Town
Welshpool (withdrew)	v	Llandrindod Wells (w/o)
Treharris	1-0	Ton Pentre
Milford Haven United	3-2	Pontlottyn

Fourth Round

Milford Haven United	1-5	Chester
Oswestry United	3-1	Treharris
Whitchurch	2-0	Rhyl
Wrexham	10-0	Welshpool

Semi-finals

Oswestry United	2-2	Chester

Played at Wrexham

Wrexham	1-1	Whitchurch

Played at Chester

Semi-final Replays

Chester	0-1	Oswestry United
Played at Wrexham		
Whitchurch	2-3	Wrexham
Played at Chester		

1907 WELSH CUP FINAL

1st April 1907 at the Racecourse, Wrexham

Oswestry United	2-0	Whitchurch

R Jones, Wynn

Oswestry United: F Williams, E Evans, S Lewis, G Richards, W Hallam, R Groves, R Jones, G Wynn, W Williams, T J Boughey, J Newbound

Whitchurch: T Pennington, G Lindop, W L Hatch, J McGinnis, A Callow, J Mitchell, G Davies, J W Foster, J Henshall, Chetwood, D Shaw

Referee: W Nunnerley (Wrexham)

Attendance: 6,000

1907/08 Welsh Cup

First Round

Nantwich	2-0	Rhyl
Connah's Quay & Shotton	bye	
Chirk	9-1	Wrexham Victoria
Brymbo Victoria	2-1	Buckley Engineers
Aberystwyth Town	8-1	Welshpool
Newtown North End	bye	
Llandrindod Wells	bye	
Llanidloes United	bye	
Wellington Town	bye	
Wellington St George	bye	
Milford United	bye	
Cardiff Corinthians	v	Ton Pentre (w/o)
Barry District	0-2	Llanbradach
Aberdare	1-2	Merthyr Vale
Cardiff Riverside	3-12	Cwm Parc

Second Round

Nantwich	1-3	Connah's Quay & Shotton
Chirk	2-1	Buckley
Aberystwyth Town	7-0	Newtown North End
Llanidloes United (w/o)	v	Llandrindod Wells (withdrew)
Wellington Town	2-1	Wellington St George
Milford Haven United	bye	
Barry District	1-1	Ton Pentre
Merthyr Vale	5-3	Cwm Park

Second Round Replay

Ton Pentre	7-0	Barry District

Third Round

Tranmere Rovers	1-1	Chester
Druids	1-1	Whitchurch
Aberystwyth Town	4-0	Llanidloes United
Wellington Town	2-3	Connah's Quay & Shotton
Wrexham	5-0	Bangor
Chirk	0-3	Oswestry United
Treharris	5-0	Merthyr Vale
Milford Haven United	0-1	Ton Pentre

Third Round Replay

Chester	2-1	Tranmere Rovers
Whitchurch	1-1	Druids

Third Round Second Replay

Druids	3-1	Whitchurch

Fourth Round

Oswestry United	2-2	Wrexham
Aberystwyth Town	2-1	Ton Pentre
Treharris	0-2	Connah's Quay & Shotton
Druids	1-6	Chester

Fourth Round Replay

Wrexham	0-2	Oswestry United

Semi-finals

Chester	4-2	Aberystwyth Town
Played at Welshpool		
Connah's Quay & Shotton	2-2	Oswestry United
Played at Wrexham		

Semi-final Replay

Oswestry United	1-3	Connah's Quay & Shotton
Played at Wrexham		

1908 WELSH CUP FINAL

20th April 1908 at the Racecourse, Wrexham

Chester	3-1	Connah's Quay & Shotton

Goode 2, Lees — *J Roberts*

Chester: Keeley, Wightman, J Russell, W Matthews, F Grainger, T Gordon, A Williams, A Lees, J Freeman, B Goode, J Lipsham

Connah's Quay: H Lloyd, Penn, T Hewitt, J Griffiths, Evans, T Lumberg, Bates, O'Neill, W `Bloomer' Jones, J Roberts, H Roberts

Referee: W Nunnerley (Wrexham)

Attendance: 8,000

1908/09 Welsh Cup

First Preliminary Round

Oak Alyn Rovers	6-1	Burntwood United

Second Preliminary Round

Saltney	0-1	Tranmere Rovers
Aston Hall	2-2	Mold Town
Johnstown Amateurs	5-0	Brymbo Victoria
Summerhill	7-0	Buckley Engineers
Oak Alyn Rovers	7-1	Rhos Rangers
Llanbradach	v	Treharris (w/o)
Barry District	0-2	Merthyr Town

Merthyr Town were disqualified following a protest.

Aberdare Town	2-1	Ton Pentre
Mardy Corinthians	8-1	Cwm Parc

Played at Cwm Parc

Second Preliminary Round Replay

Mold Town	2-1	Aston Hall

First Round

Rhyl (w/o)	v	Denbigh Town (withdrew)
Bangor	3-0	Llandudno Amateurs
Nantwich	5-1	Birkenhead
Whitchurch	3-1	Tranmere Rovers
Summerhill	1-2	Oak Alyn Rovers
Johnstown Amateurs	7-0	Mold Town
Towyn Rovers	6-0	Newtown North End
Llanidloes United	2-0	Llandrindod Wells
Treharris	1-2	Mardy Corinthians
Barry District	1-6	Aberdare

Second Round

Rhyl	2-1	Bangor
Nantwich	2-0	Whitchurch
Johnstown Amateurs	2-3	Oak Alyn Rovers
Chirk	0-0	Wellington St George
Royal Welsh Warehouse Newtown	3-2	Towyn Rovers
Llanidloes United	4-0	Builth Wells
Aberdare Town	1-1	Mardy Corinthians
Milford Haven United	bye	

Second Round Replays

Wellington St George	6-2	Chirk
Mardy Corinthians	3-0	Aberdare Town

Third Round

Welshpool	4-0	Llanidloes United
Aberystwyth Town	4-1	RWW Newtown
Rhyl	1-2	Connah's Quay & Shotton
Chester	8-2	Nantwich
Oak Alyn Rovers	0-4	Wrexham

Played at Wrexham

Oswestry United	1-1	Druids

Wellington Town (withdrew)

	v	Wellington St George (w/o)
Mardy Corinthians	5-0	Milford Haven United

Third Round Replay

Druids	2-0	Oswestry United

Fourth Round

Wellington St George	4-1	Welshpool
Connah's Quay & Shotton	2-0	Cardiff City
Druids	1-7	Wrexham
Aberystwyth Town	0-2	Chester

Semi-finals

Wrexham	2-2	Connah's Quay & Shotton

Played at Wrexham

Chester	2-1	Wellington St George

Played at Wrexham

Semi-final Replay

Connah's Quay & Shotton	0-4	Wrexham

Played at Wrexham

1909 WELSH CUP FINAL

12th April 1909 at the Racecourse, Wrexham

Wrexham	1-0	Chester

Huffadine

Wrexham: E Husbands, E Chappell, H Blew, E Huffadine, P Williams, L Davies, F C Cook, G Wynn, B Rankin, A Smith, A Hughes

Chester: Keeley, J Russell, D Davies, W Matthews, F Grainger, T Gordon, Stockton, Ben Roberts, Cotton, Lappin, T Jones

Referee: T Kirkham (Burslem)

Attendance: 9,000

1909/10 Welsh Cup

Extra Preliminary Round

Johnstown Amateurs	5-1	Coedpoeth

Johnstown disqualified for fielding ineligible players.

Cwm Parc & Treorchy United	3-1	Barry District
Ton Pentre	3-2	Barry Dock Albion
Llanbradach	1-4	Aberdare

Preliminary Round

Llandudno Amateurs	0-2	Carnarvon United
Buckley Rangers	4-1	Buckley Engineers
Rhos Rangers	7-1	Brynteg White Stars
Ruabon	2-1	Brymbo Victoria
Coedpoeth	2-1	Summerhill
Aberystwyth Town	4-2	Welshpool
Towyn Rovers (w/o)	v	Llanfyllin (withdrew)
Middlewich	4-1	Greenfield
Nantwich	3-1	Saltney
Denbigh	1-7	Northern Nomads
Mardy	0-1	Aberdare
Cwm Parc & Treorchy United	2-2	Ebbw Vale
Merthyr Town	5-1	Cardiff City
Cardiff Corinthians	1-7	Ton Pentre

Preliminary Round Replay

Ebbw Vale	1-8	Cwm Parc & Treorchy United

First Round

Beaumaris	1-10	Carnarvon United
Rhyl	3-0	Conway
Buckley Engineers	5-2	Ruabon
Rhos	3-1	Coedpoeth
Aberyswyth Town	8-0	Montgomery
Royal Welsh Warehouse Newtown	2-2	Towyn Rovers
Whitchurch	2-1	Oswestry United
Ironbridge (w/o)	v	Wellington Town (withdrew)
Middlewich	4-2	Northern Nomads
Llandrindod Wells	1-2	Llanidloes United
Aberdare	1-1	Merthyr Town
Cwm Park & Treorchy United	2-2	Ton Pentre
Nantwich	v	Tranmere Rovers

Tranmere Rovers were struck out of the competition.

First Round Replays

Towyn Rovers	3-2	RWW Newtown
Merthyr Town	3-1	Aberdare
Ton Pentre	2-0	Cwm Park & Treorchy United

Second Round

Rhyl	2-1	Carnarvon United
Buckley Engineers	3-3	Rhos
Towyn Rovers	0-4	Aberystwyth Town
Whitchurch	8-2	Ironbridge
Nantwich	4-2	Middlewich
Builth Wells	1-5	Llanidloes United
Merthyr Town	4-1	Ton Pentre
Milford Haven United	bye	

Second Round Replay

Rhos	5-0	Buckley Engineers

Third Round

Milford Haven United	3-3	Aberystwyth Town
Connah's Quay & Shotton	3-1	Bangor
Druids	4-0	Chirk
Merthyr Town	1-1	Treharris
Rhyl	2-6	Chester
Wrexham	2-1	Rhos
Nantwich	1-0	Whitchurch
Wellington St George	4-0	Llanidloes United

Third Round Replays

Aberystwyth Town	0-2	Milford Haven United
Treharris	4-0	Merthyr Town

Fourth Round

Connah's Quay & Shotton	3-1	Treharris
Wellington St George	1-2	Wrexham
Chester	3-1	Druids
Nantwich	1-1	Milford Haven United

Fourth Round Replay

Milford Haven United	2-1	Nantwich

Semi-finals

Wrexham	1-1	Connah's Quay & Shotton

Played at Chester

Chester	0-0	Milford Haven United

Played at Merthyr. Milford refused to appear for a replay and were dismissed from the competition.

Semi-final Replay

Connah's Quay & Shotton	1-3	Wrexham

Played at Chester

1910 WELSH CUP FINAL

28th March 1910 at the Racecourse, Wrexham

Wrexham	2-1	Chester
Mason, Allman		*Jones*

Wrexham: E Husbands, W Fenner, W Hancock, E Huffadine, S Corfield, L Davies, F C Cook, G Bytheway, J Mason, R Allman, P Evans

Chester: Bancroft, J Russell, H Wright, W Matthews, F Grainger, T Gordon, Whittington, Graham, Rainford, Oswald Jones, J Lipsham

Referee: T Kirkham (Burslem)

Attendance: 10,000

1910/11 Welsh Cup

Extra Preliminary Round

Llanelly	0-8	Merthyr
Aberdare	0-3	Ton Pentre
Mardy	0-1	Cardiff City
Tredegar	3-1	Cardiff Corinthians
Cwm Parc	bye	

Preliminary Round

Bagillt	0-1	Flint
Denbigh	1-11	Mold Town
Summerhill Victoria	1-3	Brymbo Victoria
Johnstown	2-1	Summerhill
Cwm Parc	2-9	Ton Pentre
Tredegar	1-4	Cardiff City

First Round

Rhyl	0-1	Llandudno Amateurs
Mold Town	8-0	Greenfield
Flint	3-0	Buckley Engineers
Rhos Rangers	3-2	Johnstown

Rhos were disqualified following a protest.

Brymbo Victoria	1-0	Ruabon
Ironbridge United	2-4	Wellington St George
7th Royal Welsh Fusiliers Newtown	2-2	Aberystwyth Town
Llanfyllin	8-1	Royal Welsh Warehouse Newtown
Ton Pentre	2-0	Merthyr Town

1911 WELSH CUP FINAL

17th April 1911 at the Racecourse, Wrexham

Wrexham 6-0 Connah's Quay & Shotton

Cook, Davies 2, Goode 3

Wrexham: G Devaney, Murray, A F Cook, E Huffadine, S Corfield, P Williams, F Cook, B Goode, Davies, J Roberts, Pedley

Connah's Quay: E Peers, T J Hewitt, Peters, Davies, Singleton, Lumberg, W J McGuffie, Hughes, W `Bloomer' Jones, A McGuffie, Dobson

Referee: J Mason (Burslem)

Attendance: 3,000

First Round Replay

Aberystwyth Town	2-4	7th Royal Welsh Fusiliers

Second Round

Llandudno Amateurs	2-2	Carnarvon United
Mold Town	5-1	Flint
Johnstown	2-0	Brymbo Victoria
Whitchurch	8-0	Wellington St George
Northern Nomads	3-2	Saltney
Llanfyllin	1-1	7th Royal Welsh Fusiliers
Llandrindod Wells	1-0	Llanidloes
Cardiff City	2-2	Ton Pentre

Second Round Replays

Carnarvon United	2-2	Llandudno Amateurs
7th Royal Welsh Fusiliers	4-3	Llanfyllin
Ton Pentre	1-0	Cardiff City

Second Round Second Replay

Llandudno Amateurs	5-2	Carnarvon United

Third Round

Bangor	3-1	Llandudno Amateurs
Connah's Quay & Shotton	3-1	Northern Nomads
Oswestry United	2-0	Druids
Ton Pentre	5-1	Treharris
Chester	1-1	Mold Town
Whitchurch	2-2	Johnstown
Wrexham	9-0	Chirk
Llandrindod Wells	1-3	7th Royal Welsh Fusiliers

Third Round Replay

Mold Town	2-0	Chester
Johnstown	2-1	Whitchurch

Fourth Round

Mold Town	0-2	Wrexham
Oswestry United	1-0	Ton Pentre
7th Royal Welsh Fusiliers	2-4	Johnstown
Connah's Quay & Shotton	5-1	Bangor

Semi-finals

Connah's Quay & Shotton	1-0	Johnstown
Played at Wrexham		
Wrexham	4-0	Oswestry United
Played at Wrexham		

1911/12 Welsh Cup

Extra Preliminary Round

Llanelly	0-0	Mond Nickel Works
High Cross Stars (withdrew)	v	Swansea United (w/o)
Barry District	0-0	Pontypridd
Aberdare	3-0	Rhymney

Extra Preliminary Round Replays

Mond Nickel Works	0-1	Llanelly
Pontypridd	3-1	Barry District

Preliminary Round

Llandudno Amateurs	5-2	Bangor
Llandudno Junction Temperance	1-0	Colwyn Bay
Llanberis United	1-1	Carnarvon United
Holyhead Swifts	11-0	Pwllheli
Tanyfron United	2-2	Eclusham White Stars
Llanfyllin	2-1	Summerhill

Llanfyllin were subsequently expelled from the competition for fielding an ineligible player.

Chirk	1-2	Druids

Druids were expelled from the competition for fielding an ineligible player following a protest by Chirk.

Ruabon	1-3	Rhos
Aberdare	2-2	Pontypridd
Swansea United	1-2	Llanelly
Risca District	1-1	Cardiff Corinthians
Tredegar	0-6	Mardy

Preliminary Round Replays

Carnarvon United	6-2	Llanberis United
Pontypridd	2-1	Aberdare

A replay was ordered following a protest about the ground being unsafe.

Cardiff Corinthians	1-0	Risca District

Preliminary Round Second Replay

Aberdare	0-1	Pontypridd
Played at Merthyr		

First Round

Holyhead Swifts	2-0	Carnarvon United
Llandudno Junction Temp.	1-1	Llandudno Amateurs
Bagillt United	1-5	Buckley Engineers

A replay at Bagillt was ordered following a protest but Bagillt subsequently withdrew from the competition.

Mold Town	5-0	Denbigh
Eclusham White Stars	2-1	Chirk
Summerhill	2-2	Rhos
Chester	9-0	Rhyl
Saltney	3-1	Northern Nomads
Aberystwyth Town	5-3	7th Royal Welsh Fusiliers
Newtown		
Mardy	2-0	Llanelly
Cardiff Corinthians	2-4	Pontypridd

First Round Replays

Llandudno Amateurs	4-1	Llandudno Junct. Temp.
Rhos	3-1	Summerhill

Second Round

Holyhead Swifts	2-2	Llandudno Amateurs
Mold Town	1-2	Buckley Engineers
Rhos	3-1	Eclusham
Whitchurch (w/o)	v	Wellington St George (withdrew)
Saltney	1-1	Chester
Llanidloes Town	0-3	Aberystwyth Town
Llandrindod Wells	1-3	Builth Wells
Pontypridd	3-1	Mardy

Second Round Replay

Llandudno Amateurs	0-0	Holyhead Swifts
Chester	4-1	Saltney

Second Round Second Replay

Holyhead Swifts	1-2	Llandudno Amateurs

Third Round

Llandudno Amateurs	1-0	Whitchurch
Johnstown	0-2	Rhyl
Oswestry United	1-3	Chester
Wrexham	3-2	Merthyr Town
Treharris	0-1	Cardiff City
Buckley Engineers	6-0	Aberystwyth Town

The match was abandoned. The rematch finished 5-0.

Builth Wells	0-4	Ton Pentre
Pontypridd	8-0	Connah's Quay & Shotton

Fourth Round

Rhos	2-0	Chester
Buckley Engineers	2-0	Ton Pentre
Llandudno Amateurs	0-2	Pontypridd
Wrexham	1-2	Cardiff City

Fourth Round Replay

Ton Pentre	8-0	Buckley Engineers

Semi-finals

Cardiff City	1-1	Chester
Played at Cardiff		
Pontypridd	0-0	Ton Pentre

Semi-final Replays

Chester	1-2	Cardiff City
Played at Wrexham		
Ton Pentre	1-3	Pontypridd
Played at Tonypandy		

1912 WELSH CUP FINAL

8th April 1912 at Ninian Park, Cardiff

Cardiff City	0-0	Pontypridd

Cardiff City: E Husbands, Douglas, W Hardy, Abley, Lawrie, Thompson, Tracey, Pinch, G Burton, J Burton, John 'Jack' Evans

Pontypridd: G Turner, E Dalton, Murray, Bevan, Shelley, Powell, Barlow, Christie, Walker, McKinley, McCall

Referee: G O Postle (Acrefair)

Attendance: 14,000

1912 WELSH CUP FINAL REPLAY

18th April 1912 at Ynys Field, Aberdare

Cardiff City	3-0	Pontypridd

Featherstone, Tracey 2

Cardiff City: E Husbands, G Latham, A Waters, Abley, Thompson, W Hardy, Tracey, G Burton, H W Featherstone, J Burton, J Evans

Pontypridd: G Turner, E Dalton, Murray, Bevan, Shelley, Powell, McDonald, McKinley, Walker, Christie, McCall

Referee: G O Postle (Acrefair)

Attendance: 7,000

1912/13 Welsh Cup

Extra Preliminary Round

Johnstown	0-1	Chirk
Southsea United	3-0	Wrexham Nomads
Eclusham White Stars	4-0	Druids
Newport County	1-0	Mardy
Gilfach	1-3	Risca District
Treharris	1-0	Barry District
Aberdare	8-0	Lysaghts Excelsiors
Cardiff Corinthians	2-1	Newport Barbarians
Troedyrhiw Stars	9-0	Abertillery Town

Preliminary Round

Llanberis United	5-0	Llanrwst
Colwyn Bay	3-0	Llandudno Junction
Carnarvon United	4-0	Llandudno Amateurs

The match was abandoned and a replay ordered.

Green United	2-2	Southsea

Rhos	2-2	Chirk
Summerhill	0-1	Gwersyllt
Frith	2-2	Eclusham White Stars
Rhyl	1-1	Connah's Quay & Shotton
Llanelly	9-1	Morriston
Swansea Town	3-1	Milford Town
Cardiff Corinthians	1-0	Mid Rhondda
Aberdare	1-1	Newport County
Rhymney	1-3	Troedyrhiw
Risca District	2-3	Treharris

Preliminary Round Replays

Carnarvon United	2-2	Llandudno Amateurs
Southsea	2-1	Green United
Chirk	2-0	Rhos
Eclusham White Stars	5-2	Frith
Connah's Quay & Shotton	2-0	Rhyl
Aberdare	1-1	Newport County

Prelminary Round Second Replays

Llandudno Amateurs	2-3 (aet)	Carnarvon United
Newport County	3-4 (aet)	Aberdare

The match was abandoned before the end and a rematch was held at Aberdare.

Preliminary Round Third Replay

Aberdare	4-0	Newport County

First Round

Colwyn Bay	3-0	Llanberis
Holyhead Swifts	2-0	Carnarvon United
Southsea	2-2	Gwersyllt
Eclusham White Stars	0-1	Chirk
Hadley Castle CW (w/o)	v	Whitchurch (withdrew)
Wellington St George	bye	
Connah's Quay & Shotton	0-4	Northern Nomads
Denbigh Town	2-3	Holywell
Towyn Rovers	2-3	Aberystwyth Town
Newtown (w/o)	v	Barmouth (withdrew)
Builth Wells	1-4	Llanidloes
Rhayader	2-0	Llandrindod Wells
Llanelly	7-1	Port Talbot
Swansea Town	5-0	Mond NW
Troedyrhiw	3-0	Cardiff Corinthians
Treharris	0-2	Aberdare

First Round Replays

Gwersyllt	4-1	Southsea
Chirk	4-0	Eclusham White Stars

Second Round

Colwyn Bay	3-1	Holyhead Swifts
Gwersyllt	2-1	Chirk
Hadley Castle CW	2-1	Wellington St George
Northern Nomads	5-1	Holywell
Aberystwyth Town	4-1	Newtown
Troedyrhiw	2-2	Aberdare
Rhayader	2-1	Llanidloes
Swansea Town	2-1	Llanelly

All other clubs given byes

Second Round Replay

Aberdare	1-2	Troedyrhiw

Third Round

Bangor	3-2	Gwersyllt
Wrexham	1-3	Swansea Town
Chester	1-1	Oswestry United
Aberystwyth	1-2	Hadley Castle CW
Cardiff City	4-2	Ton Pentre
Merthyr Town	2-0	Northern Nomads
Pontypridd	9-0	Rhayader
Troedyrhiw	1-1	Colwyn Bay

Third Round Replays

Oswestry United	1-2	Chester
Colwyn Bay	1-3	Troedyrhiw

Fourth Round

Hadley Castle CW	1-6	Pontypridd
Merthyr Town	0-3	Swansea Town
Chester	1-0	Troedyrhiw
Bangor City	0-4	Cardiff City

Semi-finals

Cardiff City	2-4	Swansea Town

Played at Merthyr

Pontypridd	3-0	Chester

Played at Cardiff

1913 WELSH CUP FINAL

19th April 1913 at Ninian Park, Cardiff

Swansea Town	0-0	Pontypridd

Swansea Town: Fisher, W J Nicholas, A Sutherland, C Duffy, J Hamilton, Jepp, Manser, Anderson, Weir, Grierson, Swarbrick

Pontypridd: G Turner, E Dalton, Murray, J Hardman, Shelley, Fell, Morley, Walker, Hall, Knight, R Davies

Referee: I Baker (Nantwich)

Attendance: 9,000

1913 WELSH CUP FINAL REPLAY

24th April 1913 at Tonypandy

Swansea Town	1-0	Pontypridd

Anderson

Swansea Town: Fisher, W J Nicholas, A Sutherland, C Duffy, J Hamilton, Jepp, Manser, Anderson, Weir, Grierson, Swarbrick

Pontypridd: G Turner, E Dalton, Murray, J Hardman, Shelley, Fell, Morley, Walker, Hall, Knight, R Davies

Referee: I Baker (Nantwich)

Attendance: 8,319

1913/14 Welsh Cup

First Preliminary Round

Caergwrle	2-3	Summerhill
Brymbo Institute	1-3	Chirk
Gilfach	7-0	Cross Keys Town

Second Preliminary Round

Carnarvon United	1-2	Holyhead Swifts
Llandudno Junction	1-3	Colwyn Bay
Druids	2-3	Summerhill
Johnstown	0-0	Gwersyllt
Rhos	1-0	Chirk
Shrewsbury Wanderers	2-3	Hadley Castle CW
Holywell United	0-5	Connah's Quay
Pembroke Dock Athletic	2-2	Port Talbot Town
Aberdare (w/o)	v	Mardy (withdrew)
Lysaghts Excelsior	1-3	Troedyrhiw Stars
Rhymney	2-2	Cardiff Corinthians
Mid Rhondda	1-1	Newport County
Treharris	1-3	Ton Pentre
Bargoed Town	2-0	Barry
Caerphilly	4-2	Gilfach

Both clubs were expelled from the competition for fielding ineligible players.

Rhiwderin	0-4	Abertillery

Second Preliminary Round Replays

Gwersyllt	5-0	Johnstown
Port Talbot Town	7-1	Pembroke Dock Athletic
Cardiff Corinthians	2-0	Rhymney
Newport County	6-0	Mid Rhondda

First Round

Llandudno FC	1-8	Dolgarrog
Holyhead Swifts	1-1	Colwyn Bay
Hadley Castle CW	4-2	Rhos
Summerhill	1-0	Gwersyllt
Connah's Quay	4-2	Rhyl
Denbigh Town (w/o)	v	Northern Nomads (withdrew)
Bala Press	1-2	Machynlleth

Machynlleth were subsequently disqualified.

Newtown	3-2	Aberystwyth Town
Llanidloes Town	4-0	Llandrindod Wells
Rhayader	2-2	Builth Wells
Port Talbot Town	1-1	Mond NW
Llanelly	5-1	Caerau
Aberdare	0-0	Troedyrhiw Stars
Cardiff Corinthians	1-3	Newport County
Abertillery	7-0	Ton Pentre

Bargoed received a bye as Gilfach and Caerphilly had both been expelled from the competition.

First Round Replays

Colwyn Bay	3-1	Holyhead Swifts
Builth Wells	2-3	Rhayader
Mond NW	0-1	Port Talbot Town
Troedyrhiw Stars	4-0	Aberdare

Second Round

Llandudno FC	3-1	Colwyn Bay
Summerhill	3-0	Hadley Castle CW
Denbigh Town	5-1	Connah's Quay
Bala Press	1-5	Newtown
Rhayader	1-3	Llanidloes Town
Port Talbot Town	3-3	Llanelly
Newport County	1-1	Troedyrhiw Stars
Abertillery	3-0	Bargoed Town

Second Round Replay

Llanelly	1-0	Port Talbot Town
Troedyrhiw Stars	3-1	Newport County

Third Round

Llanelly	0-0	Mardy
Newtown	1-0	Denbigh Town
Wrexham	5-0	Llanidloes Town
Oswestry United	2-1	Cardiff City
Summerhill	3-0	Bangor
Abertillery	0-0	Pontypridd
Swansea Town	1-0	Chester
Troedyrhiw Stars	2-3	Llandudno FC

Third Round Replays

Mardy	1-2	Llanelly
Pontypridd	2-1	Abertillery

Fourth Round

Newtown	1-1	Wrexham
Pontypridd	5-1	Llandudno FC
Swansea Town	1-1	Oswestry United
Llanelly	8-0	Summerhill

Fourth Round Replays

Wrexham	7-0	Newtown
Oswestry United	1-2	Swansea Town

Semi-finals

Llanelly	2-1	Swansea Town

Played at Pontypridd

Wrexham	0-0	Pontypridd

Played at Cardiff

Semi-final Replay

Pontypridd	1-1 (aet)	Wrexham

Played at Chester

Semi-final Second Replay

Wrexham	3-1	Pontypridd

Played at Shrewsbury

1914 WELSH CUP FINAL

28th March 1914 at the Vetch Field, Swansea

Wrexham　　　　0-0　　　　Llanelly

Wrexham: Gallagher, W E Fenner, L Davies, T J Matthias, P Williams, E Huffadine, F C Cook, B Goode, Antwis, H J Uren, J Lipsham

Llanelly: W Bailiff, James, Bracher, Gough, Martin, Norris, Osbourne, Groves, Curtis, Payne, Bird

Referee: J Mason (Burslem)

Attendance: 15,000

1914 WELSH CUP FINAL REPLAY

25th April 1914 at the Cricket Field, Oswestry

Wrexham　　　　3-0　　　　Llanelly

Cook, Hughes, Uren

Wrexham: A Devaney, W E Fenner, L Davies, T J Matthias, P Williams, E Huffadine, F C Cook, B Goode, E Hughes, H J Uren, J Lipsham

Llanelly: W Bailiff, James, Bracher, Gough, Martin, Norris, Osbourne, Groves, J Freeman, Curtis, Bird

Referee: J Mason (Burslem)

Attendance: 3,639

1914/15 Welsh Cup

Preliminary Round

Bargoed (w/o) v		All Saints YM (Newport) (withdrew)
Troedyrhiw	0-2	Mid Rhondda
Cardiff Albions	0-6	Mardy
Ystradmynach	0-11	Merthyr Town
Barry (w/o) v		Ynysddu (withdrew)
Ton Pentre	6-0	Ebbw Vale
Gilfach	3-1	Rhymney
Newport County	3-0	Abertillery

First Round

Brymbo Institute (w/o)	v	Chirk (withdrew)
Rhos Church (w/o)	v	Johnstown (withdrew)
Northern Nomads (w/o)	v	Denbigh (withdrew)
Barmouth (withdrew)	v	Aberystwyth Town (w/o)
Pant United (withdrew)	v	Newtown (w/o)
Llanidloes Town (withdrew)	v	Builth Wells (w/o)
Milford Town (w/o)	v	Mond NW (withdrew)
Port Talbot (withdrew)	v	Caerau (w/o)
Bargoed	0-1	Mid Rhondda
Merthyr	7-0	Mardy
Gilfach	0-1	Barry
Newport County (withdrew)	v	Ton Pentre (w/o)

Second Round

Llandudno FC (w/o)	v	Conway (withdrew)
Brymbo (w/o)	v	Rhos Church (withdrew)
Northern Nomads (w/o)	v	Holywell (withdrew)
Newtown	2-1	Aberystwyth Town
Llandrindod Wells (w/o)	v	Builth Wells (withdrew)
Milford Town (w/o)	v	Caerau (withdrew)
Merthyr Town	1-0	Mid Rhondda
Gilfach	1-7	Ton Pentre

Third Round

Pontypridd (w/o)	v	Cardiff City (withdrew)
Chester	5-3	Oswestry United
Bangor	1-4	Brymbo
Swansea Town (w/o)	v	Milford Town (withdrew)
Llanelly	3-1	Ton Pentre
Llandudno (w/o)	v	Newtown (withdrew)
Llandrindod Wells (withdrew)	v	Merthyr Town (w/o)
Wrexham	4-1	Northern Nomads

Fourth Round

Brymbo	2-4	Wrexham
Chester	2-2	Llandudno FC
Swansea Town	2-1	Pontypridd
Merthyr Town	0-9	Llanelly

Fourth Round Replay

Llandudno FC	1-0	Chester

Semi-finals

Swansea Town	1-0	Llanelly
Played at Swansea		
Llandudno FC	1-3	Wrexham
Played at Llandudno		

1915 WELSH CUP FINAL

10th April 1915 at the Racecourse, Wrexham

Wrexham　　　　1-1　　　　Swansea

Owen　　　　　　　　　　*Beynon*

Wrexham: A Devaney, F Hughes, L Davies, T J Matthias, P Williams, Huffadine, F C Cook, B Goode, Owen, C Davies, G Davies

Swansea Town: Fisher, T J Hewitt, Bullock, G Heath, C Duffy, D Anderson, W H Read, Ball, Ben Beynon, J Weir, J A Lloyd

Referee: A H Oakley (Wolverhampton)

Attendance: 6,000

1915 WELSH CUP FINAL REPLAY

25th April 1915 at Ninian Park, Cardiff

Wrexham	1-0	Swansea

Goode

Wrexham: A Devaney, F Hughes, L Davies, T J Matthias, P Williams, C Davies, F C Cook, B Goode, Owen, Blackburn, G Davies

Swansea Town: Fisher, T J Hewitt, W J Nicholas, G Heath, C Duffy, D Anderson, W H Read, J Bullock, B Beynon, J Weir, J A Lloyd

Referee: A H Oakley (Wolverhampton)

Attendance: 4,000

1919/20 Welsh Cup

Preliminary Round

Rhyl	5-1	Denbigh
Colwyn Bay	1-1	Conwy
Bangor Comrades	2-3	Bangor Railway Institute
Bangor Town	bye	
Barmouth Comrades	2-3	Aberystwyth Town
Machynlleth	0-8	Newtown
Llanfyllin	bye	
Welshpool	bye	
Llanidloes	bye	
Builth Wells	bye	
Llandrindod Wells	bye	
Rhayader	bye	
Vron	1-2	Eclusham White Star
Brymbo Institute	5-2	Rhosrobin
Oswestry Comrades	1-0	Llay Hall
Rhos	5-2	Chirk
Pentre United	bye	
Saltney	bye	
Northern Nomads	bye	
Connah's Quay	bye	
Barry	4-0	Cardiff Harlequins
Cardiff Corinthians	2-0	Cardiff Albion
Milford Town	2-1	Newport Barbarians
Caerau	bye	
Mid Rhondda	6-0	Aberaman Athletic
Mardy	2-1	Aberdare Amateurs
Porth Athletic	0-1	Bargoed
Caerphilly	1-1	Ton Pentre
Waen Llwyd	1-1	Rhiwderin
Rogerstone	1-3	Ebbw Vale
Cwm Town	v	Chepstow

Cwm Town failed to appear and were duly disqualified.

| Abertillery | 4-1 | Ynysddu |

Preliminary Round Replays

Conwy	3-2	Colwyn Bay
Ton Pentre	5-1	Caerphilly
Rhiwderin	3-1	Waen Llwyd

First Round

Conwy	1-1	Rhyl
Bangor Railway Institute	v	Bangor Town

Bangor Town club did not exist

Aberystwyth Town	4-1	Newtown
Llanfyllin	3-1	Welshpool
Rhayader	1-1	Llanidloes
Llandrindod Wells	1-0	Builth Wells
Brymbo Institute	2-1	Oswestry Comrades

The match was abandoned due to poor light and a replay was ordered.

Rhos	5-1	Eclusham White Stars
Pentre United	1-3	Saltney United
Northern Nomads	1-2	Connah's Quay
Barry	5-0	Milford Town
Caerau	3-1	Cardiff Corinthians
Mid Rhondda	2-1	Bargoed
Ton Pentre	1-1	Mardy
Rhiwderin	0-5	Ebbw Vale
Chepstow	4-3	Abertillery

First Round Replays

Rhyl	7-0	Conwy
Llanidloes	0-0	Rhayader
Builth Wells	0-3	Llandrindod Wells
Brymbo Institute	3-2	Oswestry Comrades
Mardy	2-1	Ton Pentre

First Round Second Replay

Rhayader	0-1	Llanidloes

Second Round

Bangor Railway Institute	3-0	Rhyl
Aberystwyth Town	4-1	Llanfyllin
Llanidloes	3-1	Llandrindod Wells
Brymbo Institute	1-1	Rhos
Connah's Quay	2-4	Saltney
Caerau	1-0	Barry

The match was not completed.

| Mardy | 0-0 | Mid Rhondda |
| Chepstow | 3-9 | Ebbw Vale |

Second Round Replays

Rhos	3-1	Brymbo Institute
Caerau	0-3	Barry
Mid Rhondda	5-0	Mardy

Third Round

Cardiff City	5-0	Merthyr Town
Rhos	1-1	Wrexham
Saltney United	1-0	Bangor RI
Pontypridd	0-1	Barry
Swansea Town	3-2	Mid Rhondda
Chester (w/o)	v	Tranmere Rovers (withdrew)
Ebbw Vale	2-0	Llanelly
Llanidloes	3-0	Aberyswyth Town

Third Round Replay

Wrexham	2-0	Rhos

Fourth Round

Wrexham	4-1	Saltney United
Ebbw Vale	3-0	Llanidloes
Cardiff City	5-0	Chester
Barry	0-1	Swansea Town

Semi-finals

Wrexham	1-0	Ebbw Vale
Played at Wrexham		
Cardiff City	2-1	Swansea Town
Played at Cardiff		

1920 WELSH CUP FINAL

21st April 1920 at the Racecourse, Wrexham

Wrexham	0-2	Cardiff City

West 2

Cardiff City: J Kneeshaw, R C Brittan, A E Layton, F C Keenor, E E Smith, W Hardy, W Grimshaw, W Cox, A A Cashmore, G West, J Evans

Wrexham: Boxley, T Jones, R H Simpson, T J Matthias, B E Foster, R Griffiths, D Jardine, Bert Goode, E D Roberts, J Noel Edwards

Referee: J Mason (Burslem)

Attendance: 6,618

1920/21 Welsh Cup

First Preliminary Round

Llandudno FC	5-2	Llanrwst
Rhos	2-3	Wellington St George
Eclusham White Stars	4-0	Graessers Monsanto
Ruabon	2-1	Johnstown
Rhosymedre	1-2	Gresford
Wrexham Comrades	1-4	Powell's Athletic
Wrexham Civil Service	0-9	Rhosrobin
Coedpoeth	3-3	Buckley United
Tryddyn Lodge	1-2	Brymbo Institute
Buckley Comrades	0-2	New Broughton
Stansty	3-4	Summerhill
Brymbo Green	2-1	Llay Hall
Gwersyllt	2-2	Broughton DS
Dolgellau	2-1	Portmadoc
Newtown	2-0	Montgomery
Cardiff Corinthians	4-1	Rhymney
Oakdale	0-1	Chepstow
Pontllanfraith	1-5	Porth Athletic
Bargoed	2-1	Treherbert
Mardy	0-0	Barry Town
Cardiff Harlequins	1-5	Abercarn
Cardiff Albion	0-5	Caerphilly

First Preliminary Round Replays

Buckley United	9-0	Coedpoeth
Broughton DS	1-2	Gwersyllt
Barry	2-0	Mardy

Second Preliminary Round

Holyhead	1-0	Conway
Llandudno FC (w/o)	v	Bangor Railway Institute (withdrew)
Bangor Athletic	4-1	Carnarvon
Ogwen Valley	0-1	Colwyn Bay
Holywell	2-0	Shotton
Pentre	1-4	Rhyl
Denbigh	2-2	Connah's Quay
Chester	0-0	Chirk
Crichton	6-0	Bagillt
Gwersyllt	14-1	Buckley United
Brymbo Institute	1-1	Rhosrobin
New Broughton	1-1	Powell's
Brymbo Green	4-1	Summerhill
Ruabon	1-6	Wellington Town
Oswestry Town	0-2	Gresford
Eclusham White Stars	5-1	Northern Nomads
Tywyn Rovers	2-2	Dolgellau
Aberystwyth Town (withdrew)	v	Barmouth (w/o)
Aberystwyth Univ. College	3-2	Machynlleth
Bala Comrades	1-2	Corwen
Llandrindod Wells	5-0	Builth Wells
Llanidloes Town	6-0	Rhayader
Newtown	8-1	Caersws
Llanfyllin	2-3	Welshpool
Caerphilly	6-0	Abercarn
Chepstow	0-6	Ton Pentre
Bargoed	1-4	Cardiff Corinthians
Porth Athletic	0-0	Barry Town
Milford	4-2	Ystalyfera
Aberdare	1-0	Aberaman Athletic
Pembroke Dock	0-4	Bridgend
Mid Rhondda	0-0	Caerau

Second Preliminary Round Replays

Connah's Quay	6-0	Denbigh
Chirk	2-2	Chester
Rhosrobin	3-3	Brymbo Institute
Powell's	3-2	New Broughton
Dolgellau	3-0	Tywyn Rovers
Barry Town	1-1	Porth Athletic
Caerau	0-1	Mid Rhondda

Second Preliminary Round Second Replays

Chester	0-2	Chirk
Brymbo Institute	7-0	Rhosrobin
Porth Athletic	1-2	Barry Town

First Round

Colwyn Bay	2-4	Bangor Athletic
Llandudno FC	1-1	Holyhead Railway Institute
Connah's Quay	5-2	Crichton's Athletic
Rhyl	6-4	Holywell
Eclusham White Stars	0-1	Gresford

Wellington St George	4-1	Chirk
Brymbo Institute	2-2	Powell's
Gwersyllt	0-0	Brymbo Green
Corwen	1-4	Aberystwyth University College
Dolgellau	0-2	Barmouth Comrades
Welshpool	1-3	Llandrindod Wells
Newtown	0-2	Llanidloes Town
Ton Pentre	5-3	Cardiff Corinthians
Caerphilly	1-0	Barry Town
Mid-Rhondda	1-0	Bridgend
Milford	0-7	Aberdare

First Round Replays

Holyhead Rail. Institute	3-1	Llandudno FC
Powell's	0-1	Brymbo Institute
Brymbo Green	0-3	Gwersyllt

Second Round

Rhyl	2-0	Holyhead Rail. Institute

A rematch was ordered after a protest over the eligibility of a player.

Connah's Quay	2-2	Bangor Athletic
Wellington St George	4-2	Brymbo Institute
Barmouth Comrades	2-3	Aberystwyth Univ. College
Llandrindod Wells	0-0	Llanidloes Town
Caerphilly	1-1	Mid Rhondda
Ton Pentre	0-0	Aberdare
Gresford	3-1	Gwersyllt

A replay was ordered following a protest that the ground was not compliant.

Second Round Replays

Rhyl	2-0	Holyhead Rail. Institute
Bangor Athletic	3-4	Connah's Quay
Llanidloes Town	6-1	Llandrindod Wells
Mid Rhondda	3-0	Caerphilly
Aberdare	0-1	Ton Pentre
Gresford	0-0	Gwersyllt

Second Round Second Replay

Gwersyllt	0-4	Gresford

Third Round

Pontypridd	3-1	Cardiff City Reserves
Newport County	4-0	Ebbw Vale
Ton Pentre	8-0	Llanelly
Mid Rhondda	1-0	Swansea Town
Merthyr Town	6-1	Wellington St George
Gresford	4-2	Connah's Quay
Rhyl	1-6	Wrexham
Aberystwyth Univ. College	2-5	Llanidloes Town

Fourth Round

Wrexham	3-1	Gresford
Ton Pentre	1-1	Mid Rhondda
Newport County	0-1	Merthyr Town
Pontypridd	2-0	Llanidloes Town

Fourth Round Replay

Mid Rhondda	1-2	Ton Pentre

Semi-finals

Ton Pentre	0-2	Pontypridd

Played at Mid Rhondda

Merthyr Town	1-2	Wrexham

Played at Wrexham

1921 WELSH CUP FINAL

16th April 1921 at Ninian Park, Cardiff

Wrexham	1-1	Pontypridd
Edwards		*Mayson*

Wrexham: L Murphy, F Blew, R H Simpson, T J Matthias, B E Foster, A Bishop, R Jones, B Goode, Taylor, J Noel Edwards, E D Roberts

Pontypridd: Wilde, A Watson, G Jackson, Tully, Milne, Parkes, C Rouse, A Foxall, Evans, T Mayson, Eugene Carney

Referee: J Mason (Burslem)

Attendance: 7,000

1921 WELSH CUP FINAL REPLAY

28th April 1921 at Gay Meadow, Shrewsbury

Wrexham	3-1	Pontypridd
Edwards 2, Goode		*Carney*

Wrexham: L Murphy, J Ellis, R H Simpson, T J Matthias, B E Foster, E D Roberts, R Jones, B Goode, Taylor, J Noel Edwards, Pickering

Pontypridd: Wilde, Barton, G Jackson, Tully, Milne, Parkes, Clack, A Foxall, J R Owens, T Mayson, E Carney

Referee: I Baker (Nantwich)

Attendance: 8,000

1921/22 Welsh Cup

Special Preliminary Round

Porth	8-3	Cardiff Bohemians
Lovell's Athletic	0-0	Chepstow
New Tredegar	2-0	Abercarn
Llanhileth	3-2	Rhymney
Cross Keys (withdrew)	v	Blackwood Town (w/o)
Llanrwst	0-5	Colwyn Bay
Conway	1-1	Caernarvon
Bangor Athletic	7-0	Buckley United
Llandudno FC	3-2	Northern Nomads
Courtaulds	1-4	Flint Town
Esclusham	2-4	Oak Alyn Rovers
Coedpoeth	2-0	Dawley
Oakengates	11-0	Garth and Trevor United
Newtown Albion	6-1	Caersws
Forden	1-5	Montgomery
Bala	5-2	Corwen

Machynlleth	0-0	Portmadoc

All other clubs byes

Special Preliminary Round Replays

Chepstow	5-1	Lovell's Athletic
Caernarvon	2-3	Conway
Portmadoc	2-1	Machynlleth

Second Preliminary Round

Rhyl	4-1	Holyhead
Ogwen Valley	1-3	Bangor Athletic
Colwyn Bay	2-4	Llandudno FC
Holywell	5-1	Conway
Buckley	1-1	Ewloe
Sealand Tenants	0-0	Shotton Institute
Flint	1-4	Connah's Quay
Summerhill	2-0	Gresford
Gwenfro	0-4	Rhosrobin
Broughton DS & S	2-3	Brymbo Green
Brymbo Institute	2-2	Mynydd Isa
Oakengates	3-0	Oswestry Town
Chirk	6-2	Whitchurch
Rhos	5-0	Oak Alyn Rovers
Rhosymedre Druids	7-1	Coedpoeth
Welshpool	3-0	Llanfyllin
Llandrindod Wells	2-1	Rhayader
Newtown Albions	1-2	Llanidloes Town
Ruthin	2-2	Denbigh
Dolgelley	2-0	Bala
Barmouth	3-2	Towyn Rovers
Porth	1-0	Cardiff Corinthians
Bargoed	2-0	Cardiff Camerons
Barry	1-0	Cardiff Amateurs
Cardiff Riverside	2-3	Cardiff Albions
Bridgend	1-0	Pemboke Dock
Chepstow	1-3	Abertillery
New Tredegar	3-0	Blackwood Town
Llanhileth	1-2	Oakdale
Rhiwderin	1-10	Ebbw Vale
Llanbradach	2-2	Treherbert
Caerphilly	9-0	Gilfach
Mid Rhondda	5-0	Mardy
Cwmbach	0-4	Aberaman
Milford Town	1-4	Caerau
Saltney (withdrew)	v	Shotton Town (w/o)
Aberystwyth Univ. College	4-4	Portmadoc

Second Preliminary Round Replays

Ewloe	3-1	Buckley

Ewloe were subsequently thrown out of the competition after fielding an ineligible player who appeared under an assumed name.

Shotton Institute	2-3	Sealand Tenants
Mynydd Isa	0-2	Brymbo Institute
Denbigh	4-0	Ruthin
Treherbert	4-1	Llanbradach
Portmadoc	2-1	Aberystwyth Univ. College

Second Preliminary Round Second Replay

Brymbo Institute	1-0	Mynydd Isa

Third Preliminary Round

Oakengates	4-4	Chirk

A replay at Shrewsbury was ordered following a protest by Chirk regarding the size of ground.

Brymbo Green	3-1	Rhosrobin
Bangor	3-1	Rhyl
Rhos	0-0	Rhosmydre Druids
Shotton Town	1-0	Sealand Tenants
Dolgelley	2-3	Denbigh
Connah's Quay	4-2	Buckley United
Holywell	5-1	Llandudno FC
Brymbo Institute	1-4	Summerhill United
Llanidloes Town	1-1	Newtown
Welshpool	3-0	Llandrindod Wells
Portmadoc	5-0	Barmouth
Bargoed	1-1	Porth Athletic
Cardiff Albion	3-5	Barry
Ystalafera	0-4	Caerau
Bridgend	4-1	Gorseinon
Abertillery	3-0	New Tredegar
Oakdale	0-6	Ebbw Vale
Caerphilly	1-2	Aberaman
Mid-Rhondda	3-0	Treherbert

Third Preliminary Round Replays

Oakengates	2-1	Chirk

Played at Shrewsbury

Rhosymdre Druids	2-2	Rhos
Newtown	0-5	Llanidloes Town
Porth Athletic	2-0	Bargoed

Third Preliminary Round Second Replay

Rhos	4-1	Rhosymdre Druids

First Round

Denbigh	2-1	Portmadoc
Bangor	3-2	Holywell
Oakengates	3-3	Rhos
Brymbo Green	4-1	Shotton Town
Welshpool	4-1	Llanidloes Town
Connah's Quay	7-2	Summerhill United
Mid Rhondda	2-2	Porth
Caerau	2-2	Barry
Abertillery	2-3	Bridgend
Caerphilly	0-1	Ebbw Vale

First Round Replays

Rhos	5-0	Oakengates
Porth	0-4	Mid Rhondda
Barry	1-2	Caerau

Second Round

Bangor	3-0	Denbigh
Brymbo Green	3-1	Rhos
Welshpool	1-2	Connah's Quay
Caerau	1-0	Mid Rhondda
Bridgend	2-1	Ebbw Vale

Third Round

Aberdare	2-3	Swansea Town
Ton Pentre	1-0	Caerau
Bridgend	0-0	Pontypridd
Cardiff City	7-1	Newport County
Llanelly Town	1-2	Merthyr Town
Shrewsbury Town	1-3	Wrexham
Brymbo Green	1-0	Wellington Town
Bangor	1-4	Connah's Quay

Third Round Replay

Pontypridd	3-1	Bridgend

Fourth Round

Cardiff City	5-0	Merthyr Town
Ton Pentre	1-0	Swansea Town
Brymbo Green	1-5	Pontypridd
Wrexham	3-1	Connah's Quay

Semi-finals

Wrexham	0-2	Ton Pentre
Played at Shrewsbury		
Cardiff City	3-0	Pontypridd
Played at Aberdare		

1922 WELSH CUP FINAL

4th May 1922 at Taff Vale Park, Pontypridd

Cardiff City	2-0	Ton Pentre AFC

Gill, L Davies

Cardiff City: B Davies, Brittan, Blair, H P Evans, B Smith, F C Keenor, Grimshaw, Gill, L Davies, Clennell, J Evans

Ton Pentre: W D Reed C S Butler, A H Tanner, C Poynton, A Gillespie, Hathaway, W Jones, E Rees, J Jones, J Woods, A Jones

Referee: E C Sambrook (Swansea)

Attendance: 8,000

1922/23 Welsh Cup

First Round

Not used

Second Round

Northern Nomads (withdrew)	v	Coedpoeth (w/o)
Broughton DS & S	1-1	Ruthin
Dolgelley	1-4	Barmouth
Pwllheli	1-4	Portmadoc
Welshpool	3-1	Newtown
Forden	1-5	Llanfyllin
Aberystwyth Univ. College	6-0	Machynlleth
Towyn Rovers	bye	
Cardiff Camerons	2-2	Cardiff Bohemians
Gorseinon	1-6	Cardiff Corinthians
Argoed	2-1	Pengam
Cardiff Albion	2-1	Cardiff Amateurs
Risca	1-2	Cwmcarn
Talywain	1-2	Rhiwderin
Llanbradach (w/o)	v	Hirwaun
Abertridwr	3-0	Trecynon

All other clubs received a bye

Second Round Replays

Ruthin	4-0	Broughton DS & S
Cardiff Bohemians	3-2	Cardiff Camerons

Third Round

Conway	2-1	Caernarvon
Penmaenmawr	1-4	Llandudno FC
Flint	1-2	Colwyn Bay
Denbigh	1-1	Bangor
Courtaulds	3-2	Holywell
Buckley	0-1	Brymbo & Green United
Oakengates	1-3	Shrewsbury Town
Coedpoeth	2-2	Oak Alyn Rovers
Chirk	2-0	Whitchurch
Ogwen Valley	2-1	Connah's Quay
Llangollen	0-6	Oswestry
Rhosymedre	2-3	Ruthin
Gresford	1-3	Rhos
Rhyl	0-0	Holyhead
Ewloe Green	2-6	Wellington Town
Welshpool	1-0	Llanfyllin
Montgomery	0-6	Llanidloes Town
Rhayader	1-3	Llandrindod Wells
Knighton	3-1	Builth
Towyn	0-4	Barmouth
Portmadoc	1-0	Aberystwyth UC
Rhymney	1-1	Barry
Ebbw Vale	4-0	Caerau
Mardy	0-1	Llanelly
Pembroke Dock	3-1	Porth
Aberaman	2-1	Llanbradach
Bargoed	3-1	New Tredegar
Cardiff Corinthians	1-0	Bridgend
Caerphilly	1-0	Abertillery

Abertillery won a protest and progressed to the next round instead of Caerphilly.

Argoed	1-3	Abertridwr
Cardiff Bohemians	1-1	Cardiff Albion
Rhiwderin	2-3	Cwmcarn

Third Round Replays

Bangor	2-2	Denbigh
Oak Alyn Rovers	3-2	Coedpoeth
Holyhead	1-0	Rhyl
Barry	0-2	Rhymney
Cardiff Albion	1-0	Cardiff Bohemians

Third Round Second Replay

Denbigh	2-0	Bangor

Fourth Round

Ogwen Valley	0-5	Shrewsbury Town
Courtaulds	1-1	Brymbo & Green United
Llandudno FC	1-3	Colwyn Bay
Ruthin	2-0	Conway
Chirk	1-0	Denbigh
Rhyl	3-1	Oak Alyn Rovers
Wellington Town	1-2	Oswestry Town
Portmadoc	2-2	Barmouth
Llandrindod Wells	1-5	Knighton
Welshpool	2-1	Llanidloes Town
Abertridwr	1-1	Cardiff Albions
Bargoed	2-6	Llanelly
Ebbw Vale	2-0	Cardiff Corinthians
Pembroke Dock	2-0	Cwmcarn
Abertillery	0-9	Aberaman

All other clubs given byes

Fourth Round Replays

Brymbo & Green United	3-0	Courtaulds
Barmouth	1-1	Portmadoc

Fourth Round Second Replay

Portmadoc	4-2	Barmouth

Extra round

Ruthin	1-0	Welshpool

Fifth Round

Oswestry Town	3-1	Shrewsbury Town
Ruthin	1-0	Portmadoc
Knighton	2-3	Brymbo & Green United
Llanelly	3-0	Ebbw Vale
Chirk	1-3	Colwyn Bay
Rhos	1-2	Rhyl
Abertridwr	3-2	Pembroke Dock
Rhymney	3-2	Aberaman

Sixth Round

Rhymney	0-7	Cardiff City
Llanelly	1-2	Swansea Town

The match was played at Swansea on FAW orders.

Aberdare	10-2	Ton Pentre
Newport County	4-1	Pontypridd
Colwyn Bay	1-1	Rhyl
Merthyr Town	4-1	Abertridwr
Wrexham	5-0	Brymbo & Green United
Oswestry Town	4-1	Ruthin

Sixth Round Replay

Rhyl	1-0	Colwyn Bay

Seventh Round

Merthyr Town	0-0	Rhyl
Wrexham	1-1	Aberdare
Cardiff City	10-0	Oswestry Town
Swansea Town	4-2	Newport County

Seventh Round Replays

Rhyl	1-0	Merthyr Town
Aberdare	4-0	Wrexham

Semi-finals

Cardiff City	3-2	Swansea Town

Played at Cardiff

Aberdare	1-1	Rhyl

Played at Shrewsbury

Semi-final Replay

Rhyl	0-1	Aberdare

1923 WELSH CUP FINAL

3rd May 1923 at the Vetch Field, Swansea

Cardiff City	3-2	Aberdare Athletic
Grimshaw, Gill, Davies		Brown, Sheldon

Cardiff City: Farquharson, Nelson, Blair, H P Evans, B Smith, F C Keenor, Grimshaw, Gill, L Davies, Clennell, Jack Evans

Aberdare: Duckworth, Brooks, Hindmarsh, Field, Gillespie, Sheldon, James, Brown, Martin, Mayson, Danskin

Referee: E C Sambrook (Swansea)

Attendance: 8,000

1923/24 Welsh Cup

Extra Preliminary Round

Tylorstown	1-1	Porth Amateurs
Risca	4-1	Abercarn
Rogerstone	3-0	Cardiff Cameronians

Extra Preliminary Round Replay

Porth Amateurs	0-0	Tylorstown

Extra Preliminary Round 2nd Replay

Tylorstown	5-0	Porth Amateurs

Preliminary Round

Ogwen Valley	2-1	Colwyn Bay Swifts
Llanrwst	2-0	Llandudno Junction
Builth	3-2	Knighton
Llanfyllin	3-1	Montgomery
Cardiff Corinthians	3-1	Cardiff Camerons
Llanbradach	5-1	Hirwaen
Tylorstown	0-0	Cwmparc
Swansea Amateurs	7-1	Aberpergwm
Oakdale	2-2	Rhymney
Bargoed Royal British Legion	2-1	Rhiwderin
Risca	1-1	Aber Valley
New Tredegar	1-2	Lovell's Athletic

All other clubs received byes

Preliminary Round Replays

Cwmparc	1-0	Tylorstown
Rhymney	3-0	Oakdale
Aber Valley	2-1	Risca

First Qualifying Round

Llangollen	7-1	Wrexham CS
Penycae	1-1	Graessers Monsanto
Llay Main (w/o)	v	Oakengates (withdrew)
Ruthin	2-2	Oak Alyn Rovers
Pwllheli	2-3	Portmadoc
Llanrwst	5-3	Llanfairfechan
Llanfyllin	0-4	Welshpool
Newtown	3-1	Machynlleth
Barmouth	1-3	Aberystwyth
Rhayader	0-3	Llanidloes Town
Llandrindod Wells	2-1	Builth Wells
Buckley	1-2	Courtaulds
Caernarvon	1-0	Bangor University College
Ogwen Valley	1-1	Penmaenmawr
Swansea Amateurs	3-2	Cardiff Camerons
Llanbradach	5-1	Rhymney
Bargoed Royal British Legion	1-0	Aber Valley
Cwmparc	2-3	Lovell's Athletic
Aberystwyth University	bye	
Dolgelley	bye	

First Qualifying Round Replays

Graessers Monsanto	3-3	Penycae
Oak Alyn Rovers	6-1	Ruthin
Penmaenmawr	2-2	Ogwen Valley

First Qualifying Round Second Replays

Penycae	3-2	Graessers Monsanto
Ogwen Valley	0-2	Penmaenmawr

Second Qualifying Round

Newtown	4-1	Welshpool
Llanidloes Town	4-3	Llandrindod Wells
Oak Alyn Rovers	3-2	Llay Main
Penycae	2-5	Courtaulds
Dolgelley	0-6	Llangollen
Aberystwyth UC	2-3	Aberystwyth Town
Caernarvon	3-0	Portmadoc
Penmaenmawr	2-1	Llanrwst
Lovell's Athletic	6-1	Bargoed Royal British Legion
Swansea Amateurs	1-1	Llanbradach

Second Qualifying Round Replay

Llanbradach	3-1	Swansea Amateurs

First Round

Barry	3-0	Caerau
Mardy	1-1	Pembroke Dock
Llanbradach	2-1	Lovell's Athletic
Mid Rhondda	5-1	Penrhiwceiber
Aberaman	0-0	Bridgend
Caernarvon	2-1	Denbigh
Mold	3-2	Courtaulds
Bangor	6-0	Acrefair
Connah's Quay	8-1	Penmaenmawr
Colwyn Bay	1-1	Druids
Llangollen	1-3	Holyhead
Brymbo Green	1-2	Chirk

The first match kicked off 20 minutes late and was abandoned due to darkness. It was played at Wrexham because the FAW had held the Brymbo ground to be unsuitable in 1921 and the ruling had never been rescinded. In fact there was no official record at the FAW! The match went ahead and as we know was cut short. Chirk withdrew their objection to the Brymbo ground and FAW ordered the replay to be held at Brymbo. Chirk lodged a further objection. FAW representatives visited the Brymbo ground and declared it unfit. Brymbo appealed but this was dismissed by FAW. Chirk's protest was therefore upheld and FAW ordered the replay to be held at Wrexham. Following protest meeting at the Church school in Brymbo, the club decided to stop playing completely!

Llandudno FC	3-1	Rhos
Oak Alyn Rovers	0-3	Flint
Newtown	1-3	Oswestry Town
Aberystwyth Town	3-2	Llanidloes Town

First Round Replays

Pembroke Dock	2-1	Mardy
Bridgend	3-0	Aberaman
Druids	0-1	Colwyn Bay

Extra Round

Pembroke Dock	0-1	Mid Rhondda

Second Round

Barry	1-1	Mid Rhondda
Llandudno FC	2-2	Mold
Flint	2-0	Holyhead
Played at Rhyl		
Carnarvon	0-0	Aberystwyth Town
Connah's Quay	1-4	Bangor
Oswestry Town	5-1	Holywell
Colwyn Bay	1-0	Chirk
Barry	0-5	Mid Rhondda
Llanbradach	2-2	Bridgend

Second Round Replays

Mid Rhondda	5-0	Barry
Mold	1-0	Llandudno FC

Llandudno FC lodged a protest regarding the size of the ground and a further replay was ordered.

Aberystwyth Town	2-1	Carnarvon
Bridgend	7-2	Llanbradach

Second Round Second Replay

Llandudno FC	0-2	Mold

Third Round

Mid Rhondda	7-0	Bridgend
Oswestry Town	6-1	Aberystwyth Town
Bangor	3-0	Flint
Mold	3-1	Colwyn Bay

Fourth Round

Newport County	5-2	Llanelly
Pontypridd	0-2	Aberdare
Swansea Town	1-0	Ebbw Vale
Shrewsbury Town	0-0	Cardiff City
Wellington Town	0-1	Wrexham
Mold	1-1	Oswestry Town
Rhyl	1-2	Bangor
Mid Rhondda	2-2	Merthyr Town

Fourth Round Replay

Cardiff City	3-0	Shrewsbury Town
Oswestry Town	2-1	Mold
Merthyr Town	2-1	Mid Rhondda

Fifth Round

Swansea Town	0-0	Wrexham
Bangor	0-4	Aberdare
Oswestry Town	1-1	Merthyr Town
Newport County	1-1	Cardiff City

Fifth Round Replays

Wrexham	1-0 (aet)	Swansea Town
Merthyr Town	2-1	Oswestry Town
Cardiff City	0-0	Newport County

Fifth Round Second Replay

Newport County	0-0	Cardiff City

Fifth Round Third Replay

Cardiff City	0-3	Newport County

Semi-finals

Wrexham	1-0	Newport County
Played at Wrexham		
Merthyr Town	2-1	Aberdare
Played at Merthyr		

1924 WELSH CUP FINAL

30th April 1924 at Taff Vale Park, Pontypridd

Merthyr Town	2-2	Wrexham
Arblaster, H L Turner		*Jackson, Cotton*

Merthyr Town: A Lindon, Partridge, Ferrans, Lewis, Sewell, Nash, T Lewis, H L Turner, E Turner, W Arblaster, V Jones

Wrexham: G Godding, A Jones, N Edwards, R W Matthews, G Savage, E Regan, W Harrison, W Cotton, W K Jackson, W Toms, J Williams

Referee: T G Bryan (Willenhall)

Attendance: 4,500

1924 WELSH CUP FINAL REPLAY

1st May 1924 at the Racecourse, Wrexham

Merthyr Town	0-1	Wrexham
		Cotton

Merthyr Town: A Lindon, Phillips, Ferrans, Thomas, Sewell, Nash, Tom Lewis, H L Turner, E Turner, W Arblaster, V Jones

Wrexham: G Godding, A Jones, N Edwards, R W Matthews, T J Matthias, W Harrison, W Cotton, W K Jackson, W Toms, J Williams

Referee: T G Bryan (Willenhall)

Attendance: 8,000

1924/25 Welsh Cup

1st Qualifying Round

Not used

2nd Qualifying Round

Not used

3rd Qualifying Round

Machynlleth	0-3	Aberystwyth Univ.College
Portmadoc	1-0	Aberystwyth Town
Llanidloes Town	8-2	Builth Wells
Rhayader Central Wales (w/o)	v	Nomads (withdrew)
Welshpool	14-0	Caersws GWR
Newtown	1-1	Llanfyllin
Cardiff Civil Service	3-1	Rhiwderin
Bargoed Royal British Legion (w/o)	v	Merthyr YMCA (withdrew)
Llanbradach	1-3	Caerau

All other clubs received byes

3rd Qualifying Round Replay

Llanfyllin	3-2	Newtown

Llanfyllin next appeared in the 6th Qualifying Round. It is not recorded why this was the case but the 5th Qualifying Round was probably regionalised for North Wales clubs only.

4th Qualifying Round

Not used

5th Qualifying Round

Llanfairfechan	1-2	Penmaenmawr
Buckley Athletic	2-0	Courtaulds
Penrhyn Quarry	0-0	Caernarfon Town
Llandudno Junction	3-1	Llanrwst

5th Qualifying Round Replay

Caernarfon Town	3-0	Penrhyn Quarry

6th Qualifying Round

Aberystwyth University	1-2	Llanidloes Town
Rhayader	2-1	Llandrindod Wells
Barmouth	3-1	Portmadoc
Llanfyllin	2-4	Welshpool
Caerau	4-3	Bargoed Royal British Legion
Cardiff Camerons	3-1	Porth Amateurs
Cardiff Civil Service	2-3	New Tredegar
Risca Town	1-3	Penrhiwceiber

First Round

Not used

Second Round

Llangollen	3-4	Graessers
Oak Alyn Rovers	1-3	Brymbo Green
Buckley	2-3	Llandudno Junction
Penmaenmawr	4-0	Caernarvon
Rhayader	1-2	Llanidloes Town
Barmouth	0-1	Welshpool
New Tredegar	2-0	Penrhiwceiber
Swansea Amateurs	v	Aberpergwm

The match was not completed after Swansea Amateurs withdrew.

Pembroke Dock	5-0	Port Talbot
Caerau	4-1	Cardiff Camerons

Third Round

Shrewsbury Town	3-2	Rhos
Mold Town	6-0	Llandudno Junction
Acrefair	0-1	Flint
Brymbo	3-1	Graessers
Chirk	1-2	Oswestry
Druids	1-3	Wellington
Rhyl	4-1	Denbigh Town
Colwyn Bay	3-1	Holywell
Llandudno FC	1-0	Penmaenmawr
Holyhead	1-1	Bangor
Welshpool	0-0	Llanidloes Town
Aberaman	0-2	New Tredegar
Pembroke Dock	0-1	Bridgend Town
Aberpergwm	2-1	Cardiff Corinthians
Caerau	1-4	Mid Rhondda
Barry	3-0	Lovell's Athletic

Third Round Replay

Bangor	0-2	Holyhead
Llanidloes Town	5-0	Welshpool

Fourth Round

Oswestry Town	0-2	Mold Town
Mid Rhondda	1-0	Bridgend Town
Brymbo Green	1-2	Llandudno FC
Holyhead	0-2	Flint
Aberpergwm	2-3	New Tredegar
Colwyn Bay	3-3	Wellington Town
Rhyl	0-2	Shrewsbury
Llanidloes Town	2-1	Barry

Fourth Round Replay

Wellington Town	5-1	Colwyn Bay

Fifth Round

Wrexham	3-0	Llanelly
Newport County	2-0	Wellington Town
Mold Town	1-0	Llandudno FC
Flint	2-1	New Tredegar
Aberdare	5-2	Llanidloes Town
Merthyr Town	3-1	Shrewsbury Town
Pontypridd	3-2	Mid Rhondda
Swansea Town	4-0	Cardiff City

Sixth Round

Swansea Town	1-0	Aberdare
Newport County	0-1	Wrexham
Mold Town	3-0	Pontypridd
Flint	1-0	Merthyr Town

Semi-finals

Mold	1-1	Flint

Played at Wrexham

Wrexham	3-1	Swansea Town

Played at Swansea

Semi-final Replay

Flint	0-0	Mold

Played at Wrexham

Semi-final Second Replay

Mold	0-1	Flint

Played at Wrexham

1925 WELSH CUP FINAL

29th April 1925 at the Racecourse, Wrexham

Wrexham	3-1	Flint Town

J Jones 2, Goode   Elliott

Wrexham: G Godding, A Jones, A Lumberg, T J Matthias, T P Griffiths, Savage, A Longmuir, B Goode, J Jones, Nock, F Jones

Flint Town: Connell, Shepherd, Steward, C Hewitt, E Jones, Millington, E Hughes, Sweeney, F Weaver, Elliott, J Roberts

Referee: I Baker (Crewe)

Attendance: 6,565

1925/26 Welsh Cup

The following teams did not enter the competition until the Fourth round:

Swansea Town, Cardiff City, Merthyr Town, Wrexham, Flint, Mold, Aberdare and Newport County.

1st & 2nd Qualifying Round   Not used

3rd Qualifying Round

Pwllheli	1-1	Penmaenmawr
Pwllheli withdrew		
Caernarvon	2-4	Llanfairfechan
Llandudno Junction (w/o)	v	Courtaulds (withdrew)
Johnstown	6-1	Acrefair
Aberystwyth Univ. College	2-2	Machynlleth
Aberystwyth Town	15-0	Barmouth
Llanfyllin	4-0	GWR Caersws
Llanidloes Town	1-1	Newtown
Builth	1-3	Rhayader
Bargoed	1-2	Llanbradach
Rhiwderin	2-2	Cardiff Camerons
Port Talbot	2-3	Swansea Amateurs

3rd Qualifying Round Replays

Machynlleth	4-1	Aberystwyth Univ. College
Newtown	0-5	Llanidloes Town
Cardiff Camerons	2-1	Rhiwderin

4th Qualifying Round   Not used

5th Qualifying Round

Rhayader	4-1	Llandrindod Wells
Aberystwyth Town	5-0	Machynlleth
Llanidloes Town	11-2	Llanfyllin
New Tredegar	6-2	Llandbradach
Swansea Amateurs	1-0	Cardiff Camerons
Johnstown	7-2	Penmaenmawr

First Round

Llandudno Junction	2-5	Llanfairfechan
Played at Llanfairfechan		
Llanidloes Town	4-1	Rhayader
Swansea Amateurs	0-6	New Tredegar

Second Round   Not used

Third Round

Welshpool	1-0	Buckley United
Conway	3-2	Oak Alyn Rovers
Bangor	7-2	Aberystwyth Town
Denbigh	1-0	Llanidloes Town
Rhyl	3-3	Oswestry Town
Colwyn Bay	7-0	Llandudno FC
Connah's Quay	4-2	Llandudno Junction
Rhos	4-1	Whitchurch
Johnstown	1-1	Druids
Chirk	1-2	Ebbw Vale
Holyhead	1-1	Holywell
Penrhiwceiber (withdrew)	v	Cardiff Corinthians (w/o)
Mid Rhondda	4-4	Barry
New Tredegar	3-1	Pembroke Dock
Aberaman	0-1	Bridgend
Pontypridd	4-1	Lovell's Athletic

Third Round Replays

Oswestry Town	2-3	Rhyl
Druids	4-2	Johnstown
Holywell	3-1	Holyhead
Barry	2-1	Mid Rhondda

Fourth Round

Connah's Quay	0-0	Bangor
Rhyl	5-2	Denbigh
Conway	2-1	Druids
Rhos	6-1	Welshpool
Colwyn Bay	7-0	Holywell
Barry	4-1	Bridgend
Cardiff Corinthians	3-1	New Tredegar
Pontypridd	2-2	Ebbw Vale

Fourth Round Replays

Bangor	2-1	Connah's Quay
Ebbw Vale	3-1	Pontypridd

Fifth Round

Rhyl	4-1	Bangor
Colwyn Bay	1-1	Swansea Town
Mold Town	3-0	Aberdare
Newport County	0-0	Barry
Cardiff City	1-2	Merthyr Town
Wrexham	1-1	Flint
Rhos	4-1	Conway
Ebbw Vale	4-1	Cardiff Corinthians

Fifth Round Replays

Swansea Town	8-2	Colwyn Bay
Barry	2-3	Newport County
Flint	1-4	Wrexham

Sixth Round

Rhyl	1-0	Rhos
Wrexham	0-1	Swansea Town
Ebbw Vale	4-0	Mold
Merthyr	1-1	Newport County

Sixth Round Replay

Newport County	2-0	Merthyr

Semi-finals

Rhyl	1-3	Swansea Town
Ebbw Vale	2-1	Newport County

1926 WELSH CUP FINAL

29th April 1926 at Ebbw Vale

Ebbw Vale AFC	3-2	Swansea Town
Jones, Smith, Price		*Thompson*

Ebbw Vale: Howells, Thomas, Foote, Codd, Ellerington, V Jones, Johnson, MacGill, Price, Smith, Billy McCandless

Swansea Town: Robson, Langford, W Milne, Collins, J Sykes, McPherson, W Hole, Deacon, Morris, Thompson, Nicholas

Referee: A J Attwood (Newport)

Attendance: 2,500

1926/27 Welsh Cup

6th Preliminary Round

Llandrindod Wells	1-1	Rhayader
Pontlottyn	6-2	Risca Town
Aberystwyth Town	5-0	Aberystwyth Uni. College
Machynlleth	8-4	Llanidloes Town
Barmouth	5-3	Portmadoc
Llanfyllin	4-4	Newtown

Llanfyllin withdrew from the competition

Llanfairfechan	2-6	Llandudno Junction
Bala Royal British Legion	4-1	Gwersyllt

6th Preliminary Round Replay

Rhayader	5-1	Llandrindod Wells

First Round

Cardiff Corinthians	1-5	Llanbradach
Llandudno Junction	2-1	Penmaenmawr
Rhayader	0-3	Llanidloes Town
Barmouth	4-3	Bala Royal British Legion
Newtown	5-3	Aberystwyth Town
New Tredegar	1-1	Pontlottyn

First Round Replay

Pontlottyn	4-1	New Tredegar

Second Round

All clubs received a bye to the Third Round.

Third Round

Oswestry Town	3-3	Connah's Quay
Llanidloes Town	3-5	Llandudno
Denbigh Town	2-2	Rhos
Buckley U	8-3	Holyhead
Welshpool	9-0	Newtown
Colwyn Bay	5-1	Bridgend
Lovell's Athletic	6-3	Llanbradach
Penrhiwceiber	2-4	Pembroke Dock
Mid Rhondda	2-2	Barry
Cardiff Corinthians	1-1	Pontlottyn
Barmouth	2-2	Druids
Flint Town	0-0	Oak Alyn
Conway	2-4	Holywell
Acrefair	1-1	Chirk
Caernarvon Athletic	2-1	Bangor City
Mold Town	7-0	Llandudno Junction

Third Round Replays

Connah's Quay	5-0	Oswestry Town
Rhos	1-2	Denbigh Town
Barry	2-1	Mid Rhondda
Pontlottyn	4-2	Cardiff Corinthians
Druids	2-1	Barmouth
Oak Alyn	0-1	Flint Town
Chirk	3-1	Acrefair

Fourth Round

Flint Town	1-1	Buckley
Mold Town	0-0	Chirk
Welshpool	4-2	Colwyn Bay
Holywell	3-2	Denbigh Town
Llandudno FC	8-1	Druids
Connah's Quay	2-5	Caernarvon Athletic
Pembroke Dock	1-9	Lovell's Athletic
Pontlottyn	2-6	Barry

Fourth Round Replays

Buckley	3-0	Flint Town

Following a protest by Flint Town, a replay was ordered, to be played at Connah's Quay.

Chirk	1-2	Mold Town

Fourth Round Second Replay

Flint Town	0-2	Buckley

Played at Connah's Quay

Fifth Round

Barry	4-1	Merthyr Town
Aberdare	3-1	Swansea Town
Lovell's Athletic	1-0	Newport County
Cardiff City	0-0	Ebbw Vale
Holywell	4-0	Buckley
Llandudno FC	1-4	Wrexham
Caernarvon Athletic	6-1	Welshpool
Mold Town	1-3	Rhyl

Fifth Round Replay

Ebbw Vale	1-6	Cardiff City

Sixth Round

Cardiff City	2-0	Barry
Aberdare	3-3	Wrexham
Rhyl	1-1	Caernarvon Athletic
Holywell	2-0	Lovell's Athletic

Sixth Round Replays

Wrexham	2-1	Aberdare
Caernarvon Athletic	2-3	Rhyl

Semi-finals

Cardiff City	2-1	Wrexham
Rhyl	5-1	Holywell

Played at Colwyn Bay

1927 WELSH CUP FINAL

5th May 1927 at the Racecourse, Wrexham

Cardiff City	2-0	Rhyl FC

L Davies, Irving

Cardiff City: Farquharson, Nelson, Watson, Blackburn, Sloan, Hardy, F Keenor, Irving, L Davies, E Curtis, McLachlan

Rhyl: Soutar, Ellison, Lorribond, Lewis, Young, Bamber, Murray, Whitelaw, F Hoddinott, Ritchie, Miller

Referee: G D Nunnerley (Ellesmere)

Attendance: 9,690

1927/28 Welsh Cup

1st & 2nd Preliminary Rounds

Not used

3rd Preliminary Round

Barmouth (withdrew) (withdrew)	v	Bala Royal British Legion
Bangor University College	1-7	Llanfairfechan
Chirk AAA	4-2	Gwersyllt Church
Aberystwyth Town	3-2	Llanidloes Town
Rhayader	0-6	Llandrindod Wells
Machynlleth	3-3	Aberystwyth Uni. College

3rd Preliminary Round Replay

Aberystwyth Univ. College	2-0	Machynlleth

First & Second Rounds

Not used

Third Round

Newtown	1-2	Llandrindod Wells
Aberystwyth Town	4-3	Aberystwyth Uni. College
Lovell's Athletic	3-1	Ebbw Vale
Cardiff Camerons (withdrew)	v	Mid Rhondda (w/o)
New Tredegar	2-2	Cardiff Corinthians
Barry	2-4	Connah's Quay
Llandudno FC	3-1	Oak Alyn Rovers
Llanfyllin	0-5	Caernarvon Athletic
Penrhiwceiber	4-1	Bridgend Town
Bala Royal British Legion	1-5	Welshpool
Flint	1-1	Bangor City
Buckley	6-0	Druids
Holyhead	9-1	Chirk
Denbigh Town	4-8	Oswestry Town
Mold Town	1-1	Colwyn Bay
Llanfairfechan	5-2	Rhos

Third Round Replays

Cardiff Corinthians	3-2	New Tredegar
Bangor City	4-1	Flint
Colwyn Bay	0-1	Mold Town

Fourth Round

Cardiff Corinthians	2-1	Penrhiwceiber
Mid Rhondda	0-3	Lovell's Athletic
Llanfairfechan	1-2	Connah's Quay
Mold Town	4-4	Caernarvon Athletic
Bangor City	3-0	Buckley
Holyhead	6-2	Welshpool
Oswestry Town	11-1	Llandudno
Llandrindod Wells	3-2	Aberystwyth Town

Fourth Round Replay

Caernarvon Athletic	6-0	Mold Town

Fifth Round

Cardiff City	7-1	Oswestry Town
Played at Oswestry by agreement		
Wrexham	1-0	Lovell's Athletic
Merthyr Town	6-0	Cardiff Corinthians
Newport County (w/o)	v	Holywell (withdrew)
Rhyl	1-0	Caernarvon Athletic
Holyhead	1-8	Swansea Town
Bangor City	3-0	Connah's Quay
Aberdare	4-2	Llandrindod Wells

Sixth Round

Cardiff City	1-0	Swansea Town
Aberdare	0-0	Bangor City
Wrexham	3-3	Merthyr Town
Newport County	1-3	Rhyl
Played at Rhyl		

Sixth Round Replays

Bangor City	7-3	Aberdare
Merthyr Town	3-2	Wrexham

Semi-finals

Bangor City	2-2	Merthyr Town
Played at Colwyn Bay		
Cardiff City	2-2	Rhyl
Played at Wrexham		

Semi-final Replays

Merthyr Town	0-2	Bangor City
Played at Oswestry		
Rhyl	0-2	Cardiff City
Played at Shrewsbury		

1928 WELSH CUP FINAL

2nd May 1928 at Farrar Road, Bangor

Cardiff City	2-0	Bangor City

Ferguson 2

Cardiff City: Farquharson, Nelson, Jennings, Fred Keenor, Sloan, Hardy, Thirlaway, Smith, Ferguson, Len Davies, McLachlan

Bangor City: J Rundell, T Sinclair, Critchlow, G Rundell, Whittaker, R Lock, Fogg, P Jeffes, G White, Smith, Cooper

Referee: G Petrie (Holywell)

Attendance: 12,000

1928/29 Welsh Cup

1st & 2nd Qualifying Rounds

Not used

3rd Qualifying Round

Gwersyllt Church	2-6	Summerhill Institute
Rhayader	5-1	Builth Wells
Aberystwyth University College (w/o)	v	Barmouth (withdrew)

All other clubs given byes

Extra Round

Aberystwyth Town	4-1	Machynlleth
Aberystwyth Univ. College	1-4	Newtown

First & Second Rounds

Not used

Third Round

Penmaenmawr	0-7	Llandudno
Shrewsbury Town	6-0	Druids
Caernarvon Athletic	4-0	Colwyn Bay
Mold Town	2-0	Holywell
Holyhead	3-2	Llanfairfechan
Welshpool	4-2	Aberystwyth Town
Connah's Quay & Shotton	5-0	Denbigh Town
Summerhill Institute	4-3	Oak Alyn Rovers
Llanelly	2-4	Llandrindod Wells
Llanidloes Town	7-1	Aberystwyth Uni. College
Buckley	6-0	Flint
Chester	1-1	Oswestry Town
New Tredegar	3-0	Cardiff Corinthians
Llanfyllin	1-5	Rhayader
Ebbw Vale	3-5	Lovell's Athletic
Penrhiwceiber	0-2	Barry

Third Round Replay

Oswestry Town	4-5 (aet)	Chester

Fourth Round

Shrewsbury Town	2-1	Llandudno FC
Connah's Quay & Shotton	11-0	Summerhill Institute
Chester	2-5	Buckley
Mold Town	0-2	Caernarvon Athletic
Welshpool	6-2	Holyhead
Llandrindod Wells	4-1	Llanidloes Town
Barry	1-5	Lovell's Athletic
Rhayader	1-1	New Tredegar

Fourth Round Replay

New Tredegar	4-0	Rhayader

Fifth Round

Merthyr Town	4-1	New Tredegar
Wrexham	2-4	Rhyl
Buckley	1-1	Llandrindod Wells
Cardiff City	3-2	Lovell's Athletic
Connah's Quay & Shotton	6-2	Welshpool
Newport County	5-1	Swansea Town
Shrewsbury Town	1-1	Bangor City
Caernarvon Athletic	3-0	New Brighton

Fifth Round Replay

Llandrindod Wells	2-0	Buckley
Bangor City	3-1	Shrewsbury Town

Sixth Round

Bangor City	0-0	Rhyl
Connah's Quay & Shotton	3-0	Caernarvon Athletic
Llandrindod Wells	1-4	Merthyr Town
Newport County	0-1	Cardiff City

Sixth Round Replay

Rhyl	4-1	Bangor City

Semi-finals

Connah's Quay & Shotton	7-0	Merthyr Town

Played at Rhyl

Rhyl	1-2	Cardiff City

Played at Rhyl

1929 WELSH CUP FINAL

1st May 1929 at the Racecourse, Wrexham

Connah's Quay & Shotton	3-0	Cardiff City

Own goal, Rand, Mercer

Connah's Quay: R Finnigan, O'Donnell, Shanks, Rushton, Jordan, Halkyard, Robson, Mercer, Guyan, Rand, Martin

Cardiff City: Farquharson, Jennings, Roberts, Wake, F C Keenor, Blackburn, Thirlaway, Harris, Ferguson, Len Davies, McLachlan

Referee: W T Harris (Wrexham)

Attendance: 9,623

1929/30 Welsh Cup

Qualifying Round

Barmouth	8-2	Aberystwyth Town

Aberystwyth Town played in the Third Round and Barmouth did not appear in the competition again this season. It is not recorded why this was the case.

Llanidloes Town	8-0	Aberystwyth Uni. College
Rhayader	3-3	Builth Wells
Welshpool	4-3	Llanfyllin
Holt	3-2	Summerhill
Gwersyllt Church	5-1	Cross Street Gwersyllt
New Broughton	4-2	Vron United

Qualifying Round Replay

Builth Wells	5-4	Rhayader

First Round

Gwersyllt Church	1-1	Holt
Penmaenmawr	3-2	Bethesda Victoria

All other clubs received byes

First Round Replay

Holt	2-2	Gwersyllt Church

The match was abandoned during extra-time.

First Round Second Replay

Gwersyllt Church	1-3	Holt

Second Round

Not used

Third Round

Lovell's Athletic	6-0	Builth Wells
New Tredegar	0-9	Barry
Llanelly	3-1	Ebbw Vale
Cardiff Corinthians	1-0	Penrhiwceiber
Welshpool	2-5	Aberystwyth Town
Llanidloes Town	3-3	Llandrindod Wells
Holt	1-12	Shrewsbury Town
Played at Shrewsbury		
Oswestry Town	5-2	Mold Town
Llanfairfechan	9-0	Druids
New Broughton	3-7	Holywell
Played at Holywell		
Denbigh	2-3	Holyhead
Penmaenmawr	0-3	Flint
Played at Flint		
Holywell Arcadians	1-2	Chester
Played at Chester		
Colwyn Bay	7-1	Bangor City
Blaenau Ffestiniog	2-7	Caernarvon Athletic
Played at Caernarvon		
Llandudno FC	1-0	Prestatyn

Third Round Replay

Llandrindod Wells	2-1	Llanidloes Town

Fourth Round

Llandudno FC	2-4	Caernarvon Athletic
Shrewsbury Town	3-2	Oswestry Town
Shrewsbury were expelled from the competition after a protest was upheld.		
Holyhead	0-8	Flint
Llandrindod Wells	0-3	Aberystwyth Town
Colwyn Bay	4-4	Chester
Llanfairfechan	1-1	Holywell
Cardiff Corinthians	0-1	Llanelly
Barry	1-2	Lovell's Athletic

Fourth Round Replay

Chester	2-2	Colwyn Bay
The match was abandoned before full-time.		
Holywell	5-1	Llanfairfechan

Fourth Round Second Replay

Colwyn Bay	4-2	Chester

Fifth Round

Holywell	0-4	Colwyn Bay
New Brighton	5-0	Oswestry Town
Flint	0-3	Rhyl
Wrexham	2-0	Connah's Quay
Aberystwyth Town	0-1	Caernarvon Athletic
Newport County	3-2	Lovell's Athletic
Llanelly	1-4	Cardiff City
Swansea Town	4-2	Merthyr Town

Sixth Round

Wrexham	4-0	New Brighton
Rhyl	4-0	Caernarvon Athletic
Cardiff City	4-0	Swansea Town
Colwyn Bay	4-0	Newport County

Semi-finals

Wrexham	0-2	Cardiff City
Played at Wrexham		
Rhyl	3-1	Colwyn Bay
Played at Llandudno		

1930 WELSH CUP FINAL

3rd May 1930 at Gay Meadow, Shrewsbury

Cardiff City	0-0 (aet)	Rhyl

Cardiff City: Farquharson, Nelson, Roberts, Helsby, R John, Blackburn, F C Keenor, Wake, Miles, Jones, L Davies

Rhyl: Williams, Burgess, Settle, Ritchie, Roy, Bamber, McGovern, Dewsnap, Williams, Harley, J Williams

Referee: H Hughes (Rhosrobin)

Attendance: 5,892

1930 WELSH CUP FINAL REPLAY

8th October 1930 at the Racecourse, Wrexham

Cardiff City	4-2	Rhyl FC
Davies 3, Jones		Peters, Ferguson

Cardiff City: Farquharson, J Smith, Hardy, Helsby, F C Keenor, Blackburn, Emmerson, Wake, L Davies, Jones, W Robbins

Rhyl: Tudor, Owen, Geddes, Edwards, Roy, Bamber, Ferguson, Ritchie, Hughes, Peters, Ellis

Referee: H Hughes (Rhosrobin)

Attendance: 7,000

1930/31 Welsh Cup

Preliminary Round

Not used

First Round

Llandrindod Wells (withdrew)	v	Rhayader Town (w/o)
Llanidloes Town	5-0	Llanfyllin
Aberystwyth Univ. College	3-5	Caersws
Machynlleth	2-1	Aberdovey
Barmouth (withdrew)	v	Dolgelley (w/o)
Cross Street Gwersyllt	0-4	Holt
Druids	0-3	Afongoch
Holywell Arcadian	2-4	Flint Town
Ewloe Celtic	14-1	Llysfaen
Bettisfield	4-1	Prestatyn
Bethesda Victoria	6-2	Blaenau Ffestiniog FC
All other clubs received byes		

Second Round

Dolgelley	1-2	Machynlleth
Llanidloes Town	6-3	Rhayader Town
Cross Street Gwersyllt	5-1	Bettisfield
Bethesda Victoria (exempt)		Penmaenmawr (w/o)
Caernarfon	bye	

Caernarfon were given a bye to the Third Round but subsequently disbanded. Their fixtures in the Combination were taken over by Bethesda Victoria and therefore also their place in the Welsh Cup draw. Bethesda duly became exempt to Third Round and therefore Penmaenmawr were given a walkover in the Second Round tie. Hence both Bethesda and Penmaenmawr appear in the Third Round.
All other clubs received byes

Third Round

Cardiff Corinthians	8-0	Caerau
New Tredegar (withdrew)	v	Barry (w/o)
Bethesda Victoria	5-3	Llandudno FC
Holyhead Town	3-1	Bangor City
Connah's Quay & Shotton	2-3	Oswestry Town
Ellesmere Port Town	4-3	Ewloe Celtic
Builth Wells	1-8	Llanelly
Penmaenmawr	2-10	Llanfairfechan
Flint Town Amateurs	3-0	Afongoch
Machynlleth	3-2	Llandidloes
Welshpool	3-2	Newtown
Aberystwyth Town	6-0	Caersws
Shrewsbury Town	10-2	Gwersyllt Church
Aberaman Athletic	2-5	Lovell's Athletic
Ebbw Vale	5-2	Penrhiwceiber
Chester	9-1	Cross Street Gwersyllt

Fourth Round

Llanfairfechan	2-11	Chester
Shrewsbury Town	11-2	Welshpool
Machynlleth	6-3	Flint Town Amateurs
Holyhead Town	2-4	Oswestry
Ellesmere Port	6-2	Bethesda Victoria
Cardiff Corinthians	1-1	Lovell's Athletic
Ebbw Vale	1-5	Barry
Aberystwyth Town	2-4	Llanelly

Fourth Round Replay

Lovell's Athletic	4-0	Cardiff Corinthians

Fifth Round

New Brighton	1-1	Chester
Wrexham	5-1	Ellesmere Port
Rhyl	2-2	Colwyn Bay
Shrewsbury Town	5-2	Newport County
Oswestry Town	14-1	Machynlleth
Cardiff City	7-3	Barry
Swansea Town	2-0	Llanelly
Lovell's Athletic	4-2	Merthyr Town

Fifth Round Replays

Chester	0-0	New Brighton
Colwyn Bay	1-0	Rhyl

Fifth Round Second Replay

New Brighton	2-4	Chester

Sixth Round

Oswestry Town	0-2	Swansea Town
Wrexham	4-0	Colwyn Bay
Shrewsbury Town	0-0	Lovell's Athletic
Chester	0-1	Cardiff City

Sixth Round Replay

Lovell's Athletic	0-1	Shrewsbury Town

Semi-finals

Shrewsbury Town	1-0	Cardiff City

Played at Shrewsbury

Swansea Town	2-5	Wrexham

Played at Chester

1931 WELSH CUP FINAL

27th April 1931 at the Racecourse, Wrexham

Wrexham	7-0	Shrewsbury Town

Bamford 2, Lewis 2, Taylor, Hughes, Mustard

Wrexham: R Finningan, A Jones, W Crompton, Clayton, Burkinshaw, Donoghue, Mustard, Hughes, T Bamford, S Taylor, Lewis

Shrewsbury Town: Allan, Sheldon, Cope, Groves, Taylor, Millington, Roberts, Burgess, Mound, Buckingham, Vaughan

Referee: A J Attwood (Newport)
Attendance: 8,868

1931/32 Welsh Cup

First Round

Bangor City (w/o)	v	Llandudno (withdrew)
Holyhead	2-2	Llanfairfechan
Penmaenmawr (withdrew)	v	Bethesda Victoria (w/o)
Vron United	3-9	Cross Street Gwersyllt
Holywell Arcadians	6-0	Mold Amateurs
Caersws	2-6	Machynlleth
Aberdovey	0-1	Dolgelley
Aberystwyth Univ. College	0-6	Aberystwyth Town
Llanidloes Town	11-2	Rhayader
Builth Wells	1-2	Llandrindod North End
Newtown	3-2	Welshpool
Rhosrobin	4-1	Gwersyllt
Gyfelia (disbanded)	v	Druids (w/o)
Oakenholt	1-2	Mold Alexandra
Bettisfield	2-2	Flint Amateurs
Catholic OB Connah's Quay	4-7	Sandycroft

All other clubs received byes

First Round Replays

Llanfairfechan	1-3	Holyhead
Flint Amateurs	2-3	Bettisfield

Second Round

Bangor City	6-3	Holyhead
Holywell Arcadians	6-0	Bethesda Victoria
Llanerch Celts	4-1	Mold Alexandra
Rhosrobin	2-2	Druids
Sandycroft	2-5	Cross Street Gwersyllt
Machynlleth	8-0	Dolgelley
Llandrindod North End	0-3	Newtown
Llanidloes Town	2-2	Aberystwyth Town

Bettisfield received a bye

Second Round Replays

Druids	0-0	Rhosrobin
Aberystwyth Town	2-3	Llanidloes Town

Second Round Second Replay

Rhosrobin	1-4	Druids

Third Round

Bettisfield	2-5	Druids
Cross Street Gwersyllt	2-2	Llanerch Celts
Bangor City	2-0	Holywell Arcadians

The match was abandoned due to heavy rain.

Newtown	3-0	Machynlleth

Llanidloes Town received a bye

Third Round Replays

Llanerch Celts	4-2	Cross Street Gwersyllt
Holywell Arcadians	2-2	Bangor City

Third Round Second Replay

Bangor City	0-3	Holywell Arcadians

Fourth Round

Druids	0-3	Colwyn Bay

Played at Colwyn Bay

Llanerch Celts	2-11	Rhyl

Played at Rhyl

Oswestry Town	5-1	Newtown
Llanidloes Town	3-2	Whitchurch
Troedyrhiw	2-2	Lovell's Athletic
Ebbw Vale	4-1	Barry Town
Llanelly	5-1	Penrhiwceiber
Merthyr Town	2-0	Aberaman

Holywell Arcadians received a bye

Fourth Round Replay

Lovell's Athletic	1-0	Troedyrhiw

Fifth Round

Rhyl	5-0	Llanidloes Town
Shrewsbury Town	5-1	Colwyn Bay
Wrexham	3-0	Holywell Arcadians
Chester	1-1	Oswestry Town
Merthyr Town	2-2	Swansea Town
Lovell's Athletic	2-1	Ebbw Vale
Cardiff Corinthians	0-2	Newport County
Cardiff City	5-3	Llanelly

Fifth Round Replays

Oswestry Town	0-4	Chester
Swansea Town	2-1	Merthyr Town

Sixth Round

Chester	2-1	Cardiff City
Wrexham	4-2	Shrewsbury Town
Lovell's Athletic	2-2	Rhyl
Newport County	0-0	Swansea Town

Sixth Round Replays

Rhyl	3-0	Lovell's Athletic
Swansea Town	2-0	Newport County

Semi-finals

Wrexham	3-3	Rhyl

Played at Chester

Chester	0-2	Swansea Town

Played at Chester

Semi-final Replay

Rhyl	1-3	Wrexham

Played at Chester

1932 WELSH CUP FINAL

5th May 1932 at the Racecourse, Wrexham

Wrexham	1-1	Swansea Town
A Jones		Lewis

Wrexham: Burrows, Jones, Buxton, Lawrence, Brown, Rogers, A Jones, Hughes, T Bamford, Taylor, Mustard

Swansea Town: Ferguson, S Lawrence, W Milne, Jones, Craven, Miller, Williams, Antiss, Pearce, Gunn, Lewis

Referee: A J Attwood (Newport)

Attendance: 8,300

1932 WELSH CUP FINAL REPLAY

6th May 1932 at the Vetch Field, Swansea

Swansea Town	2-0	Wrexham

Pearce, Williams

Wrexham: Burrows, Jones, Buxton, Lawrence, Brown, Rogers, A Jones, Hughes, T Bamford, Taylor, Mustard

Swansea Town: Ferguson, S Lawrence, W Milne, Jones, Craven, Miller, Williams, Antiss, Pearce, Gunn, Lewis

Referee: A J Attwood (Newport)

Attendance: 5,000

1932/33 Welsh Cup

First Round   Not used

Second Round

Llanrwst	1-5	Holywell Arcadians
Rhyl Corinthians	2-1	Caernarvon
Bethesda Victoria	6-1	Holyhead Town
Llanfairfechan	4-0	Llandudno FC
Mancot	2-0	Sandycroft

The match was not completed but the result stood.

Druids	2-2	Llanerch Celts
Buckley (dismissed)	v	Burntwood
Mold Alexandra	2-2	Flint
Llay Welfare	7-1	Bradley Victoria
Llay St Martin	1-4	Gwersyllt
Welshpool	1-1	Vron United
Cross Street Gwersyllt	3-4	Northern Nomads
Rhayader	2-2	Builth Wells
Aberystwyth Town	1-1	Aberdovey
Newtown	6-3	Caersws
Dolgelley	1-7	Towyn

Second Round Replays

Llanerch Celts	2-1	Druids
Flint	3-1	Mold Alexandra
Vron United	2-1	Welshpool
Builth Wells	6-0	Rhayader
Aberdovey	0-5	Aberystwyth Town

Third Round

Blaina Town	1-1	Milford Haven
Llanfairfechan	2-0	Bangor University College
Rhyl Corinthians	5-2	Holywell Arcadians
Portmadoc	6-7	Bethesda Victoria
Mancot	2-2	Llanerch Celts

Played at Rhos

Flint	3-0	Burntwood
Vron United	0-6	Northern Nomads
Llay Welfare	0-7	Gwersyllt
Towyn	6-3	Aberystwyth Uni. College
Aberystwyth Town	3-1	Newtown
Builth Wells	1-6	Hereford United

Third Round Replays

Milford Haven	2-1	Blaina Town
Llanerch Celts	6-2	Mancot

Fourth Round

Llanelly (w/o)	v	Milford Haven (withdrew)
Ebbw Vale	0-2	Merthyr Town
Barry	2-2	Aberaman Athletic
Cardiff Corinthians	0-2	Troedyrhiw
Flint	4-1	Bethesda Victoria
Llanfairfechan	1-5	Bangor City
Colwyn Bay	5-1	Rhyl Corinthians
Llanidloes Town	0-3	Shrewsbury Town
Llanerch Celts	1-0	Northern Nomads
Oswestry Town	3-1	Gwersyllt Town
Towyn	2-3	Machynlleth
Hereford United	1-2	Aberystwyth Town

Fourth Round Replay

Aberaman Athletic	0-4	Barry

Fifth Round

Colwyn Bay	6-0	Flint
Bangor City	12-2	Llanerch Celts
Shrewsbury Town	3-1	Machynlleth
Oswestry Town	5-2	Aberystwyth Town
Merthyr Town	2-2	Troedyrhiw
Lovell's Athletic	2-3	Llanelly
Barry	5-0	Penrhiwceiber

Fifth Round Replay

Treodyrhiw	0-2	Merthyr Town

Sixth Round

Barry	0-6	Llanelly
Oswestry Town	7-4	Colwyn Bay

All other clubs received byes

Sixth Round Replay

Shrewsbury Town	0-1	Bangor City

Seventh Round

Bangor City	2-0	New Brighton
Rhyl	1-2	Southport
Merthyr Town	2-3	Llanelly
Oswestry Town	2-2	Wrexham
Bristol Rovers	0-3	Swansea Town
Crewe Alexandra	3-5	Chester
Cardiff City	4-2	Tranmere Rovers
Bristol City	3-4	Newport County

Seventh Round Replay

Wrexham	4-1	Oswestry Town

Eighth Round

Bangor City	1-2	Wrexham
Llanelly	0-4	Chester
Swansea Town	1-1	Cardiff City
Newport County	0-0	Southport

Eighth Round Replay

Cardiff City	2-1	Swansea Town
Southport	4-0	Newport County

Semi-finals

Wrexham	1-1	Southport

Played at Wrexham

Chester	2-1	Cardiff City

Played at Chester

Semi-final Replay

Southport	1-3	Wrexham

Played at Chester

1933 WELSH CUP FINAL

3rd May 1933 at Sealand Road, Chester

Chester　　　　2-0　　　　Wrexham

Mercer, Cresswell

Chester: Burke, Bennett, Herod, Pitcairn, Skitt, Duckworth, Kelly, Mercer, Mantle, Cresswell, Hedley

Wrexham: Adams, Jones, Brown, Bulling, McMahon, Lawrence, Hughes, Trewin, Bamford, Lewis, Waller

Referee: G Wood (Sheffield)

Attendance: 15,000

1933/34 Welsh Cup

First Round

Portmadoc	4-1	Llanddulas
Llandudno FC	1-4	Flint
Rhyl Corinthians	4-4	Bethesda Victoria
Llanfairfechan	1-0	Holyhead
Cross Street Gwersyllt	0-1	Llay Welfare
Mold Alexandra	3-2	Gwersyllt

A Gwersyllt protest that Mold had fielded an ineligible player was upheld and Mold were dismissed from the competition.

Vron United	1-3	Llanerch Celts
Brymbo Green	5-4	Druids
Welshpool	9-0	Llanfyllin
Newtown	6-0	Caersws
Aberystwyth Univ. College	0-6	Machynlleth
Aberystwyth Town	3-2	Llanidloes Town
Bala	2-1	Dolgelley
Towyn	1-3	Aberdovey
Builth Wells	2-2	Llandrindod Wells
Milford	0-2	Blaina Town

All other clubs received byes

First Round Replay

Bethesda Victoria	7-4	Rhyl Corinthians
Llandrindod Wells	0-2	Builth Wells

Second Round

Bethesda Victoria	1-1	Bettisfield
Llanfairfechan	0-4	Flint
Llanerch Celts	6-1	Brymbo Green
Gwersyllt	1-2	Llay Welfare
Bala	1-5	Aberdovey
Knighton	5-2	Builth Wells
Aberystwyth Town	2-0	Newtown
Machynlleth	2-0	Welshpool

Blaina Town and Portmadoc both received byes

Second Round Replay

Bettisfield	1-4	Bethesda Victoria

Third Round

Knighton	2-0	Machynlleth
Aberdovey	0-2	Aberystwyth Town
Bangor City	1-1	Portmadoc
Rhyl	6-3	Llanerch Celts
Llay Welfare	1-5	Colwyn Bay
Oswestry Town	3-5	Flint
Llanelly	1-1	Lovell's Athletic
Aberaman Athletic	9-1	Blaina Town
Troedyrhiw	2-0	Cardiff Corinthians
Barry Town	5-0	Ebbw Vale
Penrhiwceiber	1-0	Porth

Bethesda Victoria received a bye

Third Round Replays

Portmadoc	0-6	Bangor City
Lovell's Athletic	2-1	Llanelly

Fourth Round

Bethesda Victoria	0-4	Colwyn Bay
Rhyl	5-0	Flint
Aberystwyth Town	7-2	Knighton
Aberaman Athletic	1-2	Troedyrhiw
Merthyr Town	4-2	Lovell's Athletic

Bangor City, Barry Town and Penrhiwceiber all received byes

Fifth Round

Barry Town	1-1	Troedyrhiw
Merthyr Town	7-0	Penrhiwceiber
Rhyl	4-0	Colwyn Bay
Aberystwyth Town	1-4	Bangor City

Fifth Round Replay

Troedyrhiw	4-1	Barry Town

Sixth Round

Chester	2-1	Swansea Town
Southport	1-3	Tranmere Rovers
New Brighton	3-2	Troedyrhiw
Rhyl	1-1	Port Vale
Bristol Rovers	2-0	Wrexham
Cardiff City	2-2	Bristol City
Bangor City	3-1	Merthyr Town
Newport County	2-2	Crewe Alexandra

Sixth Round Replays

Port Vale	2-0	Rhyl
Bristol City	1-0	Cardiff City
Crewe Alexandra	4-5	Newport County

Seventh Round

Newport County	1-1	Tranmere Rovers
New Brighton	2-2	Bristol City
Bangor City	1-0	Chester
Bristol Rovers	3-3	Port Vale

Seventh Round Replays

Tranmere Rovers	5-2	Newport County
Bristol City	2-1	New Brighton
Port Vale	2-1	Bristol Rovers

Semi-finals

Tranmere Rovers	6-1	Bangor City
Played at Bangor		
Bristol City	1-0	Port Vale
Played at Chester		

1934 WELSH CUP FINAL

24th April 1934 at the Racecourse, Wrexham

Bristol City	1-1	Tranmere Rovers
Molloy		Clasper

Bristol City: Scattergood, Roberts, Taylor, Morgan, Parker, Brinton, Banfield, Molloy, Riley, Loftus, Scriven

Tranmere Rovers: B Gray, Platt, Dawson, Barton, Meacock, Spencer, Tong, Brown, Bell, Clasper, Urmson

Referee: S F Rous (Watford)

Attendance: 4,922

1934 WELSH CUP FINAL REPLAY

3rd May 1934 at Sealand Road, Chester

Bristol City	3-0	Tranmere Rovers
Riley 2, Scriven		

Bristol City: Scattergood, Roberts, Birks, Morgan, Carter, Brinton, Homer, Molloy, Riley, Loftus, Scriven

Tranmere Rovers: B Gray, Platt, Topping, Barton, Meacock, Spencer, Brown, Clasper, Bell, Woodward, Urmson

Referee: R A Mortimer (Huddersfield)

Attendance: 4,000

1934/35 Welsh Cup

First Round

Blaenau Ffestiniog	2-2	Portmadoc

Blaenau Ffestiniog were subsequently dismissed from the competition and Portmadoc progressed.

Bethesda Victoria (withdrew)	v	Llanfairfechan (w/o)
Llandudno FC	1-1	Flint
Abergele	2-2	Llanddulas
Gwersyllt	2-3	Caergwrle
Brymbo Green	3-2	Mold Alexandra

A protest regarding an ineligible player was upheld and Brymbo Green were dismissed from the competition.

Johnstown	2-3	Druids
Stryd Isa	1-2	Cross Street Gwersyllt
Llay Welfare	2-5	Llanerch Celts
Aberystwyth Town	3-2	Welshpool
Towyn	6-2	Aberystwyth Uni. College
Aberdovey	3-0	Bala
Caersws	3-4	Llanidloes Town
Newtown	5-2	Machynlleth
Rhayader	5-1	Builth Wells
Llandrindod Wells	0-1	Knighton
Blaina Town	2-6	Milford Haven

First Round Replays

Flint	8-2	Llandudno FC
Llanddulas	0-1	Abergele

Second Round

Portmadoc	4-0	Llanfairfechan
Abergele	1-3	Flint
Holt	5-2	Caergwrle
Cross Street Gwersyllt	3-3	Druids
Llanerch Celts	11-0	Crosville
Aberdovey	4-7	Aberystwyth Town
Dolgelley	0-0	Towyn
Newtown	1-1	Rhayader
Llanidloes Town	9-0	Knighton

Second Round Replays

Druids	3-3	Cross Street Gwersyllt
Towyn	2-1	Dolgelley
Rhayader	2-1	Newtown

Second Round Second Replay

Cross Street Gwersyllt	6-1	Druids

Third Round

Portmadoc	1-1	Flint
Mold Alexandra	4-1	Holt
Llanerch Celts	6-0	Cross Street Gwersyllt
Towyn	0-4	Aberystwyth Town
Llanidloes Town	2-0	Rhayader

Third Round Replay

Flint	3-1	Portmadoc

Fourth Round

Aberdare	0-0	Aberaman Athletic
Barry Town	6-2	Cardiff Corinthians
Ebbw Vale	2-0	Lovell's Athletic
Llanelly	2-5	Milford Haven
Penrhiwceiber	2-2	Troedyrhiw
Shrewsbury Town	2-0	Kidderminster Harriers
Rhyl Athletic	1-1	Mold Alexandra
Llanerch Celts	2-2	Oswestry Town
Flint (w/o)	v	Colwyn Bay (withdrew)
Llanidloes Town	5-1	Aberystwyth Town

Fourth Round Replays

Aberaman Athletic	1-3	Aberdare
Troedyrhiw	6-0	Penrhiwceiber
Mold Alexandra	1-2	Rhyl Athletic
Oswestry Town	0-1	Llanerch Celts

Fifth Round

Troedyrhiw	4-0	Aberdare Town
Milford Haven	4-1	Porth
Llanidloes Town	1-3	Shrewsbury Town
Flint	0-0	Rhyl

All other clubs received byes

Fifth Round Replay

Rhyl	0-2	Flint

Sixth Round

Lovell's Athletic	1-1	Barry Town
Cardiff City	3-2	Newport County
Troedyrhiw	3-5	Shrewsbury Town
Milford Haven	1-4	Swansea Town
Chester	5-1	Bangor City
New Brighton	1-1	Southport
Flint	0-5	Tranmere Rovers
Llanerch Celts	2-3	Wrexham

Sixth Round Replays

Barry Town	0-3	Lovell's Athletic
Southport	1-4	New Brighton

Seventh Round

New Brighton	0-0	Shrewsbury Town
Tranmere Rovers	1-1	Lovell's Athletic
Swansea Town	6-0	Wrexham
Cardiff City	2-2	Chester

Seventh Round Replays

Shrewsbury Town	4-4	New Brighton
Lovell's Athletic	5-6	Tranmere Rovers
Chester	3-0	Cardiff City

Seventh Round Second Replay

New Brighton	0-2	Shrewsbury Town

Semi-finals

Swansea Town	0-5	Chester
Played at Wrexham		
Shrewsbury Town	0-3	Tranmere Rovers
Played at Shrewsbury		

1935 WELSH CUP FINAL

4th May 1935 at Sealand Road, Chester

Tranmere Rovers	1-0	Chester

Woodward

Tranmere Rovers: B Gray, C Platt, Warren, C Curtis, Major, Spencer, Baker, McDonald, Burgin, Woodward, Eden

Chester: J J Burke, F Bennett, E W Hall, J W Pitcairn, A Wilson, H Howarth, G Kelly, J H Hughes, Mantle, Cresswell, C Sargeant

Referee: A E Fogg

Attendance: 10,000

1935/36 Welsh Cup

First Round

Portmadoc	2-1	Holyhead
Llanfairfechan	4-2	Bethesda Penryn Quarry
Llandudno FC (w/o)	v	Ruthin (withdrew)
Mold	2-3	Flint
Caergwrle	0-2	Vron United
Coedpoeth	2-2	Cross Street Gwersyllt
Wynnstay	3-3	Llay Welfare
Gwersyllt	1-2	Druids
Llay United	2-0	Brymbo
Bala	3-2	Dolgelley Albion
Llanidloes Town	4-1	Caersws
Welshpool	0-4	Newtown
Aberystwyth Town	4-1	Towyn
Machynlleth	3-1	Aberdovey
Builth Wells (w/o)	v	Brecon (withdrew)
Llandrindod Wells	1-4	Rhayader
Blaina Town	0-1	Pontymister United

First Round Replays

Cross Street Gwersyllt	1-0	Coedpoeth
Llay Welfare	6-2	Wynnstay

Second Round

Llanidloes Town	7-0	Newtown
Aberystwyth	2-1	Machynlleth
Bala	4-3	Blaenau Ffestiniog FC
Flint	3-1	Portmadoc
Llandudno FC	4-4	Llanfairfechan
Llanerch Celts	2-0	Llay Welfare
Llay United	0-0	Cross Street Gwersyllt
Druids	5-0	Vron United
Rhayader (w/o)	v	Builth Wells (withdrew)
Pontymister United	1-3	Milford Haven

Second Round Replays

Llanfairfechan	4-6	Llandudno FC
Cross Street Gwersyllt	3-1	Llay United

Third Round

Rhayader	0-1	Aberystwyth Town
Flint	0-3	Macclesfield
Rhyl	5-1	Colwyn Bay
Cross Street Gwersyllt	2-9	Bangor City
Llanerch Celts	1-3	Druids
Llandudno FC	0-2	Oswestry Town
Llanidloes Town	2-1	Hereford United
Aberdare Town	5-0	Penrhiwceiber
Lovell's Athletic	4-1	Gelli Colliery
Barry Town	8-0	Porth United
Cardiff Corinthians	1-2	Aberaman Athletic
Milford United	3-3	Caerau
Troedyrhiw	1-3	Llanelly
Bala (w/o)	v	Kidderminster Harriers (withdrew)

Third Round Replay

Caerau	3-1	Milford United

Fourth Round

Llanidloes Town	1-0	Aberystwyth Town
Aberdare Town	2-0	Aberaman Athletic
Lovell's Athletic	1-1	Barry
Caerau	1-0	Llanelly
Rhyl	5-1	Macclesfield
Bala	1-2	Druids
Bangor City	1-1	Oswestry Town

Fourth Round Replays

Barry	1-3	Lovell's Athletic
Oswestry Town	0-1	Bangor City

Fifth Round

Aberdare	9-1	Caerau
Llanidloes Town	2-1	Druids

All other clubs received byes

Sixth Round

Swansea Town	1-0	Newport County
Cardiff City	2-1	Bristol City
Lovell's Athletic	1-4	Aberdare
New Brighton	1-8	Shrewsbury Town
Llanidloes Town	3-4	Bangor City
Chester	2-1	Southport
Wrexham	1-1	Rhyl
Tranmere Rovers (withdrew)	v	Crewe Alexandra (w/o)

Sixth Round Replay

Rhyl	2-1	Wrexham

Seventh Round

Rhyl	2-1	Cardiff City
Aberdare	3-1	Shrewsbury Town

A replay to be held at Shrewsbury was ordered following an appeal.

Chester	4-1	Swansea Town
Bangor City	1-1	Crewe Alexandra

Seventh Round Replays

Shrewsbury Town	4-1	Aberdare
Crewe Alexandra	2-0	Bangor City

Semi-finals

Rhyl	0-3	Chester

Played at Rhyl

Shrewsbury Town	0-0	Crewe Alexandra

Played at Bangor

Semi-final Replay

Crewe Alexandra	4-0	Shrewsbury Town

Played at Rhyl

1936 WELSH CUP FINAL

30th April 1936 at the Racecourse, Wrexham

Crewe Alexandra	2-0	Chester

Swindells, Rigby

Crewe Alexandra: Swift, Wilson, Kneale, Blake, Scott, Gilchrist, Waring, Armstrong, Swindells, Wood, Rigby

Chester: J J Burke, E W Common, E W Hall, J W Pitcairn, A Wilson, H Howarth, H Horsman, G Wharton, F Wrightson, Sanders, C Sargeant

Referee: S Boardman (Hale)

Attendance: 6,807

1936/37 Welsh Cup

First Round

Pwllheli	2-1	Portmadoc
Blaenau Ffestiniog	10-0	Penrhyn Quarry
Llandudno FC	6-0	Holyhead
Courtaulds Holywell	3-0	Leeswood
Flint	1-1	Buckley Town
Coedpoeth	2-1	Bala
Llay United	2-2	Cross Street Gwersyllt
Llay Welfare	4-2	Crosville Wrexham
Caergwrle	4-1	Gwersyllt
Druids	1-6	Llanerch Celts
Newtown	1-1	Welshpool
Penrhiwceiber	2-2	Caerphilly United
Blaina	2-1	Pontymister
Haverfordwest Athletic	1-2	Milford Haven
Machynlleth	1-5	Llanidloes Town
Caersws	2-6	Aberystwyth Town
Towyn	2-4	Aberdovey
Rhayader (w/o) (withdrew)	v	Llandrindod Wells

First Round Replays

Buckley Town	2-0	Flint
Cross Street Gwersyllt	1-1	Llay United
Welshpool	1-2	Newtown
Caerphilly United	2-1	Penrhiwceiber

First Round Second Replay

Llay United	1-0	Cross Street Gwersyllt

Second Round

Pwllheli FC	3-3	Aberdovey
Buckley Town	2-2	Courtaulds
Llandudno Town	2-0	Blaenau Ffestiniog
Llay Welfare	2-1	Llay United
Caergwrle	2-1	Llanerch Celts
Vron United	1-4	Coedpoeth
Aberystwyth Town	4-1	Rhayader
Newtown	0-1	Llanidloes Town

Ebbw Vale	3-3	Blaina Town
Ebbw Vale withdrew		
Milford United	0-0	Caerphilly United

Second Round Replays

Aberdovey	2-4	Pwllheli FC
Courtaulds	3-3	Buckley Town
Caerphilly United	0-6	Milford United

Second Round Second Replay

Buckley Town	4-1	Courtaulds

Third Round

Bangor City	7-0	Pwllheli
Llay Welfare	3-2	Coedpoeth
Buckley Town	3-2	Llandudno FC
Caergwrle	2-3	Colwyn Bay
Wellington Town	2-3	Oswestry Town
Kidderminster Harriers (w/o)		
	v	Northwich Victoria (withdrew)
Hereford United	4-0	Worcester City
Aberystwyth Town	2-2	Llanidloes Town
Aberdare Town	3-4	Aberaman Athletic
Lovell's Athletic	6-4	Blaina
Cardiff Corinthians	0-5	Barry Town
Llanelly	4-2	Milford United
Caerau Athletic	2-2	Gelli Colliery
Troedyrhiw	2-3	Gwynfi Colliery
Caerphilly Town	3-0	Porth Town

A replay was ordered following a protest by Porth.

Third Round Replays

Llanidloes Town	1-2	Aberystwyth Town
Gelli Colliery	1-1	Caerau Athletic
Porth Town	4-1	Caerphilly Town

Third Round Second Replay

Caerau Athletic	4-5	Gelli Colliery

Fourth Round

Kidderminster Harriers	6-1	Colwyn Bay
Oswestry Town	1-1	Bangor City
Buckley Town	1-1	Aberystwyth Town
Llay Welfare	4-3	Hereford United
Aberaman Athletic	7-2	Llanelly
Porth Town	2-2	Lovell's Athletic
Gelli Colliery	1-2	Gwynfi Colliery

Fourth Round Replays

Bangor City	2-1	Oswestry Town
Aberystwyth Town	6-1	Buckley Town
Lovell's Athletic	2-3	Porth Town

Fifth Round

Kidderminster Harriers	15-2	Aberystwyth Town
Aberaman Athletic	3-4	Barry Town
Gwynfi Colliery	3-7	Bangor City

Porth Town and Llay Welfare both received byes

Sixth Round

Llay Welfare	2-9	Crewe Alexandra
Shrewsbury Town	1-2	Kidderminster Harriers
Chester	4-1	Southport
Porth Town	0-5	Newport County
Bristol City	1-2	Swansea Town
Barry Town	3-1	Cardiff City
Wrexham	1-2	Rhyl
New Brighton	3-2	Bangor City

Seventh Round

Newport County	7-0	Swansea Town
Crewe Alexandra	2-1	Chester
Barry Town	2-0	Kidderminster Harriers
Rhyl	3-0	New Brighton

Semi-finals

Rhyl	3-2	Newport County
Played at Shrewsbury		
Crewe Alexandra	2-1	Barry Town
Played at Cardiff		

1937 WELSH CUP FINAL

29th April 1937 at Sealand Road, Chester

Crewe Alexandra	1-1	Rhyl FC
Wright		*Debbert*

Crewe Alexandra: Swift, Turnbull, Gilchrist, Blake, Scott, Goodier, Waring, Armstrong, Swindells, Wright, Rigby

Rhyl: Harford, Rodgers, J Roberts, Fantham, Jolly, Jones, F Roberts, Hamilton, Gore, Debbert, Sorenson

Referee: J E Williams (Bolton)

Attendance: 0

1937 WELSH CUP FINAL REPLAY

5th May 1937 at Sealand Road, Chester

Crewe Alexandra	3-1	Rhyl FC
Scott, Swindells, Waring		*F Roberts*

Crewe Alexandra: Swift, Turnbull, Gilchrist, Blake, Scott, Goodier, Waring, Armstrong, Swindells, Wright, Jones

Rhyl: Harford, Rodgers, J Roberts, Fantham, Jolly, Jones, F Roberts, Hamilton, Gore, Debbert, Sorenson

Referee: J E Williams (Bolton)

1937/38 Welsh Cup

First Round

Blaenau Ffestiniog	2-2	Llandudno FC
Colwyn Bay	2-3	Penrhyn Quarry
Llay Welfare	1-1	Llanerch Celts
Caergwrle	3-0	Rhosymedre
Crosville Wrexham	1-3	Castle Firebrick
Mold Alexandra	3-3	Cross Street Gwersyllt
Buckley Town	6-0	Coedpoeth
Druids	0-5	Chirk AAA
Flint Town	1-1	Gwersyllt
Courtaulds	4-1	Vron United
Towyn	0-4	Aberdovey Town
Machynlleth	3-4	Portmadoc
Aberystwyth Town	4-1	Pwllheli
Welshpool	8-0	Newtown
Dolgelley	3-1	Bala
Tredomen Works	5-1	Porth
Blaina Town	0-10	Llanelly
Ebbw Vale	0-0	Caerphilly Town
Caerphilly United (w/o)	v	Penrhiwceiber (withdrew)
Rhayader (withdrew)	v	Llanidloes Town (w/o)

First Round Replays

Llandudno FC	1-1	Blaenau Ffestiniog
Llanerch Celts	2-4	Llay Welfare
Cross Street Gwersyllt	7-0	Mold Alexandra
Gwersyllt	3-0	Flint Town
Ebbw Vale	2-2	Caerphilly Town

First Round Second Replays

Blaenau Ffestiniog	3-1	Llandudno FC
Ebbw Vale	4-1	Caerphilly Town

Second Round

Blaenau Ffestiniog	1-1	Penrhyn Quarry
Courtaulds	3-1	Buckley Town
Chirk AAA	2-1	Gwersyllt
Llay Welfare	3-0	Cross Street Gwersyllt
Castle Firebrick Works	3-5	Caergwrle United
The match was abandoned.		
Portmadoc	7-1	Dolgelley
Aberystwyth Town	5-4	Aberdovey
Llanidloes Town	7-1	Welshpool
Haverfordwest Athletic	3-1	Tredomen Works
Lovell's Athletic	4-1	Caerphilly United
Ebbw Vale	3-8	Llanelly

Second Round Replays

Penrhyn Quarry	4-1	Blaenau Ffestiniog
Castle Firebrick Works	0-0	Caergwrle United

Second Round Second Replay

Caergwrle United	2-1	Castle Firebrick Works

Third Round

Penrhyn Quarry	5-4	Portmadoc
Macclesfield Town	3-1	Bangor City
Kidderminster Harriers	1-2	Cheltenham Town
Wellington Town	6-0	Hereford United
Oswestry Town	1-1	Shrewsbury Town
Caergwrle United	4-3	Llay Welfare
Chirk AAA	3-2	Courtaulds
Aberystwyth Town	0-1	Llanidloes Town
Aberdare Town	0-3	Aberaman Athletic
Cardiff Corinthians	2-3	Gwynfi Welfare
Lovell's Athletic	3-0	Milford Haven
Haverfordwest Athletic	4-4	Troedyrhiw

Third Round Replays

Shrewsbury Town	6-3	Oswestry Town
Troedyrhiw	1-2	Haverfordwest Athletic

Fourth Round

Wellington Town	1-3	Cheltenham Town
Macclesfield Town	0-7	Shrewsbury Town
Llanidloes Town	4-1	Chirk AAA
Penrhyn Quarry	0-0	Caergwrle

Penrhyn Quarry were subsequently disqualified from the competition so Caergwrle progressed.

Llanelly	2-1	Haverfordwest Athletic
Aberaman Athletic	1-2	Worcester City
Gwynfi Welfare	0-3	Lovell's Athletic

Fifth Round

Llanidloes Town	2-1	Caergwrle
Llanelly	3-0	Lovell's Athletic

Sixth Round

Newport County	6-2	Bristol City
Worcester City	2-2	Barry Town
Swansea Town	8-0	Llanelly
Cardiff City	0-1	Cheltenham Town
New Brighton	1-5	Chester
Llanidloes Town	1-1	Rhyl
Wrexham	1-3	Shrewsbury Town
Southport	2-0	Crewe Alexandra

Sixth Round Replays

Barry Town	1-1	Worcester City
Rhyl	1-0	Llanidloes Town

Sixth Round Second Replay

Worcester City	2-0	Barry Town

Seventh Round

Newport County	1-0	Cheltenham Town
Swansea Town	1-0	Worcester City
Rhyl	3-2	Southport
Chester	0-0	Shrewsbury Town

Semi-finals

Shrewsbury Town	3-2	Newport County
Played at Shrewsbury		
Swansea Town	7-2	Rhyl
Played at Chester		

1938 WELSH CUP FINAL

4th May 1938 at Gay Meadow, Shrewsbury

Shrewsbury Town	2-2	Swansea Town
Williams, Race		Millington, Emmanuel

Shrewsbury Town: Halston, Seymour, Breeze, Harkin, Miller, Nicholls, Davies, Race, Williams, Brown, Hopley

Swansea Town: R John, Wright, T Emmanuel, Harris, Leyland, Lloyd, Lewis, Vernon, L Emmanuel, Beresford, Millington

Referee: A J Jewell (London)

Attendance: 14,500

1938 WELSH CUP FINAL REPLAY

19th September 1938 at Gay Meadow, Shrewsbury

Shrewsbury Town	2-1	Swansea Town
Brown, Roberts		Imrie

Shrewsbury Town: Sift, Seymour, Breeze, Harkin, Smith, Nicholls, Roberts, Dodd, Williams, Brown, Almond

Swansea Town: R John, S Lawrence, Davies, Rhodes, Simons, Imrie, Richardson, Lewis, Bamford, T Olsen, Millington

Referee: A J Jewell (London)

Attendance: 8,000

1938/39 Welsh Cup

First Round

Llandudno FC	4-1	Penrhyn Quarry
Holyhead	1-4	Caernarvon Town
Cross Street Gwersyllt	6-0	Llangollen
Buckley Town	3-1	Flint Town
Castle Firebrick	0-5	Druids
Gwersyllt	2-7	Flint Athletic
Llanerch Celts	2-1	Caergwrle
Mold Alexandra	2-5	Shotton Athletic
Llandrindiod Wells	1-1	Llanidloes Town
Portmadoc	6-3	Pwllheli
Machynlleth	4-2	Barmouth
Towyn Celtic	0-4	Aberdovey
Welshpool	9-1	Newtown
Aberystwyth Town	4-1	Trefechan
Blaenau Ffestiniog	10-0	Dolgelley
Caerphilly United	2-1	Pontypridd

First Round Replay

Llanidloes Town	6-2	Llandrindiod Wells

Second Round

Portmadoc	3-4	Llandudno FC
Flint Athletic	1-1	Shotton Athletic
Blaenau Ffestiniog	4-1	Caernarvon Town
Machynlleth	4-0	Aberdovey
Llanidloes Town	3-0	Aberystwyth Town
Druids FC	0-3	Cross Street Gwersyllt
Rhayader	1-2	Welshpool
Llay United	2-0	Buckley Town

Second Round Replay

Shotton Athletic	5-2	Flint Athletic

Third Round

Shotton Athletic	3-1	Blaenau Ffestiniog
Llay United	0-4	Llanidloes Town
Llanerch Celts	4-2	Machynlleth
Oswestry Town	3-2	Llandudno FC
Cross Street Gwersyllt	2-1	Welshpool
Hereford United (dismissed)	v	Kidderminster Harriers
Caerphilly United	2-4	Troedyrhiw
Aberdare Town	2-6	Aberaman Athletic
Haverfordwest Athletic	2-1	Llanelly
Barry Town	7-1	Cardiff Corinthians
Caerau Athletic	1-4	Gwynfi Welfare
Milford United	10-2	Caerphilly Town
Ebbw Vale	2-2	Lovell's Athletic

Third Round Replay

Lovell's Athletic	4-1	Ebbw Vale

Fourth Round

Oswestry Town	5-1	Hereford United
Shotton Athletic	4-1	Cross Street Gwersyllt
Llanidloes Town	5-0	Llanerch Celts
Haverfordwest Athletic	3-2	Gwynfi Welfare
Barry Town (w/o)	v	Aberaman Athletic (withdrew)
Milford United	8-2	Troedyrhiw

Lovell's Athletic received a bye

Fifth Round

Wrexham	9-0	Southport
Bangor City	0-1	New Brighton

The match was abandoned.

Cardiff City	2-2	Swansea Town
Rhyl	3-0	Shotton Athletic
Oswestry Town	2-0	Llanidloes Town
South Liverpool	2-1	Shrewsbury Town
Haverfordwest Athletic	2-3	Milford United
Barry Town	2-0	Lovell's Athletic

Fifth Round Replays

Bangor City	2-0	New Brighton
Swansea Town	1-4	Cardiff City

Sixth Round

Chester	4-0	Rhyl
Cardiff City	5-1	Newport County
South Liverpool	8-1	Bangor City

Barry Town	1-0	Wrexham
Milford United	2-2	Oswestry Town

Sixth Round Replay

Oswestry Town	4-0	Milford United

Seventh Round

Oswestry Town	4-2	Barry Town
Cardiff City	bye	
South Liverpool	bye	
Chester	bye	

Semi-finals

South Liverpool	5-2	Chester
Played at Goodison Park		
Cardiff City	1-1	Oswestry Town

Semi-final Replay

Oswestry Town	2-2	Cardiff City

Semi-final Second Replay

Cardiff City	2-1	Oswestry Town
Played at Shrewsbury		

1939 WELSH CUP FINAL

4th May 1939 at the Racecourse, Wrexham

South Liverpool	2-1	Cardiff City
G Jones 2		Collins

South Liverpool: Roper, Dodd, Hurst, Murray, Salmon, Billing, Leadbetter, G Jones, Roscoe, T Jones, Urmson

Cardiff City: Fielding, Balsam, Kelso, Corkhill, Williams, Nicholson, Hugh, Walton, Collins, Talbot, Hill

Referee: F McCarthy (Wrexham)

Attendance: 5,000

1939/40 Welsh Cup

First Round

Penrhyn Quarry (withdrew)	v	Caernarvon Town
Blaenau Ffestiniog	4-0	Portmadoc
Llandudno FC (w/o)	v	Holyhead (withdrew)
Barmouth	1-4	Pwllheli FC
Pwllheli FC subsequently withdrew from the competition so Barmouth were reinstated		
Caergwrle (w/o)	v	Buckley Town (withdrew)
Flint Athletic (w/o)	v	Northern Nomads (withdrew)
Mold Alexandra	0-2	Llanerch Celts
Cross Street Gwersyllt (w/o)	v	Druids (withdrew)
Gwersylllt	1-6	Bradley Rangers
Shotton Athletic	6-2	Liverpool Druids
Llay United	3-0	Flint Town
Rhayader (w/o)	v	Llanidloes Town (withdrew)
Trefechan (withdrew)	v	Aberdovey
Aberystwyth Town	7-1	Aberystwyth Uni. College
Machynlleth (w/o)	v	Welshpool (withdrew)
Ton Pentre (w/o)	v	Caerphilly (withdrew)
Dolgelley received a bye		

Second Round

Llandudno FC	4-1	Flint Athletic
Blaenau Ffestiniog FC	1-0	Caernarvon Town
Machynlleth	1-1	Rhayader
Aberystwyth Town (w/o)	v	Aberdovey (withdrew)
Dolgelley (withdrew)	v	Barmouth (w/o)
Shotton Athletic (withdrew)	v	Llanerch Celts (w/o)
Bradley Rangers	1-1	Llay United
Cross Street (w/o)	v	Caergwrle (withdrew)
Ton Pentre received a bye		

Second Round Replays

Rhayader	1-3	Machynlleth
Llay United	1-2	Bradley Rangers
A replay was ordered following a protest.		

Second Round Second Replay

Bradley Rangers	4-2	Llay United

Third Round

Llanerch Celts	2-1	Cross Street
Llandudno FC	8-2	Blaenau Ffestiniog FC
Aberystwyth Town	8-4	Machynlleth
Gwynfi United	v	Nantymoel (dismissed)
Aberdare Town	1-6	Ebbw Vale
Milford United	3-5	Haverfordwest
Ton Pentre (w/o)	v	Caerau (withdrew)
Cardiff Corinthians	2-7	Troedyrhiw
Cardiff Corinthians appeared in the next round so it presumed that Troedyrhiw withdrew.		
Lovell's Athletic	4-1	Aberaman Athletic
Barmouth and Bradley Rangers both received byes		

Fourth Round

Rhyl	1-4	New Brighton
Llandudno FC	2-1	Bangor City
Southport	2-1	South Liverpool
Aberystwyth Town	11-1	Barmouth
Llanerch Celts	1-2	Bradley Rangers
Barry Town	3-2	Cardiff Corinthians
Gwynfi Welfare	6-1	Ton Pentre
Newport County	1-1	Lovell's Athletic
Chester	4-2	Shrewsbury Town
Cardiff City	3-0	Ebbw Vale
Wrexham	1-2	Wellington Town
Hereford United (w/o)	v	Oswestry Town (withdrew)
Swansea Town	v	Haverfordwest Athletic (dismissed)

Fourth Round Replay

Lovell's Athletic	0-2	Newport County

Fifth Round

Wellington Town	10-1	Hereford United
New Brighton	4-1	Llandudno FC
Swansea Town	7-2	Gwynfi Welfare

Newport County	3-2	Barry Town
Aberystwyth Town	4-3	Bradley Rangers

Cardiff City, Chester and Southport all received byes

Sixth Round

Chester	1-3	Wellington Town
New Brighton	1-0	Southport
Cardiff City	1-1	Newport County
Swansea Town	2-0	Aberystwyth Town

Sixth Round Replay

Newport County	5-0	Cardiff City

Semi-finals

Swansea Town	1-0	Newport County
Played at Swansea		
New Brighton	0-0	Wellington Town
Played at Wellington		

Semi-final Replay

Wellington Town	4-2	New Brighton
Played at Shrewsbury		

1940 WELSH CUP FINAL

1st June 1940 at Gay Meadow, Shrewsbury

Wellington Town	4-0	Swansea Town

Mayer 2, Hopley, Driscoll

Wellington Town: Lovett. Lea, Hick, Heinemann, Childs, Jones, Sims, Mayer, Price, Driscoll, Hopley

Swansea Town: Harris, Davies, Mears, Briddon, Fisher, D L Emmanuel, Payne, Squires, Bamford, Allen, Edwards

Referee: F S Milner (Wolverhampton)

Attendance: 6,000

1946/47 Welsh Cup

First Round

Cardiff Corinthians	1-1	Troedyrhiw
Haverfordwest Athletic	2-1	Llanelly
Ton Pentre	8-0	Gwynfi Welfare
Caerau Athletic	0-0	Aberaman & Aberdare
Ebbw Vale	3-1	Cwm United
Llanfairfechan Town	3-1	Holyhead Town
Penrhyn Quarry	2-2	Blaenau Ffestiniog FC
Dolgellau	1-1	Barmouth & Dyffryn Utd
Pwllheli Royal British Legion	2-4	Portmadoc
Llandudno Junction	2-1	Flint Town United
Shotton (withdrew)	v	Mold Alexandra (w/o)
Dee Rangers	8-0	Lavister FC
Rhos Celts	2-1	Llay Welfare
Penycae	1-6	Chirk AAA
Brymbo Steelworks	3-3	Druids United
Llay United	2-1	Gresford Athletic
Welshpool	4-2	Llanfyllin
Llanidloes Town	6-4	Newtown
Rhayader Town	4-6	Llandrindod Wells
Aberystwyth Town	3-1	Aberayron
Machynlleth	8-2	Borth
Aberdovey Town	0-6	Bala Town

First Round Replay

Troedyrhiw	2-0	Cardiff Corinthians
Aberaman & Aberdare	8-5	Caerau Athletic
Blaenau Ffestiniog FC	5-4	Penrhyn Quarry
Barmouth & Dyffryn Utd	2-0	Dolgellau
Druids United	1-3	Brymbo Steelworks

Second Round

Welshpool	2-2	Machynlleth
Aberystwyth Town	3-2	Llandrindod Wells
Llanidloes Town	3-2	Builth Wells
Bala Town	4-2	Barmouth & Dyffryn Utd
Portmadoc	3-4	Blaenau Ffestiniog FC
Llanfairfechan Town	3-3	Llandudno Junction
Brymbo Steelworks	0-0	Rhos Celts
Chirk AAA	11-1	Dee Rangers
Llay United	2-0	Mold Alexandra
Troedyrhiw	4-1	Aberaman & Aberdare
Ton Pentre	2-2	Ebbw Vale
Milford United	3-1	Haverfordwest Athletic

Second Round Replays

Machynlleth	4-0	Welshpool
Llandudno Junction	3-2	Llanfairfechan Town
Rhos Celts	3-3	Brymbo Steelworks
Ebbw Vale	2-0	Ton Pentre

Second Round Second Replay

Brymbo Steelworks	5-3	Rhos Celts

Third Round

Llandudno Junction	3-1	Blaenau Ffestiniog FC
Llandudno Town	2-2	Caernarvon Town
Chirk AAA	3-3	Brymbo Steelworks
Colwyn Bay	1-3	Llay United
Troedyrhiw	7-1	Ebbw Vale
Milford United	1-1	Merthyr Tydfil
The match was abandoned.		
Barry Town	4-3	Lovell's Athletic
Machynlleth	5-2	Llanidloes Town
Bala Town	3-1	Aberystwyth Town
Oswestry Town	3-1	Hereford United

Third Round Replays

Caernarvon Town	2-1	Llandudno Town
Brymbo Steelworks	4-4	Chirk AAA
Milford United	1-2	Merthyr Tydfil

Third Round Second Replay

Chirk AAA	4-1	Brymbo Steelworks

Fourth Round

Troedyrhiw	2-3	Barry Town

Merthyr Tydfil	5-0	Machynlleth
Chirk AAA	2-2	Caernarvon Town
Llandudno Junction	1-2	South Liverpool
Oswestry Town	1-0	Llay United
Bala Town	1-1	Shrewsbury Town

Fourth Round Replays

Caernarvon Town	5-1	Chirk AAA
Shrewsbury Town	9-1	Bala Town

Fifth Round

Caernarvon Town	1-8	Wrexham
South Liverpool	2-0	Rhyl
Oswestry Town	2-8	Shrewsbury Town
Bangor City	3-5	Chester
Cardiff City	2-4	Merthyr Tydfil
Barry Town	3-3	Newport County

All other clubs received byes

Fifth Round Replay

Newport County	4-1	Barry Town

Sixth Round

Merthyr Tydfil	2-0	South Liverpool
Newport County	0-0	Shrewsbury Town
Swansea Town	1-3	Chester
Wrexham (w/o) (withdrew)	v	Wellington Town

Sixth Round Replay

Shrewsbury Town	0-1	Newport County

Semi-finals

Chester	3-2	Newport County
Played at Wrexham		
Wrexham	0-2	Merthyr Tydfil
Played at Cardiff		

1947 WELSH CUP FINAL

5th June 1947 at Ninian Park, Cardiff

Chester	0-0	Merthyr Tydfil

Chester: Scales, Butcher, McNeil, Marsh, T Walters, Lee, Turner, Burden, Yates, Astbury, Hamilton

Merthyr Tydfil: Reid, Avery, Pugh, Phillips, Allen, Richards, Powell, Thomas, B Hullett, Raybould, Crisp

Referee: A E Davies (Aberystwyth)

Attendance: 27,000

1947 WELSH CUP FINAL REPLAY

12th June 1947 at the Racecourse, Wrexham

Chester	5-1	Merthyr Tydfil
Burden 2, Yates, Turner, Astbury		Thomas

Chester: Scales, Butcher, McNeil, Marsh, T Walters, Lee, Turner, Burden, Yates, Astbury, Hamilton

Merthyr Town: Reid, Avery, Pugh, Phillips, Allen, Richards, Powell, Thomas, B Hullett, Raybould, Crisp

Referee: A E Davies (Aberystwyth)

Attendance: 11,190

1947/48 Welsh Cup

First Round

Portmadoc	3-5	Blaenau Ffestiniog FC
Pwllheli Royal British Legion	3-1	Holyhead Town
Penrhyn Quarry	7-2	Penmaenmawr
Conway Borough	2-5	Flint Town United
Llandudno Junction	2-1	Llanfairfechan Town
Bala Town	5-0	Rhosrobin
Corwen Amateurs	5-0	Rossett
Chirk AAA	6-1	Vron Celts
Johnstown United	1-2	Llay Welfare
Rhos Celts	2-1	Hughes & Lancaster
Holt Nomads	2-0	Druids United
Overton St Mary	6-2	Garth & Trevor
Llay United	1-2	Gresford
Llangollen	4-1	Brymbo
Llangollen B	1-7	Mold Alexandra
Barmouth & Dyffryn Utd	4-2	Harlech Town
Aberdovey	6-3	Dolgellau
Bow Street	2-5	Aberayron
Aberystwyth Town	7-2	Tregaron
Turfs Rhayader	2-5	Llanidloes Town
Llandrindod Wells	2-5	Builth Wells
Towyn	3-4	Welshpool
Llanfyllin	4-3	Newtown
Senghenydd Town	3-6	Troedyrhiw
Cwm United	3-0	Monmouth Town
Treharris Athletic	1-1	Ebbw Vale
Guest Keen Baldwins Port Talbot	1-6	Gwynfi Welfare
Briton Ferry Athletic	2-1	Ton Pentre
Haverfordwest Athletic	0-1	Milford United
Pembroke Dock	4-4	Llanelly

First Round Replays

Ebbw Vale	3-0	Treharris Athletic
Llanelly	2-1	Pembroke Dock

Second Round

Blaenau Ffestiniog FC	6-1	Barmouth & Dyffryn Utd
Penrhyn Quarry	9-6	Pwllheli Royal Brit. Legion

Flint Town United	3-2	Llandudno Junction
Corwen Amateurs	0-3	Bala Town
Gresford Athletic	3-1	Overton St Mary
Mold Alexandra	1-3	Llay Welfare
Chirk AAA	3-3	Rhos Celts
Holt Nomads	2-3	Llangollen
Aberystwyth Town	8-6 (aet)	Aberayron

Full-time score was 6-6.

Machynlleth	1-2	Aberdovey
Builth Wells	1-4	Llanidloes Town
Llanfyllin	5-2	Welshpool
Milford United	2-3	Llanelly
Ebbw Vale	1-0	Cwm United
Caerau	4-1	Aberaman Athletic
Cardiff Corinthians	0-4	Troedyrhiw
Briton Ferry Athletic	1-3	Gwynfi Welfare

Second Round Replay

Rhos Celts	2-1	Chirk AAA

Third Round

Blaenau Ffestiniog FC	1-5	Penrhyn Quarry
Llay Welfare	1-7	Flint Town United
Llangollen	5-1	Gresford Athletic
Bala Town	3-5	Rhos Celts
Aberdovey	6-3	Llanfyllin
Aberystwyth Town	5-3	Llanidloes Town
Llanelly	4-1	Caerau Athletic
Gwynfi Welfare	0-6	Troedyrhiw

Fourth Round

Penrhyn Quarry	6-3	Rhos Celts
Caernarvon Town	4-3	Aberdovey Town
Llangollen	3-2	Llandudno
Oswestry Town	2-3	Flint Town United
Colwyn Bay	3-3	Aberystwyth Town
Ebbw Vale	0-2	Troedyrhiw

Fourth Round Replay

Aberystwyth Town	5-1	Colwyn Bay

Fifth Round

Aberystwyth Town	4-1	Flint Town United
South Liverpool	2-1	Chester
Bangor City	3-1	Llangollen
Rhyl	11-0	Caernarvon Town
Penrhyn Quarry	2-6	Wrexham
Shrewsbury Town	6-3	Troedyrhiw
Lovell's Athletic	2-1	Cardiff City
Llanelly	1-4	Wellington Town
Barry Town	2-0	Swansea Town
Merthyr Tydfil	3-1	Newport County

Sixth Round

Llanelly	1-2	Barry Town
Rhyl	2-4 (aet)	Wrexham

Seventh Round

Bangor City	1-2	Shrewsbury Town
Aberystwyth Town	1-2	Barry Town
South Liverpool	3-1	Merthyr Tydfil
Lovell's Athletic	2-1	Wrexham

Semi-finals

South Liverpool	0-1	Lovell's Athletic

Played at Shrewsbury

Barry Town	1-3	Shrewsbury Town

Played at Merthyr

1948 WELSH CUP FINAL

22nd April 1948 at the Racecourse, Wrexham

Lovell's Athletic	3-0	Shrewsbury Town

Holland 2, Wood

Lovell's Athletic: Williams, Steggles, G Edmunds, Brayley, H Clarke, Bye, Hodder, Wood, T Holland, Shaw, Morgan

Shrewsbury Town: Day, Laking, Aldred, Wheatley, S Hughes, Sheen, A Hughes, Davey, Phillips, Argue, Butler

Referee: G Dodd (Shotton)

Attendance: 10,000

1948/49 Welsh Cup

First Round

Holyhead Town	1-3	Llandudno Junction
Portmadoc	2-4	Blaenau Ffestiniog FC
Penmaenmawr	1-3	Llanfairfechan Town

Played at Llanfairfechan

Pwllheli & District	3-1	Conway Borough
Mold Alexandra	2-4	Holywell Town

Holywell were disqualified following a protest.

Denbigh Town	5-3 (aet)	Corwen Amateurs

Full-time score was 3-3.

Hughes & Lancaster	1-6	Chirk AAA
Druids United	0-2	Brymbo Steelworks
Bala Town	1-5	Vron Celts
Llangollen	0-4	Rhostyllen & Bersham Royal British Legion
Overton St Marys	0-3	Llay Welfare
Rhos Celts	2-6	Gresford Athletic
Llay United	1-3	Johnstown United
Queens Park Rovers	2-1	Holt Nomads
Rosset Villa	4-2	Ruabon Athletic
Aberayron	1-4	Machynlleth
Aberdovey Town	5-1	Harlech Town
Trawsfynnydd	1-2	Dolgelley
Towyn	1-11	Barmouth & Dyffryn Utd
Welshpool	3-2	Llanfyllin
Caersws Amateurs	2-4	Newtown
Rhayader Town	0-9	Llanidloes Town
Builth Wells Town	1-0	Llandrindod Wells
Treharris Athletic	1-0	Aberaman Athletic
Caerau Athletic	1-3	Gwynfi Welfare
Ton Pentre	5-1	Cardiff Corinthians
Senghenydd Town	1-1	Cwm United
Ebbw Vale	0-1	Girling FC Cwmbran
Llanelly	0-3	Milford United

Steel Company of Wales Port Talbot
                          2-5   Pembroke Borough
Played at Pembroke
Briton Ferry Athletic   0-1   Grovesend Welfare
Cwmavon   1-6   Haverfordwest Athletic
Played at Haverfordwest

First Round Replay

Cwm United   2-3   Senghenydd Town

Second Round

Llanfairfechan Town   1-2   Llandudno Junction
Pwllheli & District   6-1   Blaenau Ffestiniog FC
Mold Alexandra   2-0   Denbigh Town
Gresford Athletic   6-4   Queens Park Rovers
Rosset Villa   0-2   Chirk AAA
Brymbo Steelworks   3-1   Vron Celts
Rhostyllen & Bersham Royal British Legion
                          1-3   Johnstown United
Llanidloes Town   2-1   Builth Wells Town
Aberdovey   3-3 (aet) Machynlleth
Barmouth & Dyffryn Utd   1-3   Dolgellau
Newtown   3-4   Welshpool
Senghenydd Town   1-2   Milford United
Ton Pentre   3-4   Treharris Ahletic
Haverfordwest Athletic   2-0   Gwynfi Welfare
Pembroke Borough   1-2 (aet) Grovesend Welfare
Full-time score was 1-1.

Second Round Replay

Machynlleth   8-1   Aberdovey

Third Round

Pwllheli & District   2-2   Colwyn Bay
Match was abandoned after 10 minutes of extra time.
Mold Alexandra   4-2   Llandudno Junction
Caernarvon Town   3-3 (aet) Flint Town United
Full-time score was 2-2.
Penrhyn Quarry   1-5   Llandudno
Brymbo Steelworks   6-1   Gresford Athletic
Welshpool   2-2   Chirk AAA
Match was abandoned after 25 minutes of extra time.
Llay Welfare   3-1 (aet) Dolgelley
Full-time score was 1-1.
Johnstown United   1-0   Oswestry Town
Llanidloes Town   3-2   Aberystwyth Town
Troedyrhiw   5-2   Treharris Athletic
Grovesend Welfare   1-5   Milford United
Girling FC Cwmbran   2-3   Haverfordwest Athletic
Machynlleth received a bye

Third Round Replays

Colwyn Bay   2-6   Pwllheli & District
Flint Town United   6-2   Caernarvon Town
Chirk AAA   3-2 (aet) Welshpool
Full-time score was 2-2.

Fourth Round

Pwllheli & District   6-0   Llay Welfare
Brymbo Steelworks   1-4   Flint Town United
Rhyl   6-1   Chirk AAA

Johnstown United   2-0   Llandudno FC
Bangor City   3-0   Mold Alexandra
Milford United   4-0   Machynlleth
Llanidloes Town   0-6   Merthyr Tydfil
Haverfordwest Athletic (w/o)
                          v   Wellington Town (disqualified)

Fifth Round

Bangor City   0-2   Rhyl
Chester   0-6   Wrexham
Pwllheli & District   4-1   Johnstown United
South Liverpool   7-4   Flint Town United
Lovell's Athletic   1-0   Shrewsbury Town
Milford United   2-0   Newport County
Cardiff City   3-1   Troedyrhiw
Merthyr Tydfil   6-4   Haverfordwest Athletic
Barry Town   1-7   Swansea Town

Sixth Round

Lovell's Athletic   2-3   Merthyr Tydfil

Seventh Round

Swansea Town   9-1   South Liverpool
Rhyl   1-0   Wrexham
Milford United   1-2   Cardiff City
Merthyr Tydfil   4-0   Pwllheli & District

Semi-finals

Swansea Town   3-0   Rhyl
Played at Wrexham
Cardiff City   1-3   Merthyr Tydfil
Played at Swansea

1949 WELSH CUP FINAL

5th May 1949 at Ninian Park, Cardiff

Merthyr Tydfil   2-0   Swansea Town
Powell 2

Merthyr Tydfil: Read, Avery, Phillips, Lowe, Tabram, Richards, McIlvenny, Davies, Jarman, G Beech, Powell

Swansea Town: Canning, Elwell, Keaner, R Paul, Weston, Burns, O'Driscoll, McGrory, F Scrine, B Lucas, Payne

Referee: G H Lewis (Abercwmboi)
Attendance: 35,000

1949/50 Welsh Cup

First Round

Barmouth & Dyffryn Utd   5-0   Dolgelley
Harlech Town   5-0   Aberdovey
Corris United   0-6   Machynlleth
Caersws Amateurs   3-3   Newtown
Builth Wells   4-0   Llandrindod Wells

Knighton Town	10-5 (aet)	Rhayader Town
Colwyn Bay	1-1	Conway Borough
Llandudno Junction	1-2	Penmaenmawr
Llanfairfechan Town	1-2	Blaenau Ffestiniog FC
Holyhead Town	7-1	Bethesda Athletic
Portmadoc	0-1	Caernarvon Town
Abergele United	1-2	Buckley Wanderers
Mold Alexandra	1-3	Holywell Town
Courtaulds Fflint	1-4	Flint Town United

This match may have been played at Flint Town United's ground.

Ebbw Vale	2-2	Chippenham United

Played at Chippenham

Abergavenny Thursdays	2-1	Monmouth Town
Cwm United	3-2	Risca United
Aberaman Athletic	0-5	Bargoed United
Senghenydd Town	1-5	Treharris Athletic

Played at Abertridwr

Troedyrhiw	1-2	Ton Pentre
Ton Boys Club	5-1	Cwm Parc
Port Talbot Athletic	0-4	Pembroke Borough

Played at Pembroke

Briton Ferry Athletic	0-7	Llanelly

Played at Llanelly

Haverfordwest Athletic	4-1	Grovesend Welfare
Gwynfi Welfare	2-3	Caerau Athletic
Midland Athletic (Swansea)	2-2	Cwmavon

Cwmavon were disqualified following a protest.

Llangollen	3-0	Rossett Villa
Bala Town	4-2	Corwen Amateurs
Ruabon Athletic	5-2	Wrexham Nomads
Ruthin Royal Brit. Legion	1-4	Denbigh Town
Rhostyllen Sports Club	3-4	Johnstown United
Rhosrobin & District	1-1	Rhostyllen & Bersham Royal British Legion
Gresford Athletic	1-2	Chirk AAA
Vron Celts	2-1	Coedpoeth
Queens Park Rovers	5-3	Brymbo Steelworks
Llay Welfare	4-2	Druids United
Welshpool	7-1	Monsanto
Overton St Mary's	4-0	Holt Nomads

First Round Replays

Newtown	4-1	Caersws Amateurs
Conway Borough	0-1	Colwyn Bay
Chippenham United	1-2	Ebbw Vale
Rhostyllen & Bersham Royal British Legion	4-1	Rhosrobin & District

Second Round

Llanelly	4-1	Pembroke Borough
Haverfordwest Athletic	10-2	Midland Athletic (Swansea)
Ton Pentre	3-6	Caerau Athletic
Ebbw Vale	3-0	Treharris Athletic
Cardiff Corinthians	10-0	Cwm Parc
Abergavenny Thursdays	1-1	Bargoed United

The match was abandoned after 20 minutes.

Denbigh Town	4-4	Bala Town
Rhostyllen & Bersham Royal British Legion	4-3	Chirk AAA
Llay Welfare	0-4	Vron Celts
Overton St.Mary's	3-3	Johnstown United
Ruabon Athletic	2-2	Llangollen

Played at Llangollen

Welshpool	8-0	Queens Park Rovers
Flint Town United	2-2	Colwyn Bay
Holywell Town	2-1	Buckley Wanderers
Penmaenmawr	2-2	Caernarvon Town
Holyhead Town	7-1	Blaenau Ffestiniog FC

Holyhead Town were disqualified following a protest.

Harlech Town	3-3	Barmouth & Dyffryn Utd
Knighton Town	4-5	Machynlleth
Builth Wells	4-2	Newtown

Second Round Replay

Abergavenny Thursdays	1-2	Bargoed United
Bala Town	2-3 (aet)	Denbigh Town
Johnstown United	1-3	Overton St.Mary's
Llangollen	4-2	Ruabon Athletic
Colwyn Bay	2-3	Flint Town United
Caernarvon Town	1-0	Penmaenmawr
Barmouth & Dyffryn Utd	2-4 (aet)	Harlech Town

Full-time score was 2-2.

Third Round

Blaenau Ffestiniog FC	1-1	Holywell Town
Llandudno	1-1	Flint Town United
Caernravon Town	2-1	Pwllheli & District
Vron Celts	3-0	Llangollen
Llay United	1-4	Denbigh Town
Rhostyllen & Bersham Royal British Legion	0-5	Overton St Mary's
Barmouth & Dyffryn Utd	2-1	Llanidloes Town
Aberystwyth Town	4-2	Builth Wells
Caerau Athletic	4-4	Haverfordwest Athletic
Ebbw Vale	3-1	Bargoed United
Cardiff Corinthians	2-0	Ton Boys Club
Milford United	2-6	Llanelly

Third Round Replays

Holywell Town	6-2	Blaenau Ffestiniog FC
Flint Town United	3-1	Llandudno
Haverfordwest Athletic	2-3	Caerau Athletic

Fourth Round

Holywell Town	1-1	Oswestry Town
Barmouth & Dyffryn Utd	3-0	Vron Celts
Caernarvon Town	3-0	Denbigh Town
Overton St Mary's	3-3	Flint Town United
Cardiff Corinthians	0-0	Caerau Athletic
Barry Town	7-2	Aberystwyth Town
Llanelly	1-3	Lovell's Athletic
Ebbw Vale	3-0	Machynlleth

Fourth Round Replays

Oswestry Town	4-0	Holywell Town
Flint Town United	9-1	Overton St Mary's
Caerau Athletic	6-0	Cardiff Corinthians

Fifth Round

Flint Town United	7-2	Barmouth & Dyffryn Utd
Rhyl	0-2	Wrexham

South Liverpool	0-0	Chester	
Oswestry Town	2-2	Bangor City	
Merthyr Tydfil	3-0	Newport County	
Caerau Athletic	1-4	Swansea Town	
Cardiff City	3-0	Ebbw Vale	
Lovell's Athletic	0-3	Barry Town	

Fifth Round Replays

Chester	2-2 (aet)	South Liverpool
Bangor City	5-0	Oswestry Town

Fifth Round Second Replay

South Liverpool	0-2	Chester

Played at Chester

Sixth Round

Flint Town United	4-2	Caernarvon Town

Seventh Round

Swansea Town	3-0	Cardiff City
Wrexham	2-0	Flint Town United
Chester	3-2	Barry Town
Bangor City	0-2	Merthyr Tydfil

Semi-finals

Swansea Town	5-1	Merthyr Tydfil

Played at Cardiff

Wrexham	0-0	Chester

Played at Wrexham

Semi-final Replay

Chester	1-5	Wrexham

Played at Chester

1950 WELSH CUP FINAL

27th April 1950 at Ninian Park, Cardiff

Swansea Town	4-1	Wrexham
Scrine 3, C Beech		*Tunnicliffe*

Swansea Town: Canning, R Paul, Ewell, G Beech, Kiley, Burns, Wookey, B Lucas, C Beech, I Allchurch, F Scrine

Wrexham: Ferguson, Tunney, L C Rowlands, Spruce, Wilson, Speed, Grainger, McLaughlin, Wynne, Rowell, J Tunnicliffe

Referee: B M Griffiths (Newport)

Attendance: 12,000

1950/51 Welsh Cup

First Round

Bargoed United	0-3	Cardiff Corinthians
Nelson	1-1	Senghenydd Town
Troedyrhiw	3-5	Treharris Athletic
Ebbw Vale	8-4	Cwm Welfare
Abergavenny Thursdays	3-1	Risca United
Gwynfi Welfare	3-3	Ton Corinthians
Port Talbot Athletic	3-1	Cwmparc
Morriston Town	1-4	Milford United
Cwmavon	2-1	Swansea Nomads
Pembroke Borough	7-0	Grovesend Welfare
Llanelly	2-0	Haverfordwest Athletic
Rhostyllen SC	2-1	Corwen Amateurs
Monsanto (Ruabon)	1-6	Ruthin Royal Brit. Legion

This match may have been played at Ruthin.

Chirk AAA	6-2	Coedpoeth
Ruabon Athletic	4-0	Queens Park Rovers
Brymbo Steelworks	3-1	Rhostyllen Royal British Legion

Played at Rhostyllen

Bala Town	1-7	Druids United
Llay Welfare	6-1	Llangollen
Wrexham Nomads	0-3	Gresford Athletic
Pentre Broughton	2-2	Johnstown United
Llay United	3-0	Holt Nomads
Buckley Wanderers	1-8	Holywell Town
Mold Alexandra	7-1	Saltney
Bethesda Athletic	5-1	Caernarvon Town
Portmadoc	0-7	Pwllheli & District
Blaenau Ffestiniog FC	1-1	Llanrwst Town

The match was abandoned after 20 minutes.

Holyhead Town	1-0	Llandudno Junction
Llandudno	1-0	Conway Borough
Colwyn Bay	4-0	Penmaenmawr
Towyn	2-2	Harlech Town

The match was abandoned after 40 minutes.

Aberdovey	0-5	Machynlleth
Aberystwyth Town	10-1	Aberayron
Welshpool	3-4	Llanidloes Town
Newtown	5-1	Caersws Amateurs
Builth Wells Town	3-1	Rhayader Town
Llandrindod Wells	2-3	Knighton Town
Ton Pentre (w/o) (withdrew)	v	Aberaman Athletic

First Round Replays

Senghenydd Town	2-1	Nelson
Ton Corinthians	6-2	Gwynfi Welfare
Johnstown United	3-1	Pentre Broughton
Blaenau Ffestiniog FC	6-0	Llanrwst Town
Towyn	2-1	Harlech Town

The match was abandoned after 40 minutes.

Second Round

Mold Alexandra	0-4	Holywell Town
Holyhead Town	3-2	Bethesda Athletic
Llandudno	3-3	Blaenau Ffestiniog FC
Pwllheli & District	5-1	Colwyn Bay
Towyn	5-1	Barmouth & Dyffryn Utd
Llanidloes Town	2-0	Newtown
Aberystwyth Town	4-3	Machynlleth
Knighton Town	8-2	Builth Wells Town
Llay Welfare	6-1	Johnstown United
Rhostyllen SC	2-2	Ruabon Athletic
Druids United	1-2	Brymbo Steelworks
Ruthin Royal Brit. Legion	3-0	Chirk AAA

Gresford Athletic	2-4	Llay United
Llanelly	8-1	Port Talbot Athletic
Milford United	1-2	Pembroke Borough
Cwmavon	0-2	Ton Corinthians
Ebbw Vale	0-0	Treharris Athletic
Ton Pentre	2-2	Cardiff Corinthians
Senghenydd Town	2-4	Abergavenny Thursdays

Second Round Replay

Blaenau Ffestiniog FC	1-1 (aet)	Llandudno

The score after full-time was 0-0.

Ruabon Athletic	1-3	Rhostyllen SC
Treharris Athletic	2-4	Ebbw Vale
Cardiff Corinthians	0-1	Ton Pentre

Second Round Second Replay

Llandudno	1-2	Blaenau Ffestiniog FC

Third Round

Llanidloes Town	0-3	Llanelly
Knighton Town	1-2	Pembroke Borough
Abergavenny Thursdays	5-3	Aberystwyth Town
Caerau Athletic	3-3	Ebbw Vale
Ton Pentre	3-1	Ton Corinthians
Llay United	1-2	Blaenau Ffestiniog FC
Ruthin Royal British Legion	1-3	Holyhead Town
Flint Town United	1-2	Pwllheli & District
Brymbo Steelworks	2-4	Holywell Town
Rhostyllen SC	1-4	Towyn
Llay Welfare	2-7	Oswestry Town

Played at Oswestry

Third Round Replay

Ebbw Vale	6-0	Caerau Athletic

Fourth Round

Oswestry Town	3-2	Blaenau Ffestiniog FC
South Liverpool	0-3	Rhyl
Pwllheli & District	1-2	Bangor City
Holywell Town	3-2	Holyhead Town
Lovell's Athletic	2-2	Abergavenny Thursdays
Pembroke Borough	3-0	Towyn
Barry Town	3-0	Ton Pentre
Llanelly	2-2	Ebbw Vale

Fourth Round Replays

Abergavenny Thursdays	2-8	Lovell's Athletic
Ebbw Vale	2-1	Llanelly

Fifth Round

Barry Town	0-8	Cardiff City

Played at Cardiff

Merthyr Tydfil	2-1	Lovell's Athletic
Swansea Town	5-0	Pembroke Borough
Ebbw Vale	1-2	Newport County
Chester	2-1	Rhyl
New Brighton	3-1	Holywell Town
Oswestry Town	1-2	Bangor City

Sixth Round

Merthyr Town	5-2	Chester
Bangor City	1-7	Cardiff City
New Brighton	1-3	Wrexham
Newport County	2-1	Swansea Town

Semi-finals

Cardiff City	1-0	Wrexham

Played at Shrewsbury

Newport County	1-1	Merthyr Tydfil

Played at Cardiff

Semi-final Replay

Merthyr Tydfil	4-1	Newport County

Played at Cardiff

1951 WELSH CUP FINAL

7th May 1951 at the Vetch Field, Swansea

Merthyr Tydfil	1-1	Cardiff City
Powell		*Grant*

Merthyr Tydfil: Elliott, Avery, Phillips, Lloyd, Lowe, D Davies, Reynolds, S Davies, Hullett, Jarman, Powell

Cardiff City: Joslin, G G Williams, A Sherwood, K Hollyman, S Montgomery, W Baker, Tiddy, McLaughlin, Grant, Blair, G Edwards

Referee: B M Griffiths (Newport)

Attendance: 12,000

1951 WELSH CUP FINAL REPLAY

17th May at the Vetch Field, Swansea

Merthyr Tydfil	3-2	Cardiff City
Powell, Lloyd, Jarman		*Tiddy, Edwards*

Merthyr Tydfil: Elliott, Avery, Phillips, Lloyd, Lowe, D Davies, Reynolds, S Davies, Hullett, Jarman, Powell

Cardiff City: R Howells, Rutter, G G Williams, K Hollyman, D Sullivan, W Baker, Tiddy, McLaughlin, Grant, Blair, G Edwards

Referee: B M Griffiths (Newport)

Attendance: 18,000

1951/52 Welsh Cup

First Round

Rhostyllen	3-1	Rubery Owen Wrexham
Connah's Quay Juniors	6-0	Rhostyllen SC
Gresford Colliery SC	2-4	Holt Nomads
Corwen Amateurs	8-4	Bala Town
Buckley Wanderers	1-1	Penycae
Llay Welfare	2-1	Llay United

Ruabon Athletic	2-2	Gresford Athletic
Coedpoeth	1-2	Overton St Mary's
Llangollen	2-3	Saltney
Johnstown United	3-3	New Broughton
Ruthin Royal Brit. Legion	3-0	Pentre Broughton
Chirk AAA	2-2	Mold Alexandra
Bersham Foundry	3-11	Druids United
Machynlleth	1-5	Aberystwyth Town
Newtown	4-1	Welshpool
Caersws	11-3	Aberayron
Harlech Town	3-2	Barmouth & Dyffryn Utd
Aberdovey	4-2	Dolgelley
Llandrindod Wells	4-6	Builth Wells Town
Llanidloes Town	4-0	Knighton Town
Cardiff Corinthians	1-3	Port Talbot Athletic
Risca United	5-1	Tredomen Works
Grovesend Welfare	0-2	Morriston Town
Swansea Nomads	0-1	Cwmavon

Played at Cwmavon

| Brymbo Steelworks (w/o) | v | Monsanto (withdrew) |

First Round Replays

Penycae	1-1 (aet)	Buckley Wanderers
Gresford Athletic	5-1	Ruabon Athletic
New Broughton	9-2	Johnstown United
Mold Alexandra	2-3	Chirk AAA

First Round Second Replays

Buckley Wanderers	5-3	Penycae

Second Round

Caernarvon Town	1-1	Portmadoc
Flint Town United	1-1	Colwyn Bay
Bethesda Athletic	3-2	Llanrwst Town
Llandudno Junction	4-1	Blaenau Ffestiniog FC
Conway Borough	2-3	Holywell Town
Pwllheli & District	6-1	Llandudno
Druids United	4-2	Buckley Wanderers
Corwen Amateurs	3-2	Llay Welfare
New Broughton	0-6	Connah's Quay Juniors
Ruthin Royal Brit. Legion	2-3	Saltney
Rhostyllen & Bersham SC	2-3	Brymbo Steelworks
Gresford Athletic	0-4	Overton St Mary's
Chirk AAA	9-5	Holt Nomads
Newtown	8-2	Caersws
Llanidloes Town	7-2	Builth Wells Town
Aberdovey	1-12	Aberystwyth Town
Senghenydd Town	3-0	Bargoed United
Treharris Athletic	3-1	Ebbw Vale
Risca United	2-4	Troedyrhiw
Abergavenny Thursdays	1-1	Nelson
Caerau Athletic	3-2	Port Talbot Athletic
Pembroke Borough	4-2	Cwmparc
Ton Pentre	7-0	Cwmavon
Milford United	1-0	Morriston Town

Second Round Replays

Portmadoc	1-4	Caernarvon Town
Colwyn Bay	1-0	Flint Town United
Nelson	3-1	Abergavenny Thursdays

Played at Abergavenny

Third Round

Colwyn Bay	2-2	Holywell Town
Caernarvon Town	3-0	Bethesda Athletic
Pwllheli & District	7-0	Llandudno Junction
Saltney	0-5	Connah's Quay Juniors

The match was abandoned after 75 minutes.

Druids United	4-0	Corwen Amateurs
Brymbo Steelworks	3-2	Overton St Mary's
Newtown	0-3	Oswestry Town
Harlech Town	2-4	Llanidloes Town
Pembroke Borough	1-0	Haverfordwest Athletic
Aberystwyth Town	2-3	Milford United
Caerau Athletic	3-1	Treharris Athletic
Ton Pentre	1-1	Senghenydd Town

Ton Pentre subsequently withdrew from the competition.

| Troedyrhiw | 1-2 | Nelson |

Third Round Replays

Holywell Town	1-3	Colwyn Bay
Saltney	1-3	Connah's Quay Juniors

Fourth Round

Bangor City	7-0	Druids United
Rhyl	2-2	Pwllheli & District
Brymbo Steelworks	1-2	Connah's Quay Juniors
Chirk AAA	3-4	Caernarvon Town
Colwyn Bay	6-2	South Liverpool
Oswestry Town	0-2	Lovell's Athletic
Milford United	2-0	Llanidloes Town
Llanelly	4-3	Caerau Athletic
Barry Town	3-1	Pembroke Borough
Nelson	1-1	Senghenydd Town

Nelson then withdrew

Fourth Round Replay

Pwllheli & District	3-3 (aet)	Rhyl

The score after full-time was 2-2.

Fourth Round Second Replay

Rhyl	2-0	Pwllheli & District

Played at Bangor

Fifth Round

Chester	3-1	Bangor City
Caernarvon Town	0-4	Rhyl
Colwyn Bay	0-0	Wrexham

The match was abandoned after 26 minutes.

Newport County	8-2	Connah's Quay Juniors
Lovell's Athletic	2-3	Barry Town
Milford United	1-3	Cardiff City
Merthyr Tydfil	2-1	Swansea Town
Senghenydd Town	2-1	Llanelly

Played at Llanelly

Fifth Round Replay

Colwyn Bay	2-7	Wrexham

Sixth Round

Newport County	2-3	Rhyl

Played at Rhyl

Wrexham	0-0	Chester
Barry Town	6-0	Senghenydd Town
Merthyr Town	3-1	Cardiff City

Sixth Round Replay

Chester	0-2	Wrexham

Semi-finals

Barry Town	1-1	Rhyl
Played at Wrexham		
Wrexham	0-0	Merthyr Tydfil
Played at Cardiff		

Semi-final Replay

Rhyl	1-0	Barry Town
Played at Cardiff		

1952 WELSH CUP FINAL

24th April 1952 at Ninian Park, Cardiff

Rhyl FC	4-3	Merthyr Tydfil
Stafford 2, Spendlove 2		*Reynolds 2, Jarman*

Rhyl: Scales, Ferguson, Cardno, McKillop, Rogers, McFarlane, Marsden, Welsh, D Spendlove, Thomson, Stafford

Merthyr Tydfil: Sellick, Avery, Jones, Lloyd, Lowe, Richards, Davies, Knight, Reynolds, Jarman, Powell

Referee: B M Griffiths (Newport)

Attendance: 10,000

1952/53 Welsh Cup

First Round

Coedpoeth	0-3	Denbigh Town
Played at Denbigh		
Rhostyllen SC	1-8	Johnstown United
Ruthin Royal Brit. Legion	5-0	Corwen Amateurs
Chirk AAA	5-1	Bala Town
Druids United	5-4	Penycae
Pentre Broughton	4-0	Tunnel SC Mold
Llangollen	0-1	Rhos Rangers
Gresford Athletic	3-3	Llay Welfare
Mold Alexandra	3-3	Brymbo Steelworks
Buckley Wanderers	1-1	Holt Nomads
Llay United	3-4	Ruabon Athletic
New Broughton	3-3	Gresford Colliery SC
Barmouth & Dyffryn Utd	2-4	55th RA Tonfannau
Aberdovey	0-3	Machynlleth
Llandrindod Wells	7-2	Knighton Town
Llanidloes Town	3-2	Welshpool
Newtown	6-0	Llanfair Caereinion
Caersws (w/o)	v	Montgomery (withdrew)
Nelson	5-2	Troedyrhiw
Godre'rgriag Athletic	3-2	Cwmavon
Swansea Nomads	4-1	Mumbles Athletic
Atlas SC Swansea	3-1	Grovesend Welfare
De Havilland SC Broughton (withdrew)	v	Bradley Rangers (w/o)
Aberayron (w/o)	v	Tregaron Turfs (withdrew)

First Round Replays

Llay Welfare	1-3	Gresford Athletic
Brymbo Steelworks	1-3	Mold Alexandra
Holt Nomads	1-5	Buckley Wanderers
Gresford Colliery SC	1-2	New Broughton

Second Round

Colwyn Bay	4-1	Conway Borough
Llandudno	3-0	Penmaenmawr
New Brighton (withdrew)	v	Holywell Town (w/o)
Flint Town United	2-0	Llanrwst Town
Connah's Quay Nomads	2-2	Llandudno Junction
Blaenau Ffestiniog FC	7-2	Bethesda Athletic
Portmadoc	4-2	Caernarvon Town
Bradley Rangers	2-1	Pentre Broughton
Chirk AAA	2-5	Johnstown United
Buckley Wanderers	4-4	New Broughton
Ruabon Athletic	3-5	Rhos Rangers
Played at Rhos		
Saltney	2-1	Gresford Athletic
Druids United	3-1	Mold Alexandra
Denbigh Town	4-2	Ruthin Royal Brit. Legion
Llanidloes Town	8-1	Llandrindod Wells
Newtown	2-2	Caersws
Aberystwyth Town	8-0	Machynlleth
Aberayron	2-7	55th RA Tonfannau
Abergavenny Thursdays	1-4	Ebbw Vale & Cwm
Caerau Athletic	1-1	Cardiff Corinthians
Bargoed Rangers	1-5	Nelson
Played at Nelson		
Haverfordwest Athletic	2-1	Pembroke Borough
Gwynfi Welfare	2-2	Atlas SC Swansea
Goedre'rgraig Athletic	8-1	Swansea Nomads
Senghenydd Town	1-6	Cwmparc

Second Round Replays

Llandudno Junction	1-2	Connah's Quay Nomads
New Broughton	6-7	Buckley Wanderers
Caersws	4-2	Newtown
Cardiff Corinthians	4-0 (aet)	Caerau Athletic
The score after 90 minutes was 0-0.		
Atlas SC Swansea	2-5 (aet)	Gwynfi Welfare

Third Round

Denbigh Town	4-7	Flint Town United
Llandudno	1-2	Colwyn Bay
Connah's Quay Nomads	6-2	Blaenau Ffestiniog FC
Holywell Town	6-0	Portmadoc
Saltney	3-4	Buckley Wanderers
Druids United	7-1	Bradley Rangers
Rhos Rangers	1-5	Johnstown United
Aberystwyth Town	6-1	Caersws
55th RA Tonfannau	3-3	Oswestry Town
Ebbw Vale	4-3	Cardiff Corinthians
Gwynfi Welfare	2-5	Godre'rgraig Athletic

Haverfordwest Athletic	3-1	Milford United
Cwmparc	2-2	Nelson

The scoreline was 2-2 after 90 minutes and extra time commenced. The match was abandoned during the second half of extra time when the scoreline stood at 4-2. Nelson subsequently withdrew.

Third Round Replay

Oswestry Town	5-2	55th RA Tonfannau

Fourth Round

Oswestry Town	0-0	Pwllheli & District
South Liverpool	4-7	Connah's Quay Nomads

Played at Connah's Quay

Druids United	3-7	Colwyn Bay
Johnstown United	2-2	Buckley Wanderers
Bangor City	2-2	Flint Town United
Ebbw Vale & Cwm	2-1	Aberystwyth Town
Lovell's Athletic	6-1	Cwmparc
Llanidloes Town	1-7	Llanelly

Played at Llanelly

Godre'rgraig Athletic	2-3	Kidderminster Harriers

Fourth Round Replays

Pwllheli & District	2-0	Oswestry Town
Buckley Wanderers	5-2	Johnstown United
Flint Town United	1-2	Bangor City

The match was abandoned after 26 minutes.

Fourth Round Second Replay

Flint Town United	1-1	Bangor City

Fourth Round Third Replay

Flint Town United	2-1	Bangor City

Played at Fflint

Fifth Round

Wrexham	3-4	Chester
Flint Town United	3-2	Holywell Town
Buckley Wanderers	1-4	Connah's Quay Nomads
Rhyl	4-0	Colwyn Bay
Haverfordwest Athletic	1-8	Newport County
Barry Town	2-0	Llanelly
Kidderminster Harriers	0-2	Swansea Town

Played at Swansea

Merthyr Tydfil	2-5	Cardiff City
Lovell's Athletic	2-0	Ebbw Vale

Pwllheli & District received a bye

Sixth Round

Chester	2-0	Pwllheli & District
Swansea Town	3-2	Newport County

Seventh Round

Chester	5-0	Lovell's Athletic
Swansea Town	2-3	Rhyl
Barry Town	2-3	Cardiff City
Connah's Quay Nomads	1-0	Flint Town United

Semi-finals

Rhyl	1-0	Cardiff City

Played at Rhyl

Chester	5-0	Connah's Quay Nomads

Played at Wrexham

1953 WELSH CUP FINAL

27th April 1953 at Farrar Road, Bangor

Rhyl FC	2-1	Chester
Spendlove 2		Travis

Rhyl: Griffiths, Ferguson, Fazackerley, McLean, McKillop, L Donaldson, Hanlon, Welsh, D Spendlove, Thomson, Stafford

Chester: Court, Molyneux, Gill, Hughes, Lee, T Astbury, Deakin, Morement, Travis, Sutcliffe, W Windle

Referee: B M Griffiths (Newport)

Attendance: 8,500

1953/54 Welsh Cup

First Round

Llay Welfare	2-4	Druids United
Rhos Rangers	9-2	Bradley Rangers
Saltney	4-0	Royal Pioneer Corps Depot Wrexham
Brymbo Steelworks	2-0	New Broughton
Llangollen	3-3	Johnstown United
Ruthin Royal Brit. Legion	5-4	Rhostyllen SC
Mold Alexandra	6-2	Holt Nomads
Ruabon Athletic	4-4	Llay United
Gresford Colliery SC	3-1	Rhos Aelwyd
Pentre Broughton	5-3	Corwen Amateurs
Denbigh Town	3-2	Gwersyllt United
Chirk AAA	1-0	Rubery Owen Wrexham
Coedpoeth	5-1	Penycae
Machynlleth	5-3	Aberayron
Barmouth & Dyffryn Utd	4-5 (aet)	Trawsfynydd

The scoreline after 90 minutes was 4-4.

Llanfair Caereinion	1-2	Welshpool
Newtown	2-4	55th RA Tonfannau
Knighton Town	6-0	Builth Wells
Caersws Amateurs	3-0	Llandrindod Wells Amat.
Troedyrhiw	3-0	Garw Welfare
Godre'rgraig Athletic	6-0	Pontardawe Athletic
Grovesend Welfare	1-2	Port Talbot Athletic
Cardiff Corinthians	1-1	Bargoed United

Cardiff Corinthians subsequently withdrew.

First Round Replays

Johnstown United	2-3 (aet)	Llangollen

The scoreline after 90 minutes was 1-1.

Llay United	7-4	Ruabon Athletic

Second Round

Caernarvon Town	3-2	Bethesda Athletic
Llanberis (withdrew)	v	Penmaenmawr (w/o)
Portmadoc	1-0	Blaenau Ffestiniog FC
South Liverpool	v	Llanrwst (w/o)
Colwyn Bay	2-2	Llandudno Junction
Conway Borough	0-7	Holyhead Town
Llandudno	2-2	Holywell Town
Llangollen	3-3	Mold Alexandra
Denbigh Town	3-2	Rhos Rangers
Gresford Colliery SC	1-5	Ruthin Royal Brit. Legion
Chirk AAA	2-2	Coedpoeth
Druids United	4-2	Llay United
Pentre Broughton	1-4	Brymbo Steelworks
Buckley Wanderers	7-4	Saltney
Caersws Amateurs	2-4	Welshpool
Llanidloes Town	2-2	Knighton Town
Machynlleth	5-3	Trawsfynnydd
Aberystwyth Town	1-1 (aet)	55th RA Tonfannau
Troedyrhiw	3-1	Bargoed United
Abergavenny Thursdays	0-3	Ebbw Vale & Cwm
Pembroke Borough	5-2	Goedre'rgraig Athletic
Treharris Athletic	5-4	Tonyrefail Welfare
Haverfordwest Athletic	1-1	Milford United
Caerau Athletic	2-0	Port Talbot Athletic

Second Round Replays

Llandudno Junction	1-3	Colwyn Bay
Holywell Town	3-1	Llandudno
Mold Alexandra	2-3 (aet)	Llangollen

The scoreline after 90 minutes was 2-2.

Coedpoeth	4-1	Chirk AAA
Knighton Town	3-4	Llanidloes Town
55th RA Tonfannau	0-5	Aberystwyth Town

Played at Aberystwyth

Milford United	2-2	Haverfordwest Athletic

Second Round Second Replay

Haverfordwest Athletic	1-6	Milford United

Third Round

Denbigh Town	4-6	Holywell Town
Llanrwst Town	1-1	Caernarvon Town
Holyhead Town	3-0	Penmaenmawr

The match was abandoned after 35 minutes.

Portmadoc	3-3	Colwyn Bay
Brymbo Steelworks	5-2	Llangollen
Buckley Wanderers	9-2	Ruthin FC

Ruthin Royal British Legion changed their name to become Ruthin FC.

Coedpoeth	1-6	Druids United
Llanidloes Town	4-2	Machynlleth
Welshpool	0-5	Aberystwyth Town
Pembroke Borough	5-4	Caerau
Milford United	1-1	Ebbw Vale & Cwm
Troedyrhiw	2-2	Treharris Athletic

Third Round Replay

Caernarvon Town	4-1	Llanrwst Town
Holyhead Town	7-1	Penmaenmawr
Colwyn Bay	2-3	Portmadoc
Ebbw Vale & Cwm	3-2 (aet)	Milford United

The scoreline after 90 minutes was 2-2.

Treharris Athletic	1-4	Troedyrhiw

Played at Troedyrhiw

Fourth Round

Caernarvon Town	1-3	Bangor City
Brymbo Steelworks	4-2	Holyhead Town

Played at Holyhead

Portmadoc	1-1	Buckley Wanderers
Druids United	0-7	Oswestry Town

Played at Oswestry

Holywell Town	2-3	Flint Town United
Kidderminster Harriers	1-1	Pembroke Borough
Lovell's Athletic	5-0	Llanidloes Town
Ebbw Vale & Cwm	2-1	Aberystwyth Town
Llanelly	9-0	Troedyrhiw

Fourth Round Replays

Buckley Wanderers	4-2 (aet)	Portmadoc

The scoreline after 90 minutes was 2-2.

Pembroke Borough	6-2	Kidderminster Harriers

Fifth Round

Newport County	6-2	Swansea Town
Llanelly	4-3	Pembroke Borough
Lovell's Athletic	1-1	Merthyr Tydfil
Barry Town	1-1	Cardiff City
Pwllheli & District	0-1	Rhyl
Buckley Wanderers	0-4	Bangor City
Chester	6-1	Brymbo Steelworks
Wrexham	5-2	Connah's Quay Nomads
Flint Town United	3-1	Oswestry Town

Fifth Round Replays

Merthyr Tydfil	4-1	Lovell's Athletic
Cardiff City	4-2	Barry Town

Sixth Round

Flint Town United	2-0	Rhyl
Llanelly	9-2	Ebbw Vale & Cwm

Seventh Round

Merthyr Tydfil	3-5	Cardiff City
Bangor City	1-5	Newport County
Flint Town United	2-1	Llanelly
Chester	1-0	Wrexham

Semi-finals

Flint Town United	2-1	Cardiff City

Played at Wrexham

Chester	2-2	Newport County

Semi-final Replay

Newport County	0-2	Chester

Played at Wrexham

1954 WELSH CUP FINAL

21st April 1954 at the Racecourse, Wrexham

Flint Town United   2-0   Chester

Lynch, Owen

Flint Town United: Pierce, Williams, Bryan, Bennison, W M Hughes, Logan, Owen, Whelan, W Davies, Lynch, A Davies

Chester: Jones, Fletcher, Gill, Hughes, Lee, Astbury, Rolfe, Ketteridge, Basford, Travis, Windle

Referee: R E Smith (Newport)

Attendance: 15,584

1954/55 Welsh Cup

First Round

Druids United	0-2	Llangollen
Bala Town	0-3	Ruthin FC
Rhostyllen SC	0-5	Chirk AAA
Johnstown United	1-1	Ruabon Athletic
Penycae	2-2	Rhos Rangers
Gresford Colliery SC	4-5	Bradley Rangers
Gwersyllt United	3-6	Mold Alexandra
Rubery Owen Wrexham	3-4	Holt Nomads
Buckley Wanderers	3-5	Llay Welfare
Denbigh Town	8-1	Coedpoeth
Brymbo Steelworks	7-5	Pentre Broughton
Llay United	7-3	Saltney
Connah's Quay Albion	4-5	Bagillt United
Machynlleth	6-3	Aberayron
Barmouth & Dyffryn Utd	10-1	Trawsfynnydd
Llanfair Caereinion	4-6	Llanfechain Athletic
Llandrindod Wells	5-1	Builth Wells
Grovesend Welfare	6-3	Pontardawe Athletic
Ferndale Athletic	v	Porth Welfare

Both clubs subsequently withdrew from the competition.

First Round Replays

Ruabon Athletic	4-4	Johnstown United
Rhos Rangers	4-2	Penycae

First Round Second Replay

Johnstown United	1-2	Ruabon Athletic

Both clubs were subsequently disqualified.

Second Round

Penmaenmawr	0-3	Borough United
Portmadoc	1-5	Holywell Town
Holyhead Town	7-3	Llanrwst Town
Bethesda Athletic	6-6	Blaenau Ffestiniog FC

Bethesda withdrew from the competition.

Connah's Quay Nomads	2-2	Llandudno
Colwyn Bay	3-3	Llanfairfechan Town
55th RA Tonfannau	1-2	Caernarvon Town
Bagillt United	0-14	Denbigh Town

Played at Denbigh

Mold Alexandra	4-1	Prestatyn Town
Rhos Rangers	4-4	Llay United
Holt Nomads	2-3	Buckley Wanderers

Played at Buckley

Ruthin FC	4-1	Brymbo Steelworks
Chirk AAA	3-1	Ruabon Athletic

Chirk AAA progressed after both Ruabon Athletic and Johnstown United were disqualified.

Caersws Amateurs	1-1	Llandrindod Wells

Caersws disqualified

Llanfechain Athletic	1-6	Llanidloes Town
Knighton Town	6-4	Barmouth & District Utd
Newtown	0-3	Welshpool
Llanfyllin	2-7	Aberystwyth Town

Played at Aberystwyth

Cardiff Corinthians	3-5	Tonyrefail Welfare
Pembroke Borough	6-2	Brecon Corinthians
Troedyrhiw	1-3	Haverfordwest Athletic
Grovesend Welfare	0-1	Ebbw Vale
Milford United	1-5	Abergavenny Thursdays

Second Round Replay

Llandudno	1-2	Connah's Quay Nomads
Llanfairfechan Town	1-3	Colwyn Bay
Llay United	1-3	Rhos Rangers

Third Round

Pwllheli & District	2-0	Blaenau Ffestiniog FC
Holywell Town	4-0	Colwyn Bay
Caernarvon Town	1-2	Connah's Quay Nomads

The match was abandoned in the 30th minute.

Borough United	1-3	Holyhead Town
Rhos Rangers	2-5	Oswestry Town
Chirk AAA	4-3	Buckley Wanderers
Ruthin FC	2-3	Llangollen
Mold Alexandra	4-2	Denbigh Town
Welshpool	4-2	Knighton Town
Llandrindod Wells	7-0	Machynlleth

The match was abandoned in the 83rd minute.

Aberystwyth Town	11-1	Llanidloes
Tonrefail Welfare	0-3	Pembroke Borough

Played at Pembroke

Haverfordwest Athletic	1-9	Abergavenny Thursdays

Third Round Replays

Caernarvon Town	6-4	Connah's Quay Nomads
Llandrindod Wells	2-1	Machynlleth

Fourth Round

Bangor City	6-1	Holyhead Town
Caernarvon Town	3-2	Llangollen
Pwllheli & District	3-2	Oswestry Town
Rhyl	2-1	Chirk AAA
Mold Alexandra	4-4	Holywell Town
Llanelly	1-1	Aberystwyth Town
Lovell's Athletic	5-0	Llandrindod Wells
Merthyr Tydfil	0-1	Barry Town
Welshpool	2-6	Pembroke Borough
Abergavenny Thursdays	1-0	Ebbw Vale

Fourth Round Replays

Holywell Town	8-0	Mold Alexandra
Aberystwyth Town	1-3	Llanelly

Fifth Round

Wrexham	2-0	Bangor City
Pwllheli & District	5-0	Rhyl
Caernarvon Town	1-1	Chester
Holywell Town	2-2	Flint Town United
Barry Town	7-2	Lovell's Athletic
Swansea Town	6-2	Llanelly
Pembroke Borough	0-7	Cardiff City
Newport County	6-0	Abergavenny Thursdays

Fifth Round Replay

Chester	9-1	Caernarvon Town
Flint Town United	4-3	Holywell Town

Sixth Round

Chester	3-0	Flint Town United
Pwllheli & District	1-3	Barry Town
Swansea Town	4-4	Wrexham
Newport County	1-3	Cardiff City

Sixth Round Replay

Wrexham	4-3 (aet)	Swansea Town

Semi-finals

Barry Town	3-1	Wrexham
Played at Cardiff		
Cardiff City	0-2	Chester
Played at Wrexham		

1955 WELSH CUP FINAL

11th May 1955 at the Racecourse, Wrexham

Barry Town	1-1	Chester
Niblett		*Brandon*

Barry Town: Morris, Williams, Lyske, Bright, Bellas, Foxton, Dyke, Allen, Niblett, Goodfellow, Cain

Chester: Jones, Gill, Molyneux, R Hughes, Morris, P Whitlock, Brandon, Morrey, G Coffin, Pye, Mayers

Referee: G O Hancock (Pontlottyn)

Attendance: 6,766

1955 WELSH CUP FINAL REPLAY

14th May 1955 at Ninian Park, Cardiff

Barry Town	4-3	Chester
Niblett 2, Dyke, Goodfellow		*Morrey, Pye, Brandon*

Barry Town: Morris, Williams, Lyske, Wright, Bellas, Foxton, Dyke, Allen, Niblett, Goodfellow, Cain

Chester: Jones, Fletcher, Gill, Lee, Morris, P Whitlock, Morrey, Pye, Molyneux, Smith, Brandon

Attendance: 8,450

1955/56 Welsh Cup

First Round

Buckley Wanderers	7-2	Prestatyn Town
Denbigh Town	0-5	31st TRRA Kinmel
Saltney Rustproof	6-5	Gwersyllt United

A replay was ordered as the ground did not comply with competition rules. The ground was put in order for the replay.

Pentre Broughton	1-5	Mold Alexandra
Llay United	1-1	Llay Welfare
Holt Nomads	2-0	Gresford Colliery SC
Coedpoeth	2-4	Rogers & Jackson (Wrexham)
Overton St Mary's	3-6	Chirk AAA
Rhostyllen SC	3-2	Ruabon Athletic
Ruthin FC	0-5	Druids United
Llangollen	2-5	Brymbo Steelworks
Corwen Amateurs	2-3	Penycae
Rhos Rangers	2-1	Bradley Rangers
Portland United (Wrexham)	0-10	Bala Town
Played at Bala		
Aberayron	1-3	Machynlleth
Barmouth & Dyffryn Utd	1-3	55th RA Tonfannau
Towyn	6-2	Corris United
Dolgelley	3-0	Trawsfynnydd
Llanidloes Town	1-1	Welshpool
Newtown	4-1	Caersws Amateurs
Llanfyllin	3-1	Llanfechain Athletic
Llandrindod Wells	3-5	Knighton Town
Troedyrhiw	1-0	Cardiff Corinthians
Port Talbot Athletic	7-2	Grovesend Welfare
Haverfordwest Athletic	6-3	Glanrhyd Ystradgynlais

First Round Replays

Saltney Rustproof	3-0	Gwersyllt United
Llay Welfare	1-4	Llay United
Welshpool	0-3	Llanidloes Town

Second Round

Penmaenmawr	2-4	Portmadoc
Connah's Quay Nomads	1-2	Borough United
31st TRRA Kinmel	5-2	Llanrwst Town
Played at Llanrwst		
Holyhead Town	5-1	Llandudno
Llanfairfechan Town	0-10	Colwyn Bay
Played at Colwyn		
Holywell Town	5-0	Mold Alexandra
Caernarvon Town	11-2	Bethesda Athletic
Rhostyllen SC	8-2	Saltney Rustproof Sports
Rogers & Jackson (Wrexham)	1-3	Holt Nomads
Buckley Wanderers	9-1	Corwen Amateurs
Chirk AAA	1-3	Druids United
Bala Town	2-5	Llay United
Rhos Rangers	2-0	Brymbo Steelworks
Newtown	6-0	Machynlleth
Knighton Town	6-1	Llanfyllin
Llanidloes Town	1-4	55th RA Tonfannau
Towyn	4-2	Dolgelley
Haverfordwest Athletic	7-1	Tonyrafail Welfare
Aberystwyth Town	2-4	Pembroke Borough
Brecon Corinthians	9-3	Troedyrhiw
Port Talbot Athletic	1-3	Ebbw Vale
Abergavenny Thursdays	2-0	Milford United

Third Round

Portmadoc	2-1	31st TRAA Kimnel	
Borough United	1-0	Buckley Wanderers	
Pwllheli & District	4-0	Holywell Town	
Caernarvon Town	6-0	Colwyn Bay	
Blaenau Ffestiniog FC	4-2	Holyhead Town	
Druids United	5-3	Rhostyllen SC	
Rhos Rangers	4-1	Holt Nomads	
Oswestry Town	4-1	Llay United	
Newtown	2-0	Knighton Town	
55th RA Tonfannau	4-1	Towyn	
Abergavenny Thursdays	1-3	Brecon Corinthians	
Ebbw Vale & Cwm	0-0	Pembroke Borough	

Played at Pembroke

Third Round Replay

Pembroke Borough	3-2	Ebbw Vale & Cwm	

Fourth Round

Blaenau Ffestiniog FC	1-2	Rhos Rangers	
Flint Town United	1-3	Pwllheli & District	
Oswestry Town	3-1	Druids United	
Caernarvon Town	2-4	Portmadoc	
Rhyl	5-2	Bangor City	
Borough United	1-2	55th RA Tonfannau	
Merthyr Tydfil	2-3	Lovell's Athletic	
Pembroke Borough	3-1	Haverfordwest County	

Haverfordwest Athletic had changed their name to Haverfordwest County.

Llanelly	5-0	Brecon Corinthians	

Fifth Round

Rhyl	0-2	Chester	
Pwllheli & District	1-2	Wrexham	
Oswestry Town	5-2	Rhos Rangers	
Portmadoc	7-3	55th RA Tonfannau	
Llanelly	1-0	Lovell's Athletic	
Swansea Town	9-4	Newtown	

Played at Newtown

Newport County	8-1	Barry Town	
Pembroke Borough	2-2	Cardiff City	

Fifth Round Replay

Cardiff City	9-0	Pembroke Borough	

Sixth Round

Newport County	5-1	Llanelly	
Swansea Town	1-0	Chester	
Oswestry Town	3-3	Portmadoc	
Cardiff City	5-3	Wrexham	

Sixth Round Replay

Portmadoc	0-0	Oswestry Town	

Sixth Round Second Replay

Oswestry Town	3-0	Portmadoc	

Semi-finals

Oswestry Town	0-7	Cardiff City	

Played at Wrexham

Swansea Town	5-2	Newport County	

Played at Cardiff

1956 WELSH CUP FINAL

30th April 1956 at Ninian Park, Cardiff

Cardiff City	3-2		Swansea Town

Walsh 2, McSeveney   *Riley, Palmer*

Cardiff City: G Vearncombe, R Stitfall, D Sullivan, A Harrington, D Malloy, W Baker, Walsh, Kirtley, T Ford, G Hitchens, McSeveney

Swansea Town: J King, Willis, D Thomas, M Charles, Kiley, B Jones, L Allchurch, H Griffiths, D Palmer, I Allchurch, C Jones

Referee: B M Griffiths (Newport)

Attendance: 37,500

1956/57 Welsh Cup

First Round

Buckley Wanderers	5-2		Denbigh Town
Prestatyn Town	0-4		Mold Alexandra
31st TRRA Kimnel	3-1		Buckley Rovers
Pentre Broughton	4-4		Llay United
Gresford Colliery SC	2-4		Llay Welfare

Played at Llay

Ruthin FC	1-2		Llangollen
Rogers & Jackson (Wrexham)	2-5 (aet)		Penycae
Rhosddu	3-5		Rhostyllen SC
Holt Nomads	4-0		Rubery Owen
Chirk AAA	4-5		Brymbo Steelworks
Druids United	7-0		Johnstown United
Ruabon Athletic	1-5		Bradley Rangers
Overton St Mary's	6-2		Corwen Amateurs
Bala Town	5-3 (aet)		Gresford Athletic
Barmouth & Dyffryn Utd	1-0		Aberayron

The match was abandoned after 45 minutes.

Caersws Amateurs	6-2		Llanfyllin

Neither Caersws Amateurs or Llanfyllin are listed as playing in the competition again this season. It is not known why this is the case.

Machynlleth	4-4		Towyn

Following a protest, Towyn were dismissed from the competition for fielding an ineligible player.

Llanidloes Town	1-2		Welshpool

Llanidloes Town appear to have progressed to the next round as well as Welshpool but it is not known why this occurred.

Knighton Town	4-3		Llandrindod Wells
Grovesend Welfare	1-0		Port Talbot Athletic

Played at Port Talbot

Neath Athletic	3-1		Glanrhyd Ystradgynlais

Played at Glanrhyd

Cardiff Corinthians	1-1		Troedyrhiw

Played at Troedyrhiw

First Round Replays

Llay United	2-6		Pentre Broughton
Barmouth & Dyffryn Utd	4-1		Aberayron
Troedyrhiw	1-2		Cardiff Corinthians

Second Round

Blaenau Ffestiniog FC	4-5	Llanrwst Town
Colwyn Bay	1-2	Holywell Town
Holyhead Town	1-0	Connah's Quay Nomads
Nantlle Vale	6-3	Mold Alexandra
31st TRRA Kinmel	3-1	Llandudno
Penmaenmawr	1-3	Borough United
Llanfairfechan Town	2-6	Bethesda Athletic
Overton St Mary's	2-5	Rhos Rangers
Pentre Broughton	1-8	Bradley Rangers
Penycae	1-4	Rhostyllen SC

Played at Rhostyllen

Brymbo Steelworks	7-0	Llangollen
Buckley Wanderers	2-0	Llay Welfare
Druids United	3-2	Holt Nomads
Bala Town	1-4	Welshpool

Played at Welshpool

Knighton Town	1-1	Barmouth & Dyffryn Utd

It is not known if a replay was held but Knighton Town appeared in the Third Round.

Llanidloes Town	1-4	55th RA Tonfannau

This match was replayed but it is not known why.

Abergavenny Thursdays	3-1	Milford United
Cardiff Corinthians	0-2	Pembroke Borough
Brecon Corinthians	1-2	Aberystwyth Town
Neath Athletic	1-5	Ebbw Vale

Played at Ebbw Vale

Haverfordwest County	8-1	Grovesend Welfare

Machynlleth did not appear in the Second Round but played in the Third Round so may have received a bye.

Second Round Replay

55th RA Tonfannau	3-2	Llanidloes Town

Third Round

Portmadoc	1-0	Llanrwst Town
Borough United	5-0	31st TRRA Kinmel
Nantlle Vale	2-5	Caernarvon Town
Flint Town United	3-1	Holywell Town
Buckley Wanderers	1-6	Pwllheli & District
Bethesda Athletic	0-6	Holyhead Town
Rhostyllen SC	0-6	Bradley Rangers
Rhos Rangers	1-3	Brymbo Steelworks
Knighton Town	0-5	Hereford United

Played at Hereford

Druids United	2-2	Machynlleth
55th RA Tonfannau	5-1	Welshpool
Aberystwyth Town	3-3	Abergavenny Thursdays
Ebbw Vale	1-1	Pembroke Borough

Haverfordwest County received a bye

Third Round Replays

Machynlleth	2-3	Druids United
Abergavenny Thursdays	3-2	Aberystwyth Town
Pembroke Borough	3-4	Ebbw Vale

Fourth Round

Caernarvon Town	4-1	Holyhead Town
Bangor City	0-3	Rhyl

Following a protest, Rhyl were dismissed from the competition.

Portmadoc	6-1	Flint Town United
Borough United	2-2	Bradley Rangers
Brymbo Steelworks	2-4	Pwllheli & District
Barry Town	7-2	Druids United
Ebbw Vale	1-4	Haverfordwest County
Llanelly	3-3	Merthyr Tydfil
55th RA Tonfannau	3-0	Lovell's Athletic
Hereford United	6-2	Abergavenny Thursdays

Fourth Round Replays

Bradley Rangers	0-1	Borough United

The match was abandoned after 30 minutes

Methyr Tydfil	6-4	Llanelly

Fourth Round Second Replay

Bradley Rangers	1-4	Borough United

Fifth Round

Bangor City	1-1	Wrexham
Oswestry Town	0-3	Chester
Caernarvon Town	2-1	Portmadoc
Pwllheli & District	7-2	Borough United
Haverfordwest County	3-3	Cardiff City
Hereford United	0-0	Swansea Town
Newport County	3-1	Merthyr Tydfil
Barry Town	1-2	55th RA Tonfannau

Fifth Round Replay

Wrexham	5-1	Bangor City
Cardiff City	8-1	Haverfordwest County
Swansea Town	2-0	Hereford United

Sixth Round

Caernarvon Town	1-4	Wrexham
Cardiff City	0-2	Chester
Swansea Town	6-0	Pwllheli & District
Newport County	3-1	55th RA Tonfannau

Semi-finals

Newport County	1-1	Swansea Town

Played at Cardiff

Wrexham	2-0	Chester

Played at Rhyl

Semi-final Replay

Swansea Town	3-0	Newport County

Played at Cardiff

1957 WELSH CUP FINAL

15th April 1957 at Ninian Park, Cardiff

Wrexham	2-1	Swansea Town
Thompson, McNab		C Jones

Wrexham: Waters, A McGowan, Parker, McNab, A Fox, Davis, G Jones, Thompson, Williams, R Hewitt, Anderson

Swansea Town: J King, D Thomas, B Jones, M Charles, Peake, Pearson, L Allchurch, H Griffiths, D Palmer, I Allchurch, C Jones

Referee: L Callaghan (Merthyr)

Attendance: 10,000

1957/58 Welsh Cup

First Round

Corwen Amateurs	2-4	Ruthin FC
Denbigh Town	11-1	Llangollen
Prestatyn Town	4-8	31st TRRA Kinmel
Overton St Mary's	3-2	Buckley Rovers
Rogers & Jackson	2-2	Penycae
Holt Nomads	1-3	Pentre Broughton
Rhostllyen SC	1-0	Rhosddu
British Celanese	1-5	Rubery Owen
Rhos Aelwyd	3-6	Llay Welfare
Mold Alexandra	5-0	Bala Town
Aberdovey	3-6	Towyn
Dolgellau	2-7	Barmouth & Dyffryn
Machynlleth	5-0	Corris United
Aberayron	0-11	Newtown
Played at Newtown		
Llanfair Caereinion	3-4	Caersws Amateurs
Llanidloes Town	4-0	Llandrindod Wells
Kington Town	9-2	Knighton Town
Garw Athletic	2-4	Briton Ferry Athletic
Hakin United	9-2	Royal Naval Mine Depot Milford Haven
Glanrhyd Ystradgynlais	0-0	Morriston Town

First Round Replays

Penycae	2-4	Rogers & Jackson Wrexham
Played at Rogers & Jackson Wrexham		
Morriston Town	7-1	Glanrhyd Ystradgynlais

Second Round

Llandudno	5-1	Penmaenmawr
31st TRRA Kinmel	7-0	Ruthin FC
Borough United	4-1	Holywell Town
Bethesda Athletic	3-0	Colwyn Bay
Denbigh Town	5-0	Mold Alexandra
Connah's Quay Nomads	7-1	Blaenau Ffestiniog FC
Nantlle Vale	6-1	Llanfairfechan Town
Rhostyllen SC	5-4	Druids United
Rubery Owen Wrexham	11-2	Bradley Rangers
Buckley Wanderers	4-4	Rogers & Jackson Wrexham
Brymbo Steelworks	10-2	Overton St. Mary's
Welshpool	7-5	Llay Welfare
Pentre Broughton	v	Chirk AAA
Chirk AAA were dismissed from the competition and Pentre Broughton progressed to the next round.		
55th RA Tonfannau	6-2	Kington Town
Llanidloes Town	4-1	Caersws Amateurs
Towyn	0-3	Newtown
Played at Newtown		
Barmouth & Dyffryn Utd	4-4	Machynlleth
Cardiff Corinthians	5-3	Hakin United
Port Talbot Athletic	2-3	Caerau Athletic
Ebbw Vale	2-0	Pembroke Borough
Aberystwyth Town	0-3	Milford United
Briton Ferry Athletic	2-6	Haverfordwest County
Played at Haverfordwest		
Brecon Corinithians	4-0	Morriston Town
Abergavenny Thursdays	3-0	Troedyrhiw

Second Round Replay

Rogers & Jackson Wrexham	3-5	Buckley Wanderers
Machynlleth	6-0	Barmouth & Dyffryn Utd

Third Round

Flint Town United	7-0	Denbigh Town
Pwllheli & District	3-3	Nantlle Vale
31st RA Kinmel	1-3	Connah's Quay Nomads
Portmadoc	1-3	Llandudno
Bethesda Athletic	2-6	Holyhead Town
Caernarvon Town	3-0	Borough United
Played at Llandudno Junction		
Rubery Owen	5-2	Brymbo Steelworks
Welshpool	10-0	Pentre Broughton
Rhostyllen SC	1-1	Buckley Wanderers
Hereford United	6-1	Machynlleth
Newtown	2-0	Llanidloes Town
Brecon Corinthians	3-8	55th RA Tonfannau
Haverfordwest County	2-0	Cardiff Corinthians
Abergavenny Thursdays	4-3	Ebbw Vale
Caerau Athletic	2-2	Milford United

Third Round Replays

Nantlle Vale	4-2	Pwllheli & District
Buckley Wanderers	2-0	Rhostyllen SC
Milford United	4-3	Caerau Athletic

Fourth Round

Buckley Wanderers	1-6	Oswestry Town
Nantlle Vale	2-4	Bangor City
Caernarvon Town	4-1	Welshpool
Rhyl	3-2	Holyhead Town
Llandudno	5-1	Connah's Quay Nomads
Rubery Owen	3-6	Flint Town United
Lovell's Athletic	2-1	Newtown
Played at Newtown		

Haverfordwest County	4-0	55th RA Tonfannau
Hereford United	4-0	Merthyr Tydfil
Llanelly	2-4	Barry Town
Abergavenny Thursdays	4-3	Milford United

Fifth Round

Wrexham	7-0	Flint Town United
Llandudno	0-2	Caernarvon Town
Rhyl	2-0	Bangor City
Oswestry Town	1-3	Chester
Barry Town	1-2	Abergavenny Thursdays
Cardiff City	0-2	Hereford United
Lovell's Athletic	2-2	Haverfordwest County
Played at Haverfordwest		
Newport County	2-5	Swansea Town

Fifth Round Replay

Haverfordwest County	1-3	Lovell's Athletic

Sixth Round

Wrexham	4-0	Abergavenny Thursdays
Caernarvon Town	4-2	Rhyl
Hereford United	2-1	Lovell's Athletic
Chester	2-0	Swansea Town

Semi-finals

Chester	1-1	Hereford United
Played at Wrexham		
Caernarvon Town	2-4	Wrexham
Played at Bangor		

Semi-final Replay

Hereford United	0-2	Chester
Played at Swansea		

1958 WELSH CUP FINAL

7th May 1958 at Sealand Road, Chester

Chester	1-1	Wrexham
Hughes (pen)		Murray

Chester: Biggins, Hughes, Gill, P Whitlock, Saunders, Mason, Foulkes, Bullock, Jepson, Pearson, Davies

Wrexham: Waters, A McGowan, Parker, Davies, A Fox, Evans, Jones, Murray, Bannan, Anderson, Jones

Referee: C W Kingston (Newport)

Attendance: 7,742

1958 WELSH CUP FINAL REPLAY

10th May 1958 at the Racecourse, Wrexham

Wrexham	2-1	Chester
Murray, Bannan		Evans

Wrexham: Waters, A McGowan, Parker, Davies, A Fox, Evans, Jones, Murray, Bannan, Anderson, Jones

Chester: Biggins, Hughes, Gill, P Whitlock, Saunders, Anderson, R Evans, Bullock, Jepson, Pearson, Croft

Referee: C W Kingston (Newport)

Attendance: 7,542

1958/59 Welsh Cup

First Round

Llay Welfare	4-3	Rhos Aelwyd
Rhostyllen SC	1-3	Holt Nomads
Llangollen	4-3	Pentre Broughton
Bradley Rangers	7-3	Mold Alexandra
Ruthin FC	3-3	Buckley Rovers
Corwen Amateurs	1-6	Bala Town
Corris United	7-0	Towyn
Aberdovey	2-7	Barmouth & Dyffryn Utd
Llandrindod Wells	6-0	Knighton Town
Llanfair Caereinion	12-4	Dolgelley
Llanidloes Town	3-3	Caersws Amateurs
Machynlleth	4-2	Llanrhaeadr
Cardiff Corinthians	6-2	Troedyrhiw
Briton Ferry Athletic	5-0	Glanrhyd Ystradgynlais
Morriston Town	5-2	Hakin United

First Round Replay

Buckley Rovers	3-1	Ruthin FC
Caersws Amateurs	5-2	Llanidloes Town

Second Round

Penmaenmawr	1-2	Prestatyn Town
Holywell Town	5-0	Nantlle Vale
Pwllheli & District	3-1	Portmadoc
Bethesda Athletic	2-1	Connah's Quay Nomads
Colwyn Bay	2-1	Llandudno
Blaenau Ffestiniog FC	4-4	Borough United
Buckley Rovers	3-1	Rubery Owen (Wrexham)
Llay Welfare	1-2	Druids United
Overton St Mary's	3-4	Bradley Rangers
Llangollen	7-3	Denbigh Town
Brymbo Steelworks	5-6	Welshpool
Chirk AAA	8-0	Holt Nomads
Newtown	2-3	Llandrindod Wells
Machynlleth	5-0	Llanfair Caereinion
Barmouth & Dyffryn Utd	4-2	Bala Town
Corris United	1-2	Caersws Amateurs

Milford Utd	6-0	Port Talbot Athletic
Caerau Athletic	6-1	Ebbw Vale
Pembroke Borough	2-3	Ton Pentre
Llanelly	7-0	Brecon Corinthians
Cardiff Corinthians	3-2	Aberystwyth Town
Played at Aberystwyth		
Briton Ferry Athletic	3-2	Morriston Town

Second Round Replay

Borough United	3-0	Blaenau Ffestiniog FC

Third Round

Prestatyn Town	2-8	Holyhead Town
Borough United	5-2	Flint Town United
Bethesda Athletic	1-6	Colwyn Bay
Played at Colwyn		
Pwllheli & District	2-3	Holywell Town
Welshpool	2-1	Bradley Rangers
Druids United	2-0	Llangollen
Buckley Rovers	1-2	Chirk AAA
Caersws Amateurs	3-1	Llandrindod Wells
Barmouth & Dyffryn United	1-1	Machynlleth
Kidderminster Harriers	2-3	Gloucester City
Haverfordwest County	5-3	Cardiff Corinthians
Ton Pentre	6-3	Abergavenny Thursdays
Briton Ferry Athletic	2-8	Llanelly
Played at Llanelly		
Caerau Athletic	1-0	Milford United

Third Round Replay

Machynlleth	2-1	Barmouth & Dyffryn Utd

Fourth Round

Holywell Town	4-2	Colwyn Bay
Druids United	0-6	Bangor City
Played at Bangor		
Oswestry Town	2-1	Borough United
Rhyl	2-2	Chirk AAA
Welshpool	4-3	Holyhead Town
Machynlleth	0-3	Merthyr Tydfil
Played at Merthyr		
Caersws Amateurs	2-3	Llanelly
Lovell's Athletic	1-1	Haverfordwest County
Barry Town	2-1	Ton Pentre
Gloucester City	2-0	Caerau Athletic

Fourth Round Replays

Chirk AAA	2-7 (aet)	Rhyl
The scoreline after 90 minutes was 2-2.		
Haverfordwest County	0-3	Lovell's Athletic

Fifth Round

Bangor City	6-1	Welshpool
Holywell Town	1-2	Oswestry Town
Chester	1-4	Rhyl
Wrexham	5-0	Caernarvon Town
Merthyr Tydfil	2-1	Llanelly
Swansea Town	3-1	Newport County
Barry Town	3-3	Lovell's Athletic
Gloucester City	1-1	Cardiff City

Fifth Round Replays

Lovell's Athletic	4-0	Barry Town
Cardiff City	3-0	Gloucester City

Sixth Round

Bangor City	3-2	Swansea Town
Cardiff City	3-1	Rhyl
Merthyr Tydfil	1-1	Wrexham
Lovell's Athletic	1-0	Oswestry Town

Sixth Round Replay

Wrexham	5-1	Merthyr Tydfil

Semi-finals

Bangor City	0-0	Lovell's Athletic
Played at Wrexham		
Cardiff City	6-0	Wrexham
Played at Shrewsbury		

Semi-final Replay

Lovell's Athletic	2-1	Bangor City
Played at Newton		

1959 WELSH CUP FINAL

30th April 1959 at Somerton Park, Newport

Cardiff City	2-0	Lovell's Athletic

Hudson, Bonson

Cardiff City: G Vearncombe, Milne, R Stitfall, Gammon, Malloy, Baker, Walsh, D Tapscott, Bonson, Moore, Hudson

Lovell's Athletic: Cross, Burch, Sullivan, Royall, Lloyd, Davies, B Evans, R Williams, R Evans, Reynolds, Grace

Referee: L Callaghan (Merthyr)

Attendance: 0

1959/60 Welsh Cup

First Round

Mold Alexandra	1-1	Overton St Mary's
Rhos Aelwyd	9-2	Thomas Marshall SC
Denbigh Town	7-1	Pontfadog YC
Buckley Rovers	6-1	Holt Nomads
Bradley Rangers	8-1	Rhostyllen SC
Bala Town	3-2	Corwen Amateurs
Towyn	2-3	Machynlleth
Barmouth & Dyffryn United	5-1	Dolgelley
Knighton Town	2-2	Felindre
Llanidloes Town	6-3	Caersws Amateurs
Llandrindod Wells	5-2	Newtown

First Round Replays

Overton St Mary's	4-1	Mold Alexandra
Felindre	3-5	Knighton Town

Second Round

Nantlle Vale	5-1	Penmaenmawr
Prestatyn Town	3-2	31st TRRA Kinmel
Llangollen	5-4	Chirk AAA
Ruthin FC	1-4	Rhos Aelwyd
Druids United	2-1	Bradley Rangers
Denbigh Town	6-2	Overton St Mary's
Buckley Rovers	1-2	Brymbo Steelworks
Connah's Quay Nomads	0-3	Llay Welfare
Aberystwyth Town	3-1	Bala Town
Machynlleth	7-2	Knighton Town
Barmouth & Dyffryn Utd	3-1	Welshpool
Llandrindod Wells	2-2	Llanidloes Town
Morriston Town	0-9	Ton Pentre
Played at Ton Pentre		
Cardiff Corinthians	8-0	Garw Athletic
Ebbw Vale	0-2	Caerau Athletic
Brecon Corinthians	6-2	Carmarthen Town
Briton Ferry Athletic	1-5	Haverfordwest County
Played at Haverfordwest		
Port Talbot Athletic	0-3	Pembroke Borough

Second Round Replay

Llanidloes Town	1-5	Llandrindod Wells

Third Round

Blaenau Ffestiniog FC	2-1	Flint Town United
Portmadoc	2-2	Holywell Town
Nantlle Vale	2-3	Llandudno
Bethesda Athletic	2-1	Caernarvon Town
Pwllheli & District	0-1	Borough United
Colwyn Bay	2-0	Prestatyn Town
Llangollen	2-1	Llay Welfare
Druids United	3-1	Brymbo Steelworks
Rhos Aelwyd	5-3	Denbigh Town
Machynlleth	2-1	Llandrindod Wells
Aberystwyth Town	6-2	Barmouth & Dyffryn Utd
Ton Pentre	6-0	Brecon Corinthians
Llanelly	4-0	Haverfordwest County
Pembroke Borough	2-5	Caerau Athletic
Abergavenny Thursdays	2-1	Cardiff Corinthians

Third Round Replay

Holywell Town	4-3	Portmadoc

Fourth Round

Rhyl	0-1	Colwyn Bay
Holywell Town	2-1	Blaenau Ffestiniog FC
Druids United	1-2	Llandudno
Bethesda Athletic	7-3	Llangollen

Following a protest, Bethesda were dismissed from the competition for fielding an ineligible player.

Borough United	4-0	Rhos Aelwyd
Abergavenny Thursdays	3-1	Llanelly
Caerau Athletic	2-1	Aberystwyth Town
Merthyr Tydfil	3-1	Barry Town
Machynlleth	2-5	Ton Pentre

Fifth Round

Chester	0-2	Holywell Town
Bangor City	5-2	Colwyn Bay
Wrexham	4-0	Llandudno
Borough Utd	8-1	Llangollen
Caerau Athletic	3-5	Newport County
Swansea Town	6-1	Merthyr Tydfil
Cardiff City	5-0	Lovell's Athletic
Abergavenny Thursdays	5-1	Ton Pentre

Sixth Round

Bangor City	5-1	Holywell Town
Swansea Town	1-2	Cardiff City
Wrexham	3-0	Newport County
Abergavenny Thursdays	3-0	Borough United

Semi-finals

Cardiff City	1-1	Bangor City
Played at Wrexham		
Wrexham	2-2	Abergavenny Thursdays
Played at Newport		

Semi-final Replays

Bangor City	1-4	Cardiff City
Played at Newport		
Abergavenny Thursdays	0-2	Wrexham
Played at Hereford		

1960 WELSH CUP FINAL

2nd May 1960 at Ninian Park, Cardiff

Cardiff City	1-1	Wrexham
Harbetson		Jenkins

Cardiff City: G Vearncombe, A Harrington, R Stitfall, Gammon, D Malloy, Baker, Hudson. D Tapscott, Moore, Jenkins, Watkins

Wrexham: Hughes, Holland, A McGowan, Davis, A Fox, Styles, Jones, Griffiths, Evans, Harbetson, R Hunter

Referee: L Callaghan (Merthyr)

Attendance: 11,172

1960 WELSH CUP FINAL REPLAY

5th May 1960 at the Racecourse, Wrexham

Wrexham	1-0	Cardiff City
Griffiths		

Wrexham: Hughes, Holland, A McGowan, Davis, A Fox, Styles, Jones, Griffiths, Evans, Harbetson, R Hunter

Cardiff City: G Vearncombe, A Harrington, R Stitfall, Gammon, D Malloy, Baker, Hudson, D Tapscott, Moore, Jenkins, Watkins

Referee: L Callaghan (Merthyr)

Attendance: 5,938

1960/61 WELSH CUP

First Round

Gresford Athletic	5-6	Overton St Mary's
Rhostyllen Villa	2-5	Rhosddu
Ruthin FC (w/o)	v	Mold Alexandra (withdrew)
Buckley Rovers	2-1	Holt Nomads
Bradley Rangers	3-1	Thomas Marshall SC Wrexham
Brymbo Steelworks	5-3	Corwen Amateurs
Llay Welfare	14-1	Queens Park Rangers (Wrexham)
Newtown	1-0	Caersws Amateurs
Machynlleth	5-2	Llanidloes Town
Llandrindod Wells	2-8	Knighton Town
Towyn	1-0	Dolgelley
Bala Town	2-3	Barmouth & Dyffryn Utd
Seven Sisters	1-1	3M Gorseinon
Played at Onllwyn		
Cwmavon	1-6	Pontardawe Athletic

First Round Replay

3M Gorseinon	7-2	Seven Sisters

Second Round

Caernarvon Town	2-3	Prestatyn Town
Nantlle Vale	3-0	Penmaenmawr
Holyhead Town	9-2	Nefyn United
Overton St Mary's	3-2	Bradley Rangers
Buckley Rovers	5-0	Denbigh Town
Ruthin FC	1-1	Brymbo Steelworks
Druids United	2-7	Chirk AAA
Rhosddu	3-11	Llay Welfare
Llangollen	0-1	Rhos Aelwyd
Towyn	1-0	Aberystwyth Town
Barmouth & Dyffryn Utd (w/o)	v	Builth (dismissed)
Welshpool	4-5	Knighton Town
Newtown	0-2	Machynlleth
Ebbw Vale	1-0	Morriston Town
Briton Ferry Athletic	1-1	Pembroke Borough
3M Gorseinon	0-10	Llanelly
Played at Llanelly		
Haverfordwest County	1-0	Ton Pentre
Port Talbot Athletic	0-3	Brecon Corinthians
Caerau Athletic	4-5	Pontardawe Athletic
Ferndale Athletic	4-2	Cardiff Corinthians

Second Round Replays

Brymbo Steelworks	3-2	Ruthin FC
Pembroke Borough	7-3	Briton Ferry Athletic

Third Round

Pwllheli & District	2-1	Borough United
Llandudno	5-2	Prestatyn Town
Bethesda Athletic	1-1	Portmadoc
Bethesda withdrew before the replay		
Nantlle Vale	1-1	Blaenau Ffestinog FC
Holyhead Town	4-1	Holywell Town
Flint Town United	1-0	Colwyn Bay
Buckley Rovers	0-5	Llay Welfare
Rhos Aelwyd	1-1	Chirk AAA
Overton St Mary's	2-0	Brymbo Steelworks
Machynlleth	1-1	Knighton Town
Towyn	2-1	Barmouth & Dyffryn Utd
Ferndale Athletic	3-4	Brecon Corinthians
Played at Brecon		
Llanelly	6-2	Pontardawe Athletic
Haverfordwest County	6-0	Ebbw Vale
Pembroke Borough	1-1	Lovell's Athletic

Third Round Replays

Blaenau Ffestiniog	0-4	Nantlle Vale
Chirk AAA	3-0	Rhos Aelwyd
Knighton Town	4-2	Machynlleth
Lovell's Athletic	7-1	Pembroke Borough

Fourth Round

Portmadoc	3-3	Nantlle Vale
Flint Town United	1-2	Holyhead Town
Llandudno	1-0	Overton St Mary's
Chirk AAA	3-2	Llay Welfare
Rhyl	0-1	Pwllheli & District
Merthyr Tydfil	2-0	Llanelly
Brecon Corinthians	0-1	Lovell's Athletic
Barry Town	2-1	Havefordwest County
Knighton Town	4-1	Towyn

Fourth Round Replay

Nantlle Vale	4-4	Portmadoc

Fourth Round Second Replay

Portmadoc	2-1	Nantlle Vale

Fifth Round

Chester	2-1	Portmadoc
Llandudno	0-1	Holyhead Town
Chirk AAA	0-8	Bangor City
Pwllheli & District	0-1	Wrexham
Abergavenny Thursdays	1-3	Newport County
Merthyr Tydfil	1-1	Lovell's Athletic
Knighton Town	0-16	Cardiff City
Played at Cardiff		
Barry Town	0-3	Swansea Town

Fifth Round Replay

Lovell's Athletic	3-1	Merthyr Tydfil

Sixth Round

Bangor City	3-1	Chester
Cardiff City	2-1	Newport County
Swansea Town	5-0	Holyhead Town
Wrexham	2-0	Lovell's Athletic

Semi-finals

Bangor City	3-0	Wrexham
Played at Bangor		
Swansea Town	1-1	Cardiff City
Played at Newport		

Semi-final Replay

Cardiff City	1-2	Swansea Town
Played at Llanelli		

1961 WELSH CUP FINAL

22nd April 1961 at Ninian Park, Cardiff

Swansea Town	3-1	Bangor City
Reynolds, B Davies, R Davies		Ellis

Swansea Town: N Dwyer, Sanders, Griffiths, P Davies, M Nurse, R Saunders, B Jones, R Davies, B Reynolds, C Webster, G Williams

Bangor City: L Davies, Soutar, Hillsdon, K Birch, E Murphy, B Wilkinson, M Hunt, Gryba, E Brown, B Ellis, Bullock

Referee: L Callaghan (Merthyr)

Attendance: 5,938

1961/62 Welsh Cup

First Round

Rhostyllen Villa	0-3	Johnstown Recreation GA
Ruthin FC	3-4	Mold Alexandra
Holt Nomads	0-2	Bradley SC
Llay Welfare	4-1	Gresford Athletic
Towyn	2-1	Bala Town
Barmouth & Dyffryn United	8-1	Harlech Town
Machynlleth	3-3	Dolgelley
Llandrindod Wells	5-2	Builth Wells
Caersws Amateurs	5-0	Welshpool
Newtown	6-1	Llanidloes Town

First Round Replay

Dolgelley	3-2	Machynlleth

Second Round

Bethesda Athletic	4-1	Prestatyn Town
Penmaenmawr	1-3	Caernarvon Town
Llay Welfare	6-1	Druids United
Brymbo Steelworks	7-2	Johnstown Recreation GA
Denbigh Town	8-1	Mold Alexandra
Bradley SC	4-2	Llangollen
Chirk AAA	3-1	Rhos Aelwyd
Buckley Wanderers	7-2	Overton St Mary's
Barmouth & Dyffryn United	4-6 (aet)	Knighton Town

The scoreline after 90 minutes was 4-4.

Towyn	3-2	Llandrindod Wells
Caersws Amateurs	6-2	Newtown
Aberystwyth Town	6-2	Dolgelley
Troedyrhiw	1-2	Brecon Corinthians
Ferndale Athletic	2-1	Gwynfi Welfare
Pembroke Borough	2-4	Haverfordwest County
Morriston Town	2-4	Seven Sisters
Ebbw Vale	5-2	Cardiff Corinthians
Llanelly	1-2	Ton Pentre

Third Round

Holyhead Town	2-1	Llandudno
Borough United	2-2	Holywell Town
Flint Town United	1-2	Caernarvon Town
Bethesda Athletic	2-0	Colwyn Bay
Blaenau Ffestiniog FC	0-1	Portmadoc
Nantlle Vale	2-2	Pwllheli & District
Denbigh Town	1-1	Brymbo Steelworks
Chirk AAA	4-0	Bradley SC
Buckley Wanderers	5-1	Llay Welfare
Knighton Town	2-1	Aberystwyth Town
Towyn	2-0	Caersws Amateurs
Lovell's Athletic	3-2	Brecon Corinthians
Haverfordwest County	9-2	Ebbw Vale
Abergavenny Thursdays	0-0	Seven Sisters
Ferndale Athletic	0-4	Ton Pentre

Third Round Replays

Holywell Town	3-0	Borough United
Pwllheli & District	0-1	Nantlle Vale

Following a protest, Nantlle Vale were dismissed from the competition for fielding an ineligible player.

Brymbo Steelworks	2-1	Denbigh Town
Seven Sisters	3-2	Abergavenny Thursdays

Fourth Round

Pwllheli & District	3-0	Caernarvon Town
Chester	1-5	Holywell Town
Portmadoc	1-0	Rhyl
Holyhead Town	6-0	Brymbo Steelworks
Buckley Wanderers	4-0	Bethesda Athletic
Knighton Town	1-2	Lovell's Athletic
Merthyr Tydfil	2-0	Ton Pentre
Seven Sisters	1-2	Havefordwest County
Towyn	2-3	Barry Town

Fifth Round

Holywell Town	5-0	Buckley Wanderers
Bangor City	1-1	Pwllheli & District
Portmadoc	0-2	Wrexham
Chester	1-2	Holyhead Town
Cardiff City	4-1	Newport County
Haverfordwest County	0-7	Swansea Town
Bristol City	4-2	Merthyr Tydfil
Lovell's Athletic	0-0	Barry Town

Fifth Round Replays

Pwllheli & District	0-4	Bangor City
Barry Town	5-3	Lovell's Athletic

Sixth Round

Bristol City	0-2	Cardiff City
Holywell Town	1-2	Swansea Town
Bangor City	1-1	Barry Town
Wrexham	4-0	Holyhead Town

Sixth Round Replay

Barry Town	0-1	Bangor City

Semi-finals

Bangor City	2-0	Cardiff City

Played at Wrexham

Wrexham	3-2	Swansea Town

Played at Cardiff

1962 WELSH CUP FINAL

1st leg

16th April 1962 at the Racecourse, Wrexham

Wrexham	3-0	Bangor City

Whitehouse, Colebridge, Pythian

Wrexham: K Keelan, R Holland, A McGowan, P Jones, A Fox, R Ambler, K Barnes, B Whitehouse, E Pythian, T Anderson, C Colebridge

Bangor City: L Davies, I Griffiths, B Soutar, K Birch, E Murphy, B Wilkinson, R Matthews, B Ellis, E Brown, J McAllister, R Hunter

Referee: L Callaghan (Merthyr)

Attendance: 7,638

2nd leg

30th April 1962 at Farrar Road, Bangor

Bangor City	2-0	Wrexham

Brown, Wilkinson

Bangor City: L Davies, I Griffiths, B Soutar, K Birch, E Murphy, B Wilkinson, R Matthews, B Ellis, E Brown, J McAllister, R Hunter

Wrexham: K Keelan, R Holland, A McGowan, P Jones, A Fox, G Evans, M Metcalf, B Whitehouse, E Pythian, T Anderson, C Colebridge

Referee: L Callaghan (Merthyr)

Attendance: 7,500

Final Play-off

7th May 1962 at Belle Vue, Rhyl

Bangor City	3-1		Wrexham
Ellis, Birch, Hunter			*K Barnes*

Bangor City: L Davies, Soutar, Griffiths, B Wilkinson, Murphy, Birch, R Hunter, J McAllister, Brown, B Ellis, Matthews

Wrexham: K Keelan, P Jones, A McGowan, K Barnes, A Fox, G Evans, R Barnes, B Whitehouse, E Pythian, T Anderson, C Colebridge

Referee: L Callaghan (Merthyr)

Attendance: 12,000

1962/63 Welsh Cup

First Round

Mold Alexandra	7-1	Llangollen
Bradley SC	5-4	Rhosddu
Buckley Rovers	2-1	Johnstown Recreation GA
Ruthin FC	6-3	Rhostyllen Villa
Towyn	8-1	Barmouth & Dyffryn Utd
Berriew	5-0	Llanfair Caereinion
Caersws Amateurs	3-4	Welshpool
Machynlleth	2-3	Newtown
Llanidloes Town	1-1	Llandrindod Wells
Builth Wells	2-6	Knighton Town
Abercynon Athletic	2-4	Ferndale Athletic
City of Cardiff TC	v	Troedyrhiw
City of Cardiff TC withdrew from the competition.		
Briton Ferry Athletic	6-2	Morriston Town
3M Gorseinon	2-1	Cwmavon

First Round Replay

Llandrindod Wells	3-2	Llanidloes Town

Second Round

Bethesda Athletic	1-3	Colwyn Bay
Nantlle Vale	5-3	Penmaenmawr
Prestatyn Town	2-6	Llandudno
Chirk AAA	2-0	Druids United
Rhos Aelwyd	1-2	Overton St Mary's
Brymbo Steelworks	2-5	Denbigh Town
Buckley Rovers	0-1	Llay Welfare
Bradley SC	2-3	Ruthin FC
Buckley Wanderers	4-2	Mold Alexandra
Berriew	1-1	Llandrindod Wells
Newtown	1-2	Aberystwyth Town
Towyn	2-1	Welshpool
Dolgelley	8-2	Knighton Town
Troedyrhiw	1-5	Milford United
Caerau Athletic	3-2	Llanelly
Ebbw Vale	3-0	Briton Ferry Athletic
Played at Briton Ferry		
3M Gorseinon	1-7	Seven Sisters
Port Talbot Athletic	1-2	Haverfordwest County
Ton Pentre	4-1	Pembroke Borough
Ferndalel Athletic	1-3	Brecon Corinthians
Gwynfi Welfare	4-2	Cardiff Corinthians

Second Round Replay

Llandrindod Wells	5-1	Berriew

Third Round

Borough United	2-1	Llandudno
Caernarvon Town	2-1	Colwyn Bay
Blaenau Ffestiniog FC	0-0	Pwllheli & District
Holywell Town	4-2	Portmadoc
Holyhead Town	3-3	Nantlle Vale
Chirk AAA	2-1	Buckley Wanderers
Ruthin FC	2-2	Llay Welfare
It is not known if a replay was held but Llay Welfare subsequently appeared in the Fourth Round.		
Overton St Mary's	4-6	Denbigh Town
Llandrindod Wells	2-1	Aberystwyth Town

Towyn	2-3	Dolgelley
Gwynfi Welfare	0-4	Caerau Athletic
Abergavenny Thursdays	3-2	Ton Pentre
Milford United	1-1	Haverfordwest County
Lovell's Athletic	5-0	Seven Sisters
Ebbw Vale	0-3	Brecon Corinthians

Played at Brecon

Third Round Replays

Pwllheli & District	2-1	Blaenau Ffestiniog FC
Nantlle Vale	0-3	Holyhead Town
Haverfordwest County	3-0	Milford United

Fourth Round

Holyhead Town	5-1	Chirk AAA
Holywell Town	2-0	Caernarvon Town
Rhyl	1-4	Borough United
Llay Welfare	0-0	Denbigh Town
Oswestry Town	0-6	Pwllheli & District
Dolgelley	2-2	Caerau Athletic
Lovell's Athletic	2-2	Abergavenny Thursdays
Barry Town	1-1	Hereford United

Played at Hereford

Brecon Corinthians	1-2	Merthyr Tydfil

Played at Merthyr

Llandrindod Wells	0-2	Haverfordwest County

Fourth Round Replays

Denbigh Town	2-1	Llay Welfare
Caerau Athletic	1-0	Dolgelley

The match was abandoned after 40 minutes

Abergavenny Thursdays	3-1	Lovell's Athletic
Hereford United	3-2	Barry Town

Fourth Round Second Replay

Caerau Athletic	3-2	Dolgelley

Fifth Round

Wrexham	1-0	Chester
Holywell Town	5-2	Holyhead Town
Denbigh Town	2-4	Borough United
Pwllheli & District	1-1	Bangor City
Swansea Town	6-0	Caerau Athletic
Merthyr Tydfil	0-4	Newport County
Hereford United	5-0	Haverfordwest County
Cardiff City	7-1	Abergavenny Thursdays

Fifth Round Replay

Bangor City	4-0	Pwllheli & District

Sixth Round

Holywell Town	2-6	Newport County
Hereford United	2-1	Wrexham
Borough United	4-1	Bangor City
Swansea Town	2-0	Cardiff City

Semi-finals

Borough United	1-0	Hereford United

Played at Wrexham

Newport County	1-0	Swansea Town

Played at Cardiff

1963 WELSH CUP FINAL

1st leg

27th May 1963 at Nant y Coed, Llandudno Junction

Borough United	2-1	Newport County
Russell, Bebb		Hunt

Borough United: D Walker, Morris, Bridge, H Hodges, Hullett, Clowry, M Pritchard, K Pritchard, Duffy, Russell, Bebb

Newport County: Weare, Bird, Frowen, Sullivan, Rathbone, Rowley, Smith, Sheffield, Bonson, Hunt, K Pring

Referee: L Callaghan (Merthyr)

Attendance: 3,500

2nd leg

30th May 1963 at Somerton Park, Newport

Newport County	0-0	Borough United

Newport County: Weare, Bird, Frowen, Sullivan, Rathbone, Rowley, Smith, Sheffield, Bonson, Hunt, K Pring

Borough United: D Walker, Morris, Harrison, H Hodges, Owen, Clowry, M Pritchard, K Pritchard, Duffy, Russell, Bebb

Referee: L Callaghan (Merthyr)

Attendance: 5,000

1963/64 Welsh Cup

First Round

Rhostllen Villa	4-4	Johnstown Recreation GA

Rhostllen Villa withdrew from the competition.

Gresford Colliery	1-7	Druids United
Llangollen	2-1	Buckley Rovers
Gresford Athletic	5-0	Bradley SC
Machynlleth	3-1	Barmouth & Dyffryn Utd
Knighton Town	5-3	Builth Wells
Llanidloes Town	3-2	Newtown Amateurs
Berriew (w/o)	v	Llanfair Caereinion (withdrew)

Second Round

Bethesda Athletic	1-0	Penmaenmawr
Rhos Aelwyd	2-3	Druids United
Llangollen	1-1	Overton St Mary's
Johnstown Recreation GA	4-6	Ruthin FC
Gresford Athletic	1-3	Brymbo Steelworks
Denbigh Town	4-1	Buckley Wanderers
Chirk AAA	1-4	Llay Welfare
Dolgelley	7-2	Machynlleth
Llanidloes Town	3-2	Llandrindod Wells
Newtown	3-0	Knighton Town

Berriew	0-1	Kington Town
Caersws Amateurs	0-0	Aberystwyth Town
Welshpool	1-2	Towyn
Seven Sisters	2-3	Llanelly
Ferndale Athletic	4-1	Brecon Corinthians
Neath	7-3	Ebbw Vale
Troedyrhiw	5-5	Abercynon Athletic
Pembroke Borough	5-3	Briton Ferry Athletic
Cardiff Corinthians	5-1	Morriston Town

Second Round Replays

Overton St Mary's	4-2	Llangollen

Following a protest, Overton were dismissed from the competition and Llangollen progressed.

Aberystwyth Town	2-1	Caersws Amateurs
Abercynon Athletic	2-2	Troedyrhiw

Second Round Second Replay

Troedyrhiw	1-3	Abercynon Athletic

Third Round

Holyhead Town	3-1	Bethesda Athletic
Colwyn Bay	8-0	Prestatyn Town
Llandudno	5-1	Pwllheli & District
Caernarvon Town	1-0	Holywell Town
Portmadoc	3-0	Blaenau Ffestiniog FC
Ruthin FC	1-4	Denbigh Town
Llay Welfare	2-1	Brymbo Steelworks
Druids United	3-2	Llangollen
Dolgelley	5-0	Towyn
Aberystwyth Town	v	Kington Town

Kington Town withdrew from the competition.

Llanidloes Town	1-3	Newtown
Ebbw Vale	5-2	Cardiff Corinthians
Abercynon Athletic	1-7	Haverfordwest County
Pembroke Borough	3-5	Lovell's Athletic
Ferndale Athletic	3-2	Ton Pentre
Llanelly	3-2	Abergavenny Thursdays

Fourth Round

Druids United	0-7	Holyhead Town
Bangor City	6-0	Portmadoc
Denbigh Town	3-9	Rhyl
Caernarvon Town	1-2	Llandudno
Llay Welfare	0-6	Colwyn Bay

Played at Colwyn Bay

Haverfordwest County	5-1	Ferndale Athletic
Ebbw Vale	2-1	Newtown

Played at Newtown

Dolgelley & District	2-3	Lovell's Athletic
Llanelly	1-0	Merthyr Tydfil
Barry Town	1-2	Aberystwyth Town

Fifth Round

Bangor City	3-0	Llandudno
Rhyl	2-1	Holyhead Town
Wrexham	2-1	Colwyn Bay
Chester	5-1	Borough United
Ebbw Vale	1-6	Cardiff City
Lovell's Athletic	1-3	Swansea Town
Aberystwyth Town	1-3	Llanelly
Newport County	5-2	Haverfordwest County

Sixth Round

Cardiff City	3-1	Chester
Newport County	1-0	Swansea Town
Bangor City	8-1	Rhyl
Wrexham	3-0	Llanelly

Semi-finals

Newport County	2-2	Cardiff City

Played at Swansea

Bangor City	3-1	Wrexham

Played at Chester

Semi-final Replay

Cardiff City	1-0	Newport County

Played at Cardiff

1964 WELSH CUP FINAL

1st leg

27th April 1964 at Farrar Road, Bangor

Bangor City	2-0	Cardiff City

Gray, Edwards

Bangor City: G Griffiths, E Ab Iorweth, T Banks, Murray, Murphy, Fitchford, Matthews, Kinsella, R Gray, Robinson, S Edwards

Cardiff City: D John, T Peck, P Rodriques, R Scott, J Charles, B Hole, B Lewis, P King, M Charles, I Allchurch, G Farrell

Referee: L Callaghan (Merthyr)

Attendance: 8,500

2nd leg

29th April 1964 at Ninian Park, Cardiff

Cardiff City	3-1	Bangor City

Allchurch, M Charles, Lewis   *Gray*

Cardiff City: G Vearncombe, C Baker, P Rodriques, G Williams, Murray, B Hole, Lewis, M Charles, J Charles, I Allchurch, P King

Bangor City: G Griffiths, E Ab Iorweth, T Banks, Murray, Murphy, Fitchford, Matthews, Kinsella, R Gray, Robinson, S Edwards

Referee: L Callaghan (Merthyr)

Attendance: 9,050

Final Play-off

4th May 1964 at the Racecourse, Wrexham

Bangor City	0-2	Cardiff City
		King 2

Bangor City: G Griffiths, E Ab Iorweth, T Banks, Murray, Murphy, Fitchford, Matthews, Kinsella, R Gray, Robinson, S Edwards

Cardiff City: G Vearncombe, C Baker, P Rodriques, G Williams, Murray, B Hole, Lewis, M Charles, J Charles, I Allchurch, P King

Referee: L Callaghan (Merthyr)

Attendance: 10,014

1964/65 Welsh Cup

First Round

Bradley SC	4-1	Chirk AAA
Cross Street	3-2	Mold Alexandra
Gresford Athletic	4-2	Rhos Aelwyd
Overton St Mary's	1-1	Buckley Rovers
Machynlleth	7-0	Pontrhydfendigaid
Berriew	3-0	Knighton Town
Llandrindod Wells	2-1	Builth Wells
Barmouth & Dyffryn Utd	0-3	Towyn

First Round Replay

Buckley Rovers	0-7	Overton St Mary's

Second Round

Bethesda Athletic	1-1	Nantlle Vale
Penmaenmawr	4-2	Prestatyn Town
Brymbo Steelworks	5-1	Cross Street
Gresford Athletic	0-6	Buckley Wanderers
Druids United	2-3	Llangollen
Ruthin FC	6-2	Llay Welfare
Bradley SC	1-3	Overton St Mary's
Welshpool	1-2	Llanidloes Town
Caersws Amateurs	3-5	Berriew
Towyn	4-0	Newtown
Machynlleth	5-5	Dolgelley
Aberystwyth Town	2-3	Llandrindod Wells
Seven Sisters	1-2	South Wales Switchgear
Ebbw Vale	9-0	Troedyrhiw
Abergavenny Thursdays	4-3	Brecon Corinthians
City of Cardiff TC	3-2	Pembroke Borough
Cardiff Corinthians	0-3	Haverfordwest County
Played at Haverfordwest		
Pontardawe Athletic	3-4	Ferndale Athletic
Played at Ferndale		
Dunlop Semtex	3-1	Briton Ferry Athletic
Ton Pentre	5-2	Aberaman Athletic

Second Round Replays

Nantlle Vale	5-3	Bethesda Athletic
Dolgelley	4-1	Machynlleth

Third Round

Caernarvon Town	3-1	Holywell Town
Colwyn Bay	3-1	Nantlle Vale
Penmaenmawr	1-2	Holyhead Town
Llandudno	1-2	Blaenau Ffestiniog FC
Portmadoc	3-3	Pwllheli & District
Oswestry Town	4-2	Buckley Wanderers
Brymbo Steelworks	1-2	Overton St Mary's
Llangollen	4-2	Ruthin FC
Hereford United	6-0	Towyn
Llandrindod Wells	4-0	Berriew
Llanidloes Town	1-1	Dolgelley
Ton Pentre	3-3	Ebbw Vale
City of Cardiff TC	3-0	Dunlop Semtex
South Wales Switchgear	1-1	Llanelly
Lovell's Athletic	4-2	Ferndale Athletic
Haverfordwest County	1-1	Abergavenny Thursdays

Third Round Replay

Pwllheli & District	7-1	Portmadoc
Dolgelley	1-0	Llanidloes Town
Ebbw Vale	0-4	Ton Pentre
Llanelly	2-0	South Wales Switchgear
Abergavenny Thursdays	2-1	Haverfordwest County

Fourth Round

Llangollen	1-1	Blaenau Ffestiniog FC
Pwllheli & District	5-0	Rhyl
Colwyn Bay	6-0	Oswestry Town
Borough United	2-2	Holyhead Town
The match was abandoned after 65 minutes.		
Overton St Mary's	1-10	Caernarvon Town
Barry Town	3-4	Abergavenny Thursdays
Ton Pentre	1-3	Lovell's Athletic
Llanelly	5-0	Dolgelley
Llandrindod Wells	1-3	Hereford United
Played at Hereford		
Merthyr Tydfil	2-0	City of Cardiff TC

Fourth Round Replays

Blaenau Ffestiniog FC	0-3	Llangollen
Borough United	5-3	Holyhead Town

Fifth Round

Borough United	8-2	Llangollen
Chester	1-1	Bangor City
Colwyn Bay	1-2	Wrexham
Newport County	2-3	Swansea Town
Lovell's Athletic	1-4	Hereford United
Played at Hereford		
Merthyr Tydfil	1-3	Cardiff City
Llanelly	1-2	Abergavenny Thursdays

Fifth Round Replay

Bangor City	0-4	Chester

Sixth Round

Cardiff City	3-1	Hereford United
Chester	0-0	Borough United
Pwllheli & District	1-3	Swansea Town
Wrexham	2-2	Abergavenny Thursdays

Sixth Round Replays

Borough United	2-2	Borough United
Abergavenny Thursdays	0-4	Wrexham

Sixth Round Second Replay

Chester	3-0	Borough United

Semi-finals

Cardiff City	1-0	Swansea Town
Played at Newport		
Wrexham	3-1	Chester
Played at Wrexham		

1965 WELSH CUP FINAL

1st leg

12th April 1965 at Ninian Park, Cardiff

Cardiff City	5-1	Wrexham

Johnston 2 Allchurch, King 2 — Murray (own goal)

Cardiff City: Wilson, P Rodriques, C Baker, G Williams, Murray, B Hole, Johnston, I Allchurch, J Charles, P King, Lewis

Wrexham: A Dunlop, H Jones, Holland, P Jones, R Mielczarek, D Powell, C Colebridge, A Griffiths, E Pythian, K Webber, G Williams

Referee: L Callaghan (Merthyr)

Attendance: 7,412

2nd leg

26th April 1965 at the Racecourse, Wrexham

Wrexham	1-0	Cardiff City

King

Wrexham: S Fleet, H Jones, Holland, P Jones, R Mielczarek, D Powell, C Colebridge, A Griffiths, M King, K Webber, S McMillan

Cardiff City: Wilson, Harris, C Baker, G Williams, Murray, B Hole, Johnston, I Allchurch, Ellis, P King, Lewis

Referee: J Lowry (Neath)

Attendance: 8,000

Final Play-off

26th April 1965 at Gay Meadow, Shrewsbury

Cardiff City	3-0	Wrexham

Allchurch 2, Own goal

Cardiff City: Wilson, Coldrick, C Baker, G Williams, Murray, B Hole, Johnston, I Allchurch, J Charles, P King, Lewis

Wrexham: S Fleet, P Jones, Holland, P Jones, R Mielczarek, D Powell, C Colebridge, S McMillan, M King, K Webber, D Campbell

Referee: J Lowry (Neath)

Attendance: 7,480

1965/66 Welsh Cup

First Round

Rhos Aelwyd	2-3	Buckley Rovers
Johnstown Recreation GA	1-1	Mold Alexandra
Chirk AAA	3-2	Druids United
Barmouth & Dyffryn Utd	4-3	Towyn
Berriew	2-1	Machynlleth
Builth Wells (withdrew)	v	Knighton Town
Pontrhydfedigaid	3-1	Rhayader Town
Pullman United	1-4	Briton Ferry Athletic
Tonrefail Welfare	5-0	Ammanford Town
Seven Sisters	1-1	Neath Athletic

First Round Replays

Mold Alexandra	2-4	Johnstown Recreation GA
Neath Athletic	2-1	Seven Sisters

Second Round

Overton St Mary's	3-0	Buckley Rovers
Llangollen	1-1	Chirk
Bradley SC	1-3	Buckley Wanderers
Johnstown Recreation GA	2-1	Ruthin FC
Brymbo Steelworks	6-2	Llay Welfare
Llandrindod Wells	6-0	Pontrhydfendigaid
Aberystwyth Town	1-2	Llanidloes Town
Newtown	1-0	Knighton Town
Welshpool	1-1	Berriew
Barmouth & Dyffryn Utd	6-3	Caersws Amateurs
Neath Athletic	3-4	Bridgend Town
South Wales Switchgear	3-4	Haverfordwest County
Briton Ferry Athletic	4-5	Pontardawe Athletic
Pembroke Borough	3-0	Cardiff Corinthians
Ferndale Athletic	2-0	Tonrefail Welfare
Ebbw Vale	3-0	City of Cardiff TC

Second Round Replays

Chirk	2-5	Llangollen
Berriew	0-1	Welshpool

Third Round

Holywell Town	4-1	Blaenau Ffestiniog FC
Portmadoc	1-0	Caernarvon Town
Llandudno	3-3	Holyhead Town
Pwllheli & District	4-0	Bethesda Athletic
Penmaenmawr	3-5	Colwyn Bay
Oswestry Town	3-1	Buckley Wanderers
Johnstown Recreation GA	0-4	Brymbo Steel Works
Llangollen	3-4	Overton St Mary's
Barmouth & Dyffryn United	0-1	Welshpool
Newtown	1-9	Hereford United

Played at Hereford

Llandrindod Wells	3-0	Llanidloes Town
Ebbw Vale	1-0	Pembroke Borough

Played at Pembroke

Haverfordwest County	2-2	Ton Pentre
Abergavenny Thursdays	3-1	Ferndale Athletic
Lovell's Athletic	2-3	Llanelly
Pontardawe Athletic	0-3	Bridgend Town

Played at Bridgend

Third Round Replays

Holyhead Town	10-0	Llandudno
Ton Pentre	2-1	Haverfordwest County

Fourth Round

Holywell Town	4-3	Brymbo Steelworks
Oswestry Town	1-6	Portmadoc
Holyhead Town	3-3	Overton St Mary's
Borough United	3-1	Pwllheli & District
Rhyl	3-2	Colwyn Bay
Hereford United	9-0	Llandrindod Wells
Merthyr Tydfil	4-0	Ton Pentre
Bridgend Town	3-3	Barry Town
Abergavenny Thursdays	2-3	Ebbw Vale
Welshpool	3-2	Llanelly

Fourth Round Replays

Overton St Mary's	1-6	Holyhead Town
Barry Town	6-3	Bridgend Town

Fifth Round

Bangor City	5-0	Holywell Town
Portmadoc	2-0	Rhyl
Chester	4-1	Wrexham
Borough United	4-1	Holyhead Town
Swansea Town	2-2	Cardiff City
Ebbw Vale	1-1	Merthyr Tydfil
Hereford United	1-2	Newport County
Welshpool	4-3	Barry Town

Fifth Round Replay

Cardiff City	2-5	Swansea Town
Merthyr Tydfil	2-0	Ebbw Vale

Sixth Round

Newport County	2-2	Chester
Borough United	0-5	Bangor City
Portmadoc	1-1	Swansea Town
Merthyr Tydfil	5-0	Welshpool

Sixth Round Replays

Chester	2-0	Newport County
Swansea Town	5-0	Portmadoc

Semi-finals

Swansea Town	3-1	Merthyr Tydfil
Bangor City	0-3	Chester

1966 WELSH CUP FINAL

1st leg

18th April 1966 at the Vetch Field, Swansea

Swansea Town	3-0	Chester

McLaughlin 2, Jones

Swansea Town: G Hayes, R Evans, D Ward, G Thomas, B Purcell, B Jones, K Pound, D Todd, L McLaughlin, I Allchurch, B Evans

Chester: D Reeves, T Singleton, M Starkey, P Hauser, J Butler, G A Evans, L Harley, M Metcalf, E Morris, H Ryden, E R Holland

Referee: G T Powell (Newport)

Attendance: 9,614

2nd leg

25th April 1966 at Sealand Road, Chester

Chester	1-0	Swansea Town

Morris

Chester: D Reeves, T Singleton, M Starkey, Chadwick, J Butler, G A Evans, L Harley, M Metcalf, E Morris, H Ryden, E R Holland

Swansea Town: G Hayes, R Evans, D Ward, M Johnson, B Purcell, Hughes, Humphries, D Todd, L McLaughlin, I Allchurch, B Evans

Referee: G T Powell (Newport)

Attendance: 6,346

Final Play-off

2nd May 1966 at Sealand Road, Chester

Chester	1-2	Swansea Town
Jones		Todd, Allchurch

Chester: D Reeves, Singleton, Starkey, P Hauser, Butler, Durie, Harley, Metcalf, H Ryden, Jones, E Morris

Swansea Town: Hayes, Evans, Hughes, Johnson, Purcell, Williams, Humphries, McLaughlin, B Todd, I Allchurch, Pound

Referee: G T Powell (Newport)

Attendance: 6,276

1966/67 Welsh Cup

First Round

Llangollen	1-2	Druids United
Llay Welfare	2-2	Rubery Owen
Rhos Aelwyd (w/o)	v	Bradley SC (withdrew)
Moss	1-2	Ruthin FC
Played at Ruthin		
Johnstown Recreation GA	2-3	Coedpoeth SC
Queensferry Wanderers	5-1	Rossett Villa
Buckley Rovers	2-3	Chirk AAA
Rhayader Town	2-4	Knighton Town
Berriew	5-3	Towyn
Barmouth & Dyffryn United	1-5	Machynlleth
Caersws Amateurs	4-2	Kington Town
Morriston Town	1-3	Neath Athletic
Briton Ferry Athletic	1-3	Caerau Athletic

First Round Replay

Rubery Owen	2-7	Llay Welfare

Second Round

Llay Welfare	3-2	Ruthin FC
Chirk AAA	4-5	Queensferry Wanderers
Overton St Mary's	3-3	Druids United
Brymbo Steelworks	3-0	Rhos Aelwyd
Coedpoeth SC	0-2	Buckley Wanderers
Aberystwyth Town	1-2	Llanidloes Town
Llandrindod Wells	7-0	Machynlleth
Knighton Town	0-2	Berriew
Caersws Amateurs	6-4	Newtown
A replay was held, probably following a protest about extra time being played.		
Prestatyn Town	3-4	Connah's Quay Nomads
Llanelli	4-0	Caerau Athletic
Abergavenny Thursdays	3-1	Haverfordwest County
Pembroke Borough	9-1	Ferndale Athletic
Cardiff College of Education	0-3	South Wales Switchgear
Bridgend Town	1-3	Ammanford Town
Tonyrefail Welfare	1-0	Ebbw Vale
Neath Athletic	0-1	Cardiff Corinthians

Second Round Replays

Druids United	0-2	Overton St Mary's
Caersws Amateurs	3-2	Newtown

Third Round

Blaenau Ffestiniog FC	1-1	Colwyn Bay
Pwllheli & District	3-2	Connah's Quay Nomads
Llandudno	2-1	Caernarvon Town
Rhyl	1-0	Penmaenmawr
Holyhead Town	2-0	Bethesda Athletic
Buckley Wanderers	1-4	Queensferry Wanderers
Oswestry Town	3-3	Brymbo Steelworks
Llay Welfare	5-2	Overton St Mary's
Llandrindod Wells	3-3	Caersws Amateurs
Hereford United	6-1	Berriew
Llanidloes Town	2-4	Welshpool
Llanelli	3-0	South Wales Switchgear
Abergavenny Thursdays	1-1	Lovell's Athletic
Barry Town	0-3	Ton Pentre
Ammanford Town	5-0	Tonrefail Welfare
Pembroke Borough	1-3	Cardiff Corinthians

Third Round Replays

Colwyn Bay	6-3	Blaenau Ffestiniog FC
Brymbo Steelworks	2-1	Oswestry Town
Caersws Amateurs	2-6	Llandrindod Wells
Lovell's Athletic	3-1	Abergavenny Thursdays

Fourth Round

Llandudno	1-1	Llay Welfare
Borough United	1-0	Portmadoc
Queensferry Wanderers	2-1	Colwyn Bay
Pwllheli & District	2-1	Brymbo Steelworks
Rhyl	4-1	Holyhead Town
Hereford United	4-2	Cardiff Corinthians
Welshpool	0-1	Ammanford Town
Llandrindod Wells	1-1	Llanelli
Ton Pentre	2-1	Lovell's Athletic

Fourth Round Replays

Llay Welfare	0-2	Llandudno
Llanelli	1-0	Llandrindod Wells

Fifth Round

Wrexham	5-0	Rhyl
Borough United	2-5	Chester
Queensferry Wanderers	0-3	Bangor City
Llandudno	0-5	Pwllheli & District
Swansea Town	0-4	Cardiff City
Ton Pentre	1-2	Merthyr Tydfil
Llanelli	2-6	Newport County
Hereford United	3-2	Ammanford Town

Sixth Round

Newport County	0-0	Bangor City
Cardiff City	6-3	Hereford United
Merthyr Tydfil	1-7	Wrexham
Played at Wrexham		
Pwllheli & District	2-3	Chester

Sixth Round Replays

Bangor City	0-1	Newport County

Semi-finals

Chester	0-0	Wrexham
Newport County	1-2	Cardiff City

Semi-final Replay

Wrexham	4-2	Chester

1967 WELSH CUP FINAL

1st leg

17th April 1967 at the Racecourse, Wrexham

Wrexham	2-2	Cardiff City
Ferguson, Own goal		King 2

Wrexham: Schofield, Wood, G Showell, T Oldfield, R Mielczarek, S Storey, M Evans, A Griffiths, A kinsey, S McMillan, D Campbell

Cardiff City: Wilson, Coldrick, Ferguson, Williams, Murray, Harris, Jones, N Dean, P King, J Toshack, L Lea

Referee: W J Gow (Swansea)

Attendance: 11,473

2nd leg

3rd May 1967 at Ninian Park, Cardiff

Cardiff City	2-1	Wrexham
Brown, King		Kinsey

Cardiff City: Wilson, Coldrick, Ferguson, Williams, Murray, Harris, Jones, Brown, Dean, P King, R Bird

Wrexham: Schofield, Lucas, Stacey, Showell, R Mielczarek, Oldfield (Campbell), A Griffiths, A Kinsey, D Weston, S McMillan, McLoughlin

Referee: W J Gow (Swansea)

Attendance: 8,299

1967/68 Welsh Cup

First Round

Buckley Rovers	2-0	Chirk AAA
Rossett Villa	0-2	Gresford Athletic
Cymau	2-1	Coedpoeth SC
Rhos Aelwyd	3-1	Denbigh Town
Mold Alexandra	2-4	Druids United
Barmouth & Dyffryn United	6-2	Towyn
Kington Town	3-2	Rhayader Town
Carmarthen Town	7-0	Seven Sisters
Ferndale Athletic	3-1	Briton Ferry Athletic
Tredomen Works	0-5	Caerleon

Second Round

Cymau	0-4	Brymbo Steelworks
Llay Welfare	3-1	Buckley Rovers
Druids United	4-1	Queensferry Wanderers
Gresford Athletic	0-4	Rhos Aelwyd
Aberystwyth Town	1-3	Kington Town
Llandrindod Wells	0-4	Llanidloes Town
Knighton Town	2-1	Newtown
Berriew	4-1	Machynlleth
Caersws Amateurs	9-2	Barmouth & Dyffryn Utd
Connah's Quay Nomads	1-2	Penmaenmawr
Prestatyn Town	2-3	Nantlle Vale
Played at Wrexham		
Cardiff College of Education	3-2	Llanelli
Ebbw Vale	2-0	South Wales Switchgear
Tonrefail Welfare	2-0	Caerleon
Neath Athletic	3-4	Ferndale Athletic
Abergavenny Thursdays	5-0	Carmarthen Town
Pembroke Borough	2-0	Cardiff Corinthians

Third Round

Colwyn Bay	0-1	Bethesda Athletic
Caernarvon Town	1-1	Penmaenmawr
Blaenau Ffestiniog FC	0-0	Nantlle Vale
Llandudno	0-7	Holyhead Town
Llay Welfare	1-4	Druids United
Brymbo Steelworks	2-1	Rhos Aelwyd
Berriew	1-1	Llanidloes Town
Knighton Town	2-0	Kington Town
Welshpool	4-3	Caersws Amateurs
Abergavenny Thursdays	0-2	Ebbw Vale
Barry Town	2-2	Lovell's Athletic
Ammanford Town	4-3	Ferndale Athletic
Tonrefail Welfare	1-0	Pembroke Borough
Ton Pentre	2-0	Cardiff College of Education

Third Round Replays

Penmaenmawr	3-0	Caernarvon Town
Nantlle Vale	3-1	Blaenau Ffestiniog FC
Llanidloes Town	4-2	Berriew
Lovell's Athletic	1-5	Barry Town

Fourth Round

Rhyl	5-1	Nantlle Vale
Bethesda Athletic	3-2	Oswestry Town
Played at Wrexham		
Holyhead Town	0-3	Pwllheli & District
Druids United	2-2	Penmaenmawr
Brymbo Steelworks	2-1	Portmadoc
Tonrefail Welfare	0-3	Barry Town
Knighton Town	0-2	Welshpool
Played at Welshpool		
Ebbw Vale	2-1	Ton Pentre
Hereford United	8-1	Llanidloes Town
Merthyr Tydfil	1-2	Ammanford Town

Fourth Round Replay

Penmaenmawr	3-1	Druids United
Played at Llandudno		

Fifth Round

Chester	2-1	Bangor City
Penmaenmawr	0-0	Brymbo Steelworks
Pwllheli & District	0-3	Rhyl
Bethesda Athletic	0-1	Wrexham
Played at Wrexham		
Barry Town	0-3	Hereford United

85

Ammanford Town	0-5	Swansea Town
Played at Swansea		
Welshpool	0-4	Newport County
Cardiff City	8-0	Ebbw Vale

Fifth Round Replay

Brymbo Steelworks	1-0	Penmaenmawr

Sixth Round

Newport County	3-1	Swansea Town
Wrexham	1-3	Cardiff City
Brymbo Steelworks	0-8	Chester
Rhyl	2-2	Hereford United

Sixth Round Replay

Hereford United	4-1	Rhyl

Semi-finals

Chester	0-3	Cardiff City
Newport County	0-1	Hereford United

1968 WELSH CUP FINAL

1st leg

6th May 1968 at Edgar St, Hereford

Hereford United	0-2	Cardiff City
		Jones, King

Hereford United: Isaac, Page, Timms, Jones, Lambden, J Charles, McIntosh, Summerhayes, Hunter, Derrick, Frazer

Cardiff City: Davies, Carver, Ferguson, Dean, Murray, Harris, Jones, M Clarke, B Clark, Toshack, Lea

Referee: I P Jones (Trelewis)

Attendance: 5,422

2nd leg

16th May 1968 at Ninian Park, Cardiff

Cardiff City	4-1	Hereford United
Bean, Clarke, Own goal, Lea		Charles

Cardiff City: Davies, Carver, Ferguson, Clarke, Murray, Harris, Jones, Dean, King, Toshack, Lea

Hereford United: Isaac, Page, Timms, Jones, Lambden, J Charles, McIntosh, Summerhayes, Hunter, Derrick, Frazer

Referee: I P Jones (Trelewis)

Attendance: 6,036

1968/69 Welsh Cup

First Round

Glynceiriog	3-6	Johnstown RGA
British Celanese	0-4	Gresford Athletic
Wrexham YCOB	0-6	Coedpoeth SC
Rossett Villa	0-2	Cymau
Machynlleth	3-1	Towyn
Pontrhydfendigaid	2-1	Rhayader Town
Neath Athletic	0-1	Ferndale Athletic
Haverfordwest County	4-0	Tonrefail Welfare
Llanelli	0-2	Pembroke Borough
Cardiff Corinthians	4-2	Abercynon Athletic
Bridgend Town	5-0	Caerleon
Briton Ferry Athletic	1-5	Aberaman Athletic

Second Round

Mold Alexandra	3-0	Coedpoeth SC
Rhos Aelwyd	2-1	Cymau
Johnstown Recreation GA	2-2	Llay Welfare
Gresford Athletic	1-3	Denbigh Town
Llandrindod Wells	3-3	Berriew
Aberystwyth Town	3-0	Machynlleth
Welshpool	5-0	Pontrhydfendigaid
Barmouth & Dyffryn Utd	1-1	Newtown
Knighton Town	0-1	Llanidloes Town
Kington Town	5-0	Caersws Amateurs
Blaenau Ffestiniog FC	3-1	Caernarvon Town
Prestatyn Town	1-2	Colwyn Bay
Nantlle Vale	1-1	Queensferry Wanderers
Connah's Quay Nomads	4-0	Llandudno
Abergavenny Thursdays	0-0	Lovell's Athletic
Pembroke Borough	1-1	Bridgend Town
Haverfordwest County	2-3	Ferndale Athletic
Aberaman Athletic	1-4	South Wales Switchgear
Cardiff College of Education	1-1	Cardiff Corinthians

Second Round Replay

Llay Welfare	2-3	Johnstown Recreation GA
Berriew	3-5	Llandrindod Wells
Newtown	1-4	Barmouth & Dyffryn Utd
Queensferry Wanderers	0-2	Nantlle Vale
Lovell's Athletic	3-2	Abergavenny Thursdays
Bridgend Town	2-1	Pembroke Borough
Cardiff Corinthians	2-3	Cardiff College of Education

Third Round

Colwyn Bay	1-4	Connah's Quay Nomads
Holyhead Town	0-1	Oswestry Town
Bethesda Athletic	3-1	Nantlle Vale
Portmadoc	7-2	Blaenau Ffestiniog FC
Johnstown Recreation GA	0-5	Denbigh Town
Brymbo Steelworks	1-0	Mold Alexandra
Druids United	3-3	Rhos Aelwyd
Kington Town	0-3	Aberystwyth Town
Llandrindod Wells	2-6	Welshpool Town
Llanidloes Town	1-5	Barmouth & Dyffryn Utd
South Wales Switchgear	0-1	Bridgend Town
Barry Town	0-2	Ferndale Athletic

Cardiff College of Education	2-0	Ammanford Town
Ton Pentre	1-2	Lovell's Athletic

Third Round Replay

Rhos Aelwyd	4-1	Druids United

Fourth Round

Pwllheli & District	1-0	Denbigh Town
Connah's Quay Nomads	2-2	Portmadoc
Bethesda Athletic	1-1	Penmaenmawr
Oswestry Town	4-0	Rhos Aelwyd
Brymbo Steelworks	2-2	Rhyl
Cardiff College of Education	2-2	Welshpool
Aberystwyth Town	1-0	Barmouth & Dyffryn Utd
Lovell's Athletic	3-0	Ferndale Athletic
Merthyr Tydfil	0-0	Bridgend Town

Fourth Round Replays

Portmadoc	8-0	Connah's Quay Nomads
Penmaenmawr	0-2	Bethesda Athletic
Rhyl	2-1	Brymbo Steelworks
Welshpool	0-2	Cardiff College of Education
Bridgend Town	0-1	Merthyr Tydfil

Fifth Round

Portmadoc	2-0	Oswestry Town
Rhyl	0-3	Chester
Bangor City	2-2	Wrexham
Bethesda Athletic	3-0	Pwllheli & District
Hereford United	2-1	Cardiff College of Education
Swansea Town	0-0	Newport County
Lovell's Athletic	1-0	Merthyr Tydfil
Aberystwyth Town	0-3	Cardiff City

Fifth Round Replays

Wrexham	4-3	Bangor City
Newport County	0-0	Swansea Town

Fifth Round Second Replay

Swansea Town	2-1	Newport County

Sixth Round

Wrexham	1-1	Swansea Town
Lovell's Athletic	1-5	Chester
Played at Chester		
Cardiff City	6-0	Bethesda Athletic
Portmadoc	1-3	Hereford United

Sixth Round Replay

Swansea Town	2-1	Wrexham

Semi-finals

Swansea Town	1-0	Hereford United
Chester	0-2	Cardiff City

1969 WELSH CUP FINAL

1st leg

22nd April 1969 at the Vetch Field, Swansea

Swansea City	1-3	Cardiff City
H Williams		Toshack 2, Own goal

Swansea City: Hayes, Lawrence, Gomersall, C Slee, M Nurse, Hughes, Grey, Thomas, H Williams, A Williams, B Evans

Cardiff City: Davies, Derrett, Carver, King, Murray, Harris, Sharp, Clark, L Lea, J Toshack, Jones

Referee: L Callaghan (Merthyr)

Attendance: 10,207

2nd leg

29th April 1969 at Ninian Park, Cardiff

Cardiff City	2-0	Swansea City
Toshack, Lea		

Cardiff City: Davies, Derrett, Carver, King, Murray, Harris, Sharp, Clark, L Lea, J Toshack, Jones

Swansea City: Hayes, Lawrence, Gomersall, C Slee, M Nurse, Hughes, Grey, Thomas, H Williams, A Williams, B Evans

Referee: L Callaghan (Merthyr)

Attendance: 12,617

1969/70 Welsh Cup

First Round

Maesdre Athletic (w/o)	v	Glynceiriog (withdrew)
New Quay (withdrew)	v	Towyn
Kington Town	6-3	Rhayader Town
Wrockwardine Wood	2-1	Knighton Town
Machynlleth	3-1	Llandrindod Wells
Ton Pentre	3-1	Tonrefail Welfare
Seven Sisters	2-9	Neath Athletic
Played at Neath		
Llanelli	5-1	Port Talbot Athletic
Haverfordwest County	9-0	Morriston Town
Briton Ferry Athletic	0-2	Ammanford Town
Caerau Athletic	1-0	Clydach United
Aberaman	3-1	Cardiff Corinthians
Caerleon	3-2	Ebbw Vale
Ferndale Athletic	1-1	Cwmbran Town

First Round Replay

Cwmbran Town	1-2	Ferndale Athletic

Second Round

Chirk AAA	2-1	Coedpoeth SC
Mold Alexandra	1-2	Brymbo Steelworks
Maesdre Athletic	0-2	Gresford Athletic
Johnstown Recreation GA	0-5	Whitchurch Alport
Druids United	3-1	Rhos Aelwyd
Caersws Amateurs	2-1	Wrockwardine wood
Berriew	0-1	Newtown
Kington Town	0-3	Welshpool
Towyn	2-5	Llanidloes Town
Barmouth & Dyffryn Utd	5-1	Machynlleth
Flint Town United	1-1	Llandudno Borough
Colwyn Bay	1-4	Prestatyn Town
Blaenau Ffestiniog FC	6-2	Caernarvon Town
Queensferry Wanderers	4-3	Nantlle Vale
Abergavenny Thursdays	4-4	Ferndale Athletic
Neath Athletic	1-1	Aberaman Athletic
Ton Pentre	0-0	Haverfordwest County
Llanelli	3-0	Ammanford Town
Caerau Athletic	0-3	Caerleon

Second Round Replays

Llandudno Borough	1-0	Flint Town United
Ferndale Athletic	1-3	Abergavenny Thursday
Aberaman Athletic	3-2	Neath Athletic
Haverfordwest County	2-1	Ton Pentre

Third Round

Holyhead Town	0-2	Pwllheli & District
Queensferry Wanderers	1-7	Prestatyn Town
Llandudno Borough	2-1	Connah's Quay Nomads
Penmaenmawr	2-2	Blaenau Ffestiniog FC
Played at Blaenau Ffestininog		
Oswestry Town	3-2	Whitchurch Alport
Gresford Athletic	2-0	Brymbo Steelworks
Chirk AAA	7-2	Druids United
Barmouth & Dyffryn Utd	3-1	Newtown
Aberystwyth Town	2-1	Caersws Amateurs
Llanidloes Town	3-5	Welshpool
Barry Town	1-0	Abergavenny Thursdays
Llanelli	2-1	Caerleon
Haverfordwest County	1-0	Bridgend Town
Cardiff College of Education	4-0	Aberaman Athletic

Third Round Replay

Blaenau Ffestiniog FC	4-2	Penmaenmawr

Fourth Round

Portmadoc	0-4	Blaenau Ffestiniog FC
Chirk AAA	1-2	Llandudno Borough
Prestatyn Town	0-1	Gresford Athletic
Pwllheli & District	2-0	Rhyl
Bethesda Athletic	3-5	Oswestry Town
Barmouth & Dyffryn Utd	4-0	Haverfordwest County
Cardiff College of Education	1-1	Llanelli
Merthyr Tydfil	4-0	Welshpool
Barry Town	3-0	Aberystwyth Town

Fourth Round Replay

Llanelli	5-0	Cardiff Coll. of Education

Fifth Round

Blaenau Ffestiniog FC	0-1	Wrexham
Played at Wrexham		
Llandudno Borough	0-6	Chester
Played at Chester		
Pwllheli & District	0-2	Bangor City
Oswestry Town	6-0	Gresford Athletic
Newport County	2-2	Hereford United
Barry Town	0-4	Swansea City
Played at Swansea		
Cardiff City	6-1	Barmouth & Dyffryn Utd
Merthyr Tydfil	2-3	Llanelli

Fifth Round Replay

Hereford United	2-1	Newport County

Sixth Round

Cardiff City	3-0	Wrexham
Swansea City	8-0	Oswestry Town
Chester	3-1	Llanelli
Bangor City	1-2	Hereford United

Semi-finals

Cardiff City	2-2	Swansea City
Hereford United	3-3	Chester

Semi-final Replays

Swansea City	0-2	Cardiff City
Chester	3-0	Hereford United

1970 WELSH CUP FINAL

1st leg

8th May 1970 at Sealand Road, Chester

Chester	0-1	Cardiff City

Bird

Chester: T Carling, R Cheetham, N Edwards, B Ashworth, G Turner, M Sutton, A Tarbuck, T Bradbury, K Webber, D Draper, S McMillan, sub A Spence

Cardiff City: F Davies, D Carver, G Bell, M Sutton, D Murray, B Harris, P King, J Toshack, A Woodruff, B Clark, R Bird, sub L Lea

Referee: C Thomas (Treorchy)

Attendance: 3,087

2nd leg

13th May 1970 at Ninian Park, Cardiff

Cardiff City   4-0   Chester
Woodruff, Bird, Lea, Clark

Cardiff City: F Davies, D Carver, G Bell, M Sutton, D Murray, B Harris, P King, A Woodruff, L Lea, B Clark, R Bird

Chester: T Carling, R Cheetham, N Edwards, B Ashworth, G Turner, M Sutton, A Spence, A Tarbuck, K Webber, D Draper, S McMillan

Referee: C Thomas (Treorchy)

Attendance: 5,567

1970/71 Welsh Cup

First Round

Guilsfield Amateurs	3-7	Welshpool Amateurs
Machynlleth	1-0	Rhayader Town
Knighton Town	4-1	Llandrindod Wells
Caerleon	2-0	Cardiff Corinthians
Pembroke Borough	7-2	Briton Ferry Athletic
Cwmbran Town	1-0	Ebbw Vale
Milford United	1-0	Skewen Athletic
Tonrefail Welfare	2-4	Ferndale Athletic

Second Round

Coedpoeth SC	2-0	Flint Town United
Whitchurch Alport (withdrew)	v	Llay Welfare
Chirk AAA	4-4	Rhos Aelwyd
Barmouth & Dyffryn Utd	2-1	Knighton Town
Berriew	3-2	Welshpool
Welshpool Amateurs	0-1	Caersws Amateurs
Llanidloes Town	2-0	Machynlleth
Newtown	7-2	Towyn
Llandudno Swifts	1-2	Caernarvon Town
Played at Caernarvon		
Nantlle Vale	2-2	Prestatyn Town

Prestatyn Town were dismissed from the competition following a protest.

Pembroke Borough	1-2	Abergavenny Thursdays
Ferndale Athletic	6-0	Milford United
Cwmbran Town	0-2	Haverfordwest County
Ammanford Town	1-0	Ton Pentre
Bridgend Town (withdrew)		
Queensferry Wanderers (withdrew)		

Second Round Replay

Rhos Aelwyd	3-1	Chirk AAA

Third Round

Llandudno Borough	2-3	Blaenau Ffestiniog FC
Penmaenmawr	0-5	Connah's Quay Nomads
Caernarvon Town	3-3	Colwyn Bay
Nantlle Vale	1-5	Portmadoc
Bethesda Athletic	3-1	Pwllheli & District
Coedpoeth SC	1-2	Gresford Athletic
Oswestry Town	3-0	Rhos Aelwyd
Llay Welfare	1-1	Brymbo Steelworks
Aberystwyth Town	4-4	Barmouth & Dyffryn Utd
Berriew	0-0	Newtown
Llanidloes Town	3-2	Caersws Amateurs
Caerleon	3-6	Abergavenny Thursdays
Llanelli	1-0	Cardiff Coll. of Education
Ammanford Town	1-1	Ferndale Athletic

Third Round Replays

Colwyn Bay	4-3	Caernarvon Town
Brymbo Steelworks	4-1	Llay Welfare
Barmouth & Dyffryn Utd	2-0	Aberystwyth Town
Newtown	3-1	Berriew
Ferndale Athletic	0-3	Ammanford Town

Fourth Round

Brymbo Steelworks	0-2	Blaenau Ffestiniog FC
Colwyn Bay	0-5	Portmadoc
Bethesda Athletic	4-2	Connah's Quay Nomads
Oswestry Town	7-2	Holyhead Town
Rhyl	0-0	Gresford Athletic
Merthyr Tydfil	3-1	Abergavenny Thursdays
Barmouth & Dyffryn Utd	0-4	Llanelli
Ammanford Town	8-0	Newtown
Llanidloes Town	0-0	Haverfordwest County

Fourth Round Replays

Gresford Athletic	2-2	Rhyl
Played at Wrexham		
Haverfordwest County	4-5	Llanidloes Town

Fourth Round Second Replay

Rhyl	3-0	Gresford Athletic
Played at Wrexham		

Fifth Round

Blaenau Ffestiniog FC	2-2	Oswestry Town
Portmadoc	3-6	Wrexham
Played at Wrexham		
Bethesda Athletic	1-1	Bangor City
Chester	1-1	Rhyl
Hereford United	2-2	Merthyr Tydfil
Llanidloes Town	2-4	Swansea City
Newport County	1-1	Cardiff City
Llanelli	1-1	Ammanford Town

Fifth Round Replays

Oswestry Town	3-0	Blaenau Ffestiniog FC
Bangor City	6-3	Bethesda Athletic
Rhyl	0-2	Chester
Merthyr Tydfil	1-0	Hereford United
Cardiff City	4-0	Newport County
Ammanford Town	3-2	Llanelli

Sixth Round

Merthyr Tydfil	0-1	Wrexham
Chester	2-1	Swansea City
Cardiff City	5-0	Bangor City
Ammanford Town	0-0	Oswestry Town

Sixth Round Replay

Oswestry Town	5-1	Ammanford Town

Semi-finals

Cardiff City	0-0	Chester
Oswestry Town	0-2	Wrexham

Semi-final Replay

Chester	1-2	Cardiff City

1971 WELSH CUP FINAL

1st leg

10th May 1971 at the Racecourse, Wrexham

Wrexham	0-1	Cardiff City

Woodruff

Wrexham: D Gaskell, M Evans, T Vansittart, B Ashcroft, E May, A Griffiths (S Mason), I Moir, R Park, R J Smith, A Kinsey, A Provan

Cardiff City: J Eadie, D Carver, G Bell, M Sutton, D Murray, L Phillips, P King, I Gibson, A Warboys (B Clark), A Woodruff, R Bird

Referee: R Jones (Deganwy)

Attendance: 14,101

2nd leg

12th May 1971 at Ninian Park, Cardiff

Cardiff City	3-1	Wrexham

Gibson 2, Bird   Smith

Cardiff City: J Eadie, D Carver, G Bell, M Sutton, D Murray, L Phillips, P King, I Gibson, B Clark, A Woodruff, R Bird

Wrexham: D Gaskell, S Mason, T Vansittart, B Ashcroft, E May, M Evans, I Moir, R Park, R J Smith, A Kinsey (S Ingle), A Provan

Referee: R Jones (Deganwy)

Attendance: 7,000

1971/72 Welsh Cup

First Round

B.I.C.C.Wrexham	6-2	British Celanese (Wrexham)
Rhayader Town	0-6	Bridgnorth Town
Knighton Town	6-1	Llanwyddyn
Llansantffraid	0-1	Llandrindod Wells
Welshpool Amateurs	4-3	Machynlleth
Cwmbran Town	1-0	Cardiff Corinthians
Briton Ferry Athletic	1-2	Milford United
Pembroke Borough	5-1	Tonyrefail Welfare
Caerleon	4-1	Cwmbran Catholics
Ebbw Vale	3-1	Seven Sisters

Second Round

Denbigh Town	5-7	Whitchurch Alport
Llay Welfare	2-2	Brymbo Steelworks
Rhos Aelwyd	2-1	Chirk AAA
Flint Town United (withdrew)	v	Cymau
Mold Alexandra	0-5	Gresford Athletic
Coedpoeth SC	1-3	B.I.C.C. Wrexham
Llandrindod Wells	4-3	Barmouth & Dyffryn Utd
Knighton Town	1-2	Welshpool Amateurs
Berriew	2-3	Towyn
Llanidloes Town	0-2	Bridgnorth Town
Aberystwyth Town	4-2	Caersws Amateurs
Newtown	2-8	Welshpool
Hawarden Rangers	3-1	Caernarvon Town
Holyhead Town	6-1	Llandudno Swifts
Nantlle Vale	2-2	Llandudno Borough
Rhos United	1-2	Penmaenmawr
Pwllheli & District	2-1	Prestatyn Town
Ton Pentre	2-1	Pembroke Borough
Bridgend Town	2-2	Cwmbran Town
Caerleon	4-1	Milford United
Haverfordwest County	1-0	Ferndale Athletic
Ebbw Vale	3-2	Abergavenny Thursdays

Second Round Replays

Brymbo Steelworks	0-1	Llay Welfare
Llandudno Borough	0-2	Nantlle Vale
Cwmbran Town	1-0	Bridgend Town

Third Round

Hawarden Rangers	3-3	Blaenau Ffestiniog FC
Nantlle Vale	3-0	Portmadoc

Played at Portmadog. The match was abandoned after 80 minutes as Portmadoc had been reduced to 6 players. Nantlle Vale progressed to the next round.

Pwllheli & District	0-0	Connah's Quay Nomads

The match was abandoned after 4 minutes due to bad weather.

Colwyn Bay	3-2	Penmaenmawr
Holyhead Town	0-0	Bethesda Athletic
Llay Welfare	1-0	Cymau
B.I.C.C. Wrexham	0-2	Whitchurch Alport
Gresford Athletic	4-3	Rhos Aelwyd
Welshpool	5-2	Llandrindod Wells
Aberystwyth Town	4-1	Welshpool Amateurs
Towyn	1-6	Bridgnorth Town
Ebbw Vale	3-0	Caerleon
Ammanford Town	1-1	Cwmbran Town

The match was abandoned during the second half due to a waterlogged pitch.

Haverfordwest County	3-1	Barry Town

The match was abandoned after 45 minutes due to a waterlogged pitch.

Cardiff University	1-1	Llanelli
Cardiff College of Education	3-2	Ton Pentre

Third Round Replays

Blaenau Ffestiniog FC	1-0	Hawarden Rangers
Pwllheli & District	1-1	Connah's Quay Nomads
Bethesda Athletic	0-2	Holyhead Town
Ammanford Town	6-1	Cwmbran Town
Haverfordwest County	3-0	Barry Town
Llanelli	3-0	Cardiff University

Third Round Second Replay

Connah's Quay Nomads	0-2	Pwllheli & District

Fourth Round

Bangor City	5-1	Gresford Athletic
Whitchurch Alport	0-4	Blaenau Ffestiniog FC
Llay Welfare	0-7	Rhyl
Colwyn Bay	2-1	Nantlle Vale
Pwllheli & District	2-2	Holyhead Town
Bridgnorth Town	4-0	Cardiff College of Education
Ebbw Vale	4-2	Welshpool
Merthyr Tydfil	1-1	Ammanford Town
Haverfordwest County	1-2	Llanelli
Hereford United	2-2	Aberystwyth Town

Fourth Round Replays

Holyhead Town	1-0	Pwllheli & District
Ammanford Town	0-0	Merthyr Tydfil
Aberystwyth Town	1-0	Hereford United

Fourth Round Second Replay

Merthyr Tydfil	1-2	Ammanford Town

Fifth Round

Holyhead Town	0-0	Chester
Bangor City	5-1	Colwyn Bay
Wrexham	2-0	Oswestry Town
Blaenau Ffestiniog FC	0-1	Rhyl
Aberystwyth Town	2-0	Ammanford Town
Swansea City	0-2	Cardiff City
Newport County	3-1	Ebbw Vale
Bridgnorth Town	1-5	Llanelli

Fifth Round Replay

Chester	7-2	Holyhead Town

Sixth Round

Llanelli	0-1	Cardiff City
Rhyl	2-1	Chester
Bangor City	1-2	Newport County
Wrexham	6-2	Aberystwyth Town

Semi-finals

Rhyl	1-2	Cardiff City
Wrexham	2-0	Newport County

1972 WELSH CUP FINAL

1st leg

8th May 1972 at the Racecourse, Wrexham

Wrexham	2-1	Cardiff City
Whittle, Own goal		Woodruff

Wrexham: B Lloyd, S Mason, Fogg, G Davies, E May, M Evans, B Tinnion, G Whittle, R J Smith, A Kinsey, M Thomas, sub B Ashcroft

Cardiff City: W Irwin, D Carver, G Bell, W Kellock, R Morgan, L Phillips, T Villars, B Clark, I Gibson (A Woodruff), A Warboys, P King

Referee: W J Reynolds (Swansea)

Attendance: 6,984

2nd leg

12th May 1972 at Ninian Park, Cardiff

Cardiff City	1-1	Wrexham
Foggon		Kinsey

Cardiff City: W Irwin, D Carver, G Bell, M Sutton, D Murray, L Phillips, A Foggon, B Clark, P King, A Warboys, T Villars, sub A Woodruff

Wrexham: B Lloyd, S Mason, D Fogg, G Davies, E May, M Evans, B Tinnion, G Whittle, B Ashcroft, A Kinsey, A Griffiths (R J Smith)

Referee: W J Reynolds (Swansea)

Attendance: 6,508

1972/73 Welsh Cup

First Round

Holyhead Town	3-2	Bethesda Athletic
Rhos United	6-0	Llandudno
Colwyn Bay	3-0	Caernarfon Town
Nantlle Vale	2-1	Portmadoc
Pwllheli & District	2-3	Barmouth & Dyffryn Utd
Gresford Athletic	5-3	Mold Alexandra
Brymbo Steelworks	3-1	Whitchurch Alport
Rhos Aelwyd	0-2	Johnstown Recreation GA
Llay Welfare	1-1	Chirk AAA
Denbigh Town	2-1	Connah's Quay Nomads
Brierley Hill Alliance	3-2	Bridgnorth Town
UCW Aberystwyth (withdrew)	v	Llanwddyn
Llanidloes Town	1-0	Llandrindod Wells
Kington Town	2-2	Rhayader Town
Knighton Town	2-0	Caersws Amateurs
Berriew	1-4	Newtown
Abermule	1-1	Welshpool Amateurs
Welshpool	2-1	Towyn
Tonyrefail Welfare	1-2	Cardiff Corinthians
Barry Town	2-1	Cardiff Coll. of Education

Ebbw Vale	3-0	Abergavenny Thursdays
Ammanford Town	4-4	Pembroke Borough
Briton Ferry Athletic	1-1	Haverfordwest County
Pontardawe Athletic	4-0	Skewen Athletic
Bridgend Town	2-0	Port Talbot Athletic
Cwmbran Town	4-2	Cwmbran Celtic
Spencer Works Newport	3-2	Caerleon
Ferndale Athletic	2-3	Ton Pentre

First Round Replays

Chirk AAA	4-0	Llay Welfare
Rhayader Town	0-4	Kington Town
Welshpool Amateurs	3-0	Abermule
Pembroke Borough	2-1	Ammanford Town
Haverfordwest County	2-1	Briton Ferry Athletic

Second Round

Blaenau Ffestiniog FC	2-1	Nantlle Vale
Gresford Athletic	0-0	Rhos United
Colwyn Bay	1-2	Holyhead Town
Brymbo Steelworks	0-0	Denbigh Town
Chirk AAA	3-1	Johnstown Recreation GA
Welshpool	1-1	Kington Town
Welshpool Amateurs	1-3	Barmouth & Dyffryn Utd
Played at Barmouth		
Brierley Hill Alliance	8-0	Newtown
Aberystwyth Town	11-1	Llanwyddyn
Llanidloes Town	3-2	Knighton Town
Pembroke Borough	2-1	Llanelli
Bridgend Town	4-0	Ebbw Vale
Barry Town	4-1	Spencer Works Newport
Pontardawe Athletic	3-2	Ton Pentre
Haverfordwest County	3-4	Cardiff Corinthians
Cwmbran Town	1-2	Merthyr Tydfil

Second Round Replays

Rhos United	2-5	Gresford Athletic
Denbigh Town	2-1	Brymbo Steelworks
Kington Town	2-3	Welshpool

Third Round

Gresford Athletic	0-9	Bangor City
Played at Bangor		
Barmouth & Dyffryn Utd	1-5	Blaenau Ffestiniog FC
Denbigh Town	2-0	Chirk AAA
Brierley Hill Alliance	0-2	Welshpool
Aberystwyth Town	3-2	Llanidloes
Barry Town	1-2	Merthyr Tydfil
Pembroke Borough	0-0	Cardiff Corinthians
Bridgend Town	3-2	Pontardawe Athletic
Oswestry Town	v	Holyhead Town
Holyhead failed to appear and the tie was awarded to Oswestry Town.		

Third Round Replay

Cardiff Corinthians	1-4	Pembroke Borough

Fourth Round

Chester	1-0	Wrexham
Welshpool	1-0	Blaenau Ffestiniog FC
Oswestry Town	4-0	Denbigh Town
Rhyl	2-2	Bangor City
Aberystwyth Town	1-7	Cardiff City
Bridgend Town	0-4	Merthyr Tydfil
Swansea City	0-0	Newport County
Hereford United	6-1	Pembroke Borough

Fourth Round Replays

Bangor City	2-0	Rhyl
Newport County	3-0	Swansea City

Fifth Round

Hereford United	0-0	Merthyr Tydfil
Welshpool	1-1	Chester
Oswestry Town	1-8	Bangor City
Newport County	1-3	Cardiff City

Fifth Round Replays

Merthyr Tydfil	0-3	Hereford United
Played at Hereford		
Chester	1-0	Welshpool

Semi-finals

Bangor City	2-0	Hereford United
Chester	0-1	Cardiff City

1973 WELSH CUP FINAL

1st leg

4th April 1973 at Farrar Road, Bangor

Bangor City	1-0	Cardiff City

Marsden

Bangor City: Clarke, K Williams, Jones, A Smith, R Hughes, D Atherton, C Penrose, Crossley, Marsden, J Hughes, Brodie, sub Nicklin

Cardiff City: W Irwin, P Dwyer, G Bell, A Couch, D Murray, L Phillips, W Kellock, A McCulloch, D Showers, A Woodruff, W Anderson, sub D Powell

Referee: J D Williams (Rhyl)

Attendance: 5,005

2nd leg

11th April 1973 at Ninian Park, Cardiff

Cardiff City	5-0	Bangor City

Bell 3, Reece, Phillips

Cardiff City: W Irwin, P Dwyer, G Bell, A Larmour, D Murray, D Powell, G Reece, A McCulloch, L Phillips, Vincent, W Anderson, sub D Showers

Bangor City: Clarke, Crossley, Jones, K Williams, R Hughes, D Atherton, C Penrose, Nicklin, Marsden, J Hughes, Brodie, sub A Smith

Referee: J D Williams (Rhyl)

Attendance: 4,679

1973/74 Welsh Cup

First Round

Llandudno	1-7	Nantlle Vale
Blaenau Ffestiniog FC	5-0	Caernarvon Town
Pwllheli & District	2-1	Rhyl
Colwyn Bay	0-1	Bethesda Athletic
Porthmadog	8-1	Rhos United
Llandudno Swifts	1-4	Holyhead Town
Buckley Wanderers	1-1	Connah's Quay Nomads
Brymbo Steelworks	6-1	Llay Welfare
Gresford Athletic	4-1	Rhos Aelwyd

Following a protest, Gresford were found to have fielded an ineligible player and falsified their teamsheet so were dismissed from the competition. Rhos Aelwyd progressed to the next round.

Llanwyddyn	2-2	Chirk AAA
Mold Alexandra	2-1	Rhosddu
Caersws Amateurs	5-1	GKN Sports
Llanidloes Town	4-3	Towyn
Aberystwyth Town (w/o)	v	Machynlleth (withdrew)
GKN Sankey	1-2	Bridgnorth Town
Ebbw Vale	0-7	Worcester City

Played at Worcester

Merthyr Tydfil	5-0	Tonyrefail Welfare
Barry Town	0-1	Caerleon
Bridgend Town	3-1	Cardiff College of Education
Cwmbran Town	1-1	Cardiff Corinthians
Ferndale Athletic	3-1	Cwmbran Celtic
Ton Pentre	2-1	Spencer Works Newport
Ammanford Town	0-0	BP Llandarcy
Berriew	2-6	Welshpool
Dolgellau Athletic	1-4	Llansantffraid
Welshpool Amateurs	7-2	Newtown
Llandrindod Wells (w/o)	v	Kington Town (withdrew)
Knighton Town	5-0	Rhayader Town
Brierley Hill Alliance	3-1	Whitchurch Allport
Stourbridge	2-1	Kidderminster Harriers
Haverfordwest County	3-1	Llanelli
Pontardawe Athletic	0-2	Briton Ferry Athletic
Pembroke Borough	6-1	Skewen Athletic

First Round Replays

Connah's Quay Nomads	0-3	Buckley Wanderers
Chirk AAA	7-0	Llanwyddyn

Chirk AAA were found to have fielded ineligible players in replay amd Llanwddyn were duly awarded the tie.

Cardiff Corinthians	2-4	Cwmbran Town
BP Llandarcy	2-2	Ammanford Town

BP Llandarcy won 5-4 on penalties.

Second Round

Oswestry Town	1-0	Nantlle Vale
Blaenau Ffestiniog FC	1-1	Pwllheli & District
Buckley Wanderers	0-0	Rhos Alewyd
Porthmadog	9-2	Holyhead Town
Bethesda Athletic	5-0	Llanwyddyn
Brymbo Steelworks	2-0	Mold Alexandra
Llanidloes Town	3-1	Llandrindod Wells
Caersws Amateurs	1-3	Aberystwyth Town
Welshpool Amateurs	4-0	Llansantffraid
Worcester City	7-2	Knighton Town
Welshpool	1-0	Brierley Hill Athletic
Bridgnorth Town	0-2	Stourbridge
Caerleon	1-4	Ton Pentre
Merthyr Tydfil	5-2	Cwmbran Town
Pembroke Borough	1-1	Ferndale Athletic
Haverfordwest County	3-2	Bridgend Town
BP Llandarcy	1-2	Briton Ferry Athletic

Second Round Replays

Pwllheli & District	2-5	Blaenau Ffestiniog FC
Rhos Aelwyd	1-0	Buckley Wanderers

Rhos Aelwyd were subsequently disqualified for fielding an inegigible player so Buckley Wanderers progressed.

Ferndale Athletic	0-1	Pembroke Borough

Third Round

Welshpool Amateurs	0-2	Bethesda Athletic
Porthmadog	0-2	Shrewsbury Town
Aberystwyth Town	1-2	Blaenau Ffestiniog FC
Buckley Wanderers	1-1	Oswestry Town

Played at Oswestry

Welshpool	3-1	Brymbo Steelworks
Llanidloes Town	3-3	Ton Pentre
Briton Ferry Athletic	0-3	Worcester City

Played at Worcester

Stourbridge	6-0	Haverfordwest County
Merthyr Tydfil	2-1	Pembroke Borough

Third Round Replay

Oswestry Town	1-0	Buckley Wanderers
Ton Pentre	4-2	Llanidloes Town

Fourth Round

Blaenau Ffestiniog FC	0-0	Wrexham

Played at Wrexham The match was abandoned after 27 minutes due to fog.

Shrewsbury Town	5-0	Welshpool
Chester	2-1	Bethesda Athletic
Worcester City	2-1	Hereford United
Swansea	1-2	Stourbridge
Cardiff City	1-0	Ton Pentre
Newport County	1-0	Merthyr Tydfil
Bangor City	2-2	Oswestry Town

Fourth Round Replays

Blaenau Ffestiniog FC	3-6	Wrexham

Played at Wrexham

Oswestry Town	1-0	Bangor City

Fifth Round

Stourbridge	5-2	Worcester City
Newport County	0-1	Shrewsbury Town
Oswestry Town	1-3	Cardiff City
Wrexham	1-0	Chester

Semi-finals

Wrexham	1-2	Stourbridge
Shrewsbury Town	1-2	Cardiff City

1974 WELSH CUP FINAL

1st leg

24th April 1974 at the War Memorial Ground, Stourbridge

Stourbridge 0-1 Cardiff City
Showers

Stourbridge: Moore, Richards, Taylor, Pridgeon, Green, J Davies, McGrath, Bates, Haywood, J Chambers, Booth, sub Saint

Cardiff City: W Irwin, A Larmour, F Pethard, C Charles, D Murray, R Morgan, J Farrington, G Smith, J Whitham, D Showers, A Woodruff, sub J Impey

Referee: I P Jones (Treharris)

Attendance: 5,726

2nd leg

24th April 1974 at Ninian Park, Cardiff

Cardiff City 1-0 Stourbridge
Reece

Cardiff City: R Healey, P Dwyer, F Pethard C Charles, R Morgan, T Villars, G Reece, Vincent, L Phillips, J Impey, W Anderson, sub D Showers

Stourbridge: Moore, Richards, Taylor, Pridgeon, Green, J Davies, McGrath, Bates, Haywood, J Chambers, Booth, sub Saint

Referee: I P Jones (Treharris)

Attendance: 4,000

1974/75 Welsh Cup

Qualifying Round

Lex XI	0-1	Buckley Rovers
Bala Town	5-2	New Broughton
Rhyl Wanderers	1-2	Point of Ayr
Flint Town United	3-1	Hawarden Rangers
Brecon Corinthians	4-2	Aberaman
Cardiff College of Education	1-3	Pontardawe Athletic
Tredomen Works	0-0	Caerau Athletic

Qualifying Round Replay

Caerau Athletic	7-5	Tredomen Works

First Round

Nantlle Vale	3-2	Colwyn Bay
Caernarvon Town	9-0	Holyhead Town
Bethesda Athletic	1-5	Porthmadog
Rhos United	0-2	Pwllheli & District
Played at Pwllheli		
Blaenau Ffestiniog FC	1-6	Rhyl
Point of Ayr	4-2	Connah's Quay Nomads
Rhosddu	0-1	Brymbo Steelworks
Llay Welfare	1-1	Buckley Wanderers
Druids United	1-3	Mold Alexandra
Rhos Aelwyd	1-2	Bala Town
Flint Town United	0-1	Buckley Rovers
Gresford Athletic	3-4	Chirk AAA
Welshpool	0-2	Newtown
Towyn	2-2	Llanidloes Town
Llanwyddyn	0-3	Llanfair Caereinion
Caersws	5-2	Berriew
Machynlleth	0-12	Aberystwyth Town
Rhayader Town	1-2	Llandrindod Wells
Kington Town	2-4	Knighton Town
Worcester City	0-1	Kidderminster Harriers
GKN Sankey	1-0	Bridgnorth Town
Caerleon	0-1	Everwarm Bridgend
Ebbw Vale	3-6	Ferndale Athletic
Played at Ferndale		
Pontardawe Athletic	2-1	Tonyrefail Welfare
Cardiff Corinthians	2-1	Cwmbran Town
Caerau Athletic	3-0	Brecon Corinthians
Merthyr Tydfil	0-4	Ton Pentre
Sully	0-1	Barry Town
Pembroke Borough	1-0	Ammanford Town
Briton Ferry Athletic	4-2	Haverfordwest County
Llanelli	5-0	BP Llandarcy

First Round Replays

Buckley Wanderers	1-0	Llay Welfare
Llanidloes Town	3-0	Towyn

Second Round

Mold Alexandra	0-3	Porthmadog
Played at Porthmadog		
Bala Town	1-0	Point of Ayr
Chirk AAA	4-4	Buckley Rovers
Nantlle Vale	1-1	Rhyl
Buckley Wanderers	0-2	Caernarvon Town
Pwllheli & District	4-0	Brymbo Steelworks
Llanidloes Town	3-1	Llanfair Caereinon
Knighton Town	3-0	Caersws
Oswestry Town	2-0	Llandrindod Wells
GKN Sankey	0-4	Kidderminster Harriers
Aberystwyth Town	1-2	Newtown
Pembroke Borough	0-1	Ferndale Athletic
Briton Ferry Athletic	4-1	Llanelli
Caerau Athletic	0-3	Barry Town
Cardiff Corinithians	1-0	Pontardawe Athletic
Ton Pentre	2-2	Everwarm Bridgend

Second Round Replays

Buckley Rovers	4-2	Chirk AAA
Rhyl	3-1	Nantlle Vale
Everwarm Bridgend	3-1	Ton Pentre

Third Round

Oswestry Town	1-0	Caernarfon Town
Rhyl	8-1	Newtown
Pwllheli & District	0-1	Bangor City

Buckley Rovers	0-3	Porthmadog
Played at Porthmadog		
Llanidloes Town	1-0	Bala Town
Cardiff Corinthians	2-0	Knighton Town
Everwarm Bridgend	2-2	Briton Ferry Athletic
Hereford United	1-0	Barry Town
Ferndale Athletic	2-4	Kidderminster Harriers

Third Round Replay

Briton Ferry Athletic	3-1	Everwarm Bridgend

Fourth Round

Shrewsbury Town	9-0	Llanidloes Town
Bangor City	3-2	Porthmadog
Rhyl	0-2	Wrexham
Chester	1-3	Oswestry Town
Stourbridge	2-2	Newport County
Cardiff City	2-0	Hereford United
Briton Ferry Athletic	5-4	Cardiff Corinthians
Kidderminster Harriers	0-0	Swansea City

Fourth Round Replays

Newport County	5-1	Stourbridge
Swansea City	3-0	Kidderminster Harriers

Fifth Round

Cardiff City	4-0	Oswestry Town
Wrexham	8-0	Briton Ferry Athletic
Newport County	1-1	Swansea City
Shrewsbury Town	1-1	Bangor City

Fifth Round Replays

Swansea City	1-2	Newport County
Bangor City	0-1	Shrewsbury Town

Semi-finals

Wrexham	2-1	Shrewsbury Town
Newport County	0-1	Cardiff City

1975 WELSH CUP FINAL

1st leg

5th May 1975 at the Racecourse, Wrexham

Wrexham	2-1	Cardiff City
Tinnion, Lyons		*Buchanan*

Wrexham: B Lloyd, Jones, D Fogg, M Evans, B Scott, Gareth Davies, B Tinnion, M Sutton, B Ashcroft, J Lyons, G Whittle, sub Geoff Davies

Cardiff City: W Irwin, B Attley, F Pethard, J Buchanan, K Pontin, A Larmour, D Giles, P Dwyer, Rees, J McClelland, W Anderson, sub T Villars

Referee: W J Gow (Swansea)

Attendance: 6,862

2nd leg

12th May 1975 at Ninian Park, Cardiff

Cardiff City	1-3	Wrexham
Reece		*Whittle, Ashcroft 2*

Cardiff City: W Irwin, B Attley, F Pethard, J Buchanan, K Pontin, A Larmour, T Villars, P Dwyer, D Showers, J McClelland, W Anderson, sub G Reece

Wrexham: B Lloyd, Jones, D Fogg, M Evans, B Scott, Gareth Davies, B Tinnion, M Sutton, B Ashcroft, M Thomas, A Griffiths, sub Geoff Davies

Referee: W J Gow (Swansea)

Attendance: 3,280

1975/76 Welsh Cup

Qualifying Round

Druids United	6-0	Hawarden Rangers
Rhosddu	0-1	Courtaulds Greenfield
Machynlleth	0-6	Berriew
Played at Berriew		
Montgomery Town	3-2	Guilsfield United

First Round

Holyhead Town (withdrew)	v	Portmadog (w/o)
Pwllheli & District	1-2	Flint Town United
The match was abandoned after 55 minutes.		
Nantlle Vale	1-2	Bethesda Athletic
Blaenau Ffestiniog FC	1-1	Prestatyn Town
Point of Ayr	1-1	Caernarvon Town
Colwyn Bay	3-1	Rhos United
Mold Alexandra	1-3	Chirk AAA
Welshpool	4-1	Connah's Quay Nomads
Gresford Athletic	6-1	Buckley Wanderers
Bala Town	3-1	Ruthin FC
Brymbo Steelworks	2-2	Courtaulds Greenfield
Llay Welfare	1-0	Druids United
Berriew	2-3	Llanidloes Town
Montgomery Town	0-2	Towyn
Llandrindod Wells	1-2	Newtown
Llanfair Caereinion	1-1	Aberystwyth Town
Talgarth	3-1	Rhayader Town
GKN Sankey	0-1	Knighton Town
Worcester City	2-2	Brierley Hill Alliance
Bridgnorth Town	1-1	Kidderminster Harriers
Tonyrefail Welfare	2-3	Cardiff Corinthians
Ebbw Vale	2-0	Caerau Athletic
Caerleon	2-1	Aberaman Athletic
Spencer Works Newport	0-2	Cardiff College of Education
Cwmbran Town	0-1	Merthyr Tydfil
Pontardawe Athletic	1-2	Ton Pentre

Sully	1-1	Everwarm Bridgend
Ferndale Athletic	3-1	Cwmbran Celtic
Barry Town	2-0	Pontllanfraith
Llanelli	1-0	Milford United
BP Llandarcy	0-4	Ammanford Town
Pembroke Borough	0-1	Haverfordwest County

First Round Replays

Pwllheli & District	2-2	Flint Town United
Prestatyn Town	2-3	Blaenau Ffestiniog FC
Caernarvon Town	1-0	Point of Ayr
Courtaulds Greenfield	3-2	Brymbo Steelworks
Aberystwyth Town	1-0 (aet)	Llanfair Caereinion
Brierley Hill Alliance	1-3	Worcester City
Kidderminster Harriers	5-2	Bridgnorth Town
Everwarm Bridgend	1-2	Sully

First Round Second Replay

Flint Town United	4-3	Pwllheli & District

Second Round

Chirk AAA	2-6	Rhyl
Played at Porthmadog		
Llay Welfare	1-2	Blaenau Ffestiniog FC
Caernarvon Town	1-1	Bala Town
Gresford Athletic	1-4	Bethesda Athletic
Colwyn Bay	2-3	Courtaulds (Greenfield)
Porthmadog	3-1	Flint Town United
Kidderminster Harriers	1-1	Newtown
Oswestry Town	2-0	Welshpool
Knighton Town	0-1	Worcester City
Llanidloes Town	3-0	Towyn
Stourbridge	5-0	Aberystwyth Town
Sully	3-0	Caerleon
Cardiff Corinthians	4-2	Briton Ferry Athletic
Llanelli	3-4	Haverfordwest County
Ton Pentre	4-2	Merthyr Tydfil
Ebbw Vale	0-2	Barry Town
Cardiff College of Education	5-1	Ammanford Town
Talgarth	1-2	Ferndale Athletic

Second Round Replays

Bala Town	7-3	Caernarvon Town
Courtaulds Greenfield	3-2	Colwyn Bay
Newtown	0-3	Kidderminster Harriers

Third Round

Llanidloes Town	6-1	Bangor City
Oswestry Town	1-2	Porthmadog
Bala Town	0-3	Courtaulds Greenfield
Bethesda Athletic	2-2	Rhyl
Blaenau Ffestiniog FC	1-1	Kidderminster Harriers
The match was abandoned after 17 minutes.		
Cardiff College of Education	1-1	Worcester City
Played at Worcester		
Stourbridge	1-2	Hereford United
Cardiff Corinthians	4-1	Haverfordwest County
Ferndale Athletic	1-1	Barry Town
Ton Pentre	2-5	Sully

Third Round Replays

Rhyl	5-1	Bethesda Athletic
Blaenau Ffestiniog FC	2-2	Kidderminster Harriers
Worcester City	0-0 (aet)	Cardiff College of Education
Played at Worcester		
Worcester City won 4-2 on penalties.		
Barry Town	2-3 (aet)	Ferndale Athletic
The scoreline after 90 minutes was 1-1.		

Third Round Second Replay

Kidderminster Harriers	3-2	Blaenau Ffestiniog FC

Fourth Round

Chester	8-1	Kidderminster Harriers
Courtaulds Greenfield	0-5	Shrewsbury Town
Rhyl	0-2	Porthmadog
Wrexham	8-0	Llanidloes Town
Worcester City	4-0	Ferndale Athletic
Newport County	1-2	Hereford United
Sully	0-5	Cardiff City
Swansea City	6-0	Cardiff Corinthians

Fifth Round

Cardiff City	1-1	Swansea City
Wrexham	0-0	Chester
Porthmadog	0-4	Hereford United
Played at Hereford		
Worcester City	2-2	Shrewsbury Town

Fifth Round Replays

Swansea City	0-3	Cardiff City
Chester	2-1	Wrexham
Shrewsbury Town	3-0	Worcester City

Semi-finals

Hereford United	1-1	Shrewsbury Town
Chester	0-0	Cardiff City

Semi-finals Replays

Shrewsbury Town	1-1 (aet)	Hereford United
Hereford United won 5-4 on penalties		
Cardiff City	1-0	Chester

1976 WELSH CUP FINAL

1st leg

29th April 1976 at Ninian Park, Cardiff

Cardiff City	2-2	Hereford United

The match was declared void after Spiring, the scorer of both of Hereford United's goals, was ruled to be ineligible to play. A replay was ordered.

1st leg Replay

18th May 1976 at Edgar Street, Hereford

Hereford United	3-3	Cardiff City
Davey, Paine, McNeil		Evans, Dwyer 2

Hereford United: K Charlton, S Emery, A Byrne, W Tucker, J Galley, J Lindsay, T Paine, L Briley, S Davey, D McNeil, R Carter

Cardiff City: R Healey, F Pethard, C Charles, D Giles, P Dwyer, A Larmour, P Sayer, D Livermore, A Evans, B Clark, W Anderson

Referee: C Thomas (Treorchy)

Attendance: 3,709

2nd leg

19th May 1976 at Ninian Park, Cardiff

Cardiff City	3-2	Hereford United
Pethard, Clark, Evans		Lindsay, Byrne

Cardiff City: W Irwin, F Pethard, C Charles, D Giles, P Dwyer, A Larmour, P Sayer, D Livermore, A Evans, B Clark, W Anderson

Hereford United: K Charlton, S Emery, S Ritchie, W Tucker, J Galley, J Lindsay, T Paine, D Tyler, S Davey, D McNeil, R Carter, S Byrne

Referee: C Thomas (Treorchy)

Attendance: 2,648

1976/77 Welsh Cup

Qualifying Round

Pilkingtons St Asaph	5-0	Courtaulds Flint
Burntwood & Drury	5-1	BICC Wrexham
New Broughton (w/o)	v	Coedpoeth SC (withdrew)
Llanfair Caereinion	1-1	Caersws
Llanfechain	1-1	Llanfyllin Town
Treharris Athletic	4-6	Morriston Town
Afan Lido	3-0	Seven Sisters
Brecon Corinthians	4-3	Aberaman Athletic

Qualifying Round Replays

Caersws	1-0	Llanfair Caereinion
Llanfyllin Town	2-1	Llanfechain

First Round

Colwyn Bay	1-2	Nantlle Vale
Point of Ayr	6-1	Llandudno Swifts
Holyhead Town	1-1	Blaenau Ffestiniog FC
Prestatyn Town (withdrew)	v	Caernarvon Town (w/o)
Courtaulds Greenfield	4-1	Denbigh Town
Pilkingtons St Asaph	1-2	Rhos United
Pwllheli & District	6-1	Flint Town United
Rhos Aelwyd	1-1	Ruthin FC
Bala Town	2-1	Buckley Wanderers
Burntwood & Drury	1-2	Gresford Athletic
Druids United	1-1	Connah's Quay Nomads
Chirk AAA	2-3	Mold Alexandra
New Broughton	1-3	Welshpool
Brymbo Steelworks	2-4	Oswestry Town
Towyn	0-0	Aberystwyth Town
Newtown	1-1	Llandrindod Wells
Caersws	1-2	Knighton Town
Berriew	4-0	Rhayader Town
Llanfyllin	2-5	Llanidloes Town
Stourbridge	1-0	Kidderminster Harriers
Bridgnorth Town	3-1	Brierley Hill Alliance
Ferndale Athletic	1-0	Pontardawe Athletic
Cardiff College of Education	2-5	Merthyr Tydfil
Brecon Corinthians	0-8	Ton Pentre
Caerau Athletic	1-3	Cardiff Corinthians
Caerleon	2-0	Talgarth
Spencer Works Newport	2-0	Blaenrhondda
Barry Town	2-0	Cwmbran Town
Everwarm Bridgend	4-0	Ebbw Vale
Sully	6-0	Tonyrefail Welfare
Briton Ferry Athletic	0-3	Pembroke Borough
Llanelli	0-3	Afan Lido
BP Llandarcy	0-2	Haverfordwest County
Morriston Town	2-1	Ammanford Town

First Round Replays

Blaenau Ffestiniog	3-1	Holyhead Town
Ruthin FC	0-1	Rhos Aelwyd
Connah's Quay Nomads	4-2	Druids United
Aberystwyh Town	2-0	Towyn
Llandrindod Wells	3-1	Newtown

Second Round

Porthmadog	2-0	Rhos Aelwyd
Blaenau Ffestiniog FC	1-0	Connah's Quay Nomads
Pwllheli & District	5-0	Gresford Athletic
Rhos United	0-2	Rhyl
Point of Ayr	2-3	Courtaulds Greenfield
Bethesda Athletic	4-1	Mold Alexandra
Oswestry Town	0-0	Bala Town
Knighton Town	1-4	Bridgnorth Town
Nantlle Vale	2-1	Caernarvon Town
Stourbridge	5-2	Llanidloes Town
Berriew	2-0	Aberystwyth Town
Llandrindod Wells	2-4	Welshpool
Barry Town	3-1	Spencer Works Newport
Sully	2-2	Ton Pentre
Pembroke Borough	1-5	Merthyr Tydfil
Afan Lido	1-1	Ferndale Athletic
Haverfordwest County	4-0	Morriston Town
Everwarm Bridgend	4-2	Cardiff Corinthians
Caerleon	1-2	Worcester City
Played at Worcester		

Second Round Replays

Bala Town	2-3	Oswestry Town
Ton Pentre	2-1	Sully
Ferndale Athletic	5-3 (aet)	Afan Lido

The scoreline after 90 minutes was 3-3.

Third Round

Blaenau Ffestiniog FC	2-2	Bridgnorth Town
Bethesda Athletic	2-1	Nantlle Vale
Oswestry Town	2-3	Pwllheli & District
Porthmadog	3-1	Courtaulds Greenfield
Rhyl	0-1	Bangor City
Welshpool	1-1	Stourbridge
Merthyr Tydfil	3-0	Worcester City
Ton Pentre	0-2	Barry Town
Ferndale Athletic	1-2	Haverfordwest County
Berriew	0-1	Everwarm Bridgend

Everwarm Bridgend played under that name from the First Round until the Third Round. On 6th December 1976, Everwarm reverted to their former name of Bridgend Town and the Fourth Round match against Haverfordwest County was therefore played as Bridgend Town.

Third Round Replays

Bridgnorth Town	3-0	Blaenau Ffestiniog FC
Stourbridge	4-0	Welshpool

Fourth Round

Wrexham	4-1	Bridgnorth Town
Porthmadog	0-2	Bangor City
Shrewsbury Town	3-3	Chester
Bethesda Athletic	0-4	Pwllheli & District
Swansea City	4-1	Newport County
Stourbridge	0-2	Cardiff City
Played at Cardiff		
Merthyr Tydfil	2-0	Barry Town
Haverfordwest County	1-1	Bridgend Town

Fourth Round Replays

Chester	1-2	Shrewsbury Town
Bridgend Town	4-0	Haverfordwest County

Fifth Round

Wrexham	4-1	Swansea City
Bangor City	0-2	Cardiff City
Pwllheli & District	1-6	Shrewsbury Town
Bridgend Town	1-2	Merthyr Tydfil

Following a protest, the tie was awarded to Bridgend Town.

Semi-finals

Bridgend Town	1-2	Cardiff City
Wrexham	1-1	Shrewsbury Town

Semi-final Replay

Shrewsbury Town	4-1	Wrexham

1977 WELSH CUP FINAL

1st leg

16th May 1977 at Ninian Park, Cardiff

Cardiff City	2-1	Shrewsbury Town

Pethard, Friday — *Hornsby*

Cardiff City: R Healey, P Dwyer, F Pethard, A Campbell, K Pontin, A Larmour, S Grapes, D Livermore, P Sayer, R Friday, J Buchanan (D Showers)

Shrewsbury Town: K Mulhearn, J King, C Leonard, G Turner, C Griffin, I Atkins, S Irvine, B Hornsby, C Bates, L Lawrence, P Maguire

Referee: W J Gow (Swansea)

Attendance: 3,178

2nd leg

18th May 1977 at Gay Meadow, Shrewsbury

Shrewsbury Town	3-0	Cardiff City

Griffin, Own goal, L Roberts

Shrewsbury Town: K Mulhearn, J King, C Leonard, G Turner, C Griffin, I Atkins, S Irvine, B Hornsby, L Roberts, C Bates, P Maguire (L Lawrence)

Cardiff City: R Healey, P Dwyer, F Pethard, A Campbell, K Pontin, A Larmour, D Giles, P Sayer, D Showers, R Friday, J Buchanan (S Grapes)

Referee: W J Gow (Swansea)

Attendance: 2,907

1977/78 Welsh Cup

Qualifying Round

Buckley FC	2-2	Coedpoeth SC
Cwmbran Celtic	2-0	Aberaman Athletic
Seven Sisters	2-3	Garw Athletic
Milford United	1-1	Port Talbot Athletic

Qualifying Round Replays

Coedpoeth SC	3-6	Buckley FC
Port Talbot Athletic	2-0	Milford United

First Round

Denbigh Town	0-4	Courtaulds Greenfield
Caernarvon Town	1-3	Point of Ayr
Nantlle Vale	1-3	Conwy United

Connah's Quay Nomads	7-0	Llandudno Swifts
Porthmadog	3-1	Flint Town United
Rhos United	0-3	Colwyn Bay
Prestatyn Town	1-1	Blaenau Ffestiniog FC

Prestatyn Town subsequently withdrew.

Brymbo Steelworks	1-1	Mold Alexandra
New Broughton	5-0	Druids United
Rhosddu	1-3	Bala Town
Gresford Athletic	0-2	Ruthin FC
Chirk AAA	0-7	Buckley FC
Newtown	4-0	Llandrindod Wells
Llanidloes Town	2-0	Aber AC
Aberystwyth Town	2-1	Talgarth
Knighton Town	1-2	Caersws
Llanfair Caereinion	1-2	Presteigne St Andrews
Welshpool	2-1	Rhayader Town
Berriew	1-1	Towyn
Stourbridge	1-1 (aet)	Worcester City

Worcester City won 6-4 on penalties.

Brierley Hill Alliance	0-0	Oswestry Town

Played at the ground of Lye Town

Kidderminster Harriers	2-1	Bridgnorth Town
Cwmbran Celtic	1-1	Caerleon
Cardiff Corinthians	0-2	Ferndale Athletic
Merthyr Tydfil	2-1	Caerau Athletic
Cardiff College of Education	0-1	Afan Lido
Blaenrhondda	0-4	Barry Town
Sully	2-1	Ebbw Vale
Tonyrefail Welfare	0-4	Ton Pentre
Ammanford Town	2-1	Briton Ferry Athletic
Morriston Town	1-2	BP Llandarcy
Llanelli	3-1	Pontardawe Athletic
Garw Athletic	1-1	Port Talbot Athletic
Haverfordwest County	1-0	Pembroke Borough

First Round Replays

Mold Alexandra	2-3	Brymbo Steelworks
Towyn	4-1	Berriew
Oswestry Town	4-0	Brierley Hill Alliance
Caerleon	0-1	Cwmbran Celtic
Port Talbot Athletic	1-0	Garw Athletic

Second Round

Courtaulds Greenfield	2-2	Buckley FC
Rhyl	0-0 (aet)	Conwy United

Conwy United won 7-6 on penalties.

Point of Ayr	3-3	Porthmadog
Bala Town	2-3	Connah's Quay Nomads
Colwyn Bay	1-2	Ruthin FC
New Broughton	2-3	Brymbo Steelworks
Blaenau Ffestiniog FC	2-0	Pwllheli & District
Towyn	6-0	Newtown
Kidderminster Harriers	5-1	Aberystwyth Town
Worcester City	3-0	Llanidloes Town
Presteigne St Andrews	2-1	Welshpool
Caersws	3-2	Oswestry Town
BP Llandarcy	0-2	Ton Pentre
Llanelli	0-1	Port Talbot Athletic
Ammanford Town	1-4	Barry Town
Cwmbran Celtic	1-8	Merthyr Tydfil
Haverfordwest County	2-1	Afan Lido
Ferndale Athletic	5-3	Sully

Second Round Replays

Buckley FC	0-2	Courtaulds Greenfield
Porthmadog	1-0	Point of Ayr

Third Round

Connah's Quay Nomads	1-1	Brymbo Steelworks
Courtaulds Greenfield	3-1	Porthmadog

Courtaulds were dismissed from the competition following a protest and Porthmadog progressed.

Bangor City	9-0	Conwy United
Ruthin FC	2-3	Blaenau Ffestiniog FC
Kidderminster Harriers	2-0	Barry Town
Towyn	1-1	Bridgend Town
Haverfordwest County	2-5	Merthyr Tydfil
Caersws	0-2	Sully
Presteigne St Andrews	0-3	Worcester City
Port Talbot Athletic	0-0	Ton Pentre

Third Round Replays

Brymbo Steelworks	2-1	Connah's Quay Nomads
Bridgend Town	4-2	Towyn
Ton Pentre	1-2	Port Talbot Athletic

Fourth Round

Porthmadog	0-3	Shrewsbury Town

Played at Shrewsbury

Kidderminster Harriers	2-2	Brymbo Steelworks
Chester	0-2	Wrexham
Bangor City	9-0	Blaenau Ffestiniog FC
Merthyr Tydfil	2-0	Port Talbot Athletic
Worcester City	2-2	Cardiff City
Swansea City	0-0	Newport County
Sully	1-2	Bridgend Town

Fourth Round Replays

Brymbo Steelworks	0-2	Kidderminster Harriers
Cardiff City	3-0	Worcester City
Newport County	1-0	Swansea City

Fifth Round

Newport County	1-3	Bangor City
Wrexham	3-0	Merthyr Tydfil
Bridgend Town	1-2	Shrewsbury Town
Cardiff City	1-1	Kidderminster Harriers

Fifth Round Replay

Kidderminster Harriers	1-3	Cardiff City

Semi-finals

Bangor City	4-2	Shrewsbury Town
Cardiff City	0-2	Wrexham

1978 WELSH CUP FINAL

1st leg

7th May 1978 at Farrar Road, Bangor

Bangor City	1-2	Wrexham
Telford		Shinton, Cartwright

Bangor City: M Craven, D Atherton, P Lunn, D Elliott, J McClelland, J Smith, P Olney, T Broadhead, (J Hughes), B Telford, S Mason, Hipwell

Wrexham: D Davies, M Evans, A Dwyer, G Davies, J Roberts, M Thomas, B Shinton, M Sutton, A Griffiths, G Whittle, L Cartwright

Referee: C Thomas (Treorchy)

Attendance: 10,000

2nd leg

9th May 1978 at the Racecourse, Wrexham

Wrexham	1-0	Bangor City
Lyons		

Wrexham: D Davies, M Evans, A Dwyer, G Davies, J Roberts, M Thomas, B Shinton, M Sutton, J Lyons (W Gegielski) G Whittle, L Cartwright

Bangor City: M Craven, D Atherton, P Lunn, D Elliott, J McClelland, J Smith, P Olney, J Hughes, B Telford, S Mason, Hipwell

Referee: C Thomas (Treorchy)

Attendance: 13,959

1978/79 Welsh Cup

Qualifying Round

Rhos United	1-3	British Steel Deeside
Bangor Athletic	0-8	Conwy United
Abergele United	2-0	Llandudno Swifts
Machynlleth	1-0	Penrhyncoch
Llanfair Caereinion	2-3	Aber AC
New Quay	1-3	Montgomery Town
Ffostrasol Wanderers	1-0	Rhayader Town
Maesteg Park Athletic	3-2	Brecon Corinthians
Garw	1-4	Pontllanfraith
Cwmbran Town	0-3	Abercynon Athletic
Pontyclun	1-2	Newport YMCA

First Round

Blaenau Ffestiniog FC	0-5	Pwllheli & District
Colwyn Bay	3-0	Caernarvon Town
Conwy United	2-5	Porthmadog
Courtaulds Greenfield	4-1	British Steel Deeside
Nantlle Vale	3-1	Connah's Quay Nomads
Flint Town United	4-1	Abergele United
Mold Alexandra	0-0	Denbigh Town
Brymbo Steelworks	2-0	Llay Welfare
Druids United	3-3	Chirk AAA
Gresford Athletic	2-0	Ruthin FC
Caersws	5-1	Ffostrasol Wanderers
Knighton Town	0-1	Newtown
Berriew	1-1	Aberystwyth Town
Towyn	4-0	Montgomery Town
Llanidloes Town	3-1	Talgarth
Aber AC	1-1	Presteigne St Andrews
Machynlleth	3-0	Llandrindod Wells
Welshpool	2-3	Oswestry Town
Bridgnorth Town	0-4	Worcester City
Played at Worcester		
Stourbridge	4-4	Brierley Hill Alliance
Maesteg Park Athletic	4-1	Ebbw Vale
Ferndale Athletic	4-1	South Glamorgan Institute
Cardiff Corinthians	1-1	Afan Lido
Caerau Athletic	4-2	Abercynon Athletic
Caerleon	1-1	Newport YMCA
Pontllanfraith	3-1	Sully
Aberaman Athletic	1-3	Barry Town
Briton Ferry Athletic	2-2	Ton Pentre
Ammanford Town	4-0	Milford United
BP Llandarcy	2-2	Llanelli
Morriston Town	2-3	Pembroke Borough
Pontardawe Athletic	0-5	Haverfordwest County

First Round Replays

Denbigh Town	1-0	Mold Alexandra
Chirk AAA	0-4	Druids United
Aberystwyth Town	4-0	Berriew
Presteigne St Andrews	6-1	Aber AC
Brierley Hill Alliance	3-2	Stourbridge
Played at Stourbridge		
Afan Lido	2-1	Cardiff Corinthians
Newport YMCA	3-1	Caerleon
Ton Pentre	4-0	Briton Ferry Athletic
Llanelli	2-0	BP Llandarcy

Second Round

Colwyn Bay	0-2	Kidderminster Harriers
Pwllheli & District	2-1	Nantlle Vale
Denbigh Town	3-2	Druids United
Gresford Athletic	1-2	Rhyl
Courtaulds Greenfield	1-1	Brymbo Steelworks
Porthmadog	3-2	Flint Town United
Brierley Hill Alliance	2-5	Worcester City
Played at Worcester City FC		
Machynlleth	1-2	Newtown
Presteigne St Andrews	1-3	Oswestry Town
Llanidloes Town	1-0	Caersws
Towyn	0-2	Aberystwyth Town
Afan Lido	2-2	Ton Pentre
Ferndale Athletic	1-3	Pembroke Borough
Barry Town	1-2	Ammanford Town
Merthyr Tydfil	3-0	Newport YMCA
Maesteg Park Athletic	0-2	Pontllanfraith
Bridgend Town	5-2	Caerau Athletic
Llanelli	0-1	Haverfordwest County

Second Round Replays

Brymbo Steelworks	0-2	Courtaulds Greenfield
Ton Pentre	2-1	Afan Lido

Third Round

Aberystwyth Town	1-7	Oswestry Town
Denbigh Town	0-2	Rhyl
Courtaulds Greenfield	2-1	Llanidloes Town
Pwllheli & District	0-2	Kidderminster Harriers
Porthmadog	0-0	Newtown

The match was abandoned after 65 minutes.

Ton Pentre	2-1	Pembroke Borough
Pontllanffraith	1-5	Worcester City

Played at Worcester

Merthyr Tydfil	2-1	Haverfordwest County
Ammanford Town	1-2	Bridgend Town

Third Round Replay

Porthmadog	4-1	Newtown

Fourth Round

Chester	0-0	Bangor City
Wrexham	4-1	Porthmadog
Courtaulds Greenfield	1-6	Oswestry Town
Shrewsbury Town	6-0	Rhyl
Bridgend Town	0-3	Worcester City
Swansea City	6-1	Kidderminster Harriers
Newport County	0-2	Ton Pentre
Cardiff City	2-1	Merthyr Tydfil

Fourth Round Replay

Bangor City	0-1	Chester

Fifth Round

Chester	4-3	Oswestry Town
Shresbury Town	4-0	Ton Pentre
Worcester City	3-2	Cardiff City
Wrexham	3-2	Swansea City

Semi-finals

Shrewsbury Town	2-0	Worcester City
Chester	0-1	Wrexham

1979 WELSH CUP FINAL

1st leg

21st May 1979 at the Racecourse, Wrexham

Wrexham	1-1	Shrewsbury Town
Fox		*Biggins*

Wrexham: E Niedzwiecki, M Sutton, A Dwyer, W Cegielski, J Roberts, D Giles, B Shinton, G Whittle, J Lyons, S Buxton, S Fox (M Williams)

Shrewsbury Town: B Wardle, J King, A Larkin, S Cross, S Hayes, J Keay, T Birch, I Atkins, D Tong, S Biggins, J Lindsay

Referee: G P Owen (Menai Bridge)

Attendance: 6,174

2nd leg

24th May 1979 at Gay Meadow, Shrewsbury

Shrewsbury Town	1-0	Wrexham
Maguire		

Shrewsbury Town: B Wardle, J King, A Larkin, S Cross, C Griffin, J Keay, J Lindsay, I Atkins, D Tong, S Biggins, P Maguire

Wrexham: E Niedzwiecki, M Sutton, G Whittle, W Cegielski, I Edwards, D Giles, B Shinton, P Williams, D McNeil, J Lyons, S Fox

Referee: G P Owen (Menai Bridge)

Attendance: 8,889

1979/80 Welsh Cup

Qualifying Round

Llandudno Town	1-3	Rhos United
Conwy United	11-1	British Steel
Llandudno Amateurs	1-2	Abergele United
Llanfair Caereinion	5-1	Ffostrasol Wanderers
Barmouth & Dyffryn Utd	0-2	Aber AC
Rhayader Town	4-3	Montgomery Town
Abergavenny Thursdays	1-2	Spencer Works
Talgarth	1-8	Taff's Well
Trelewis	1-3	Brecon Corinthians

First Round

Pwllheli & District	2-0	Porthmadog
Connah's Quay Nomads	6-2	Abergele United
Rhos United	0-6	Colwyn Bay

Played at Colwyn Bay

Conwy United	1-0	Caernarfon Town
Courtaulds Greenfield	0-3	Flint Town United
Blaenau Ffestiniog FC	0-1	Nantlle Vale
Llay Welfare	1-2	Gresford Athletic
Ruthin FC	2-2	Chirk AAA
Mold Alexandra	0-5	Brymbo Steelworks
Denbigh Town	1-3	Druids United
Bridgnorth Town	0-1	Kidderminster Harriers
Stourbridge	2-1	Brierley Hill Alliance
Newtown	8-0	Rhayader Town
Caersws	1-1	Towyn

Towyn were dismissed from the competition after fielding an ineligible player.

Presteigne St Andrews	6-2	Knighton Town
Machynlleth	2-0	Welshpool
Llanfair Caereinion	2-1	Aberystwyth Town

Played at Aberystwyth

Berriew	4-2	Aber AC
Llanidloes Town	3-2	Llandrindod Wells
Brecon Corinthians	2-3	Afan Lido
Taff's Well	1-5	Bridgend Town

Played at Bridgend

Sully	0-3	Barry Town

Cardiff Corinthians	0-0	Ferndale Athletic
Caerau Athletic	2-1	Abercynon Athletic
Aberaman Athletic	2-0	Caerleon
Ebbw Vale	0-2	Pontllanfraith
Newport YMCA	2-4	Maesteg Park Athletic
Spencer Works Newport	7-0	South Glamorgan Institute
Merthyr Tydfil	2-1	Briton Ferry Athletic
Pontardawe	1-4	Pembroke Borough
Haverfordwest County	4-1	Morriston Town
Milford United	4-0	Llanelli
BP Llandarcy	1-0	Ammanford Town

First Round Replays

Chirk AAA	0-2	Ruthin FC
Ferndale Athletic	3-1	Cardiff Corinthians

Second Round

Rhyl	2-3	Colwyn Bay
Connah's Quay Nomads	5-0	Gresford Athletic
Flint Town United	0-3	Brymbo Steelworks
Ruthin FC	1-1	Druids United
Conwy United	2-6	Oswestry Town
Pwllheli & District	0-3	Nantlle Vale
Machynlleth	0-1	Berriew
Newtown	4-0	Llanfair Caereinion
Caersws	1-2	Kidderminster Harriers
Presteigne St Andrews	2-1	Llanidloes Town
Maesteg Park Athletic	3-2	Haverfordwest County
Bridgend Town	3-0	Spencer Works
Merthyr Tydfil	3-1	Aberaman Athletic
Stourbridge	2-3	Llandarcy
Ferndale Athletic	0-1	Caerau Athletic
Ton Pentre	2-1	Pembroke Borough
Milford United	1-1	Barry Town
Afan Lido	2-4	Pontllanfraith

Second Round Replays

Druids United	3-1	Ruthin FC
Barry Town	4-0	Milford United

Third Round

Oswestry Town	6-0	Berriew
Bangor City	3-0	Presteigne St Andrews
Nantlle Vale	3-0	Newtown
Druids United	1-2	Connah's Quay Nomads
Brymbo Steelworks	4-0	Colwyn Bay
Merthyr Tydfil	4-0	Caerau Athletic
Kidderminster Harriers	2-1	Maesteg Park Athletic
Worcester City	7-0	BP Llandarcy
Pontllanffraith	3-1	Ton Pentre
Barry Town	4-1	Bridgend Town

Fourth Round

Wrexham	5-0	Connah's Quay Nomads
Nantlle Vale	2-1	Brymbo Steelworks
Shrewsbury Town	2-2	Oswestry Town
Chester	1-1	Bangor City
Swansea City	2-0	Pontllanfraith
Newport County	2-0	Cardiff City
Kidderminster Harriers	1-0	Worcester City
Merthyr Tydfil	4-2	Barry Town

Fourth Round Replays

Oswestry Town	1-6	Shrewsbury Town
Bangor City	0-2	Chester

Fifth Round

Merthyr Tydfil	1-0	Chester
Wrexham	0-1	Newport County
Swansea City	2-0	Kidderminster Harriers
Nantlle Vale	1-4	Shrewsbury Town

Played at Shrewsbury

Semi-finals

Newport County	3-1	Merthyr Tydfil
Swansea City	2-2	Shrewsbury Town

Semi-final Replay

Shrewsbury Town	2-2	Swansea City

Shrewsbury Town won 6-5 on penalties.

1980 WELSH CUP FINAL

1st leg

6th May 1980 at Somerton Park, Newport

Newport County	2-1	Shrewsbury Town

Tynan 2   *Own goal*

Newport County: G Plumley, R Walden, T Tynan, G Davies, K Oakes, N Bailey, N Vaughan, S Lowndes, D Gwyther, J Aldridge, K Moore (R Ward)

Shrewsbury Town: R Wardle, J Keay, C Leonard, G Turner, C Griffin, J King, D Tong, I Atkins, W Biggins, J Dungworth, P Maguire (S Cross)

Referee: R Bridges (Deeside)

Attendance: 9,950

2nd leg

12th May 1980 at Gay Meadow, Shrewsbury

Shrewsbury Town	0-3	Newport County

                        Tynan, Lowndes, Gwyther

Shrewsbury Town: R Wardle, J King, C Leonard, B Coyne, C Griffin, J Keay, D Tong, I Atkins, W Biggins, J Dungworth, P Maguire (S Cross)

Newport County: G Plumley, R Walden, T Tynan, G Davies, K Oakes, N Bailey, N Vaughan, S Lowndes, D Gwyther, J Aldridge, K Moore (R Ward)

Referee: R Bridges (Deeside)

Attendance: 8,993

1980/81 Welsh Cup

First Round

Menai Bridge Tigers	4-2	Porthmadog
Conwy United	1-3	Caernarvon Town
Abergele United	0-4	Llandudno Amateurs
Denbigh Town	1-3	Pwllheli & District
Courtaulds Greenfield	0-2	Flint Town United
Buckley FC	0-1	Chirk AAA
Llay Welfare	1-0	Bala Town
Mold Alexandra	1-1	Druids United
Gresford Athletic	0-0	Ruthin Town
Montgomery Town	1-2	Brierley Hill Alliance
Bridgnorth Town	0-4	Stourbridge
Ffostrasol Wanderers	2-5	Aberystwyth Town
Llandrindod Wells	1-2	Knighton Town
Aber AC	0-3	Talgarth
Llanidloes Town (w/o)	v	Machynlleth (withdrew)
Caersws	2-4	Welshpool
Towyn	3-1	Rhayader Town
Aberaman Athletic	0-2	Cardiff Corinthians
Taff's Well	1-1	Bryntirion Athletic
South Glamorgan Institute	1-1	Newport YMCA
Afan Lido	2-0	Spencer Works Newport
Sully	1-1	Caerleon
Pontyclun	1-2	Ferndale Athletic
Cwmbran Celtic	0-4	Abercynon Athletic
Llanelli	2-1	Briton Ferry Athletic
Pembroke Borough	2-0	Morriston Town
Coedffranc	0-4	Pontardawe Athletic
Played at Pontardawe		
Milford United	0-1	Ammanford Town

First Round Replays

Druids United	1-2	Mold Alexandra
Ruthin Town	2-3 (aet)	Gresford Athletic

The scoreline after 90 minutes was 2-2.

Bryntirion Athletic	1-2	Taff's Well
Newport YCMA	0-1	South Glamorgan Institute
Caerleon	1-0 (aet)	Sully

Second Round

Rhyl	0-1	Brymbo Steelworks
Welshpool	2-1	Oswestry Town
Colwyn Bay	1-0	Menai Bridge Tigers
Flint Town United	1-1	Towyn
Knighton Town	1-1	Caernarvon Town
Chirk AAA	1-1	Pwllheli & District
Aberystwyth Town	1-2	Connah's Quay Nomads
Blaenau Ffestiniog FC	4-2	Mold Alexandra
Gresford Athletic	0-3	Llanidloes Town
Played at Llandiloes		
Newtown	7-1	Llay Welfare
Presteigne St Andrews (w/o)	v	Nantlle Vale (withdrew)
Llandudno Amateurs	5-1	Berriew
Caerleon	1-1	Afan Lido
Stourbridge	1-1	Pontllanfraith
Caerau Athletic	1-3	Amrnanford Town
Bridgend Town	0-1	South Glamorgan Institute
Ton Pentre	3-2	Taff's Well
Maesteg Park	2-2	BP Llandarcy
Pembroke Borough	4-3	Talgarth
Haverfordwest County	7-0	Ferndale Athletic
Kidderminster Harriers	0-2	Worcester City
Brierley Hill Alliance	1-1	Cardiff Corinthians

Brierley Hill withdrew from the competition.

Abercynon Athletic	4-1	Pontardawe Athletic
Llanelli	1-1	Barry Town

Second Round Replays

Towyn	1-0	Flint Town United
Caernarvon Town	1-1 (aet)	Knighton Town

Knighton Town won 5-4 on penalties

Pwllheli & District	3-0 (aet)	Chirk AAA
Afan Lido	0-2	Caerleon
Pontllanfraith	0-1	Stourbridge
BP Llandarcy	0-6	Maesteg Park
Barry Town	2-1	Llanelli

Third Round

Brymbo Steelworks	1-4	Bangor City
Towyn	2-2	Presteigne St Andrews
Llandudno Amateurs	1-0	Colwyn Bay
Wrexham	6-0	Pwllheli & District
Connah's Quay Nomads	1-0	Blaenau Ffestiniog FC
Hereford United	1-0	Newtown
Llanidloes Town	0-5	Shrewsbury Town
Played at Shrewsbury		
Knighton Town	2-1	Welshpool
Abercynon Athletic	4-0	Ammanford Town
Cardiff Corinthians	0-6	Cardiff City
Played at Cardiff City		
Newport County	2-2	Worcester City
Caerleon	1-5	Swansea City
Played at Swansea		
Maesteg Park	5-2	South Glamorgan Institute
Stourbridge	2-3	Ton Pentre
Merthyr Tydfil	2-0	Haverfordwest County
Barry Town	2-2	Pembroke Borough

Third Round Replays

Presteigne St Andrews	2-1	Towyn
Worcester City	2-3	Newport County
Pembroke Borough	1-2	Barry Town

Fourth Round

Presteigne St Andrews	0-2	Bangor City
Wrexham	3-0	Cardiff City
Llandudno Amateurs	1-1	Connah's Quay Nomads
Newport County	3-0	Ton Pentre
Knighton Town	1-4	Hereford United
Maesteg Park	3-2	Barry Town
Shrewsbury Town	6-1	Abercynon Athletic
Merthyr Tydfil	0-2	Swansea City

Fourth Round Replay

Connah's Quay Nomads	2-1	Llandudno Amateurs

Fifth Round

Swansea City	4-1	Maesteg Park
Shrewsbury Town	2-2	Hereford United
Wrexham	2-1	Connah's Quay Nomads
Newport County	3-1	Bangor City

Fifth Round Replay

Hereford United	5-0	Shrewsbury Town

Semi-finals – 1st leg

Hereford United	2-1	Newport County
Wrexham	2-2	Swansea City

Semi-finals – 2nd leg

Newport County	1-1	Hereford United

Hereford United won 3-2 on aggregate.

Swansea City	1-1	Wrexham

Aggregate 3-3. Swansea City won on the away goals rule.

1981 WELSH CUP FINAL

1st leg

4th May 1981 at the Vetch Field, Swansea

Swansea City	1-0	Hereford United

R James

Swansea City: D Stewart, W Evans, D Hadziabdic, N Robinson, J Mahoney, D Lewis, A Curtis, R James, L James, J Charles, T Craig

Hereford United: R Cashley, Price, D Bartley, K Hicks, S Cornes, P Spiring, J Harvey, J Laidlaw, D Showers, F McGrellis, W White

Referee: C Thomas (Porthcawl)

Attendance: 13,182

2nd leg

11th May 1981 at Edgar Street, Hereford

Hereford United	1-1	Swansea City

Laidlaw   R James

Hereford United: R Cashley, Price, D Bartley, K Hicks, S Cornes, P Spiring, J Harvey, J Laidlaw, D Showers, F McGrellis, W White

Swansea City: D Stewart, N Robinson, B Attley, W Evans, J Mahoney, D Lewis, D Giles, R James, L James, J Charles, T Craig

Referee: C Thomas (Porthcawl)

Attendance: 7,038

1981/82 Welsh Cup

First Round

Menai Bridge Tigers	0-4	Conwy United
Greenfield	0-0	Flint Town United
Porthmadog	2-1	UCNW Bangor
Druids United	1-0	Gresford Athletic
Bala Town	3-2	Ruthin Town
St Mary's Ruabon	2-0	Denbigh Town
Bargoed Rangers	3-1	Llandrindod Wells
Montgomery Town	1-9	Caersws

Played at Caersws

Cheltenham Town	3-3	Oswestry Town
Stafford Rangers	2-1	Kidderminster Harriers
Sully	1-0	Garw
Spencer Works Newport	4-2	Milford United
Briton Ferry Athletic	8-0	Aberaman Athletic
Lake United	2-0	Ebbw Vale
Abergavenny Thursdays	3-2	Carmarthen Town
Pontlottyn Blast Furnace	1-1	Newport YMCA

First Round Replays

Flint Town United	0-1	Greenfield
Oswestry Town	0-2	Cheltenham Town
Newport YMCA	2-0	Pontlottyn Blast Furnace

Second Round

Conwy United	0-0	Bangor City
Newtown	5-0	Porthmadog
Caernarfon Town	4-2	Llandudno Amateurs
Knighton Town	1-3	Presteigne St Andrews
Caersws	1-2	Connah s Quay Nomads
Bargoed Rangers	0-5	Stourbridge
Rhyl	0-1	Colwyn Bay
Bala Town	2-5	Greenfield
Towyn	1-0	Druids United
Blaenau Ffestiniog FC	7-2	Aberystwyth Town
St Mary's Ruabon	0-2	Oswestry Town

Played at Oswestry

Llanidloes Town	4-0	Welshpool
Pwllheli & District	3-0	Brymbo Steelworks
Llanelli	1-0	Briton Ferry Athletic
Spencer Works Newport	1-2	Haverfordwest County
Lake United	2-2	Worcester City

Played at Worcester

Sully	2-2	Cardiff Corinthians
South Glamorgan Institute	1-2	BP Llandarcy
Taff's Well	3-1	Ton Pentre
Ammanford Town	4-1	Abercynon Athletic
Abergavenny Thursdays	0-3	Bridgend Town
Pontllanfraith	4-0	Pembroke Borough
Caerleon	2-0	Newport YMCA
Stafford Rangers	1-0	Merthyr Tydfil
Ferndale Athletic	0-3	Barry Town
Maesteg Park	0-1	Pontardawe Athletic

Second Round Replays

Bangor City	8-1	Conwy United
Worcester City	2-1	Lake United
Cardiff Corinthians	1-0	Sully

Third Round

Towyn	0-8	Hereford United
Played at Hereford		
Llanidloes Town	0-2	Colwyn Bay
Greenfield	2-1	Presteigne St Andrews
Caernarfon Town	4-2	Blaenau Ffestiniog FC
Connah's Quay Nomads	1-0	Pwllheli & District
Shrewsbury Town	4-1	Oswestry Town
Stourbridge	2-4	Wrexham
Bangor City	4-2	Newtown
Stafford Rangers	0-4	Swansea City
Taff's Well	0-5	Newport County
Barry Town	5-0	Caerleon
Llanelli	1-1	Worcester City
Ammanford Town	1-1	Haverfordwest County
Pontllanfraith	2-1	BP Llandarcy
Bridgend Town	1-4	Cardiff City
Cardiff Corinthians	0-1	Pontardawe Athletic

Third Round Replays

Worcester City	5-1	Llanelli
Haverfordwest County	0-4	Ammanford Town

Fourth Round

Cardiff City	3-1	Newport County
Swansea City	6-0	Worcester City
Caernarfon Town	1-8	Shrewsbury Town
Bangor City	1-0	Ammanford Town
Greeenfield	3-0	Connah's Quay Nomads
Pontllanffraith	0-2	Colwyn Bay
Pontardawe Athletic	1-5	Wrexham
Hereford United	3-1	Barry Town

Fifth Round

Cardiff City	4-1	Wrexham
Bangor City	2-1	Shrewsbury Town
Swansea City	2-2	Colwyn Bay
Greenfield	1-2	Hereford United
Played at Hereford		

Fifth Round Replay

Colwyn Bay	0-3	Swansea City
Played at Swansea		

Semi-finals – 1st leg

Bangor City	1-2	Swansea City
Hereford United	0-0	Cardiff City

Semi-finals – 2nd leg

Swansea City	0-0	Bangor City
Swansea City won 2-1 on aggregate		
Cardiff City	2-1	Hereford United
Cardiff City won 2-1 on aggregate		

1982 WELSH CUP FINAL

1st leg

11th May 1982 at Ninian Park, Cardiff

Cardiff City	0-0	Swansea City

Cardiff City: A Dibble, L Jones, M Henderson, K Pontin, C Micallef, J Mullen, Lythgoe, T Gilbert, G Bennett, D Bennett, G Stevens

Swansea City: D Davies, C Marustik, D Habziabdic, M Thompson, R Kennedy, A Rajovic, A Curtis, R James, L James, N Stevenson, R Latchford

Referee: G P Owen (Anglesey)

Attendance: 11,960

2nd leg

19th May 1982 at the Vetch Field, Swansea

Swansea City	2-1	Cardiff City
Latchford 2		G Bennett

Swansea City: D Davies, N Robinson, D Habziabdic, G Stanley, R Kennedy, A Rajovic, A Curtis, R James, L James, N Stevenson, R Latchford

Cardiff City: A Dibble, L Jones, M Henderson, K Pontin, C Micallef, J Mullen, Lythgoe, T Gilbert, McEwan, G Bennett, D Bennett

Referee: G P Owen (Anglesey)

Attendance: 15,828

1982/83 Welsh Cup

First Round

Llandudno Amateurs	0-3	Conwy United
Flint Town United	0-0	UCNW Bangor
Porthmadog	0-2	Bala Town
Brymbo Steel Works	2-1	Lex XI
Chirk AAA	2-1	St Mary's Ruabon
Gresford Athletic	3-0	Druids United
Ruthin Town	0-3	Buckley FC
Brecon Corinthians	3-0	Welshpool
Kidderminster Harriers	4-0	Aberystwyth Town
Stourbridge	3-0	Montgomery Town
Caersws	2-6	Oswestry Town
Llandrindod Wells	2-1	Knighton Town
Biaenrhondda (w/o)	v	Tredomen Works (withdrew)
Clydach United	2-3	Milford United
Ebbw Vale	1-3	Cheltenham Town
Cwmbran Town	1-4	South Glamorgan Institute
Aberaman Athletic	1-5	Afan Lido

First Round Replay

UCNW Bangor	1-2	Flint Town United

Second Round

Gresford Athletic	0-3	Colwyn Bay
Pwllheli & District	2-1	Brymbo Steelworks
Bala Town	1-6	Rhyl
Chirk AAA	1-7	Conwy United
Blaenau Ffestiniog FC	2-5	Flint Town United
Connah's Quay Nomads	1-3	Caernarfon Town
Greenfield	3-3	Buckley FC
Brecon Corinthians	6-1	Presteigne St Andrews
Newtown	1-1	Oswestry Town
Llanidloes Town	3-1	Stourbridge
Llandrindod Wells	11-0	Towyn
Kidderminster Harriers	3-1	Worcester City
Milford United	3-4	Taff's Well
Newport YMCA	2-2	Pontardawe Athletic
Cheltenham Town	3-1	Sully
Bridgend Town	6-0	Afan Lido
Ammanford Town	1-1	South Glamorgan Institute
Llanelli	4-1	Pembroke Borough
Lake United	1-1	Barry Town
Pontllanfraith	0-0	Maesteg Park Athletic
Spencer Works Newport	2-1	Caerleon
Haverfordwest County	2-1	Blaenrhondda
Abercynon Athletic	2-1	Ton Pentre
Mierthyr Tydfil	5-2	BP Llandarcy
Cardiff Corinthians	2-1	Briton Ferry Athletic

Second Round Replays

Buckley FC	0-3	Greenfield
Oswestry Town	3-3 (aet)	Newtown

The scoreline after 90 minutes was 2-2.
Oswestry Town won 5-3 on penalties.

Pontardawe Athletic	3-3 (aet)	Newport YMCA

Newport YMCA won 4-3 on penalties.

South Glamorgan Institute	4-5	Ammanford Town
Barry Town	3-2	Lake United
Maesteg Park Athletic	3-2	Pontllanfraith

Third Round

Llandrindod Wells	1-6	Bangor City
Caernarfon Town	3-0	Greenfield
Flint Town United	2-5	Pwllheli & District
Rhyl	1-1	Shrewsbury Town
Colwyn Bay	2-1	Conwy United
Brecon Corinthians	3-4	Kidderminster Harriers
Wrexham	4-0	Oswestry Town
Llanidloes Town	1-1	Hereford United
Cardiff Corinthians	0-2	Haverfordwest County
Newport County	1-0	Cardiff City
Llanelli	0-2	Cheltenham Town
Merthyr Tydfil	0-1	Taff's Well
Bridgend Town	3-1	Newport YMCA
Maesteg Park Athletic	2-3	Barry Town
South Glamorgan Institute	1-2	Abercynon Athletic
Spencer Works	0-3	Swansea City

Third Round Replays

Shrewsbury	3-0	Rhyl
Hereford United	7-0	Llanidloes Town

Fourth Round

Bangor City	1-2	Colwyn Bay
Bridgend Town	1-1	Kidderminster Harriers
Cheltenham Town	6-0	Pwllheli & District
Haverfordwest County	2-1	Barry Town
Hereford United	6-0	Abercynon Athletic
Swansea City	2-1	Shrewsbury Town
Taff's Well	2-3	Caernarfon Town
Wrexham	4-1	Newport County

Fourth Round Replay

Kidderminster Harriers	2-2 (aet)	Bridgend Town

Bridgend Town won 4-2 on penalties.

Fifth Round

Colwyn Bay	0-0	Haverfordwest County
Swansea City	3-1	Hereford United
Wrexham	3-2	Cheltenham Town
Bridgend Town	1-2	Caernarfon Town

Fifth Round Replay

Haverfordwest County	1-2	Colwyn Bay

Semi-finals – 1st leg

Colwyn Bay	0-1	Swansea City

Played at Rhyl

Caernarfon Town	0-2	Wrexham

Semi-finals – 2nd leg

Swansea City	3-0	Colwyn Bay

Swansea City won 3-0 on aggregate.

Wrexham	0-0	Caernarfon Town

Wrexham won 2-0 on aggregate

1983 WELSH CUP FINAL

1st leg

10th May 1983 at the Racecourse, Wrexham

Wrexham	1-2	Swansea City

Dowman   *Latchford, Giles*

Wrexham: E Niedzwiecki, J King, A Hill,
R Savage, S Dowman, J Keay, S Cunnington,
S Buxton, S Hunt, J Muldoon (M Evans), D Gregory

Swansea City: C Sander, D Lewis, G Richards,
J Charles (C Pascoe), N Stevenson, A Rajovic,
G Stanley, R James, D Gale, R Kennedy,
R Latchford

Referee: H King (Troedyrhiw)

Attendance: 2,295

2nd leg

17th May 1983 at the Vetch Field, Swansea

Swansea City	2-0	Wrexham

Latchford 2

Swansea City: C Sander, C Marustik, G Richards, J Charles, R Kennedy, D Lewis, C Pascoe (N Stevenson), R James, D Gale, G Stanley, R Latchford

Wrexham: E Niedzwiecki, J King, P Bater, R Savage, M Evans, J Keay, A Hill, S Buxton, S Hunt, J Muldoon (R Savage), A Edwards

Referee: H King (Troedyrhiw)

Attendance: 5,630

1983/84 Welsh Cup

First Round

Llandudno Amateurs	1-4	Rhos United

Rhos United were dismissed from the competition for fielding an ineligible player.

Bala Town	0-1	Flint Town United
Blaenau Ffestiniog FC	0-1	Greenfield
Connah Quay Nomads (w/o)	v	Porthmadog (withdrew)
Llanfairpwll	2-3	Conwy United
St Mary's Ruabon	1-6	Lex XI
Ruthin Town	2-3	Oswestry Town
Brymbo Steelworks	1-2	Cefn Albion
Druids United	1-3	Chirk AAA
Buckley FC	1-1	Grapes Moss
Knighton Town	1-0	Caersws
UCW Aberystwyth (withdrew)	v	Machynlleth (w/o)
Newtown	3-3	Llandrindod Wells
Welshpool	2-1	Aberystwyth Town
Llanidloes Town	6-0	Towyn
Lake United	5-1	South Glamorgan Institute
Ferndale Athletic	3-2	Newport YMCA
Port Talbot Athletic	3-1	Sully
Afan Lido	0-6	Stourbridge
Played at Stourbridge		
Clydach United	0-4	Abercynon Athletic
Tredomen Works	1-2	BP Llandarcy
Pontlottyn Blast Furnace	1-2	Abergavenny Thursdays
Pontyclun	0-2	Cardiff Corinthians
Aberaman Athletic	0-3	Spencer Works Newport
Pontardawe Athletic	0-1	Ammanford Town

All other clubs received byes

First Round Replays

Grapes Moss	1-4	Buckley FC
Llandrindod Wells	3-2	Newtown

Second Round

Conwy United	1-3	Llandrindod Wells
Pwllheli & District	0-1	Welshpool
Rhyl	2-0	Knighton Town
Bangor City	6-0	Cefn Albion
Kidderminster Harriers	9-1	Machynlleth
Llanidloes Town	2-4	Buckley FC
Connah's Quay Nomads	2-1	Brecon Corinthians
Llandudno Amateurs	0-6	Lex XI
Oswestry Town	3-2	Greenfield
Flint Town United	1-2	Chirk AAA
BP Llandarcy	1-1	Ton Pentre
Maesteg Park Athletic	2-0	Abergavenny Thursdays
Bridgend Town	0-0	Blaenrhondda
Ebbw Vale	0-1	Abercynon Athletic
Pontllanfraith	4-0	Llanelli
Worcester City	4-0	Lake United
Pembroke Borough	1-1	Spencer Works Newport
Ammanford Town	2-2	Cwmbran Town
Taff's Well	3-0	Caerau Athletic
Milford United	0-1	Caerleon
Haverfordwest County	1-3	Merthyr Tydfil
Port Talbot Athletic	3-2	Briton Ferry Athletic
Cardiff Corinthians	1-1	Stourbridge
Barry Town	3-0	Ferndale Athletic

All other clubs received byes

Second Round Replays

Ton Pentre	2-3	BP Llandarcy
Blaenrhondda	0-3	Bridgend Town
Spencer Works Newport	3-0	Pembroke Borough
Cwmbran Town	3-2 (aet)	Ammanford Town

The scoreline after 90 minutes was 1-1.

Stourbridge	1-3	Cardiff Corinthians

Third Round

Bangor City	4-0	Llandrindod Wells
Wrexham	1-1	Worcester City
Llanidloes Town	0-0	Rhyl
Hereford United	4-0	Caernarfon Town
Lex XI	3-2	Chirk AAA
Kidderminster Harriers	2-0	Oswestry Town
Connah's Quay Nomads	0-1	Shrewsbury Town
Colwyn Bay	1-0	Welshpool
Swansea City	5-2	Abercynon Athletic
Merthyr Tydfil	1-0	Caerleon
Port Talbot Athletic	1-2	Maesteg Park Athletic
BP Llandarcy	2-0	Spencer Works Newport
Cardiff Corinthians	1-1	Cwmbran Town
Bridgend Town	1-5	Newport County
Played at Newport		
Cardiff City	5-0	Taff's Well
Barry Town	1-1	Pontllanfraith

All other clubs received byes

Third Round Replays

Worcester City	1-2	Wrexham
Rhyl	3-0	Llanidloes Town
Cwmbran Town	3-2	Cardiff Corinthians
Pontllanfraith	1-4	Barry Town

Fourth Round

Merthyr Tydfil	2-2	Barry Town
Swansea City	4-2	Bangor City
Newport County	6-0	Lex XI
Wrexham	1-1	Rhyl
Shrewsbury Town	5-2	Colwyn Bay
Cwmbran Town	3-4	Hereford United
Kidderminster Harriers	4-1	BP Llandarcy
Cardiff City	4-0	Maesteg Park Athletic

Fourth Round Replays

Barry Town	1-1	Merthyr Tydfil

Merthyr Tydrfil won 6-5 on penalties.

Rhyl	1-3	Wrexham

Fifth Round

Barry Town	1-1	Swansea City
Kidderminster Harriers	1-1	Shrewsbury Town
Newport County	0-1	Wrexham
Cardif City	1-3	Hereford United

Fifth Round Replay

Swansea City	2-1	Barry Town
Shrewsbury Town	1-0	Kidderminster Harriers

Semi-finals – 1st leg

Shrewsbury Town	2-0	Swansea City
Hereford United	0-0	Wrexham

Semi-finals – 2nd leg

Swansea City	1-0	Shrewsbury Town

Shrewsbury Town won 2-1 on aggregate.

Wrexham	1-0	Hereford United

Wrexham won 1-0 on aggregate.

1984 WELSH CUP FINAL

1st leg

18th May 1984 at Gay Meadow, Shrewsbury

Shrewsbury Town	2-1	Wrexham

Cross, Robinson *Edwards*

Shrewsbury Town: S Perks, W Williams, P Johnson, A Kerr, G Stevens, P Petts, B McNally, C Bates, S Cross, C Robinson, P Tester (G Hackett)

Wrexham: R Sinclair, N Salathiel, S Cunnington, S Hunt, J Keay, S Wright, J Muldoon, D Gregory, J Steel, A Edwards, J King

Referee: R Bridges (Hawarden)

Attendance: 2,607

2nd leg

25th May 1984 at the Racecourse, Wrexham

Wrexham	0-0	Shrewsbury Town

Wrexham: R Sinclair, J King, S Cunnington (S Jones), S Hunt, J Keay, S Wright, J Muldoon, D Gregory, J Steel, A Edwards, N Salathiel

Shrewsbury Town: S Perks, W Williams, P Johnson, C Griffin, G Stevens, P Petts, G Turner, C Bates, S Cross, C Robinson, P Tester (G Hackett)

Referee: R Bridges (Hawarden)

Attendance: 3,148

1984/85 Welsh Cup

First Round

Llandudno Amateurs	1-1	Pwllheli & District
Bethesda Athletic	2-1	Llanfairpwll
Connah's Quay Nomads	1-2	Blaenau Ffestiniog FC
Rhos United	2-7	Conwy United
Flint Town United	0-2	Portmadoc
Grapes Moss	1-2	Bala Town
Rhos Aelwyd	2-2	Oswestry Town
Played at Oswestry		
Brymbo Steelworks	2-0	Ruthin Town
Druids United	1-5	Cefn Albion
Gresford Athletic	1-2	Buckley FC
Denbigh Town	0-5	Llangollen
Presteigne St Andrews	0-0	Aberystwyth Town
Machynlleth	1-3	Montgomery Town
Newtown	3-1	Caersws
Llandrindod Wells	1-4	Towyn
Knighton Town	2-0	Rhayader Town
AFC Cardiff	1-0	Ammanford Town
Ferndale Athletic	3-0	Abercynon Athletic
Aberaman Athletic	0-1	Sully
Carmarthen Town	1-1	South Glamorgan Institute
Newport YMCA	1-1	Cardiff Corinthians
Abergavenny Thursdays	3-6 (aet)	Spencer Works
Pontlottyn Blast Furnace	3-0	Tondu Robins
Pontardawe Athletic (w/o)	v	Garw (withdrew)
Taff's Well	0-2	Afan Lido

First Round Replays

Pwllheli & District	3-2 (aet)	Llandudno Amateurs

The scoreline after 90 minutes was 2-2.

Oswestry Town	4-3	Rhos Aelwyd
Aberystwyth Town	3-1	Presteigne St Andrews
South Glamorgan Institute	5-0	Carmarthen Town
Cardiff Corinthians	3-0	Newport YMCA

Second Round

Pwlheli & District	0-2	Worcester City
Bangor City	4-0	Knighton Town
Conwy United	2-2	Brecon Corinthians
Oswestry Town	1-4	Chirk AAA

Cefn Albion	1-3	Colwyn Bay
Aberystwyth Town	4-0	Bala Town
Brymbo Steelworks	8-2	Buckley FC
Lex XI	2-0	Porthmadog
Blaenau Ffestiniog FC	0-5	Towyn
Bethesda Athletic	1-0	Montgomery Town
Llanidloes Town	1-0	Newtown
Kidderminster Harriers	0-1	Rhyl
Llangollen	1-4	Caernarfon Town
BP Llandarcy	0-0	Barry Town
Caerleon	2-0	Ebbw Vale
Merthyr Tydfil	1-0	Pontiottyn
Caerau Athletic	0-1	Cardiff Corinthians
Afan Lido	1-1	Haverfordwest County
Ton Pentre	4-1	South Glamorgan Institute
Maesteg Park	1-1	Spencer Works Newport
Pembroke Borough	1-1	Cwmbran Town
AFC Cardiff	1-0	Ferndale Athletic
Pontardawe Athletic	5-2	Llanelli
Briton Ferry Athletic	5-2	Milford United
Pontllanfraith	1-1	Bridgend Town
Sully	3-0	Port Talbot Athletic

Second Round Replays

Brecon Corinthians	4-3	Conwy United
Barry Town	3-2 (aet)	BP Llandarcy

The scoreline after 90 minutes was 1-1.

Haverfordwest County	4-0	Afan Lido
Spencer Works Newport	7-4	Maesteg Park
Cwymbran Town	1-2	Pembroke Borough
Bridgend Town	1-4	Pontllanfraith

Third Round

Bethesda Athletic	1-3	Shrewsbury Town

Played at Bangor City FC

Hereford United	4-1	Colwyn Bay
Aberystwyth Town	1-1	Caernarfon Town
Chirk AAA	1-4	Wrexham

Played at Wrexham

Lex XI	2-1	Brecon Corinthians
Llanidloes Town	0-2	Rhyl
Bangor City	4-0	Worcester City
Brymbo Steelworks	0-2	Towyn
Ton Pentre	0-2	Caerleon
Pontllanfraith	1-2	AFC Cardiff
Pembroke Borough	0-2	Newport County
Sully	4-0	Pontardawe Athletic
Haverfordwest County	0-3	Cardiff Corinthians
Briton Ferry Athletic	0-1	Barry Town
Cardiff City	5-0	Merthyr Tydfil
Swansea City	1-1	Spencer Works Newport

Third Round Replays

Caernarfon Town	3-2	Aberystwyth Town
Spencer Works Newport	0-5	Swansea City

Fourth Round

Swansea City	7-1	Sully
Rhyl	2-1	Caernarfon Town
Wrexham	3-0	Barry Town
Shrewsbury Town	6-0	AFC Cardiff
Caerleon	0-0	Bangor City
Towyn	3-0	Lex XI
Newport County	4-0	Cardiff Corinthians
Cardiff City	0-4	Hereford United

Fourth Round Replay

Bangor City	2-0	Caerleon

Fifth Round

Swansea City	2-0	Hereford United
Newport County	3-2	Wrexham
Rhyl	1-7	Shrewsbury Town
Bangor City	6-1	Towyn

Semi-finals – 1st leg

Swansea City	2-2	Shrewsbury Town
Bangor City	1-0	Newport County

Semi-finals – 2nd leg

Shrewsbury Town	2-1	Swansea City

Shrewsbury Town won 4-3 on aggregate.

Newport County	0-0	Bangor City

Bangor City won 1-0 on aggregate.

1985 WELSH CUP FINAL

1st leg

14th May 1985 at Gay Meadow, Shrewsbury

Shrewsbury Town	3-1	Bangor City

Tester 2, Hackett *Urquhart*

Shrewsbury Town: Perks, W Williams,
P Johnson, R McLaren, C Griffin, Cross, G Hackett,
Petts (Nardiello), Stevens, C Robinson, P Tester

Bangor City: B Lloyd, Gunn, P Lunn, G Evans,
J Banks, N Powell, B Urquhart, P Whelan,
V Williams, E Williams, A Morris (G Williams)

Referee: H King (Troedyrhiw)

Attendance: 1,507

2nd leg

19th May 1985 at Farrar Road, Bangor

Bangor City	0-2	Shrewsbury Town

McLaren, Stevens

Bangor City: B Lloyd, Gunn, P Lunn, G Williams,
J Banks, N Powell, B Urquhart, P Whelan,
V Williams (Fuller), E Williams, A Morris

Shrewsbury Town: Perks, W Williams,
P Johnson, R McLaren, C Griffin, Cross, G Hackett,
Petts (Nardiello), Stevens, C Robinson, P Tester

Referee: H King (Troedyrhiw)

Attendance: 1,800

1985/86 Welsh Cup

First Round

Llanrwst United	1-3	BSC Shotton
Flint Town United	3-3	Connah's Quay Nomads
Conwy United	2-3	Holywell Town
Bethesda Athletic	1-1	Llanfairpwll
Blaenau Ffestiniog FC	2-0	Llandudno Amateurs
Pwllheli & District	2-1	Pilkingtons St Asaph
Rhos United (withdrew)	v	Porthmadog (w/o)
Druids United	2-2	Mold Alexandra
Grapes Moss	1-0	Denbigh Town
Cefn Albion	1-1	Brymbo Steelworks
Chirk AAA	1-0	Rhos Aelwyd
Bala Town	1-2	Gresford Athletic
Llandrindod Wells	0-1	Newtown
Machynlleth	2-7	Caersws
Oswestry Town	3-1	Llanidloes Town
Aberystwyth Town	3-1	Presteigne St Andrews
Kidderminster Harriers	2-0	Montgomery Town
Knighton Town	1-1	Rhayader Town
Afan Lido	0-1	Taff's Well
Ammanford Town	2-4	South Glamorgan Institute
Ferndale Athletic	2-1	Spencer Works
Abercynon Athletic	5-0	Pontawdawe Athletic
Aheraman	3-1	BP Llandarcy
Newport YMCA	0-3	Abergavenny Thursdays

First Round Replays

Connah's Quay Nomads	2-3	Flint Town United
Llanfairpwll	3-2	Bethesda Athletic
Mold Alexandra	9-1	Druids United
Brymbo Steelworks	4-2	Cefn Albion
Rhayader Town	3-0	Knighton Town

Second Round

Lex XI	2-0	Colwyn Bay
Oswestry Town	1-0	Newtown
Caernarfon Town	2-0	Tywyn
BSC Shotton	0-1	Holywell Town
Following a protest, Holywell were dismissed from the competition so BSC Shotton progressed.		
Brymbo Steelworks	2-0	Rhayader Town
Chirk AAA	2-2	Kidderminster Harriers
Worcester City	2-1 (aet)	Rhos United
Caersws	1-1 (aet)	Flint Town United
Mold Alexandra	3-1	Aberystwyth Town
Gresford Athletic	2-3	Pwllheli & District
Grapes Moss	0-5	Rhyl
Played at Rhyl		
Blaenau Ffestiniog FC	0-3	Llanfairpwll
Pembroke Boro	0-4	AFC Cardiff
Taff's Well	1-2	Barry Town
Caerleon	1-0	Cardiff Corinthians
Ferndale Athletic	1-2	Ebbw Vale Town
Ton Pentre	1-1	Abergavenny Thursdays
Caerau	0-0	Brecon Corinthians
Aberaman	1-3	Maesteg Park
Milford United	2-0	Llanelli
Carmarthen Town	1-2	Sully
Bridgend Town	2-2	South Glamorgan Institute
Abercynon Athletic	1-1	Briton Ferry Athletic
Played at Briton Ferry		
Pontllanfraith	0-1	Haverfordwest County
Port Talbot Athletic	0-6	Merthyr Tydfil

Second Round Replays

Kidderminster Harriers	10-1	Chirk AAA
Flint Town United	1-2	Caersws
Abergavenny Thursdays	1-2	Ton Pentre
Brecon Corinthians	5-2	Caerau
South Glamorgan Institute	0-1	Bridgend Town
Briton Ferry Athletic	1-0	Abercynon Athletic

Third Round

Caernarfon Town	0-1	Caersws
Hereford United	0-2	Bangor City
Llanfairpwll	3-1	Pwllheli & District
Kidderminster Harriers	3-1	Shrewsbury Town
Brymbo Steelworks	2-3	Mold Alexandra
Rhyl	1-2	BSC Shotton
Worcester City	1-2	Wrexham
Oswestry Town	5-2	Lex XI
Ton Pentre	2-4	Newport County
Brecon Corinthians	2-2	Bridgend Town
Caerleon	2-3	Cardiff City
AFC Cardiff	2-2 (aet)	Sully
Briton Ferry Athletic	0-1	Ebbw Vale
Merthyr Tydfil	5-0	Milford United
Haverfordwest County	2-6	Swansea City
Maesteg Park	0-2	Barry Town

Third Round Replays

Bridgend Town	2-0	Brecon Corinthians
Sully	1-1	AFC Cardiff
Sully won 10-9 on penalties.		

Fourth Round

Cardiff City	4-1	Mold Alexandra
Wrexham	8-0	Bridgend Town
Hereford United	10-1	BSC Shotton
Barry Town	6-3	Oswestry Town
Merthyr Tydfil	2-0	Ebbw Vale
Newport County	3-3	Kidderminster Harriers
Llanfairpwll	0-2	Caersws
Sully	1-2	Swansea City

Fourth Round Replay

Kidderminster Harriers	2-1	Newport County

Fifth Round

Merthyr Tydfil	1-3	Hereford United
Wrexham	3-0	Caersws
Cardiff City	0-0	Barry Town
Swansea City	1-1	Kidderminster Harriers

Fifth Round Replays

Barry Town	0-2	Cardiff City
Kidderminster Harriers	4-0	Swansea City

Semi-finals – 1st leg

Kidderminster Harriers	4-1	Hereford United
Wrexham	4-1	Cardiff City

Semi-finals – 2nd leg

Hereford United	3-1	Kidderminster Harriers

Kidderminster Harriers won 5-4 on aggregate

Cardiff City	1-2	Wrexham

Wrexham won 6-2 on aggregate

1986 WELSH CUP FINAL

18th May 1986 at the Racecourse, Wrexham

Wrexham	1-1	Kidderminster Harriers
Horne		Casey

Wrexham: D Davies, N Salathiel, S Cunnington, M Williams, F Jones, P Comstive, N Hencher (D Gregory), B Horne, J Steel, S Charles, A Edwards

Kidderminster Harriers: T Campbell, M Buckland, J Barton, C Boxall, C Jones, M Woodhall, G Mackenzie, K Casey, M Rosegreen, M Tuohy, O'Dowd

Referee: K Cooper (Pontypridd)

Attendance: 5,035

1985/86 REPLAY

21st May 1986 at Aggborough, Kidderminster

Kidderminster Harriers	1-2	Wrexham
Casey		Steel 2

Kidderminster Harriers: T Campbell, M Buckland, J Barton, C Boxall, C Jones, M Woodhall, G Mackenzie, K Casey, M Rosegreen, M Tuohy, O'Dowd

Wrexham: D Davies, N Salathiel, S Cunnington, M Williams, F Jones, P Comstive, S Buxton, B Horne, J Steel, S Charles, A Edwards

Referee: K Cooper (Pontypridd)

Attendance: 4,304

1986/87 Welsh Cup

First Round

Conwy United	2-4	Prestatyn Town
Holywell Town	2-0	CPD Porthmadog
Bethesda Athletic	5-0	Llanfairfechan
Pwllheli & District (withdrew)	v	Denbigh Town (w/o)
Holyhead United Juniors (withdrew)	v	Llanrwst United (w/o)
Pilkingtons St. Asaph	3-3	Connah's Quay Nomads
Rhos United	0-0	Rhydymwyn
Fflint Town United	1-1	Shotton Westminster
Tywyn (withdrew)	v	Gresford Athletic (w/o)
Presteigne St Andrews	3-1	Corwen Amateurs
Machynlleth	0-1	Brymbo Steelworks
Ruthin Town	5-2	Penycae
Cefn Albion	2-0	Knighton Town
Chirk AAA	5-1	Bala Town
Druids United	0-3	Lex XI
Rhos Aelwyd	4-1	Llangollen
Newtown AFC	8-0	Llanidloes Town
Llandrindod Wells	1-0	Abergavenny Thursdays
Ferndale Athletic	3-0	Pontardawe Athletic
Maesteg Park AFC	1-0	Pontllanfraith
Aberaman Athletic	1-0	Ammanford Town
Port Talbot Athletic	1-3	Afan Lido
South Glamorgan Institute	0-2	Cardiff Corinthians
Carmarthen Town	1-3	AFC Cardiff
Llanelli AFC	0-1	Abercynon Athletic
Pembroke Borough	0-1	Caerleon
BP Llandarcy	1-2	Worcester City
Spencer Works Newport	0-0	Taff's Well
Newport YMCA	0-0	Caerau FC

First Round Replays

Connah's Quay Nomads	1-2	Pilkingtons St. Asaph
Rhydymwyn	2-1	Rhos United
Shotton Westminster	3-4	Fflint Town United
Taff's Well	2-0	Spencer Works Newport
Caerau FC	1-2	Newport YMCA

Second Round

Bethesda Athletic	1-1	Brecon Corinthians
Denbigh Town	0-5	Brymbo Steelworks
Colwyn Bay	2-0	Oswestry Town
Holywell Town	4-2	Llanrwst United
Prestatyn Town	0-0	Ruthin Town
BSC Shotton	0-1	Aberystwyth Town
Rhydymwyn FC	1-3	Caernarfon Town
Cefn Albion	2-1	Fflint Town United
Mold Alexandra	0-1	Rhos Aelwyd
Gresford Athletic	1-1	Llanfairpwll FC
Chirk AAA	0-1	Pilkingtons St.Asaph
Lex XI	2-0	Caersws FC
Newtown AFC	1-3	Rhyl
Presteigne St Andrews	1-2	Bangor City
Milford United	1-1	AFC Cardiff
Newport YMCA	2-2	Afan Lido
Cwmbran Town	1-2	Haverfordwest County
Aberaman Athletic	1-1	Caerleon FC
Abercynon Athletic	1-2	Briton Ferry Athletic
Sully FC	2-0	Llandrindod Wells
Ferndale Athletic	1-1	Taff's Well
Ton Pentre AFC	2-1	Ebbw Vale
Cardiff Corinthians	0-0	Merthyr Tydfil
Maesteg Park AFC	1-0	Bridgend Town
Barry Town	2-2	Worcester City

Second Round Replays

Brecon Corinthians	7-2	Bethesda Athletic
Ruthin Town	1-2	Prestatyn Town

Llanfairpwll FC	4-1	Gresford Athletic
AFC Cardiff	2-1	Milford United
Afan Lido	2-0	Newport YMCA
Caerleon FC	1-0	Aberaman Athletic
Taff's Well	3-1	Ferndale Athletic
Merthyr Tydfil	2-0	Cardiff Corinthians
Worcester City	0-2	Barry Town

Third Round

Colwyn Bay	1-1	Caernarfon Town
Rhyl FC	1-0	Holywell Town
Kidderminster Harriers	0-1	Llanfairpwll
Cefn Albion	0-10	Shrewsbury Town
Hereford United	0-1	Wrexham
Rhos Aelwyd	1-1	Lex XI
Brecon Corinthians	1-1	Aberystwyth Town
Brymbo Steelworks	6-0	Pilkingtons St.Asaph
Bangor City	3-1	Prestatyn Town
Cardiff City	4-0	Taff's Well
Swansea City	1-3	Newport County
Caerleon	1-2	Sully
Afan Lido	0-1	Ton Pentre
Haverfordwest County	4-2	AFC Cardiff
Merthyr Tydfil	1-0	Maesteg Park
Barry Town	2-1	Briton Ferry Athletic

Third Round Replays

Caernarfon Town	0-0 (aet)	Colwyn Bay

Caernarfon Town won 4-1 on penalties.

Lex XI	3-2	Rhos Aelwyd
Aberystwyth Town	3-1	Brecon Corinthians

Fourth Round

Shrewsbury Town	0-1	Newport County
Caernarfon Town	1-1	Merthyr Tydfil
Brymbo Steelworks	4-1	Sully
Bangor City	3-0	Ton Pentre
Wrexham	1-0	Cardiff City
Llanfairpwll	1-3	Aberystwyth Town
Rhyl FC	2-2	Haverfordwest County
Barry Town	2-0	Lex XI

Fourth Round Replays

Merthyr Tydfil	3-1	Caernarfon Town
Haverfordwest County	0-1	Rhyl FC

Fifth Round

Bangor City	2-1	Rhyl FC
Merthyr Tydfil	4-2	Barry Town
Aberystwyth Town	2-2	Newport County
Wrexham	1-0	Brymbo Steelworks

Fifth Round Replay

Newport County	1-0	Aberystwyth Town

Semi-finals – 1st leg

Newport County	2-1	Wrexham
Merthyr Tydfil	1-0	Bangor City

Semi-finals – 2nd leg

Wrexham	2-2	Newport County

Newport County won 4-3 on aggregate.

Bangor City	1-0	Merthyr Tydfil

Merthyr Tydfil won on penalties.

1987 WELSH CUP FINAL

17th May 1987 at Ninian Park, Cardiff

Merthyr Tydfil	2-2	Newport County
Latchford, Webley		Thackeray 2

Merthyr Tydfil: G Wager, Tong, G Baird, Holvey, Mullen, S Williams, K Rogers, D Webley, R Latchford, Beattie, C Williams

Newport County: J Dillon, L Jones, S Sherlock, A Thackeray, Compton, R Carter, Staniforth, Gibbins (Mills), R Jones, S Taylor, J Lewis

Referee: F Roberts (Prestatyn)

Attendance: 7,000

1987 WELSH CUP FINAL REPLAY

21st May 1987 at Ninian Park, Cardiff

Merthyr Tydfil	1-0	Newport County
Baird		

Newport County: J Dillon, L Jones, S Sherlock, Mills, Compton, R Carter, Staniforth, Gibbins, R Jones, S Taylor, J Lewis

Merthyr Tydfil: G Wager, Tong, G Baird, Holvey, Mullen, S Williams, K Rogers, D Webley, R Latchford, Beattie, C Williams

Referee: F Roberts (Prestatyn)

Attendance: 6,010

1987/88 Welsh Cup

First Round

Porthmadog	3-1	Conwy United
Llanfairpwll	3-1	Rhos United
Llanrwst United	3-1	Llandudno Amateurs
Bala Town	0-6	Shotton Westminster
Denbigh Town	2-3	Rhydymwyn
Cionnahs Quay Nomads	0-2	Holywell Town
Flint Town United	1-1	Prestatyn Town
Pilkingtons St Asaph	1-0	Hawarden Rangers
Lex XI	0-0	Gresford Athletic
Corwen Amateurs	0-1	Llay Welfare
Llay Royal British Legion	2-0	Bradley Sports Club
Druids United	1-4	Penycae
Overton Athletic	1-3	Rhos Aelwyd
Ruthin Town	4-1	Cefn Albion

Kidderminster Harriers	3-0	Oswestry Town
Caersws	3-0	Llanidloes Town
Knighton Town (w/o)	v	Rhayader Town (withdrew)
Llandrindod Wells	4-2	Presteigne St Andrews
Machynlleth	1-2	Chirk AAA
Pontllanfraith	1-1	Sully
Cardiff Corinthians	4-2 (aet)	Pembroke Borough
Ebbw Vale	1-0	Maesteg Park Athletic
Afan Lido	3-0	South Wales Police
Caldicot Town	2-1	Caerau
Spencer Works	1-2	BP Llandarcy
Taff's Well	3-0	Ammanford United
S Glamorgan Institute	0-1	Carmarthen Town
Port Talbot Athletic	1-1	Brecon Corinthians
Bridgend Town	6-4	Aberaman
Llanelli	0-3	Milford United
Caerleon	2-3	Ferndale Athletic
Worcester City	1-0	Forest Green Rovers
Risca United	1-4	Briton Ferry Athletic
Abergavenny Thursdays	2-0	AFC Cardiff
Skewen Athletic	4-1	Abercynon Athletic
Newport YMCA	4-1	Pontardawe Athletic

First Round Replays

Prestatyn Town	1-3	Flint Town United
Gresford Athletic	0-1	Lex XI
Sully	3-2	Pontllanfraith
Brecon Corinthians	1-3	Port Talbot Athletic

Second Round

Caernarfon Town	2-1	Bethesda Athletic
Llanrwst United	3-3	Rhydymwyn
Rhyl	4-0	Holywell Town
Porthmadog	2-1	Flint Town United
Llanfairpwll	5-1	Shotton Westminster
Colwyn Bay	4-1	Pilkingtons St Asaph
Kidderminster Harriers	1-1	Penycae
Newtown	1-0	Chirk AAA
Lex XI	0-4	Brymbo Steelworks
Rhos Aelwyd	0-3	Llay Royal British Legion
Mold Alexandra	2-0	Caersws
Ruthin Town	3-0	Llay Welfare
Port Talbot Athletic	2-1	Sully
Taff's Well	1-2	Worcester City
Presteigne St Andrews	1-2	Bangor City
Played at Worcester		
Skewen Athletic	2-1	BP Llandarcy
Haverfordwest County	1-0	Barry Town
Caldicot Town	1-1	Cwmbran Town
Newport YMCA	1-2	Ebbw Vale
Ton Pentre	3-1	Abergavenny Thursdays
Milford United	2-1	Bridgend Town
Llandrindod Wells	1-6	Aberystwyth Town
Knighton Town	2-0	Cardiff Corinthians
Ferndale Athletic	4-1	Carmarthen Town
Afan Lido	1-1	Briton Ferry Athletic

Second Round Replays

Rhydymwyn	2-3	Llanrwst United
Cwmbran Town	2-2 (aet)	Caldicot Town
Cwmbran Town won 4-2 on penalties.		
Briton Ferry Athletic	1-0	Afan Lido

Third Round

Hereford United	0-3	Kidderminster Harriers
Wrexham	3-0	Ruthin Town
Caernarfon Town	4-1	Mold Alexandra
Llanfairpwll	2-1	Shrewsbury Town
Brymbo Steelworks	2-1	Rhyl
Porthmadog	1-4	Colwyn Bay
Llay Royal British Legion	0-0	Newtown
Llanrwst United	0-3	Bangor City
Ebbw Vale	0-1	Cardiff City
Cwmbran Town	0-4	Swansea City
Newport County	2-4	Haverfordwest County
Milford United	0-1	Aberystwyth Town
Merthyr Tydfil	3-0	Knighton Town
Worcester City	3-1	Briton Ferry Athletic
Port Talbot Athletic	0-0	Ferndale Athletic
Skewen Athletic	0-5	Ton Pentre

Third Round Replays

Newtown	1-0	Llay Royal British Legion
Ferndale Athletic	2-4	Port Talbot Athletic

Fourth Round

Brymbo Steelworks	1-1	Bangor City
Caernarfon Town	3-1	Shrewsbury Town
Newtown	1-1	Colwyn Bay
Haverfordwest County	0-1	Kidderminster Harriers
Wrexham	4-1	Worcester City
Cardiff City	3-1	Port Talbot Athletic
Swansea City	0-2	Merthyr Tydfil
Ton Pentre	1-1	Aberystwyth Town

Fourth Round Replays

Bangor City	5-1	Brymbo Steelworks
Colwyn Bay	3-1	Newtown
Aberystwyth Town	1-3	Ton Pentre

Fifth Round

Wrexham	2-1	Ton Pentre
Caernarfon Town	0-0	Colwyn Bay
Bangor City	2-2	Kidderminster Harriers
Cardiff City	3-1	Merthyr Tydfil

Fifth Round Replays

Colwyn Bay	0-0 (aet)	Caernarfon Town 0-0
Caernarfon Town won 5-4 on penalties.		
Kidderminster Harriers	3-1	Bangor City

Semi-finals – 1st leg

Cardiff City	2-1	Caernarfon Town
Kidderminster Harriers	1-2	Wrexham

Semi-finals – 2nd leg

Caernarfon Town	0-1	Cardiff City
Cardiff City won 3-1 on aggregate.		
Wrexham	3-2	Kidderminster Harriers
Wrexham won 5-3 on aggregate.		

1988 WELSH CUP FINAL

18th May 1988 at the Vetch Field, Swansea

Cardiff City 2-0 Wrexham
Gilligan, Curtis

Cardiff City: G Wood, P Bater, N Plautner, M Ford, N Stevenson, T Boyle, A Curtis, B McDermott, J Gilligan, M Kelly, K Bartlett, (Wheeler), sub (not used) S Mardenborough

Wrexham: M Salmon, N Salathiel, D Wright, J Jones, M Williams (S Massey), B Flynn, R Preece (J Bowden), G Hunter, S Buxton, K Russell, M Carter

Referee: R B Gifford (Llanbradach)

Attendance: 5,465

1988/89 Welsh Cup

First Round

Conwy United	2-0	Rhydymwyn
Llanfairpwll	2-0	Rhos United
Porthmadog	2-0	Mold Alexandra
Bethesda Athletic	4-1	Lanrwst United
Llandudno	0-1	Flint Town United
Howarden Rangers	1-3	Shotton Westminster
Connah's Quay Nomads	0-0	Mostyn
Pilkington	1-3	Holywell Town
Ruthin Town	3-0	Corwen Amateurs
Lex XI	2-2	Buckley FC
Overton Athletic	0-2	Llay Welfare
Cefn Albion	3-2	Penycae
Chirk AAA	9-0	Bala Town
Llay Royal British Legion	0-1	Gresford Athletic
Rhos Aelwyd	0-4	Bradley SC
Builth Wells	0-4	Brecon Corinthians
Caersws	6-1	Llandridod Wells
Presteigne St Andrews	2-0	Machynlleth
Knighton Town	0-0	Rhayader Town
Carno	0-2	Llandidloes Town
Tonyrefail Welfare	3-2	Sully
Abercynon Athletic	1-4	Abergavenny Thursdays
South Glamorgan Institute	0-9	Llanwern FC
Trelewis	0-3	Ferndale Athletic
Barry Town	2-1	Briton Ferry Athletic
Afan Lido	2-2	Maesteg Park Athletic
Risca United	1-1	Pontllanfraith
Cwmbran Town	0-3	AFC Cardiff
Caerleon	0-0	Newport YMCA
Caldicot Town	3-0	Cardiff Corinthians
Clydach United	2-0	Port Talbot Athletic
Skewen Athletic	5-2	South Wales Police
Carmarthen Town	1-0	Llanelli
BP Llandarcey	0-1	Caerau
Milford United	2-5	Bridgend Town
Pontardawe Athletic	0-5	Haverfordwest County
Pembroke Borough	2-0	Ammanford Town
Forest Green Rovers	1-1	Bath City
Cheltenham Town	0-2	Worcester City

First Round Replays

Mostyn	1-1	Connah's Quay Nomads
Rhayader Town	1-2	Knighton Town
Maesteg Park Athletic	2-3	Afan Lido
Pontllanfraith	1-1	Risca United
Newport YMCA	1-0	Caerleon
Bath City	2-1	Forest Green Rovers

First Round Second Replays

Connah's Quay Nomads	1-2	Mostyn
Risca United	4-1	Pontllanfraith

Second Round

Colwyn Bay	1-1	Bangor City
Llanfairpwll	2-1	Conwy United
Holywell Town	1-3	Porthmadog
Flint Town United	2-2	Rhyl
Bethesda Athletic	3-1	Mostyn
Brymbo Steelworks	0-1	Chirk AAA
Newtown	4-4	Gresford Athletic
Lex XI	2-0	Cefn Albion
Rhos Aelwyd	2-1	Ruthin Town
Caersws	4-1	Llanidloes Town
Llay Welfare	3-3	Shotton Westminster
Skewen Athletic	0-3	Bath City
Haverfordwest County	2-0	Pembroke Borough
Worcester City	3-0	Carmarthen Town
Ferndale Athletic	0-2	Risca United
Abergavenny Thursdays	1-1	Caldicot Town
AFC Cardiff	0-6	Merthyr Tydfil
Ton Pentre	0-3	Barry Town
Presteigne St Andrews	1-3	Clydach Town
Caerau	0-1	Newport YMCA
Aberystwyth Town	1-0	Afan Lido
Ebbw Vale	1-0	Brecon Corinthians
Tonyrefail Welfare	3-1	Knighton Town
Llanwern FC	0-2	Bridgend Town

Second Round Replays

Bangor City	2-0	Colwyn Bay
Rhyl	2-1	Flint Town United
Gresford Athletic	1-4	Newtown
Shotton Westminster	6-0	Llay Welfare
Caldicot Town	0-2	Abergavenny Thursdays

Third Round

Shrewsbury Town	2-0	Caernarfon Town
Porthmadog	0-2	Bangor City
Rhos Aelwyd	0-4	Hereford United
Lex XI	0-8	Wrexham
Newtown	5-0	Shotton Westminster
Rhyl	2-2	Caersws
Kidderminster Harriers	3-0	Llanfairpwll
Merthyr Tydfil	0-3	Swansea City
Cardiff City	3-0	Bath City
Barry Town	5-1	Clydach United
Haverfordwest County	2-0	Newport YMCA
Newport County	6-1	Bridgend Town
Tonyrefail Welfare	0-2	Worcester City
Abergavenny Thursdays	2-1	Risca United
Ebbw Vale	2-1	Aberystwyth Town

Third Round Replay

Caersws	1-0	Rhyl

Fourth Round

Worcester City	0-1	Cardiff City
Barry Town	2-0	Haverfordwest County
Newport County	3-0	Caernarfon Town
Newtown	0-1	Bangor City
Swansea City	0-0	Caersws
Bethesda Athletic	0-2	Hereford United
Abergavenny Thursdays	1-2	Kidderminster Harriers
Ebbw Vale	1-2	Wrexham

Fourth Round Replay

Caersws	0-2	Swansea City

Fifth Round

Newport County	0-1	Hereford United
Wrexham	1-3	Swansea City
Barry Town	1-0	Bangor City
Kidderminster Harriers	3-1	Cardiff City

Semi-finals – 1st leg

Barry Town	0-1	Swansea City
Kidderminster Harriers	1-0	Hereford United

Semi-finals – 2nd leg

Swansea City	3-1	Barry Town
Swansea City won 4-1 on aggregate		
Hereford United	0-0	Kidderminster Harriers
Kidderminster Harriers won 1-0 on aggregate		

1989 WELSH CUP FINAL

21st May 1989 at the Vetch Field, Swansea

Swansea City	5-0	Kidderminster Harriers

Wade, James, Raynor, Hutchinson, Thornber

Swansea City: L Bracey, A Melville, C Coleman, D Lewis, A Knill, S Thornber, R James, A Davies, P Raynor, B Wade (A Legg), T Hutchinson (D Hough)

Kidderminster Harriers: P Jones, Pearson, J Barton, C Brazier, M Weir, Bancroft (G McKenzie), Dearlove (Howell), K Casey, P Davies, M Tuohy, R Jones

Referee: J W Lloyd (Wrexham)

Attendance: 5,100

1989/90 Welsh Cup

First Round

Conwy United	3-3	Y Felinheli
Porthmadog	3-0	Llanerchymedd
Llanrwst United	1-3	Nantlle Vale
Llanfairpwll	1-2	Bethesda Athletic
Shotton Westminster	1-7	Connah's Quay Nomads
Mostyn	5-2	Llandudno
Flint Town United	4-0	Holywell Town
Pilkington's St Asaph	3-1	Rhydymwyn
Tywyn and Bryncryg	3-1	Knighton Town
Druids United	2-1	Bradley Sport Club
Brymbo Steelworks	4-1	Buckley FC
Mold Alexandra	2-4	Gresford Athletic
Llay Royal British Legion	1-0	British Aerospace
Bala Town	1-2	Penycae
Corwen Amateurs	1-4	Morda United
Rhos Aelwyd	1-1	Cefn Albion
Chirk AAA	2-1	Ruthin Town
Lex XI	10-0	Llay Welfare
Llanidloes Town	1-1	Rhayader Town
Builth Wells	5-1	Llandrindod Wells
Penrhyncoch	8-0	Machynlleth
Bridgend Town	2-2	Cwmbran Town
AFC Cardiff	3-1	Tonyrefail Welfare
Pontyclun	2-1	Risca United
Trelewis	1-2	Skewen Athletic
South Glamorgan Institute of Higher Education	0-3	Brecon Corinthians
Ferndale Athletic	10-0	Newport YMCA
Caerau	2-3	Taff's Well
Port Talbot Athletic	1-0	Caldicot Town
Caerleon	1-4	Briton Ferry Athletic
Pontllanfraith	2-2	Abergavenny Thursdays
BP Llandarcy	0-2	Ammanford Town
Afan Lido	4-0	Abercynon Athletic
Seven Sisters	3-4	Cardiff Corinthians
Carmarthen Town	2-1	Llanwern
Haverfordwest County	1-1	Sully
Pembroke Borough	0-0	Ponterdawe Athletic
Llanelli	2-0	Milford United
Bath City	1-1	Cheltenham Town
Stoubridge	0-2	Worcester City
AFC Newport	3-1	Stroud FC

First Round Replays

Y Felinheli	0-1	Conwy United
Cefn Albion	5-3	Rhos Aelwyd
Rhayader Town	3-2	Llanidloes Town
Cwmbran Town	2-3	Bridgend Town
Abergavenny Thursdays	1-2	Pontllanfraith
Sully	3-2	Haverfordwest County
Pontardawe Athletic	1-2	Pembroke Borough
Cheltenham Town	0-2	Bath City

Second Round

Pilkingtons St Asaph	1-3	Rhyl
Bethsda Athletic	0-3	Porthmadog
Nantlle Vale	0-3	Colwyn Bay
Conwy United	1-1	Bangor City
Flint Town United	1-0	Caernarfon Town
Penycae	2-0	Cefn Albion
Lex XI	2-1	Gresford Athletic
Connah's Quay Nomads	2-1	Llay Royal British Legion
Druids United	0-1	Chirk AAA
Mostyn	2-2	Brymbo Steelworks
Builth Wells	0-3	Caersws

Rhayader Town	0-5	Morda United
Aberystwyth Town	3-0	Penrhyncoch
Tywyn & Bryncrug	2-0	Newtown
Port Talbot Athletic	1-0	Briton Ferry Athletic
Worcester City	4-0	Ebbw Vale
Pontllanfraith	0-3	Llanelli
Bridgend Town	2-3	AFC Cardiff
Sully	1-1	Maesteg Park
Taff's Well	0-2	Ton Pentre
Skewen Athletic	0-0	Cardiff Corinthians
Carmarthen Town	1-2	Ammanford
Pontyclun	0-9	Bath City
Ferndale Athletic	0-4	Pembroke Borough
AFC Newport	1-0	Brecon Corinthians
Afan Lido	2-3	Merthyr Tydfil

Second Round Replays

Bangor City	8-0	Conwy United
Brymbo Steelworks	4-1	Mostyn
Maesteg Park	2-1	Sully
Cardiff Corinthians	5-1	Skewen Athletic

Third Round

Ton Pentre	0-2	Port Talbot Athletic
Ammanford Town	1-3	Llanelli
Aberystwyth Town	2-1	Cardiff Corinthians
Swansea City	1-7	Merthyr Tydfil
Pembroke Borough	1-7	AFC Cardiff
Cardiff City	1-0	AFC Newport
Barry Town	3-2	Bath City
Hereford United	9-0	Connah's Quay Nomads
Porthmadog	1-4	Wrexham
Penycae	0-2	Caersws
Bangor City	7-1	Flint Town United
Brymbo Steelworks	1-8	Colwyn Bay
Morda United	1-2	Kidderminster Harriers
Tywyn & Bryncrug	2-1	Lex XI
Chirk AAA	1-6	Rhyl
Maesteg Park	1-1	Worcester City

Third Round Replay

Worcester City	1-0	Maesteg Park

Fourth Round

Rhyl	3-1	Llanelli
Caersws	3-0	Tywyn & Bryncrug
Port Talbot Athletic	1-4	Cardiff City
AFC Cardiff	2-2	Aberystwyth Town
Colwyn Bay	0-1	Barry Town
Merthyr Tydfil	0-3	Bangor City
Kidderminster Harriers	1-3	Hereford United
Worcester City	0-1	Wrexham

Fourth Round Replays

Aberystwyth Town	1-0	AFC Cardiff

Fifth Round

Caersws	1-2	Barry Town
Wrexham	1-1	Rhyl FC
Cardiff City	2-0	Aberystwyth Town
Bangor City	1-1	Hereford United

Fifth Round Replays

Rhyl FC	0-2	Wrexham
Hereford United	4-0	Bangor City

Semi-finals – 1st leg

Barry Town	0-1	Wrexham
Cardiff City	0-3	Hereford United

Semi-finals – 1st leg

Wrexham	0-0	Barry Town

Wrexham won 1-0 on aggregate.

Hereford United	1-3	Cardiff City

Hereford United won 4-3 on aggregate.

1990 WELSH CUP FINAL

13th May 1990 at the National Stadium, Cardiff

Hereford United	2-1	Wrexham
Robinson, Benbow		Worthington

Hereford United: T Elliott, M A Jones, S Devine, M Pejic, D Peacock, Bradley, S Jones (P Tester), M Jones, I Benbow, Robinson, I Bowyer

Wrexham: V O'Keefe, N Salathiel, A Kennedy, S Reck, N Beaumont, W Phillips, Morgan, A Thackeray, M Sertori (C Armstrong), G Worthington, J Bowden

Referee: J C Deakin (Llantwit Major)

Attendance: 4,182

1990/91 Welsh Cup

First Round

Ammanford Town	1-1	Skewen Athletic
BP Llandarcy	1-0	South Wales Police
Bala Town	5-0	Rubery Owen
Brecon Corries	1-2	Carmarthen Town
Bridgend Town	4-1	Seven Sisters
British Aerospace	1-8	Mochdre
Briton Ferry	1-0	Afan Lido
Brymbo Steelworks	2-0	Llay Welfare
Buckley FC	1-1	Lex XI
Builth Wells	2-1	Llansantffraid
Caerleon	0-1	Caldicot Town
Caersws	2-1	Tywyn & Bryncrug
Cardiff Institute of Higher Education	0-3	Pontllanfraith
Carno	0-1	Worcester City
Chirk AAA	1-1	New Broughton
Colwyn Bay	2-0	Bethesda Athletic
Connay's Quay Nomads	5-2	Pilkingtons St Asaph
Conwy United	3-2	Llanrwst United
Corwen Amateurs	1-2	Llay Royal British Legion

Ebbw Vale	3-0	Tonyrefail Welfare
Ferndale Athletic	1-1	Cheltenham Town
Fflint Town United	2-1	Ruthin Town
Knighton Town	3-1	Llanidloes Town
Llandudno	1-1	Llanfairpwll
Llangefni Town	5-1	Pwllheli Borough
Locomotive Llanberis	1-1	Porthmadog
Morda United	0-2	Hednesford Town
Mostyn	4-2	Rhyl Victory Club
Newport YMCA	2-2	Inter Cardiff
Newtown	5-0	Penrhyncoch
Penycae	1-1	Gresford Athletic
Pontardawe Athletic	1-0	Pembroke Borough
Pontlottyn Blast Furnace	0-9	Newport AFC
Port Talbot Athletic	2-0	Caerau
Rhos Aelwyd	3-5	Cefn Albion
Rhyl	9-0	Holywell Town
Risca United	1-1	Cardiff Civil Service
Stourbridge	4-1	Welshpool Town
Stroud	3-0	Llanwern
Taff's Well	8-0	Abercynon Athletic
Trelewis Welfare	0-2	Cardiff Corinthians

First Round Replays

Lex XI	3-0	Buckley FC
New Broughton	0-1	Chirk AAA
Llanfairpwll	1-0	Llandudno
Porthmadog	4-1 (aet)	Locomotive Llanberis

The scoreline after 90 minutes was 1-1.

Inter Cardiff	4-2	Newport YMCA

Second Round

Abergavenny Thursdays	4-0	Carmarthen Town
Aberystwyth Town	5-1	Knighton Town
Ammanford Town	3-2	Cardiff Civil Service
Builth Wells	1-5	Cheltenham Town
Caldicot Town	0-0	Cardiff Corinthians
Chirk AAA	5-0	Brymbo Steelworks
Connah's Quay Nomads	0-1	Colwyn Bay
Conwy United	0-3	Llangenfi Town
Cwmbran Town	1-1	Maesteg Park
Haverfordwest County	3-0	Ebbw Vale
Hednesford Town	1-3	Stourbridge
Inter Cardiff	0-2	Ton Pentre
Lex XI	3-0	Bala Town
Llanelli	2-1	Morriston Town
Llanfairpwll	1-4	Caernarfon Town
Llay Royal British Legion	2-0	Gresford Athletic
Mochdre	0-3	Fflint Town United
Newport AFC	3-0	Pembroke Borough
Newtown	6-2	Cefn Albion
Pontllanfraith	0-3	Bridgend Town
Port Talbot Athletic	1-1	Briton Ferry Athletic
Porthmadog	0-4	Bangor City
Rhyl	2-0	Mostyn
Stroud	3-3	Kidderminster Harriers
Taff's Well	0-2	BP Llandarcy
Worcester City	4-1	Caersws FC

Second Round Replays

Cardiff Corinthians	2-0	Caldicot Town
Maesteg Park	0-1	Cwmbran Town

Third Round

Ammanford Town	2-1	Haverfordwest County
Bangor City	2-1	Stourbridge
Bridgend Town	1-1	Abergavenny Thursdays

Bridgend withdrew from the competition.

Briton Ferry Athletic	0-1	BP Llandarcy
Cardiff City	1-4	Merthyr Tydfil
Cardiff Corinthians	0-3	Newport AFC
Chirk AAA	0-3	Stroud
Colwyn Bay	3-1	Rhyl
Cwmbran Town	1-7	Cheltenham Town
Fflint Town United	1-2	Aberystwyth Town
Hereford United	1-1	Newtown AFC
Lex XI	4-3	Llangefni Town
Llay Royal British Legion	0-2	Caernarfon Town
Swansea City	8-1	Llanelli
Ton Pentre	0-1	Barry Town
Wrexham	3-1	Worcester City

Third Round Replay

Newtown AFC	1-1	Hereford United

Hereford United won 4-3 on penalties.

Fourth Round

Aberystwyth Town	1-3	Hereford United
Ammanford Town	0-5	Wrexham
BP Llandarcy	0-5	Stroud
Bangor City	4-1	Lex XI
Barry Town	3-1	Cheltenham Town
Caernarfon Town	1-2	Abergavenny Thursdays
Merthyr Tydfil	0-1	Swansea City
AFC Newport	0-1	Colwyn Bay

Fifth Round

Barry Town	1-1	Abergavenny Thursdays
Colwyn Bay	1-1	Swansea City
Hereford United	1-1	Bangor City
Stroud	1-2	Wrexham

Fifth Round Replays

Abergavenny Thursdays	0-1	Barry Town
Bangor City	0-0	Hereford United

Hereford won 5-4 on penalties.

Swansea City	2-1	Colwyn Bay

Semi-finals – 1st leg

Barry Town	2-2	Swansea City
Wrexham	1-1	Hereford United

Semi-finals – 1st leg

Swansea City	1-0	Barry Town

Swansea won 3-2 on aggregate.

Hereford United	1-2	Wrexham

Wrexham won 3-2 on aggregate.

1991 WELSH CUP FINAL

19th May 1991 at the National Stadium, Cardiff

Swansea City　　2-0　　Wrexham

Penney, Raynor

Swansea City: Kendall, Williams, Coleman, Hough, Trick, Legg, Watson (Charles), Raynor, Coughlin, Connor, Penney

Wrexham: Morris, Thackeray (Owen), Hardy, Sertori, Phillips, J Jones, Bowden, Murray (Beaumont), L Jones, Preece, Griffiths

Referee: K Burge (Rhondda)

Attendance: 5,000

1991/92 Welsh Cup

First Round

Afan Lido	3-0	Seven Sisters
Ammanford Town	3-4	Carmarthen Town
Bala Town	1-1	New Broughton
Bridgend Town	1-0	Ebbw Vale
Buckley FC	2-1	Brymbo FC
Caerau	0-4	Llanwern
Caerleon	2-1	Pontlottyn Blast Furnace
Cardiff Civil Service	3-0	Cardiff Corinthians
Carno	1-2	Llansantffraid
Cefn Albion	1-2	Gresford Athletic
Cemaes Bay	1-0	Conwy United
Chirk AAA	1-0	Lex XI
Connah's Quay Nomads	4-1	Pilkingtons St Asaph
Cwmbran Town	3-2	Newport YMCA
Ferndale Athletic	10-2	Cardiff Institute of Higher Education
Haverfordwest County	3-0	BP Llandarcy
Inter Cardiff	3-3	Caldicot Town
Kidderminster Harriers	5-1	Rhayader Town
Knighton Town	0-0	Llanidloes Town
Llandrindod Wells	1-3	Brecon Corinthians
Llandudno	5-0	Pwllheli Borough
Llanelli	1-2	Port Talbot Athletic
Llanrwst United	1-2	Rhyl
Llay Royal British Legion	1-0	Rhos Aelwyd
Maesteg Park Athletic	8-0	Trelewis Welfare
Marchwiel Villa	0-0	Llay Welfare
Morriston Town	2-2	Pembroke Borough
Nefyn United	1-3	Llanfairpwll
Newcastle Emlyn	3-5	Stourbridge
Penrhyncoch	1-0	Builth Wells
Penycae	5-1	Johnstown Athletic
Pontllanfraith	3-0	Aberaman Athletic
Porthcawl Town	6-1	Ponterdawe Athletic
Porthmadog	2-1	Locomotive Llanberis
Rhydymwyn	0-2	Holywell Town
Risca United	1-3	Abercynon Athletic
Rubery Owen Rockwell	1-9	Morda United
Ruthin Town	0-1	British Aerospace
Skewen Athletic	0-3	Briton Ferry Athletic
Taff's Well	4-0	Pontyclun FC
Ton Pentre	1-0	Stroud
Tonyrefail Welfare	3-0	South Wales Constabulary
Welshpool Town	0-2	Hednesford Town

Played at Hednesford

First Round Replays

New Broughton	4-0	Bala Town
Caldicot Town	0-3	Inter Cardiff
Llanidloes Town	3-2	Knighton Town
Llay Welfare	2-4	Marchwiel Villa
Pembroke Borough	1-2	Morriston Town

Second Round

Bangor City	3-1	Porthmadog
Brecon Corinthians	1-4	Caersws
British Aerospace	1-2	Chirk AAA
Briton Ferry Athletic	2-1	Afan Lido
Buckley FC	0-3	Llay Royal British Legion
Carleon FC	2-1	Ton Pentre
Cardiff Civil Service	1-0	Port Talbot Athletic
Cemaes Bay	3-2	Llanfairpwll
Connah's Quay Nomads	1-1	Colwyn Bay
Cwmbran Town	4-1	Taff's Well
Flint Town United	2-2	Caernarfon Town
Gresford Athletic	0-2	Marchwiel Villa
Haverfordwest County	3-0	Abercynon Athletic
Hednesford Town	3-1	Penrhyncoch
Holywell Town	2-2	Llandudno FC
Inter Cardiff	2-1	Ferndale Athletic
Kidderminster Harriers	7-1	Morda United
Llansantffraid FC	3-1	Llanidloes Town
Maesteg Park Athletic	4-2	Llanwern AFC
Morriston Town	3-0	Tonyrefail Welfare
Mostyn	2-1	Rhyl
New Broughton	1-0	Pencae
Newport AFC	3-1	Bridgend Town
Newtown AFC	1-2	Aberystwyth Town
Pontllanfraith	0-4	Abergavenny Thurdays
Porthcawl Town	1-4	Merthyr Tydfil
Stourbridge	7-1	Carmarthen Town

Second Round Replays

Colwyn Bay	6-0	Connah's Quay Nomads
Llandudno FC	0-3	Holywell Town

Third Round

Barry Town	2-3	Aberystwyth Town
Briton Ferry Athletic	3-2	Abergavenny Thurdays
Caersws FC	1-2	Cemaes Bay
Cardiff City	3-0	Newport AFC
Chirk AAA	2-1	Llay Royal British Legion
Colwyn Bay	5-1	Holywell Town
Cwmbran Town	2-5	Maesteg Park Athletic
Haverfordwest County	4-1	Morriston Town
Hednesford Town	3-0	New Broughton
Inter Cardiff	1-2	Caerleon FC
Kidderminster Harriers	4-1	Llansantffraid FC
Marchwiel Villa	0-3	Caernarfon Town
Merthyl Tydfil	0-2	Swansea City
Mostyn	1-3	Hereford United

Played at Fflint Town United

Stourbridge	0-0	Cardiff Civil Service
Wrexham	3-2	Bangor City

Third Round Replay

Cardiff Civil Service	1-3	Stourbridge

Fourth Round

Briton Ferry Athletic	2-4	Colwyn Bay
Caernarfon Town	0-1	Aberystwyth Town
Cardiff City	3-3	Stourbridge
Cemaes Bay	1-2	Haverfordwest County
Hereford United	1-2	Maesteg Park AFC
Kidderminster United	1-3	Swansea City
Llay Royal British Legion	0-0	Hednesford Town
Wrexham	2-0	Caerleon FC

Fourth Round Replays

Stourbridge	1-2	Cardiff City
Hednesford Town	3-0	Llay Royal British Legion

Fifth Round

Haverfordwest County	0-0	Hednesford Town
Wrexham	0-1	Colwyn Bay

The match was abandoned after 63 minutes due to fog.

Maesteg Park AFC	2-0	Aberystwyth Town
Swansea City	0-1	Cardiff City

Fifth Round Replays

Hednesford Town	4-0	Haverfordwest County
Wrexham	1-3	Colwyn Bay

Semi-finals – 1st leg

Cardiff City	0-0	Maesteg Park Athletic
Hednesford Town	1-0	Colwyn Bay

Semi-finals – 2nd leg

Maesteg Park Athletic	0-4	Cardiff City

Cardiff City 4-0 on aggregate.

Colwyn Bay	2-3	Hednesford Town

Hednesford Town 4-2 on aggregate.

1992 WELSH CUP FINAL

7th May 1992 at the National Stadium, Cardiff

Cardiff City	1-0	Hednesford Town

Dale

Cardiff City: Hansbury, Perry, Searle, Gibbins (Gill), Bellamy, Abraham, Ramsay, Griffith (Miller), Pike, Dale, Blake

Hednesford Town: Hayward, White (Snaith), Collins, Freeman, Foster, Rudge, Turley (Brown), Walsh, Knight, Burr, O'Connor

Referee: H King (Merthyr)

Attendance: 10,300

1992/93 Welsh Cup

Preliminary Round

Abbey Life	2-2	British Aerospace
Buckley FC	0-3	Ruthin Town
Cardiff Institute of Higher Education	0-6	Treowen Stars
Carmarthen Town	3-2	Pontyclun
Llandrindod Wells	0-2	Builth Wells
Llay Welfare	1-0	Penley

Played at Brymbo FC

Nantlle Vale	0-1	Nefyn United
Overton Athletic	1-2	Rhos Aelwyd
Panteg	3-2	Skewen Athletic
Penpacau	6-1	Newcastle Emlyn
Pontarwade Athletic	0-1	Porthcawl Town
Rockwell	2-4	New Broughton

Played at New Broughton

South Wales Constabulary	0-2	Tonyrefail Welfare
Trelewis Welfare	0-2	Abercynon Athletic

Preliminary Round Replay

British Aerospace	2-1	Abbey Life

Played at Mostyn FC

First Round

Aberaman Athletic	1-2	Risca United
AFC Porth	5-1	Panteg
Ammanford Town	2-2	Porthcawl Town
Bala Town (withdrew)	v	Llay Royal British Legion (w/o)
BP Llandarcy	1-1	Abercynon Athletic
Bridgend Town	1-1	Caerleon
British Aerospace	3-0	Marchwiel Villa
Brymbo	3-2	New Broughton
Caldicot Town	2-0	Tonyrefail Welfare
Cardiff Civil Service	4-3	Treowen Stars
Cemaes Bay	3-2	Locomotive Llanberis
Chirk AAA	1-3	Cefn Druids
Y Felinheli	3-2	Nefyn United
Ferndale Athletic	0-2	Ton Pentre
Fields Park Pontllanfraith	0-0	Cardiff Corinthians
Goytre United	1-4	Brecon Corinthians
Knighton Town	4-2	Penparcau
Lex XI	3-0	Penycae
Llandyrnog United	0-4	Mostyn
Llanfairpwll	3-0	Llanrwst United
Llansantffraid	8-0	Presteigne St Andrews
Morda United	4-0	Penrhyncoch
Morriston Town	2-2	Caerau
Pembroke Borough	6-2	Newport YMCA
Pontlottyn Blast Furnace	1-2	Llanwern
Rhayader Town	2-1	Carno
Rhos Aelwyd	2-2	Gresford Athletic
Rhyl FC	3-0	Pilkingtons
Seven Sisters	0-3	Carmarthen Town

Played at Carmarthen

Taff's Well	1-5	Port Talbot Athletic
Welshpool Town	10-1	Builth Wells

First Round Replays

Parthcawl Town	1-0		Ammanford Town
Abercynon Athletic	0-2		BP Llandarcy
Caerleon	3-0		Bridgend Town
Cardiff Corinthians	1-0		Fields Park Pontllanfraith
Caerau	3-0		Morriston Town
Gresford Athletic	2-0		Rhos Aelwyd

Second Round

Aberystwyth Town	6-0		Knighton Town
AFC Porth	3-1		Cardiff Civil Service
Bangor City	7-1		Mostyn
BP Llandarcy	0-1		Cardiff Corinthians
Brecon Corinthians	0-3		Ton Pentre
British Aerospace	2-2		Llay Royal British Legion
Briton Ferry Athletic	4-1		Caldicot Town
Caerau	5-1		Afan Lido
Caersws	2-2		Kidderminster Harriers
Carno	4-3		Morda United
Cefn Druids	1-2		Connah's Quay Nomads
Conwy United	1-0		Holywell Town
Cwmbran Town	0-1		Merthyr Tydfil
Ebbw Vale	3-1		Abergavenny Thursdays
Haverfordwest County	2-0		Pembroke Boro
Inter Cardiff	5-1		Porthcawl Town
Lex XI	0-1		Gresford Athletic
Llanfairpwll	2-4		Llandudno
Llansantffraid	5-1		Welshpool
Llanwern	1-5		Llanelli
Mold Alexandra	1-0		Brymbo
Newtown	0-2		Llanidloes Town
Port Talbot Athletic	3-0		Carmarthen Town
Porthmadog	2-7		Cemaes Bay
Rhyl FC	6-0		Y Felinheli
Risca United	3-2		Caerleon
Ruthin Town	0-1		Flint Town United

Second Round Replays

Llay Royal British Legion	2-1		British Aerospace
Kidderminster Harriers	4-3		Caersws

Third Round

AFC Porth	2-0		Llanelli
Briton Ferry Athletic	2-6		Aberystwyth Town
Caerau	4-3		Ebbw Vale
Cemaes Bay	2-1		Carno
Connah's Quay Nomads	4-2		Conwy United
Haverfordwest County	5-1		Cardiff Corinthians
Hereford United	6-0		Flint Town United
Kidderminster Harriers	2-2		Bangor City
Llandudno	1-0		Llay Royal British Legion
Llanidloes Town	0-3		Wrexham
Llansantffraid	1-1		Mold Alexandra
Maesteg Park Athletic	5-1		Inter Cardiff
Merthyr Tydfil	2-0		Swansea Town
Port Talbot Athletic	0-0		Risca United
Rhyl FC	3-1		Gresford Athletic
Ton Pentre	0-2		Cardiff City

Third Round Replays

Bangor City	2-1		Kidderminster Harriers
Mold Alexandra	1-2		Llansantffraid
Risca United	0-2		Port Talbot Athletic

Fourth Round

Aberystwyth Town	1-2		AFC Porth
Caerau	0-9		Cardiff City
Cemaes Bay	0-1		Connah's Quay Nomads
Haverfordwest County	0-2		Rhyl FC
Hereford United	2-3		Wrexham
Llansantffraid	2-1		Llandudno
Maesteg Park Athletic	3-0		Port Talbot Athletic
Merthyr Tydfil	3-2		Bangor City

Fifth Round

AFC Porth	0-3		Connah's Quay Nomads
Cardiff City	4-0		Maesteg Park Athletic
Llansantffraid	0-4		Rhyl FC
Wrexham	1-0		Merthyr Tydfil

Semi-finals – 1st leg

Rhyl FC	2-0		Connah's Quay Nomads
Cardiff City	2-0		Wrexham

Semi-finals – 2nd leg

Connah's Quay Nomads	1-0		Rhyl FC

Rhyl FC won 3-0 on aggregate.

Wrexham	1-0		Cardiff City

Cardiff City won 2-1 on aggregate.

1993 WELSH CUP FINAL

16th May 1993 at the National Stadium, Cardiff

Cardiff City	5-0		Rhyl

Stant 3, Griffith 2

Cardiff City: G Ward, R James, D Searle, D Brazil (C Pike), J Perry, P Millar (C Dale), P Ramsey, N Richardson, P Stant, N Blake, C Griffith

Rhyl: G Lichfield, A Lee, R Jones, S Epsley, P Lacey, S Jones, S Cross (D Norman), L Congerton, I McMullen, S Taylor (P Marriott), A Jones

Referee: K Burge (Tonypandy)

Attendance: 16,443

1993/94 Welsh Cup

Preliminary Round

BP Llandarcy	4-0		South Wales Constabulary
British Aerospace	0-1		Chirk AAA
Chepstow Town	3-4		Cardiff Corinthians
Y Felinheli	2-0		Penmaenmawr Phoenix
Fields Park/Pontllanfraith	2-4		Pontlottyn Blast Furnace
Goytre United	5-2		Port Tywyn Suburbs
Llanfairpwll	3-0		Llandyrnog United

Llanrwst United	1-1	Nefyn United
Played at Nefyn		
Llay Welfare	0-4	Bala Town
Morda United	3-1	New Broughton
Newcastle Emlyn	1-4	Pontyclun
Newport YMCA	2-1	Trelewis Welfare
Overton/Marchwiel	6-1	Presteigne St Andrews
Penparcau	1-3	Llangeinor
Penycae	3-0	Llay Royal British Legion
Pontardawe Athletic	2-1 (aet)	Seven Sisters
Played at Seven Sisters. The scoreline after 90 minutes was 1-1.		
Porthcawl Town	2-1	British Steel
Played at British Steel		
Pwllheli Borough	1-4	Nantlle Vale
Rhydymwyn	1-0	Locomotive Llanberis
Rhyl Delta	1-4	Llangefni Town
Skewen Athletic	5-0	Milford United
Taff's Well	2-1	Panteg
Tonyrefail Welfare	2-3	Abercynon Athletic
Treowen Stars	3-0	Tredomen

Preliminary Round Replay

Nefyn United	4-1	Llanrwst United

First Round

Aberaman Athletic	3-0	Llanwern
Abergavenny Thursday	0-2	Risca United
AFC Porth	3-1	Brecon Corinthians
Ammanford Town	1-2	Bridgend Town
Bala Town	2-4	Morda United
Barry Town	2-0	Abercynon Athletic
BP Llandarcy	1-0	Pontardawe
Buckley Town	2-4	Cefn Druids
Caerau	1-1	Llangeinor
Caerleon	1-1	Ferndale Athletic
Cardiff Corinthians	4-5	Caldicot Town
Carno	2-1	Penrhyncoch
Chirk AAA	2-0	Penley
Goytre United	1-0	Porthcawl Town
Gresford Athletic	2-4	Penycae
Llandrindod Wells	2-6	Taff's Well
Llandudno	2-3	Mostyn
Llangefni Town	3-0	Cemaes Bay
Llanidloes Town	1-1	Lex XI
Nefyn United	1-4	Ruthin Town
Overton/Marchwiel	0-3	Brymbo
Pembroke Borough	0-1	Skewen Athletic
Pontlottyn Blast Furnace	0-2	Cardiff Civil Service
Pontyclun FC	2-1	Carmarthen Town
Port Talbot Athletic	0-1	Morriston Town
Rhos Aelwyd	0-3	Rhayader Town
Rhydymwyn	3-0	Nantlle Vale
Treowen Stars	3-0	Newport YMCA
Welshpool	5-0	Knighton Town
Y Felinheli	0-3	Llanfairpwll

First Round Replays

Llangeinor	1-2	Caerau
Ferndale Athletic	3-1	Caerleon
Lex XI	1-0	Llanidloes Town
Morriston Town	0-2	Port Talbot Athletic

Second Round

Aberaman Athletic	1-2	Ton Pentre
Afan Lido	5-2	BP Llandarcy
Bangor City	2-0	Porthmadog
Briton Ferry Athletic	7-1	Cardiff Civil Service
Caerau	1-1	Barry Town
Caersws	1-1	Newtown
Caldicot Town	2-0	AFC Porth
Carno	6-0	Chirk AAA
Cefn Druids	0-0	Mold Alexandra
Ebbw Vale	5-0	Bridgend Town
Ferndale Athletic	0-0	Treowen Stars
Haverfordwest County	2-1	Maesteg Park Athletic
Lex XI	3-4	Llanfairpwll
Llanelli	2-1	Risca United
Llangefni Town	1-1	Brymbo
Llansantffraid	1-1	Aberystwyth Town
Morda United	1-0	Conwy United
Mostyn	1-0	Ruthin Town
Penycae	1-5	Holywell Town
Porthcawl Town	2-2	Pontyclun
Rhayader Town	1-5	Flint Town United
Skewen Athletic	3-2 (aet)	Port Talbot Athletic
Taff's Well	1-7	Merthyr Tydfil
Welshpool	4-3	Rhydymwyn

Second Round Replays

Barry Town	3-2	Caerau
Newtown	7-1	Caersws
Mold Alexandra	2-3	Cefn Druids
Treowen Stars	3-2	Ferndale Athletic
Brymbo	5-1	Llangefni Town
Aberystwyth Town	4-1	Llansantffraid
Pontyclun	0-3	Porthcawl Town

Third Round

Bangor City	2-0	Llanfairpwll
Barry Town	3-1	Cwmbran Town
Brymbo	0-3	Connah's Quay Nomads
Cardiff City	2-0	Afan Lido
Cefn Druids	0-5	Rhyl
Ebbw Vale	1-0	Skewen Athletic
Flint Town United	2-1	Welshpool
Haverfordwest County	1-6	Briton Ferry Athletic
Hereford United	3-0	Mostyn
Holywell Town	3-2	Aberystwyth Town
Inter Cardiff	2-1	Caldicot Town
Morda United	1-7	Newtown AFC
Swansea City	0-0	Merthyr Tydfil
Ton Pentre	2-1	Llanelli
Treowen Stars	1-1	Porthcawl Town
Wrexham	6-1	Carno

Third Round Replays

Merthyr Tydfil	1-2	Swansea City
Porthcawl Town	4-3	Treowen Stars

Fourth Round

Barry Town	4-0	Holywell Town
Briton Ferry Athletic	2-2	Flint Town United
Ebbw Vale	1-1	Connah's Quay Nomads

Hereford United	4-0	Newtown
Porthcawl Town	1-1	Inter Cardiff
Rhyl	1-2	Swansea City
Wrexham	0-2	Cardiff City

Fourth Round Replay

Flint Town United	3-0	Briton Ferry Athletic
Connah's Quay Nomads	1-2	Ebbw Vale
Inter Cardiff	3-0	Porthcawl Town
Swansea City	3-0	Rhyl

Fifth Round

Bangor City	1-1	Inter Cardiff
Barry Town	1-0	Flint Town United
Ebbw Vale	1-1	Cardiff City
Swansea City	1-0	Hereford United

Fifth Round Replays

Inter Cardiff	0-1	Bangor City
Cardiff City	3-0	Ebbw Vale

Semi-finals – 1st leg

Bangor City	1-1	Barry Town
Swansea City	2-1	Cardiff City

Semi-finals – 1st leg

Barry Town	1-0	Bangor City
Barry Town won 2-1 on aggregate.		
Cardiff City	4-1	Swansea City
Cardiff City won 5-3 on aggregate.		

1994 WELSH CUP FINAL

13th May 1994 at the National Stadium, Cardiff

Cardiff City	1-2	Barry Town
Stant		D'Auria, Hough

Cardiff City: S Williams, W Fereday, J Perry, M Aizelwood, D Searle, P Millar, N Richardson (D Adams 60), K Brock, C Griffith, P Stant, G Thompson (T Bird 75)

Barry Town: Morris, Hough, Griffiths, T Boyle, Williams, A Curtis (A Smith), Wimbleton, A Beattie, D'Auria, C Lillygreen, Bertschin (Sanderson 71)

Referee: J Lloyd (Wrexham)

Attendance: 14,500

1994/95 Welsh Cup

Preliminary Round

Abercynon Athletic	1-2	Chepstow Town
Albion Rovers	3-2	Fields Park Pontllanffraith
Bala Town	2-3	Llay Welfare
British Steel	0-2	BP Llandarcy
Cardiff Corinthians	3-1	Cardiff Institute
Y Felinheli	0-0	Llanrwst United
Goytre United	6-1	Seven Sisters
Newport YMCA	4-4	Pontlottyn Blast Furnace
Panteg	2-1	Trelewis Welfare
Porthcawl Town	6-0	Newcastle Emlyn
Presteigne St Andrews	7-2	Penparcau
Rhyl Delta	2-1	British Aerospace
Skewen Athletic	1-2	Pontardawe Athletic
Tondu Robins	4-0	South Wales Constabulary

Preliminary Round Replays

Llanrwst United	3-4	Y Felinheli
Pontlottyn Blast Furnace	7-0	Newport YMCA

First Round

Abergavenny Thursdays	1-1	Panteg
AFC Porth	3-0	Pontardawe Athletic
Albion Rovers	0-3	Tondu Robins
BP Llandarcy	2-0	Morriston Town
Brecon Corinthians	1-1	Goytre United
Briton Ferry Athletic	0-0	Carmarthen Town
Brymbo	2-2	Llanfairfechan Town
Buckley Town	3-5	Penycae
Cardiff Corinthians	2-1	Caerau
Cardiff Civil Service	3-1	Caldicot Town
Carno	7-1	Llanidloes Town
Chepstow Town	3-0	Bridgend Town
Ferndale Athletic	0-1	Ammanford Town
Lex XI	1-2	Cemaes Bay
Llandrindod Wells	0-3	Welshpool Town
Llandudno	7-0	Llay Welfare
Locomotive Llanberis	0-0	Gresford Athletic
Mostyn FC	2-2	Llanfairpwll
Nantlle Vale	2-6	Llangefni Town
Nefyn United	3-0	Knighton Town
New Broughton	0-2	Cefn Druids
Oswestry Town	1-0	New Brighton Villa
Pembroke Borough	0-5	Haverfordwest County
Pontlottyn Blast Furnace	2-0	Caerleon FC
Pontypridd Town	3-1	Porthcawl Town
Port Talbot Athletic	0-1	Aberaman Athletic
Presteigne St Andrews	2-1	Penrhyncoch
Rhos Aelwyd	2-2	Chirk AAA
Rhyl Delta	1-2	Rhayader Town
Risca United	2-2	Llanwern
Ruthin Town	0-3	Llandyrnog United
Treowen Stars	1-2	Taff's Well
Y Felinheli	0-5	Prestatyn Town

First Round Replays

Panteg	1-2	Abergavenny Thursdays
Goytre United	2-1	Brecon Corinthians
Carmarthen Town	2-1	Briton Ferry Athletic
Llanfairfechan Town	2-2	Brymbo
Llanfairpwll	6-1	Mostyn FC
Chirk AAA	1-3	Rhos Aelwyd
Llanwern	1-4	Risca United

First Round Second Replay

Brymbo	2-0	Llanfairfechan Town

Second Round

Ebbw Vale	3-0	Aberaman Athletic
Cardiff Corinthians	2-0	Llanelli
Carmarthen Town	0-3	Cwmbran Town
Cefn Druids	1-0	Llansantffraid
Connah's Quay Nomads	3-2	Mold Alexandra
Flint Town United	2-2	Brymbo
Gresford Athletic	1-2	Aberystwyth Town
Llandyrnog United	0-3	Rhos Aelwyd
Llangefni Town	3-0	Welshpool Town
Maesteg Park Athletic	2-1	BP Llandarcy
Merthyr Tydfil	5-0	Goytre United
Nefyn United	1-2	Llandudno
Newtown	6-0	Penycae
Oswestry Town	1-1	Caersws
Pontlottyn Blast Furnace	1-1	Afan Lido
Pontypridd Town	3-2	AFC Porth
Porthmadog	3-0	Conwy United
Prestatyn Town	0-4	Cemaes Bay
Presteigne St Andrews	3-3	Carno
Rhayader Town	0-2	Holywell Town
Rhyl	3-0	Llanfairpwll
Risca United	3-0	Ammanford Town
Taff's Well	2-0	Chepstow Town
Tondu Robins	0-2	Abergavenny Thursdays

Second Round Replays

Brymbo	3-1	Flint Town United
Caersws	3-1	Oswestry Town
Afan Lido	5-0	Pontlottyn Blast Furnace
Carno	6-1	Presteigne St Andrews

Third Round

Taff's Well	0-7	Swansea City
Bangor City	2-0	Carno
Brymbo	1-3	Aberystwyth Town
Caersws	4-0	Rhos Aelwyd
Cardiff Corinthians	0-1	Afan Lido
Carmarthen Town	2-3	Barry Town
Cefn Druids	0-2	Connah's Quay Nomads
Holywell Town	1-3	Porthmadog
Llandudno	3-1	Llangefni Town
Maesteg Park Athletic	1-0	Inter Cardiff
Merthyr Tydfil	5-0	Cwmbran Town
Rhyl	3-0	Cemaes Bay
Risca United	2-0	Pontypridd Town
Ton Pentre	2-1	Abergavenny Thursdays
Ebbw Vale	1-1	Cardiff City
Newtown	1-1	Wrexham

Third Round Replays

Cardiff City	7-1	Ebbw Vale
Wrexham	2-0	Newtown

Fourth Round

Afan Lido	0-3	Ton Pentre
Bangor City	12-1	Maesteg Park Athletic
Barry Town	1-1	Llandudno
Cardiff City	4-0	Risca United
Merthyr Tydfil	1-0	Aberystwyth Town
Porthmadog	0-0	Caersws
Swansea City	5-1	Rhyl
Wrexham	4-0	Connah's Quay Nomads

Fourth Round Replays

Llandudno	3-1	Barry Town
Caersws	1-2	Porthmadog

Fifth Round

Bangor City	2-2	Wrexham
Merthyr Tydfil	2-0	Ton Pentre
Swansea City	8-0	Porthmadog
Llandudno	0-1	Cardiff City

Fifth Round Replay

Wrexham	1-0	Bangor City

Semi-finals – 1st leg

Wrexham	3-1	Merthyr Tydfil
Swansea City	0-1	Cardiff City

Semi-finals – 2nd leg

Merthyr Tydfil	0-1	Wrexham

Wrexham won 4-1 on aggregate.

Cardiff City	0-0	Swansea City

Cardiff City won 1-0 on aggregate.

1995 WELSH CUP FINAL

21st May 1995 at the National Stadium, Cardiff

Wrexham	2-1	Cardiff City
Bennett 2		Dale

Wrexham: A Marriott, D Brace, B Jones, B Hunter, P Hardy, Durkin, G Owen, B Hughes, K Connolly, S Morris (S Watkin 84), G Bennett. Subs D Phillips, M Cartwright (g)

Cardiff City: S Williams, D Brazil, J Perry, L Baddeley, D Searle, C Griffith, N Wigg, N Richardson, P Millar (Oatway 84), C Dale, T Bird (S Young 77), Sub: Mountain (g)

Referee: V J Reed (Aberdare)

Attendance: 11,200

1995/96 Welsh Cup

Preliminary Round

Abercynon Athletic	1-2	Cambrian United
Bala Town	0-2	Penley FC
British Steel	3-1	Bryntirion Athletic
Grange Harlequins	3-2	Pontlottyn Blast Furnace
Panteg FC	0-2	Newport YMCA
Porthcawl Town	2-2	Llangeinor
Porth Tywyn Suburbs	6-0	Pontyclun FC
Trelewis Welfare	0-5	Albion Rovers

Preliminary Round Replay

Llangeinor	2-3	Porthcawl Town

First Round

Aberaman Athletic	3-1	Risca United
Abergavenny Thursdays	1-0	Caerleon AFC
Albion Rovers	0-2	Treowen Stars
Ammanford AFC	2-0	Bridgend Town
Brecon Corinthians	0-1	Cardiff Corinthians
British Steel	0-1	BP Llandarcy
Buckley Town	1-1	New Brighton Villa
Cambrian United	0-4	Newport YMCA
Carmarthen Town	2-4	Pontardawe Athletic
Carno FC	1-2	Rhayader Town
Cefn Druids	0-2	Oswestry Town
Ferndale Athletic	1-12	Taff's Well AFC
Fields Park Pontllanfraith	2-2	AFC Porth
Goytre United	3-0	Haverfordwest County
Grange Harlequins	5-1	Caldicot Town
Gresford United	1-2	Chirk A.A.A.
Knighton Town	1-3	Llandrindod Wells FC
Llandudno FC	1-0	Llangefni Town
Llandyrnog United	2-0	Prestatyn Town
Llanrwst United	3-2	Rhyl Delta
Llanwern AFC	0-4	Pontypridd Town
Maesteg Park AFC	2-1	Caerau FC
Mostyn FC	3-2	Denbigh Town
Nantlle Vale FC	2-1	Nefyn United
New Broughton FC	1-3	Ruthin Town
Newcastle Emlyn FC	1-5	Morriston Town
Penley FC	2-2	Mold Alexandra
Penparcau FC	1-1	Llanidloes Town
Penrhiwceiber Rangers	2-1	Cardiff Civil Service
Penycae FC	1-6	Brymbo FC
Porthcawl Town	0-3	Porth Tywyn Suburbs
Port Talbot Athletic	2-0	Skewen Athletic
Rhos Aelwyd	0-2	Lex XI
Welshpool AFC	2-1	CPD Penrhyncoch

First Round Replays

New Brighton Villa	0-3	Buckley Town
AFC Porth	2-1	Fields Park Pontllanfraith
Mold Alexandra	5-2	Penley FC
Llanidloes Town	2-3	Penparcau FC

Second Round

Ebbw Vale AFC	3-3	BP Llandarcy
Aberaman Athletic	1-1	Llandrindod Wells
AFC Porth	3-3	Grange Harlequins
Ammanford AFC	1-4	Cardiff Corinthians
Briton Ferry Athletic	3-1	Pontardawe Athletic
Brymbo FC	1-3	Conwy United
Connah's Quay Nomads	5-1	Welshpool AFC
Goytre United	4-2	Penrhiwceiber Rangers
Llandudno FC	3-2	Mostyn FC
Llandyrnog United	2-1	Buckley Town
Llanrwst United	2-6	Cemaes Bay FC
Maesteg Park AFC	2-1	Morriston Town
Nantlle Vale FC	1-3	Caersws FC
Newport YMCA	2-4	Pontypridd Town
Oswestry Town	1-0	Chirk A.A.A.
CPD Porthmadog	2-1	Mold Alexandra
Porth Tywyn Suburbs	0-0	Taff's Well AFC
Port Talbot Athletic	2-7	Aberystwyth Town
Rhayader Town	1-2	Abergavenny Thursdays
Ruthin Town	0-3	Lex XI
Penparcau FC	0-2	Rhyl FC
Treowen Stars	1-3	Llanelli AFC

Second Round Replays

Llandrindod Wells	4-1	Aberaman Athletic
Grange Harlequins	3-2	AFC Porth
Taff's Well AFC	1-0	Porth Tywyn Suburbs

Third Round

Ebbw Vale AFC	1-0	Briton Ferry Athletic
Abergavenny Thursdays	3-2	Caersws FC
Aberystwyth Town	1-1	Newtown AFC
Bangor City	2-3	Cwmbran Town
Cemaes Bay FC	3-0	Maesteg Park AFC
Connah's Quay Nomads	1-3	Llandudno FC
Conwy United	0-2	Barry Town
Goytre United	8-2	Llanelli AFC
Llandrindod Wells AFC	1-0	Afan Lido FC
Holywell Town	0-2	Grange Harlequins
Lex XI FC Wrexham	0-0	Ton Pentre AFC
Llansantffraid FC	2-1	Llandyrnog United
Oswestry Town	2-1	Fflint Town United
CPD Porthmadog	1-0	Cardiff Corinthians
Rhyl FC	1-0	Inter Cardiff

Rhyl FC were disqualified for fielding an ineligible player.

Taff's Well AFC	0-1	Pontypridd Town

Third Round Replays

Newtown AFC	0-1 (aet)	Aberystwyth Town
Ton Pentre AFC	3-2	Lex XI FC Wrexham

Fourth Round

Grange Harlequins	1-2	Ebbw Vale AFC
Cwmbran Town	3-0	Goytre United
Llansantffraid FC	4-0	Abergavenny Thursdays
Aberystwyth Town	0-0	Oswestry Town
CPD Porthmadog	2-1	Llandrindod Wells FC
Inter Cardiff	2-0	Llandudno FC
Ton Pentre AFC	0-1	Barry Town
Pontypridd Town	1-0	Cemaes Bay FC

Fourth Round Replay

Oswestry Town	3-2	Aberystwyth Town

Fifth Round

Ebbw Vale AFC	0-1	Inter Cardiff
Cwmbran Town	2-0	CPD Porthmadog
Oswestry Town	0-2	Barry Town
Pontypridd Town	1-2	Llansantffraid FC

Semi-finals – 1st leg

Barry Town	1-0	Cwmbran Town
Inter Cardiff	0-1	Llansantffraid FC

Semi-finals – 1st leg

Cwmbran Town	3-2	Barry Town

Aggregate 3-3. Barry Town won on the away goals rule.

Llansantffraid FC	3-1	Inter Cardiff

Llansantffraid FC won 4-1 on aggregate.

1996 WELSH CUP FINAL

19th May 1996 at National Stadium, Cardiff

Llansantffraid FC	3-3 (aet)	Barry Town

Morgan 29', G.Evans 54', C.Whelan 95'
Lloyd 35', Mulliner 61'o.g.
Bird 118'

Llansantffraid FC won 3-2 on penalties.

Llansantffraid: Mulliner, J Whelan, Curtiss, Brown, Jones, O'Brien (Watt 112'), I Evans (Nunnerley 112'), G Evans, Morgan, C. Whelan, Abercrombie. Sub not used: Barrett

Barry Town: Ovendale, Evans, Lloyd, Mayer, Batchelor, Barnett (Griffith 105'), Giles (Withers 96'), Bird, Hunter (Pike 58'), Jones, O'Gorman.

Referee: R B Gifford (Llanbradach)

Attendance: 2,666

1996/97 Welsh Cup

Preliminary Round

Berriew	2-3	Carno
Chirk AAA	2-2	British Aerospace
Corweb Amateurs	2-0	Rhostyllen Villa
Gresford Athletic	4-3	Rhos Aelwyd
Llandyrnog United	2-2	Prestatyn Town
Nantlle Vale	5-0	Llangefni Town
Penparcau	2-4	Montgomery Town

Following a protest, Montgomery were dismissed from the competition and Penparcau progressed.

Penycae	5-2	Penley
Trelewis Welfare	1-4	Pontlottyn Blast Furnace

Preliminary Round Replays

British Aerospace	5-4	Chirk AAA
Prestatyn Town	2-0	Llandyrnog United

First Round

Abercynon Athletic	2-4	Hoover Sports
Brecon Corinthians	1-5	Newport YMCA
Caerau United	2-2	Abergavenny Thursdays
Caerleon	1-0	Panteg
Caldicot Town	4-0	Pontypridd Town
Cardiff Civil Service	1-1	Bridgend Town
British Aeropsace	1-2	Cefn Druids
Ferndale Athletic	1-5	Port Talbot Athletic
Garw	1-3	Ponyclun
Goytre United	0-1	Maesteg Park
Grange Harlequins	3-0	Cardiff Corinthians
Gresford Athletic	1-3	Buckley Town
Haverfordwest County	6-2	Penrhiwceiber Rangers
Knighton Town	7-0	Carno
Lex XI	6-0	Mold Alexandra
Llandrindod Wells	3-1	Denbigh Town
Llandudno	2-2	Mostyn
Llanelli	1-1	Skewen Athletic
Llanidloes Town	1-1	Brymbo Broughton
Llanwern	3-0	UWIC Cardiff
Nantlle Vale	1-4	Penycae
Oswestry Town	8-1	Corwen Amateurs
CPD Penrhyncoch	1-2	Ruthin Town
Pontardawe Athletic	2-0	AFC Rhondda
Porth Tywyn Suburbs	2-0	Afan Lido
Porthcawl Town	4-2	Blaenrhondda
Rhayader Town	3-1	Prestatyn Town
Rhydymwyn	5-0	Penparcau
South Wales Police	3-0	Aberaman Athletic
Taff's Well	2-0	Ammanford
Tonyrefail Welfare	0-3	BP Llandarcy
Treharris Athletic	4-0	Morriston Town
Pontlottyn Blast Furnace	0-0	Treowen Stars

Treowen Stars progressed to the next round, presumably following a replay though no record of a replay is available.

First Round Replays

Abergavenny Thursdays	4-3	Caerau United
Bridgend Town	4-2 (aet)	Cardiff Civil Service

The scoreline after 90 minutes was 2-2.

Mostyn	0-0 (aet)	Llandudno

Mostyn won 10-9 on penalties.

Skewen Athletic	3-4 (aet)	Llanelli
Broughton Town	4-2	Llanidloes Town

Second Round

Abergavenny Thursdays	1-2	BP Llandarcy
Aberystwyth Town	9-0	Penycae
Brymbo Broughton	0-2	Caersws
Caldicot Town	1-4	Ton Pentre
Carmarthen Town	1-2	Briton Ferry Athletic
Cefn Druids	5-1	Oswestry Town
Cemaes Bay	3-0	Mostyn
Grange Harlequins	2-1	Risca United
Haverfordwest County	1-1	Bridgend Town
Hoover Sports	1-2	Maesteg Park Athletic
Holywell Town	0-0	Rhydymwyn
Knighton Town	0-1	Lex XI
Llanwern	3-0	Newport YMCA
Pontadawe Athletic	0-0	Ebbw Vale
Porth Tywyn Suburbs	5-0	Caerleon
Porthcawl Town	3-2	Pontyclun
CPD Porthmadog	6-1	Buckley Town
Rhayader Town	1-0	Ruthin Town
Rhyl	0-1	Connah's Quay Nomads
South Wales Police	1-5	Taff's Well
Treharris Athletic	2-2	Llanelli
Treowen Stars	0-1	Port Talbot Athletic
Welshpool Town	2-2	Llandrindod Wells

Second Round Replays

Bridgend Town	2-1	Haverfordwest County
Ebbw Vale	2-1 (aet)	Pontadawe Athletic

The scoreline after 90 minutes was 0-0.

Rhydymwyn	1-2	Holywell Town
Llanelli	4-0	Treharris Athletic
Llandrindod Wells	0-5 (aet)	Welshpool Town

Third Round

Briton Ferry Athletic	1-1	Rhayader Town
Caersws	3-2	Bangor City
BP Llandarcy	3-0	Llanwern
Flint Town United	1-4	Cwmbran Town
Cefn Druids	1-1	Ebbw Vale
Caernarfon Town	4-0	Ton Pentre
Conwy Utd	2-0	InterCable-Tel
Newtown AFC	3-4	Maesteg Park
Porthcawl Town	3-0	Connah's Quay Nomads
Bridgend Town	0-1	Aberystwyth Town
Port Talbot Athletic	4-3	Welshpool Town
Grange Harlequins	1-0	Llanelli
Holywell Town	1-0	Taff's Well FC
Porth Tywyn Suburbs	4-1	Lex XI
Llansantffraid	0-2	Barry Town
Cemaes Bay	3-2	Porthmadog

Third Round Replays

Rhayader Town	1-2	Briton Ferry Athletic
Ebbw Vale	3-0	Cefn Druids

Fourth Round

Aberystwyth Town	2-2	Ebbw Vale
Briton Ferry Athletic	1-2	BP Llandarcy
Porthcawl Town	1-0	Port Talbot Athletic
Grange Harlequins	1-3	Cwmbran Town
Porth Tywyn Suburbs	1-3	Caersws
Maesteg Park	0-1	Holywell Town

The match was abandoned.

Barry Town	2-0	Cemaes Bay
Caernarfon Town	1-1	Conwy United

Fourth Round Replays

Ebbw Vale	1-2	Aberystwyth Town
Maesteg Park	2-2	Holywell Town
Conwy United	2-0	Caernarfon Town

Fourth Round Second Replay

Holywell Town	2-0	Maesteg Park

Fifth Round

Barry Town	3-1	Caersws
Porthcawl Town	0-2	Aberystwyth Town
BP Llandarcy	0-2	Conwy United
Holywell Town	1-1	Cwmbran Town

Fifth Round Replay

Cwmbran Town	2-0	Holywell Town

Semi-finals

Aberystwyth Town	0-2	Cwmbran Town

Played at Stebonheath Park, Llanelli

Barry Town	1-0	Conwy United

Played at Latham Park, Newtown

1997 WELSH CUP FINAL

18th May 1997 at Ninian Park, Cardiff

Barry Town	2-1	Cwmbran Town

Griffith 7', 73'   *Watkins 48'*

Barry Town: Ovendale, T.Evans, Knott (Pike 66'), Lloyd, York, Jones, Barnett, Loss, Bird, Griffith, Ryan. Subs not used: C.Evans, O'Gorman.

Cwmbran Town: O'Hagan, Walker (Battle 85'), Powell, Gibbins (Payne 78'), Parfitt, Blackie, Carter, Goodridge, Davies (Summers 55'), Dyer, Watkins.

Referee: A C Howells (Port Talbot)

Attendance: 1560

1997/98 Welsh Cup

Preliminary Round

Abercynon Athletic	0-2	Ferndale Athletic
British Aerospace Broughton	4-1	Penley FC
Halkyn United	1-4	Colwyn Bay YMCA
Montgomery Town	3-1	Berriew
Morriston Town	0-2	Ely Rangers
Panteg FC	2-3	Skewen Athletic
Pontlottyn Blast Furnace	2-5	Newport YMCA
South Wales Police Bridgend	5-2	Tonyrefail Welfare

First Round

Hoover Sports Merthyr	2-0	Taff's Well AFC
Maesteg Park Athletic	0-2	Porthcawl Town
Grange Harlequins	4-3	Caerau United
Aberaman Athletic	2-2	Porth Tywyn Suburbs
Abergavenny Thursdays	0-7	Treharris Athletic
AFC Rhondda	5-5	Briton Ferry Athletic
Ammanford AFC	1-0	Risca United
Blaenrhondda AFC	2-2	Pontypridd Town
Brecon Corinthians	0-5	Afan Lido FC
Bridgend Town	4-2	Port Talbot Athletic
Brymbo Broughton FC	1-0	Colwyn Bay YMCA
Caerleon FC	2-7	Goytre United
Cardiff Civil Service	2-4	Ferndale Athletic
Castell Alun Colts	1-7	Buckley Town
Cefn Druids	4-1	Prestatyn Town
Chepstow Town	2-2	Penrhiwceiber Rangers
Chirk AAA	3-2	CPD Glantraeth
Corwen Amateurs	3-6	Lex XI FC
Denbigh Town	2-4	Presteigne St Andrews
Ely Rangers	5-4	Newport YMCA
Fields Park Pontllanfraith	5-1	Albion Rovers

Garw Athletic	1-1	UWIC Cardiff
Holyhead Hotspur	2-1	Rhydymwyn FC
Llandyrnog United	2-2	Mold Alexandra
Llangefni Town	3-2	British Aerospace Broughton
Llanidloes Town	3-6	Knighton Town
Llanwern AFC	3-1	Llanelli AFC
Mostyn FC	0-4	Llandrindod Wells
Nantlle Vale FC	3-1	Llandudno FC
Oswestry Town	5-1	Montgomery Town
CPD Penrhyncoch	0-1	Holywell Town
Penycae FC	0-1	Guilsfield FC
Pontardawe Athletic	4-1	Caldicot Town
Pontyclun FC	1-2	BP Llandarcy
Ruthin Town	3-1	Rhos Aelwyd
Skewen Athletic	2-1	Gwynfi United
Ton Pentre	5-0	South Wales Police Bridgend
Treown Stars	2-0	Cardiff Corinthians

First Round Replays

Porth Tywyn Suburbs	5-0	Aberaman Athletic
Briton Ferry Athletic	3-1	AFC Rhondda
Pontypridd Town	1-4	Blaenrhondda AFC
Penrhiwceiber Rangers	0-5	Chepstow Town
UWIC Cardiff	3-2	Garw Athletic
Mold Alexandra	3-1	Llandyrnog United

Second Round

Afan Lido FC	0-0	Ton Pentre
BP Llandarcy	1-1	Haverfordwest County
Brymbo Broughton	1-3	Flint Town United
Buckley Town	2-5	Lex XI
Caernarfon Town	6-1	Chirk AAA
Carmarthen Town	1-0	Porth Tywyn Suburbs
Cefn Druids	4-1	Nantlle Vale FC
Connah's Quay Nomads	4-1	CPD Porthmadog
Ely Rangers	5-1	Blaenrhondda FC
Fields Park Pontllanfraith	0-1	Briton Ferry Athletic
Goytre United	6-1	Chepstow Town
Guilsfield FC	0-4	Holywell Town
Knighton Town	3-0	Oswestry Town
Llandrindod Wells	0-4	Holyhead Hotspur
Llanwern AFC	2-0	Skewen Athletic
Mold Alexandra	1-0	Llangefni Town
Pontardawe Athletic	2-6	Hoover Sports Merthyr
Porthcawl Town	1-1	Bridgend Town
Presteigne St Andrews	1-8	Caersws FC
Rhayader Town	2-2	Total Network Solutions
Ruthin Town	3-1	Cemaes Ynys Mon
Treharris Athletic	4-0	Ferndale Athletic
Treowen Stars	4-1	Ammanford AFC
UWIC Cardiff	5-1	Grange Harlequins
Welshpool Town	0-7	Bangor City

Second Round Replays

Ton Pentre	3-0	Afan Lido FC
Haverfordwest County	2-1 (aet)	BP Llandarcy

The scoreline after 90 minutes was 1-1.

Bridgend Town	0-2	Porthcawl Town
Total Network Solutions	3-3 (aet)	Rhayader Town

Total Network Solutions won 5-4 on penalties.

Third Round

Hoover Sports Merthyr	2-2	Holywell Town
Newtown AFC	2-0	Treowen Stars
Llanwern AFC	1-0	Treharris Athletic
UWIC Cardiff	0-4	Caersws FC
Ton Pentre	5-0	Mold Alexandra
Haverfordwest County	2-3	Ebbw Vale
Holyhead Hotspur	2-3	Cwmbran Town
Knighton Town	4-1	Conwy United
Total Network Solutions	4-1	Ruthin Town
Connah's Quay Nomads	1-1	Goytre United
Caernarfon Town	0-0	Cefn Druids
Porthcawl Town	2-3	Aberystwyth Town
Briton Ferry Athletic	1-7	Inter CableTel
Lex XI	0-3	Barry Town
Flint Town United	0-3	Bangor City
Carmarthen Town	2-0	Ely Rangers

Third Round Replays

Holywell Town	0-1	Hoover Sports Merthyr
Goytre United	0-2	Connah's Quay Nomads
Cefn Druids	0-2	Caernarfon Town

Fourth Round

Aberystwyth Town	1-3	Bangor City
Caernarfon Town	2-1	Carmarthen Town
Cwmbran Town	6-1	Hoover Sports Merthyr
Ebbw Vale AFC	0-4	Newtown AFC
Played at Newtown		
Connah's Quay Nomads	4-0	Llanwern AFC
Inter CableTel	2-3	Caersws FC
Knighton Town	0-8	Barry Town
Ton Pentre	1-2	Total Network Solutions

Fifth Round

Bangor City	2-0	Caernarfon Town
Connah's Quay Nomads	3-2	Cwmbran Town
Caersws FC	1-1	Newtown AFC
Barry Town	3-1	Total Network Solutions

Fifth Round Replay

Newtown AFC	4-2	Caersws FC

Semi-finals

Barry Town	1-2	Connah's Quay Nomads
Played at Newtown		
Newtown	1-2 (aet)	Bangor City

The scoreline was 90 minutes after extra time.
Played at Rhyl

1998 WELSH CUP FINAL

10th May 1998 at the Racecourse, Wrexham

Bangor City   1-1 (aet)   Connah's Quay
McKenna 89'   Futcher 73'

Bangor City won 4-2 on penalties

Bangor City: Williams, Humphreys (McGoona 44'), Edwards, Allen, Whelan, Ashton, Waring, Lloyd-Williams, Brookman, McKenna, Noble. Subs not used: Highdale, Dulson

Connah's Quay Nomads: Collister Thomas (Cody 93'), Carroll, Hutchinson, Jardine, Smyth, Futcher, C.Davies (N.Davies 60'), Hughes, Keep (Allen 67'), D.Wynne.

Referee: D C Richards (Llangennech)

Attendance: 2,023

1998/99 Welsh Cup

First Round

Aberaman Athletic	2-1	Porthcawl Town
AFC Rhondda	7-1	Caerau Athletic
Ammanford AFC	3-2	Blaenrhondda
BP Llandarcy	4-2	Cardiff Corinthians
Bridgend Town	3-1	Cardiff Civil Service
Buckley Town	0-3	Ruthin Town
Caerleon AFC	4-1	Briton Ferry Athletic
Chepstow Town	5-2	Llanwern AFC
Chirk AAA	2-3	British Aerospace
Corwen Amateurs	0-5	Denbigh Town
Flexys Cefn Druids	4-0	Mostyn FC
Goytre United	4-1	Caldicot Town
Guilsfield FC	2-0	Llanidloes Town
Halkyn United	0-1	Brymbo Broughton
Holyhead Hotspur	6-0	Bala Town
Hoover Sports Merthyr	2-1	Penrhiwceiber Rangers
Knighton Town	1-2	CPD Penrhyncoch
Lex XI	3-4	Rhydymwyn FC
Llandyrnog United	2-5	Llangefni Town
Maesteg Park AFC	1-2	Grange Harlequins
Mold Alexandra (withdrew)	v	Colwyn Bay YMCA (w/o)
Morriston Town	4-3	Pontyclun FC
Oswestry Town	2-1	Rhos Aelwyd
Owens Corning FC (w/o)	v	Prestatyn Town (withdrew)
Penycae FC	1-1 (aet)	Castell Alun Colts
Pontardawe Town	4-1	Skewen Athletic
Ponlottyn Blast Furnace	2-1	Garw Athletic
Pontypridd Town (w/o)	v	Gwynfi Utd (withdrew)
Porth Tywyn Suburbs	2-1	Caerau Ely
Risca United	1-2	Ely Rangers
Taff's Well AFC	1-2	Tredegar Town
UWIC Cardiff	6-1	Llandrindod Wells

First Round Replays

Castell Alun Colts	1-0	Penycae FC

Second Round

Total Network Solutions	2-2	Aberystwyth Town
Afan Lido FC	5-1	Caerleon FC
Caernarfon Town	3-0	Llangefni Town
Carmarthen Town	2-1	Hoover Sports Merthyr
Cwmbran Town	2-0	Goytre United
Haverfordwest County	6-0	Bridgend Town
Guilsfield FC	0-5	Caersws FC
CPD Porthmadog	0-2	Holywell Town
Rhayader Town	3-1	Welshpool Town
Rhydymwyn FC	2-2	Conwy United
Rhyl FC	5-4	Denbigh Town
Aberaman Athletic	2-3	Llanelli AFC
AFC Rhondda	1-1 (aet)	Ammanford AFC

The scoreline after 90 minutes was 0-0. The clubs had agreed before the game that they would not replay. Ammanford AFC won 3-2 on penalties.

British Aerospace	5-1	Brymbo Broughton
Chepstow Town	4-0	Morriston Town
Flexys Cefn Druids	3-1	Cemaes Bay
Flint Town United	6-2	Castell Alun Colts
Gwynfi United	0-2	BP Llandarcy
Owens Corning FC	1-4	Holyhead Hotspur
CPD Penrhyncoch	3-2	Oswestry Town
Pontlottyn Blast Furnace	0-3	Tredegar Town
Porth Tywyn Suburbs	2-1	Ton Pentre
Port Talbot Athletic	2-1	Grange Harlequins
Ruthin Town	0-1	Colwyn Bay YMCA
Treowen Stars	5-0	Ely Rangers
UWIC Cardiff	1-1	Pontardawe Town

Second Round Replays

Aberystwyth Town	2-3 (aet)	Total Network Solutions
Conwy United	2-1	Rhydymwyn FC
Pontardawe Town	4-3	UWIC Cardiff

Third Round

Ammanford AFC	w/o	Ebbw Vale
Barry Town	2-0	Haverfordwest County
British Aerospace	2-2	BP Llandarcy
Caersws FC	3-4	Cwmbran Town
Carmarthen Town	2-2	Chepstow Town
Connah's Quay Nomads	2-2	Newtown AFC
CPD Penrhyncoch	2-4	Colwyn Bay YMCA
Flexys Cefn Druids	1-5	Caernarfon Town
Holyhead Hotspur	1-3	Conwy United
Inter CableTel	1-0	Holywell Town
Llanelli AFC	2-1	Tredegar Town
Porth Tywyn Suburbs	1-1	Port Talbot Athletic
Rhayader Town	3-0	Bangor City
Rhyl FC	2-2	Flint Town United
Total Network Solutions	2-0	Afan Lido FC
Treowen Stars	1-2	Pontardawe Town

Third Round Replays

BP Llandarcy	3-2	British Aerospace
Chepstow Town	2-5	Carmarthen Town
Newtown AFC	0-1	Connah's Quay Nomads
Port Talbot Athletic	1-0	Porth Tywyn Suburbs
Flint Town United	1-1 (aet)	Rhyl FC

Flint Town United won 5-4 on penalties.

Fourth Round

Inter CableTel	1-1	Pontardawe Town
Total Network Solution	2-1	Rhayader Town
Ammanford FC	1-0	Colwyn Bay YMCA
Port Talbot Athletic	2-0	Flint Town United
Carmarthen Town	2-0	Caernarfon Town
Llanelli AFC	1-2	Cwmbran Town
Conwy Utd	7-0	Llandyrnog
Barry Town	0-1	Connah's Quay Nomads

Fourth Round Replay

Pontardawe	0-3	Inter CableTel

Fifth Round

Ammanford	0-0	Conwy United
Total Network Solutions	1-2	Cwmbran Town
Connah's Quay Nomads	1-1	Inter CableTel
Carmarthen Town	1-0	Port Talbot Athletic

Fifth Round Replays

Conwy United	1-0	Ammanford
Inter CableTel	3-1	Connah's Quay Nomads

Semi-finals

Carmarthen Town	1-0	Conwy United

Played at Latham Park, Newtown

Cwmbran Town	3-4	Inter CableTel

Played at Jenner Park, Barry

1999 WELSH CUP FINAL

9th May 1999 at Penydarren Park, Merthyr

Inter CableTel	1-1 (aet)	Carmarthen Town
Porretta 116'		Meredith 114'

Inter CableTel won 4-2 on penalties.

Inter CableTel: Wager, Parselle, Wile, Brazil, Richards (Williams 79'), Dyson, Davies, Porretta, Mardenborough, Evans (Tyler 108'), Dyer (Misbah 62')

Carmarthen Town: Fitzgerald, Nicholas (Burrows 91'), Jones, Barnhouse, Cable, Thomas, Rees (Vaughan 97'), Rossiter, Nichols, Williams, Meredith. Sub not used: Evans

Referee: K Burge (Tonypandy)

Attendance: 1,100

1999/2000 Welsh Cup

First Round

Aberaman Athletic	0-4	Ammanford AFC
Blaenrhondda	1-0	Skewen Athletic
British Aerospace FC	2-1	CPD Porthmadog
Briton Ferry Athletic	1-0	AFC Llwydcoed
Brymbo Broughton	2-3	Lex XI FC
Caerleon AFC	2-1	Fields Park Pontllanfraith
Cemaes Bay FC	1-4	Amlwch Town
Chirk AAA	1-2	Llandyrnog United
Corwen Amateurs	2-2 (aet)	Holyhead Hotspur

Corwen won 4-2 on penalties

Garden Village	3-0	Pontyclun
Garw Athletic	4-4 (aet)	Porthcawl Town

The scoreline after 90 minutes was 3-3.
Garw won 4-3 on penalties.

Glan Conwy	3-4	Halkyn United
Guilsfield FC	5-0	Knighton Town
Hoover Sports	7-2	Chepstow Town
Kerry FC	1-4	Oswestry Town
Llandudno FC	8-0	Mold Alexandra
Llandudno Junction FC	2-1	Castell Alun Colts
Llanfairpwll FC	0-1	Ruthin Town
Llangefni Town (w/o)	v	Rhyl Delta (withdrew)
Llanidloes Town	4-0	Llandrindod Wells
Llanwern AFC	4-2	Caerau FC
Maesteg Park AFC	2-0	Gwynfi United
Penrhiwceiber Rangers	1-2	Goytre United
CPD Penrhyncoch	3-0	Welshpool Town
Penycae FC	1-2	Denbigh Town
Porth Tywyn Suburbs	2-2 (aet)	Pontlottyn Blast Furnace

Porth Tywyn Suburbs won 4-2 on penalties.

Port Talbot Athletic	2-1	Cardiff Civil Service FC
Prestatyn Town	2-0	Bala Town
Rhos Aelwyd	0-2	Buckley Town
Risca United	0-4	Bridgend Town
Taff's Well AFC	0-3	Treowen Stars
Treharris Athletic	0-6	Ely Rangers
UWIC Cardiff	6-0	Caldicot Town
Tredegar Town	3-0	Pontardawe Town

Second Round

Ely Rangers	1-2	Garden Village
Blaenrhondda FC	2-1	BP Llandarcy
AFC Rhondda	1-2	Afan Lido FC
Ton Pentre AFC	1-2	Haverfordwest County
Garw Athletic	6-1	Goytre United
Maesteg Park AFC	1-3	Caerleon FC
Llanelli AFC	6-0	Briton Ferry Athletic
Rhayader Town	3-1	Tredegar Town
Hoover Sports	2-2 (aet)	Port Talbot Athletic

Port Talbot Athletic won 5-4 on penalties.

Llanwern AFC	2-1	Ammanford AFC
Bridgend Town	0-1	UWIC Cardiff
Treowen Stars	1-2	Porth Tywyn Suburbs
Corwen Amateurs	1-2	Bangor City
Buckley Town	1-3	Rhydymwyn FC
Oswestry Town	0-1	Rhyl FC
Llandyrnog United	0-7	Total Network Solutions
Newtown AFC	11-0	Holywell Town
British Aerospace	3-5 (aet)	Llandudno FC

The scoreline after 90 minutes was 3-3.

Flexsys Cefn Druids	2-0	Flint Town United
Ruthin Town	0-0 (aet)	Amlwch Town

Amlwch Town won 4-2 on penalties.

Halkyn United	6-2 (aet)	Prestatyn Town

The scoreline after 90 minutes was 2-2.

Guilsfield FC	3-3 (aet)	Connah's Quay Nomads

Guilsfield FC won 5-4 on penalties.

Llanidloes Town	0-1 (aet)	Penrhyncoch FC
Lex XI FC	0-5	Caernarfon Town
Denbigh Town	1-2	Llangefni Town
Caersws FC	5-0	Llandudno Junction

Third Round

UWIC Cardiff	0-2	Afan Lido FC
CPD Penrhyncoch	2-1 (aet)	Blaenrhondda FC

The scoreline after 90 minutes was 1-1.

Llanelli AFC	7-1	Porth Tywyn Suburbs
Llanwern AFC	0-1	Amlwch Town
Aberystwyth Town	3-1	Garw Athletic
Cwmbran Town	0-0 (aet)	Caernarfon Town

Cwmbran Town won 5-3 on penalties.

Inter Cardiff AFC	5-0	Garden Village
Rhyl FC	1-0	Guilsfield FC
Port Talbot Athletic	0-1	Carmarthen Town
Total Network Solutions	2-0	Newtown AFC
Caersws FC	1-0	Flexsys Cefn Druids
Llangefni Town	1-3	Caerleon FC
Barry Town	2-0	Rhydymwyn FC
Conwy United	2-4 (aet)	Rhayader Town

The scoreline after 90 minutes was 2-2.

Bangor City	5-0	Llandudno FC
Haverfordwest County	0-1	Halkyn United

Fourth Round

Afan Lido FC	1-0	Total Network Solutions
Bangor City	4-0	Inter Cardiff AFC
Barry Town	3-0	Rhayader Town
Caersws FC	1-2	Cwmbran Town
Carmarthen Town	4-1	Aberystwyth Town
Halkyn United	2-3	Caerleon FC
Llanelli AFC	3-0	Rhyl FC
CPD Penrhyncoch	6-1	Amlwch Town

Fifth Round

Afan Lido FC	3-1 (aet)	Llanelli AFC

The scoreline after 90 minutes was 1-1.

Barry Town	5-0	CPD Penrhyncoch
Caerleon FC	1-4	Bangor City
Carmarthen Town	2-3	Cwmbran Town

Semi-finals

Barry Town	1-1 (aet)	Cwmbran Town

Cwmbran won 4-2 on penalties. Played at Llanelli

Afan Lido FC	2-4 (aet)	Bangor City

The scoreline after 90 minutes was 2-2.
Played at Newtown

2000 WELSH CUP FINAL

7th May 2000 at The Racecourse, Wrexham

Bangor City	1-0	Cwmbran Town

Roberts 29'

Bangor City: Mulliner, Johnson, Rowlands, Brett, Bird, S Williams, R Williams (Comley-Excell 83') Coady, Roberts, Allen, E Williams.
Subs not used: Hazelden, Cross.

Cwmbran Town: Wager, Carter (Davies 45'), Wigley (Powell 87'), Aizlewood, Blackie, O'Brien, Summers, Moore, Graham, Futcher (Pattimore 67'), James.

Referee: B Lawlor (Holyhead)

Attendance: 1,125

2000/01 Welsh Cup

First Round

Ammanford AFC	3-1	Seven Sisters
Blaenrhondda AFC	3-1	Taff's Well
Bridgend Town	2-0	Pontyclun FC
Briton Ferry Athletic	0-1	Cardiff Civil Service
Caerleon FC	0-1	Chepstow Town
Caernarfon Town	5-1	Cemaes Bay

Played at Cemaes Bay

Caldicot Town	2-0	Risca United
Cardiff Corinthians	2-1	Pontypridd Town
Dinas Powys	0-0 (aet)	Pontlottyn Blast Furnace

Pontlottyn Blast Furnace won 3-1 on penalties.

Fields Park Pontllanfraith	7-0	Abergavenny Thursdays
Garw Athletic	1-3 (aet)	Ely Rangers

The scoreline after 90 minutes was 1-1.

Glan Conwy	6-2	Llandyrnog United
Halkyn United	0-1	Bethesda Athletic
Holyhead Hotspur	2-3	CPD Porthmadog
Lex XI FC	3-5	Buckley Town
Llanidloes Town	4-0	Meifod FC
Merthyr Saints	0-5	Penrhiwceiber Rangers
Mold Alexandra	1-3	Llangefni Town
Newport YMCA	2-0	Tredegar Town
CPD Penrhyncoch	3-1 (aet)	Newcastle Emlyn

The scoreline after 90 minutes was 1-1.

Rhostyllen United	2-6	Brickfield Rangers
Rhydymwyn FC	0-3	Welshpool Town
Ruthin Town	3-1	Flint Town United
Skewen Athletic	3-2	Porth Tywyn Suburbs
Ton Pentre AFC	5-1	AFC Llwydcoed
Abercynon Athletic	0-2	Neath AFC
AFC Rhondda	3-6	Maesteg Park AFC
Airbus UK	2-3	Brymbo Broughton
Caerau	3-3 (aet)	Aberaman Athletic

The scoreline after 90 minutes was 2-2.
Aberaman Athletic won 4-3 on penalties.

Chirk AAA	0-3	Bala Town
Conwy United	0-4	CPD Glantraeth
Corwen Amateurs	3-3	Rhos Aelwyd
Gresford Athletic	2-0	Penycae FC
Guilsfield FC	1-0	Presteigne St. Andrews
Gwynfi United	1-1	Goytre United
Llandudno FC	2-3	Denbigh Town
Llanfairpwll FC	2-1	Holywell Town
Llanwern AFC	1-2	Treowen Stars
Pontardawe Town	2-0	Garden Village
Portos Grange Quins	3-2	Porthcawl Town

Second Round

Bethesda Athletic	2-3	Bala Town
Ruthin Town	3-2	Denbigh Town
CPD Porthmadog	1-2	Newtown AFC
Rhayader Town	4-2	Llanidloes Town
CPD Penrhyncoch	1-0	CPD Glantraeth
Caersws FC	6-2	Brymbo Broughton
Connah's Quay Nomads	3-0	Gresford Athletic
Rhos Aelwyd	2-3	Llanfairpwll
Guilsfield FC	0-4	Buckley Town
Rhyl FC	2-1	Flexsys Cefn Druids
Oswestry Town	0-2	Caernarfon Town
Welshpool Town	2-3	Brickfield Rangers
Ammanford AFC	2-4	Maesteg Park AFC
Bridgend Town	0-2	Ton Pentre AFC
Pontlottyn Blast Furnace	3-5	Neath AFC
Haverfordwest County	8-0	Skewen Athletic
Newport YMCA	1-3	Caldicot Town
Blaenrhondda AFC	4-1	Penrhiwceiber Rangers
Cardiff Civil Service	4-5	Caerleon FC
UWIC Inter Cardiff	1-2	Aberystwyth Town
Cardiff Corinthians	1-2	Llanelli AFC
Gwynfi United	2-3	Treowen Stars
Aberaman Athletic	1-3	Fields Park Pontllanfraith
Pontardawe Town	3-1	Pontardawe Town
Llangefni Town	10-2	Glan Conwy

Third Round

Neath AFC	1-2	Welshpool Town
Llanelli AFC	4-1	Ruthin Town
Ton Pentre AFC	1-0 (aet)	Pontardawe Town
Newtown AFC	2-1	Rhyl FC
Caerleon AFC	0-4	Carmarthen Town
Rhayader Town	3-1	Buckley Town
Port Talbot Athletic	1-2	Total Network Solutions
Treowen Stars	0-3	Bangor City
Fields Park Pontllanfraith	0-2	Caersws FC
CPD Penrhyncoch	1-2 (aet)	Barry Town

The scoreline after 90 minutes was 0-0.

Caernarfon Town	2-4	Cwmbran Town
Blaenrhondda AFC	1-0	Bala Town
Haverfordwest County	1-2	Afan Lido FC
Connah's Quay Nomads	1-2	Maesteg Park AFC
Llanfairpwll FC	2-1	Caldicot Town

The match was abandoned after 30 minutes. Caldicot Town withdrew from the competition then lodged a protest regarding opponents' ground. The protest was rejected.

Aberystwyth Town	3-1	Llangefni Town

Fourth Round

Total Network Solutions	2-1 (aet)	Cwmbran Town

The scoreline after 90 minutes was 1-1.

Bangor City	3-2 (aet)	Newtown AFC

The scoreline after 90 minutes was 1-1.

Blaenrhondda AFC	0-5	Llanelli AFC
Caersws FC	3-0	Afan Lido FC
Welshpool Town	2-4	Aberystwyth Town
Rhayader Town	2-1	Carmarthen Town
Maesteg Park Athletic	1-0	Ton Pentre AFC
Llanfairpwll FC	0-4	Barry Town

Fifth Round

Barry Town	3-0	Bangor City
Llanelli AFC	0-4	Aberystwyth Town
Total Network Solutions	2-1	Rhayader Town
Maesteg Park AFC	3-1	Caersws FC

Semi-finals

Maesteg Park AFC	1-2	Total Network Solutions

Played at Park Avenue, Aberystwyth

Aberystwyth Town	1-2	Barry Town

Played at Stebonheath Park, Llanelli

2001 WELSH CUP FINAL

25th May 2001 at The Racecourse, Wrexham

Barry Town	2-0	Total Net. Solutions

Moralee 77' Lloyd 87'

Barry Town: Digby, Evans, Lloyd, Kennedy, York, Sharpe, Phillips, French, Moralee, Davies (Flynn 62'), Staton (Jenkins 62'). Not used: Burke

Total Network Solutions: Deegan, Holmes, Coathup, Morgan, Edwards, Alexander (McKenna 77'), G.Powell, Wright, Toner (Welton 66'), Evans (Edge 50'), Ward.

Referee: R A Jones (Caernarfon)

Attendance: 1,022

2001/02 Welsh Cup

Preliminary Round

Caerau Ely	3-0	Troedyrhiw
R.T.B. Ebbw Vale	4-0	Pontypool Town

First Round

Aberaman Athletic	5-1	Abercynon Athletic
Ammanford AFC	3-5	Pontardawe Town
Bala Town	1-5	Mold Alexandra
Bettws FC	2-1 (aet)	Ely Rangers

The scoreline after 90 minutes was 0-0.

Brickfield Rangers	1-2	Brymbo Broughton
Briton Ferry Athletic	4-2	Pontlottyn Blast Furnace
Buckley Town	0-1	Gresford Athletic

Caerleon FC	2-2 (aet)	Caerau Ely

Caerleon won 6-5 on penalties.

Cemaes Bay FC	2-3	Lex XI FC
Corwen Amateurs	0-6	Llandudno FC
Flint Town United	1-2	Denbigh Town
Garden Village	3-1	Seven Sisters
Goytre United	1-3	Dinas Powys
Guilsfield FC	0-5	CPD Penrhyncoch
Gwynfi United	6-2	Bridgend Town
Holyhead Hotspur	7-4	Prestatyn Town
Llandyrnog United	1-2	Halkyn United
Llanfairpwll FC	2-0	Caerwys
Meifod FC	3-2	Llanidloes Town
Merthyr Saints	2-4	Garw Athletic
Neath AFC	4-3	Porth Tywyn Suburbs
Newcastle Emlyn	0-2	Llanrhaeadr Ym Mochnant
Penrhiwceiber Rangers	3-1	AFC Rhondda
Pontyclun FC	1-1	Taff's Well AFC
Pontypridd Town	3-1	AFC Llwydcoed
Porthcawl Town	3-3 (aet)	Newport YMCA

The scoreline after 90 minutes was 2-2.
Newport YMCA won 5-4 on penalties.

CPD Porthmadog	2-1	Conwy United
Portos Grange Quins	1-3	Cardiff Corinthians
Presteigne St. Andrews	5-0	Llandrindod Wells
Risca & Gelli United	2-4	Fields Park Pontllanfraith
Ruthin Town	2-0	Rhos Aelwyd
Skewen Athletic	5-0	Morriston Town
Tredegar Town	0-1	RTB Ebbw Vale
Treharris Athletic	0-2	Cardiff Civil Service
Treowen Stars	1-3	Blaenrhondda AFC
Welshpool Town	3-0	Chirk AAA

Second Round

Bettws FC	5-2	Garw Athletic
Blaenrhondda	3-1 (aet)	UWIC Inter Cardiff
Brymbo Broughton	1-4	Llandudno FC
Caerleon AFC	1-3	Aberaman Athletic
Caernarfon Town	1-4	Caersws FC
Cardiff Civil Service	2-1	Pontyclun FC
Fields Park/Pontllanfraith	2-4	Afan Lido FC
Flexsys Cefn Druids	6-2	Llangefni/Glantraeth
Gresford Athletic	1-2	Lex XI FC
Halkyn United	5-1	Holyhead Hotspur
Haverfordwest County	3-2	Neath AFC
Llanelli AFC	8-1	Cardiff Corinthians
Llanfairpwll FC	7-2	Presteigne St. Andrews
Llanrhaeadr Ym Mochnant FC	1-7	Newtown AFC
Llanidloes Town	1-2	Ruthin Town
Newport YMCA	4-4 (aet)	Garden Village

Newport YMCA won 5-3 on penalties.

Oswestry Town	1-3	Rhayader Town
CPD Penrhyncoch	1-5	Connah's Quay Nomads
Pontardawe Town	2-0	Dinas Powys FC
Pontypridd Town	2-3 (aet)	Briton Ferry Athletic

The scoreline after 90 minutes was 2-2.

CPD Porthmadog	3-1	Denbigh Town
Rhyl FC	1-2	Rhyl FC
RTB Ebbw Vale	2-3	Gwynfi United
Skewen Athletic	0-3	Port Talbot Town
Ton Pentre AFC	7-0	Penrhiwceiber Rangers
Welshpool Town	2-0	Mold Alexandra

Third Round

Blaenrhondda AFC	1-3	Cwmbran Town
Cardiff Civil Service	2-1	Llanelli AFC
Afan Lido FC	0-2	Carmarthen Town
Ton Pentre AFC	2-1	Briton Ferry Athletic
Aberystwyth Town	0-1	Aberaman Athletic
Haverfordwest County	0-2	Pontardawe Town
Bettws FC	1-0	Newport YMCA
Maesteg Park AFC	2-3	Gwynfi United
Connah's Quay Nomads	3-2	Newtown AFC
Flexsys Cefn Druids	2-1	Ruthin Town
CPD Porthmadog	1-5	Bangor City
Halkyn United	2-1	Rhayader Town
Caersws FC	5-1	Lex XI FC Wrexham
Welshpool Town	3-2	Llanfairpwll FC
Total Network Solutions	1-0	Llandudno FC

Fourth Round

Bangor City	9-1	Cardiff Civil Service
Barry Town	4-3	Caersws FC
Bettws FC	0-3	Ton Pentre AFC
Carmarthen Town	2-1	Connah's Quay Nomads
Cwmbran Town	8-1	Aberaman Athletic
Flexsys Cefn Druids	1-0	Halkyn United
Gwynfi United	0-1 (aet)	Total Network Solutions
Pontardawe Town	0-1	Welshpool Town

Fifth Round

Barry Town	3-0	Total Network Solutions
Carmarthen Town	0-4	Bangor City
Ton Pentre AFC	3-2 (aet)	Cwmbran Town

The scoreline after 90 minutes was 2-2.

Welshpool Town	0-4	Flexsys Cefn Druids

Semi-finals

Barry Town	2-0	Ton Pentre AFC

Played at Stebonheath Park, Llanelli

Bangor City	5-0	Flexsys Cefn Druids

Played at Belle Vue, Rhyl

2002 WELSH CUP FINAL

5th May 2002 at Park Avenue, Aberystwyth

Barry Town	4-1	Bangor City

Moralee 51' 90' French 8' Flynn 35'   *Griffiths 41'*

Barry Town: Rayner, Jarman, Lloyd, Kennedy, Morgan, Phillips (Toomey 28'), York, French, Moralee, Flynn, Ramasut (86'). Not used: Brown

Bangor City: Priestley, Jones (Cooper 70'), Goodall, Short, Rowlands (C.Roberts 70'), Griffiths, Lloyd-Williams, Blackmore, P.Roberts, Davies, Burgess. Sub not used: Hazelden

Referee: R J Ellingham (Pontprennau)

Attendance: 2,256

2002/03 Welsh Cup

Preliminary Round

Caerau Ely	5-2	RTB Ebbw Vale
Caerwys	2-0	Rhos Aelwyd
Cwmaman United	2-1	Pontlottyn Blast Furnace
Glantraeth	10-2	Bala Town

First Round

AFC Llwydcoed	1-0	Newport YMCA
AFC Rhondda	4-1	Porthcawl Town
Airbus UK	2-0	Ruthin Town
Amlwch Town	0-3	Buckley Town
Glantraeth	7-0	Corwen Amateurs
Bettws FC	2-3	Caerau Ely
Briton Ferry Athletic	2-6 (aet)	Blaenrhondda

The scoreline after 90 minutes was 2-2.

Brymbo Broughton	3-2	Conwy United
Caerwys FC	3-3 (aet)	Brickfield Rangers

Brickfield Rangers won 6-5 on penalties.

Caldicot Town	2-1	Morriston Town
Cardiff Civil Service	2-1	Tredegar Town
Cemaes Bay	2-1	Llandyrnog United
Cwmaman United	3-2 (aet)	Newcastle Emlyn

The scoreline after 90 minutes was 2-2.

Denbigh Town	0-3	CPD Porthmadog
Ely Rangers	1-2	Aberaman Athletic
Garden Village	5-3	Merthyr Saints
Garw Athletic	4-3	Seven Sisters
Goytre United	7-1	Milford United
Gwynfi United (w/o)	v	Penrhiwceiber Rangers (withdrew)
Halkyn United	3-0	Flint Town United
Holyhead Hotspur	3-1	Castell Alun Colts
Llandudno FC	0-0	Mold Alexandra

The match was abandoned after 45 minutes.

Llanfairpwll	3-0	Chirk AAA
Llanrhaeadr Ym Mochnant	4-1	Llanidloes Town
Maesteg Park AFC	3-0	Risca & Gelli United
Meifod FC (withdrew)	v	Presteigne St.Andrews (w/o)
Neath AFC	2-1	Dinas Powys
Penrhyncoch	4-0	Guilsfield FC
Pontyclun FC	0-2	Treowen Stars
Pontypridd Town	3-3 (aet(	Grange Harlequins

Grange Harlequins won 4-3 on penalties.

Porth Tywyn Suburbs	3-0	Caerleon FC
Prestatyn Town	1-3 (aet)	Lex XI FC

The scoreline after 90 minutes was 1-1.

Taff's Well	4-0	Cardiff Corinthians
Troedyrhiw	4-2	Fields Park Pontllanfraith
Gresford Athletic	6-0	Holywell Town

First Round Replay

Llandudno FC	4-0	Mold Alexandra

Second Round

Goytre United	0-1	Haverfordwest County
Aberystwyth Town	3-0	Welshpool Town
AFC Rhondda	2-2 (aet)	AFC Llwydcoed

The scoreline after 90 minutes was 1-1.
AFC Rhondda won 3-2 on penalties.

Airbus UK	2-0	Buckley Town
Blaenrhondda	0-1	Cwmaman United
Brymbo Broughton	2-1	Caernarfon Town
Caerau Ely	3-0	Grange Harlequins
Caldicot Town	1-3	Garw Athletic
Cardiff Civil Service	0-1	UWIC Inter Cardiff
Carmarthen Town	4-1	Gwynfi United
Cemaes Bay	4-6	Lex XI FC
Connah's Quay Nomads	3-0	Brickfield Rangers
Glantraeth	4-3	CPD Porthmadog
Llanelli AFC	1-4	Cwmbran Town
Llanfairpwll	3-3 (aet)	Halkyn United

The scoreline after 90 minutes was 1-1.
Halkyn United won 6-5 on penalties.

Llangefni Town	3-5	Pontardawe Town
Neath AFC	1-1 (aet)	Afan Lido FC

The scoreline after 90 minutes was 0-0.
Neath AFC won 5-4 on penalties.

Newtown AFC	6-1	Llanrhaeadr Ym Mochnant
Oswestry Town	2-1	Presteigne St. Andrews
Porth Tywyn Suburbs	3-0	Garden Village
Port Talbot Town	1-0	Taff's Well AFC
Rhayader Town	0-5	CPD Penrhyncoch
Rhyl FC	5-0	Holyhead Hotspur
Treowen Stars	2-0	Maesteg Park AFC
Troedyrhiw	0-2	Aberaman Athletic
Llandudno FC	3-1	Gresford Athletic

Third Round

Aberaman Athletic	0-4	Barry Town
Aberystwyth Town	6-0	Lex XI FC
AFC Rhondda	0-5	Pontardawe Town
Bangor City	6-0	Halkyn United
Brymbo Broughton FC	0-1	Llandudno
Caersws FC	1-0	Total Network Solutions
Connah's Quay Nomads	1-0	Newtown AFC
Cwmbran Town	3-1	Cwmaman United
Flexsys Cefn Druids	4-3	Airbus UK
Garw Athletic	1-3	Haverfordwest County
Glantraeth	1-2	Oswestry Town
Port Talbot Town	2-1	Neath AFC
Porth Tywyn Suburbs	1-2	Ton Pentre AFC
Rhyl FC	2-1	CPD Penrhyncoch
Treowen Stars	0-4	Carmarthen Town
UWIC Inter Cardiff	3-0	Caerau Ely

Fourth Round

Barry Town	4-1	Pontardawe Town
Caersws FC	0-3	Bangor City
Carmarthen Town	0-1	Cwmbran Town
Llandudno FC	1-3	Connah's Quay Nomads
Oswestry Town	2-1	Haverfordwest County
Port Talbot Town	2-3	Aberystwyth Town
Ton Pentre AFC	2-1	Flexsys Cefn Druids
UWIC Inter Cardiff	0-1	Rhyl FC

Fifth Round

Aberystwyth Town	2-3	Barry Town
Bangor City	0-0 (aet)	Cwmbran Town

Cwmbran Town won 5-3 on penalties.

Rhyl FC	1-0	Connah's Quay Nomads
Ton Pentre AFC	3-0	Oswestry Town

Semi-finals

Barry Town	1-0	Rhyl FC

Played at Park Avenue, Aberystwyth

Cwmbran Town	2-1	Ton Pentre AFC

Played at Jenner Park, Barry

2003 WELSH CUP FINAL

11th May 2003 at Stebonheath Park, Llanelli

Barry Town	2-2 (aet)	Cwmbran Town

Ramasut 28' (pen), Phillips 86'   Welsh 34' Moore 39'

Barry Town won 4-3 on penalties.

Barry Town: Baruwa, Brown (York 72'), Lloyd, Kennedy, Morgan (Burke 118'), Phillips, Jenkins (Cotterrall 77'), French, Moralee, Ramasut, Akinfenwa

Cwmbran Town: Ellacott, Carter, Smothers (David 90'), Wigg, Warton, Jones, Morris (Davies 77'), Moore, Welsh, Watkins (Dunn 56'), Hurlin.

Referee: B Bevan (Wrexham)
Attendance: 852

2003/04 Welsh Cup

First Round

Aberaman Athletic	2-4	Fields Park/Pontllanfraith
AFC Llwydcoed	3-2	Penrhiwceiber Rangers
Ammanford FC	1-2	Cardiff Corinthians
Blaenrhondda FC	3-1	Tredegar Town
Bodedern FC	2-1	Prestatyn Town
Brickfield Rangers	1-0	Conwy United
Bridgend Town	0-0 (aet)	Garden Village

Bridgend won 6-5 on penalties.

Bryntirion Athletic	3-4 (aet)	Treharris Athletic

The scoreline after 90 minutes was 3-3.

Caldicot Town	1-3	Merthyr Saints
Cemaes Bay FC	2-3	Holyhead Hotspur
Chirk AAA	2-2 (aet)	Penrhyncoch

Penrhyncoch won 3-2 on penalties.

Flint Town United	5-0	Brynteg Village
Gresford Athletic	5-2	Corwen Amateurs
Guilsfield FC	3-1	Rhayader Town
Gwynfi United	1-0	Caerau Ely FC
Holywell Town	1-4	CPD Glantraeth
Llanfairpwll FC	2-1	Rhos Aelwyd
Llanidloes Town	1-2	Newcastle Emlyn FC
Llanwern FC	2-3	Ely Rangers
Mold Alexandra	2-0	Bala Town
Morriston Town	0-0 (aet)	Dinas Powys FC

Morriston Town won 4-3 on penalties.

Newport YMCA	0-1 (aet)	Treowen Stars
Pontyclun FC	0-2	Grange Harlequins
Pontypridd Town	1-2	Caerleon FC
Porth Tywyn Suburbs	3-2	Troedyrhiw FC
Porthcawl Town	1-2 (aet)	Cwmaman United

The scoreline after 90 minutes was 1-1.

Presteigne St. Andrews	1-0	Llanrhaeadr FC
Risca & Gelli United (w/o)	v	Pontlottyn Blast Furnace (withdrew)
Taff's Well FC	0-4	Skewen Athletic

Second Round

Aberystwyth Town	12-1	Lex XI
Bangor City	0-0 (aet)	CPD Glantraeth

Glantraeth won 7-6 on penalties.

Barry Town	1-2	Risca & Gelli United
Brickfield Rangers	0-2	Buckley Town
Briton Ferry Athletic	3-1	Blaenrhondda AFC
Caerleon FC	0-0 (aet)	Skewen Athletic

Caerleon FC won 5-3 on penalties.

Caernarfon Town	5-0	Llandudno
Cardiff Corinthians	0-3 (aet)	AFC Llwydcoed

The scoreline after 90 minutes was 0-0.

CPD Bodedern	5-1	CPD Penrhyncoch
Cwmbran Town	5-1	Merthyr Saints
Ely Rangers	0-2	Port Talbot Town
Flint Town United	2-1	Ruthin Town
Grange Harlequins	0-1 (aet)	Ton Pentre
Guilsfield FC	1-8	Connah's Quay Nomads
Gwynfi United	1-4	Bridgend Town
Halkyn United	1-3	Llangefni Town
Haverfordwest County	0-2	Afan Lido FC
Holyhead Hotspur	3-0	Gresford Athletic
Llanelli AFC	5-0	Morriston Town
Maesteg Park AFC	0-1	Goytre United
Mold Alexandra	1-4	Welshpool Town
Neath AFC	0-0 (aet)	Cwmaman United

Neath AFC won 4-3 on penalties.

Newcastle Emlyn	0-1	Pontardawe Town
NEWI Cefn Druids	3-0	Porthmadog FC
Newtown AFC	3-0	Amlwch Town
Porth Tywyn Suburbs	1-0	Garw Athletic
Presteigne St. Andrews	1-4	Llanfairpwll FC
Rhyl FC	2-0	Airbus UK
Total Network Solutions	2-0	Caersws FC
Treharris Athletic	0-0 (aet)	Bettws FC

Treharris Athletic won 3-1 on penalties.

Treowen Stars	3-1	Fields Park Pontllanfraith
UWIC Inter Cardiff	2-1	Carmarthen Town

Third Round

Bodedern FC	1-2	Connah's Quay Nomads
Bridgend Town	3-2	Treowen Stars
Buckley Town	0-7	NEWI Cefn Druids
Caerleon FC	0-1 (aet)	Porth Tywyn Suburbs
Caernarfon Town	3-2	Holyhead Hotspur
Flint Town United	0-3	CPD Glantraeth
Llanelli AFC	0-1	Cwmbran Town
Llanfairpwll FC	1-4	Rhyl FC
Pontardawe Town	0-2	Afan Lido FC
Port Talbot Town	2-1 (aet)	Aberystwyth Town
Risca & Gelli United	0-1	AFC Llwydcoed
Ton Pentre	4-1	Neath AFC
Total Network Solutions	5-1	Llangefni Town

Treharris Athletic	0-2	Goytre United
UWIC Inter Cardiff	2-0	Briton Ferry Athletic
Welshpool Town	3-1	Newtown AFC

Fourth Round

Caernarfon Town	1-2	Cwmbran Town
Connah's Quay Nomads	0-1	Total Network Solutions
AFC Llwydcoed	0-2	Rhyl FC
NEWI Cefn Druids	3-0	Goytre United
Porth Tywyn Suburbs (wthdrew)	v	Afan Lido (w/o)
Ton Pentre	0-1	Port Talbot Town
UWIC Inter Cardiff	2-0	Bridgend Town
Welshpool Town	3-2 (aet)	CPD Glantraeth

Welshpool Town withdrew from the competition after discovering they had fielded played an ineligible player.

Quarter-finals

Afan Lido FC	1-2	Rhyl FC
Cwmbran Town	2-1 (aet)	UWIC Inter Cardiff
NEWI Cefn Druids	0-1	Port Talbot Town
Total Network Solutions	4-1	CPD Glantraeth

Semi-finals

Cwmbran Town	2-4 (aet)	Rhyl FC

The scoreline after 90 minutes was 0-0.
Played at Latham Park, Newtown

Port Talbot Town	0-1	Total Network Solutions

Played at Park Avenue, Aberystwyth

2004 WELSH CUP FINAL

9th May 2004 at Latham Park, Newtown

Rhyl FC   1-0 (aet)   Total Net. Solutions

Taylor 91' og

Rhyl: Smith, Brewerton, M.Powell, Atherton, Edwards, Walters (McGinn 32'), Wilson, Limbert, Moran, G.Powell (Jackson 106'), Graves (Adamson 82')

Total Network Solutions: Acton, Naylor (Bridgewater 19' (Perry 84')), Hogan, Holmes, Evans, Taylor, Ruscoe, Wilde, Toner, Wood, Davies (Aggrey 106')

Referee: J A Collins (Llangyfelach)

Attendance: 1,534

2004/05 Welsh Cup

First Round

Ammanford	0-9	Goytre United
Bala Town	5-2 (aet)	Conwy United

The scoreline after 90 minutes was 2-2.

Barry Town	3-0	Gwynfi United
Blaenrhondda	3-2	Ystradgynlais
Bodedern	5-0	Brynteg Village
Bridgend	2-0	Neath
Caldicot Town	2-2 (aet)	Croesyceiliog

Caldicot Town won 5-4 on penalties.

Cardiff Corinthians	3-2	Maesteg Park Athletic
Carmarthen Town	7-2	Bryntirion Athletic
Carno	3-2	Caerwys
Cefn United	1-2	Denbigh Town
Chirk AAA	2-4 (aet)	Gresford Athletic

The scoreline after 90 minutes was 2-2.

Corwen	0-5	Ruthin Town
Dinas Powys	6-0	AFC Porth
Garden Village Youth	v	Llanrug United (w/o)
Glan Conwy	1-3	Penmaenmawr Pheonix
Goytre	0-3	Caerau Ely
Grange Harlequins	7-0	Morriston Town
Guilsfield (w/o)	v	Sealand Leisure (withdrew)
Halkyn United	2-0	Flint Town United
Holyhead Hotspur	4-0	Cemaes Bay
Holywell Town	1-0	Mold Alexandra
Lex XI	5-4	Llanberis
Llandudno Junction (w/o)	v	Amlwch Town (withdrew)
Llandudno Town	1-0	Llanfyllin Town
Llangollen Town	4-1	Rhostyllen United
Llanidloes	0-10	Llangefni Town
Llanrhaeadr Ym Mochnant	2-1	Llandyrnog
Llantwit Fardre	0-1	Garden Village
Meifod	1-8	Glantraeth
Newport YMCA	1-2	Briton Ferry Athletic
Penrhiwceiber	1-2	AFC Llwydcoed
Penrhiwfer	4-2 (aet)	Llanwern

The scoreline after 90 minutes was 2-2.

Penycae	1-3	Penrhyncoch
Pontyclun	3-1	Newcastle Emlyn
Pontypridd Town	0-1	Llanelli AFC
Porthcawl Town	0-3	Bettws
Prestatyn Town	1-4	Airbus UK
Rhayader Town	1-0	Rhos Aelwyd
Rhydymwyn	4-2	Llanfairpwll
Risca & Gelli United	2-0	Ento Aberaman Athletic
Skewen Athletic	6-0	Garw Athletic
Summerhill United	1-2	Buckley Town
Taff's Well	7-0	Cwmamman United
Ton Pentre	2-1	Ely Rangers
Tredegar Town	0-1	Caerleon
Troedyrhiw	1-0	Fields Park Pontllannfraith
UWIC Inter Cardiff	1-0	Treowen Stars
Y Felinheli	1-3	Mynydd Isa

Second Round

Afan Lido	1-0	Caldicot Town
Airbus UK	2-1	Rhydymwyn FC
Bala Town	3-0	Denbigh Town
Barry Town	3-0	Blaenrhondda FC
Bettws	0-2	Aberystwyth Town
Bodedern	3-1	Carno
Briton Ferry Athletic	1-2	Garden Village
Buckley Town	1-1 (aet)	Gresford Athletic

Gresford Athletic won 8-7 on penalties.

Caerau Ely	0-2	Penrhiwfer
Caerleon	3-3 (aet)	Taff's Well

The scoreline after 90 minutes was 2-2.
Caerleon won 5-4 on penalties.

Caersws	5-1	Ruthin Town
Carmarthen Town	3-0	Bridgend Town

Dinas Powys	2-1	Risca & Gelli United
Glantraeth	2-0	NEWI Cefn Druids
Goytre United	0-1	AFC Llwydcoed
Llandudno	1-3	Rhyl
Llandudno Junction	1-5	Welshpool Town
Llanelli	2-3	Cwmbran Town
Llangefni Town	3-1	Guilsfield
Llangollen Town	0-8	Caernarfon Town
Llanrhaeadr Ym Mochnant	1-5	Lex XI
Llanrug United	2-3	Halkyn United
Mynydd Isa	1-2 (aet)	Holywell Town

The scoreline after 90 minutes was 1-1.

Newtown	0-1	Porthmadog FC
Penmaenmawr Phoenix	0-2	Bangor City
Penrhyncoch	2-2 (aet)	Holyhead Hotspur

Holyhead won 4-3 on penalties.

Rhayader Town	2-4	Port Talbot Town
Skewen Athletic	0-2	Grange Quins
Ton Pentre	2-0	Cardiff Corries
Total Network Solutions	5-0	Connah's Quay Nomads
Troedyrhiw	2-3	Haverfordwest County
UWIC Inter Cardiff	4-3	Pontyclun

Third Round

AFC Llwydcoed	1-2	Welshpool Town
Airbus UK	0-2	Afan Lido
Bala Town	2-2 (aet)	Ton Pentre

Bala Town won 5-3 on penalties.

Barry Town	2-1	Garden Village
Caernarfon Town	2-1 (aet)	Grange Harlequins

The scoreline after 90 minutes was 1-1.

Dinas Powys	2-3	Bangor City
Gresford Athletic	2-2 (aet)	Carmarthen Town

The scoreline after 90 minutes was 1-1.
Carmarthen Town won 4-1 on penalties.

Haverfordwest County	3-0	Glantraeth
Holywell Town (Disqualified)	v	Aberystwyth Town (w/o)
Lex XI	0-1	Caersws
Llangefni	1-0	Bodedern
Port Talbot Town	0-1	Halkyn United
Porthmadog	1-3 (aet)	Cwmbran Town

The scoreline after 90 minutes was 1-1.

Rhyl	9-0	Holyhead Hotspur
Total Network Solutions	11-0	Penrhiwfer
UWIC	3-1	Caerleon

Fourth Round

Aberystwyth Town	3-2 (aet)	Caernarfon Town

The scoreline after 90 minutes was 2-2.

Barry Town	2-5	Afan Lido
Carmarthen Town	1-0	Cwmbran Town
Halkyn United	0-4	Caersws
Rhyl	4-0	Llangefni Town
Total Network Solutions	2-1	Bangor City
UWIC Inter Cardiff	1-4	Haverfordwest County
Welshpool Town	1-2	Bala Town

Quarter-finals

Aberystwyth Town	0-2	Haverfordwest County
Caersws	0-1	Carmarthen Town
Rhyl	4-0	Bala Town
Total Network Solutions	4-1	Afan Lido

Semi-finals

Carmarthen Town	1-0	Haverfordwest County

Played at Stebonheath Park, Llanelli

Rhyl	1-3	Total Network Solutions

Played at Racecourse Ground, Wrexham

2005 WELSH CUP FINAL

8th May 2005 at Stebonheath Park, Llanelli

Carmarthen Town	0-1	Total Network Solutions

John Lawless 75'

Carmarthen Town: Pennock, Hardy, Lloyd, Giles, Carter, Jones, Smothers (Cotterrall 78'), Kennedy (Abdillahi 78'), Burke (James 89'), Dodds, Aherne-Evans

Total Network Solutions: Doherty, Naylor, Holmes, Leah, Evans, Taylor, Ruscoe, Lloyd-Williams (King 83'), Wilde, Wood, Lawless (Toner 89'). Sub not used: Beck

Referee: S Jones (Swansea)

Attendance: 1,126

2005/06 Welsh Cup

First Round

Afan Lido	0-3	West End
AFC Llwydcoed	5-0	Blaenrhondda
AFC Porth	0-1	Pontyclun
Bethesda Athletic	1-5	Mynydd Isa
Bridgend Town	1-4	UWIC
Briton Ferry Athletic	5-2	Llantwit Fadre
Buckley Town	4-2	Flint Town United
Caerleon	5-6 (aet)	Bettws
Caerwys	0-2	Llanrwst United
Caldicot Town	4-0	Porthcawl Town
Cefn United	0-2	Connah's Quay Nomads
Chirk AAA	3-2	Brynteg Village
Coedpoeth United	0-3	Caernarfon Town
Conwy United (w/o)	v	Y Felinheli (withdrew)
Corwen	0-6	Glantraeth
Croesyceiliog	2-1	Garden Village
Cwmbran Celtic	2-4	Ystradgynlais
Denbigh Town	1-4	Prestatyn Town
Dinas Powys	0-2	Port Talbot Town
Ely Rangers	4-2 (aet)	Cambrian & Clydach Boys & Girls Club
Ento Aberaman	2-0	Barry Town
Garw Athletic	0-3	Taff's Well
Glan Conwy	0-3	Bala Town
Goytre United	7-1	Llanwern
Grange Harlequins	2-0 (aet)	Penrhiwceiber Rangers
Gresford Athletic	2-1	Bodedern
Hawarden Rangers	2-3	Mold Alexandra
Holywell Town	0-1	NEWI Cefn Druids

Knighton Town	0-4	Penrhyncoch
Llandudno Junction	0-3	Airbus UK
Llandyrnog United	3-2	Llanrhaeadr Ym Mochnant
Llanfairpwll	1-3	Llangefni Town
Llanfyllin Town	2-1	Carno
Llangollen Town	0-2	Llanberis
Llanidloes Town	0-7	Guilsfield
Llanrug United	2-6	Llandudno
Maesteg Park Athletic	7-0	Ammanford
Morriston Town	0-1	Bryntirion Athletic
Neath Athletic	0-1	Llanelli
Nefyn United	1-0	Halkyn United
Newcastle Emlyn	1-6	Cardiff Corinthians
Newport YMCA	2-1	Caerau Ely
Penmaenmawr Pheonix	1-1 (aet)	Summerhill Brymbo
Summerhill Brymbo won 4-5 on penalties.		
Penrhiwfer	2-4	Risca United
Pontypridd Town	3-2	Pontardawe Town
Presteigne St Andrews (w/o)	v	Meifod (disqualified)
Rhayader Town	5-1	Four Crosses
Rhydymwyn	0-6	Holyhead Hotspur
Ruthin Town	3-4	Lex XI
Sealand Rovers	0-4	Rhos Aelwyd
Tredegar Town	0-4	Ton Pentre
Treharris Athletic	4-2	Goytre
Troedyrhiw	3-0 (aet)	Treowen Stars

Second Round

Aberystwyth Town	2-0	Bettws FC
Airbus UK	4-1	Conwy United
Bala Town	3-2 (aet)	Penrhyncoch
Bangor City	4-0	Llanberis
Caersws FC	5-3	Cardiff Grange Quins
Caldicot Town	1-3	Cwmbran Town
Cardiff Corinthians	0-11	Carmarthen Town
Chirk AAA	1-2	Nefyn United
Croesyceiliog FC	3-2	West End
Ento Aberaman	0-1	Briton Ferry Athletic
Glantraeth	6-1	Guilsfield
Gresford Athletic	1-2	Porthmadog FC
Haverfordwest County	1-2	Goytre United
Holyhead Hotspur	1-3	Caernarfon Town
Lex XI	4-2	Connah's Quay Nomads
Llanelli AFC	8-2	Risca United
Llanfyllin Town	1-3	Buckley Town
Llanrwst United	3-2	Llandudno
Mold Alexandra	4-3	Mynydd Isa
Newtown AFC	5-1	Llandyrnog United
Pontyclun	2-1 (aet)	Maesteg Park Athletic
Pontypridd Town	2-2 (aet)	Ton Pentre
Pontypridd Town won 7-6 on penalties.		
Port Talbot Town	3-2	Newport YMCA
Presteigne St Andrews	2-4 (aet)	Prestatyn Town
Rhayader Town	2-4	Llangefni Town
Rhyl FC	4-0	Sealand Rovers
Summerhill Brymbo	2-3 (aet)	NEWI Cefn Druids
Total Network Solutions	4-1	Welshpool Town
Treharris Athletic	1-3	Ely Rangers
Troedyrhiw	3-2 (aet)	Taff's Well
UWIC	2-1	AFC Llwydcoed
Ystradgynlais	2-3	Bryntirion Athletic

Third Round

Bala Town	4-3 (aet)	Buckley Town
Bangor City	4-2	Airbus UK
Caersws FC	3-1	Croesceiliog
Carmarthen Town	4-0	Briton Ferry Athletic
Ely Rangers	1-4	Cwmbran Town
Glantraeth	2-5	Rhyl FC
Goytre United	6-3	Troedyrhiw
Llangefni Town	3-0	Llanrwst
Mold Alexandra	0-5	Prestatyn Town
NEWI Cefn Druids	3-1	Nefyn United
Newtown AFC	6-0	Pontyclun
Pontypridd Town	1-0 (aet)	Aberystwyth Town
Port Talbot Town	3-0	Bryntirion Athletic
Porthmadog FC	0-3	Caernarfon Town
Total Network Solutions	4-0	Lex XI
UWIC	1-3	Llanelli AFC

Fourth Round

Bangor City	2-1	Newtown AFC
Caernarfon Town	4-0	Bala Town
Caersws FC	1-3	Llangefni Town
Cwmbran Town	1-3	Port Talbot Town
Llanelli AFC	1-0	Total Network Solutions
NEWI Cefn Druids	3-5	Rhyl FC
Pontypridd Town	0-5	Goytre United
Prestatyn Town	1-2	Carmarthen Town

Quarter-finals

Bangor City	1-0	Carmarthen Town
Llanelli AFC	3-0	Caernarfon Town
Port Talbot Town	3-0	Llangefni Town
Rhyl FC	5-2	Goytre United

Semi-finals

Llanelli AFC	0-1	Bangor City
Played at Aberystwyth		
Rhyl FC	2-2 (aet)	Port Talbot Town
Rhyl won 5-4 on penalties.		
Played at Aberystwyth		

2006 WELSH CUP FINAL

Racecourse Ground, Wrexham

Bangor City	0-2	Rhyl FC

Andy Moran 48' pen, Gareth Wilson 78'

Bangor City: Havard, Blackmore, O'Neil, K.Jones, Beattie, C.Jones, Killackey, Priest, Linnacre, Roberts, Lamb. Subs not used: Maxwell, Burke, Ogilvey.

Rhyl: Gann, Connolly (Limbert 88'), Graves (Adamson 82'), Horan, Edwards, Wilson, Moran, Hunt (Sharp 84'), M. Powell, Brewerton.

Referee: Mark Whitby (Penllergaer)

Attendance: 1,743

2006/07 Welsh Cup

First Round

Afan Lido	3-1	Penrhiwceiber Rangers
Ammanford AFC	4-1 (aet)	Pontyclun
Barry Town	3-2 (aet)	Croesyceiliog
Bridgend Town	2-0	Taff's Well
Briton Ferry Athletic	0-1	Bettws
Buckley Town	3-1	Castell Alun Colts
Caerleon	2-1	Garw Athletic
Caldicot Town	0-1	Cwmbran Celtic
Cambrian and Clydach Vale	1-3	Morriston Town
Cardiff Corinthians	3-1	Maesteg Park

Cardiff Corinthians were dismissed from the competition and Maesteg Park progressed to the next round.

Chirk AAA	1-3	Conwy United
Coedpoeth United	0-3	Bethesda Athletic
Rhydymwyn	1-3	Penycae
Denbigh Town	6-0	Glyn Ceiriog
Dinas Powys	1-0	Bryntirion Athletic
ENTO Aberaman Athletic	1-2	Neath Athletic
Flint Town United	4-0	Nefyn United
Garden Village	6-0	AFC Llwydcoed
Glantraeth	3-3 (aet)	Bodedern

Bodedern won 4-3 on penalties.

Gresford Athletic	6-3	Halkyn United
Guilsfield	3-2	Four Crosses
Hawarden Rangers	0-1	Llanrwst United
Holyhead Hotspur	2-1	Lex XI
Holywell Town	3-3 (aet)	Brickfield Rangers

Brickfield Rangers won 5-3 on penalties.

Llanberis	0-3	Mynydd Isa
Llandudno	4-0	Ruthin Town
Llandudno Junction	3-4	Llanrug United
Llanfyllin Town	3-2	Carno
Llanrhaeadr Ym Mochnant	3-4 (aet)	Penrhyncoch
Goytre	2-3 (aet)	UWIC
Llantwit Fardre	0-1	Newport YMCA
Llanwern	7-0	Aberbargoed Buds
Mold Alexandra	1-2	Llanfairpwll
Pentwyn Dynamos	3-4	Caerau Ely
Pontardawe Town	4-1	Porthcawl Town
Pontypridd Town	4-0	Treharris Athletic
Prestatyn Town	5-0	Llandyrnog United
Presteigne St Andrews	4-0	Kerry
Pwllheli	2-1	Cefn United
Queens Park	3-7 (aet)	Brymbo
Rhos Aelwyd	2-4	Bala Town
AFC Porth	2-4 (aet)	West End
Ton Pentre	1-0	Merthyr Saints
Tredegar Town	0-1	Llangeinor
Troedyrhiw	1-2 (aet)	Ely Rangers

Second Round

Barry Town	0-4	Afan Lido
Bodedern	3-3 (aet)	Bethesda Athletic

Bodedern won 4-3 on penalties.

Brickfield Rangers	1-4	Airbus UK
Bridgend Town	5-2	Garden Village
Brymbo	1-1 (aet)	NEWI Cefn Druids

Brymbo won 5-3 on penalties.

Buckley Town	2-1	Llanfyllin Town
Caerleon	2-1 (aet)	UWIC
Connah's Quay Nomads	2-1	Aberystwyth Town
Cwmbran Celtic	2-3 (aet)	Maesteg Park
Cwmbran Town	1-7	Carmarthen Town
Denbigh Town	2-4	Newtown AFC
Dinas Powys	3-0	Morriston Town
Ely Rangers	2-2 (aet)	Caerau Ely

Ely Rangers won 4-2 on penalties.

Goytre Utd	1-2	West End
Guilsfield	0-5	Bala Town
Llandudno	3-0	Flint Town United
Llanelli AFC	5-0	Bettws
Llanfairpwll	0-6	Rhyl FC
Llangefni	0-2	Holyhead Hotspur
Llanrug Utd	0-2	Bangor City
Mynydd Isa	0-5	Caersws FC
Neath Athletic	2-0	Llanwern
Newport YMCA	2-1 (aet)	Ammanford
Penrhyncoch	2-0	Conwy United
Pontardawe Town	1-2 (aet)	Pontypridd Town
Port Talbot Town	3-2	Haverfordwest County
Prestatyn	2-4	Porthmadog FC
Presteigne St Andrews	1-1 (aet)	Penycae

Presteigne St Andrews won 4-3 on penalties.

Pwllheli	2-0	Gresford Athletic
The New Saints	3-1	Llanrwst United
Ton Pentre	6-0	Llangeinor
Welshpool Town	4-1	Caernarfon Town

Third Round

Afan Lido	3-0	Bodedern
Bridgend Town	1-1 (aet)	Airbus UK

Bridgend Town won 5-4 on penalties.

Carmarthen Town	2-0	West End
Caerleon	1-1 (aet)	Ely Rangers

Ely Rangers won 4-2 on penalties.

Caersws FC	3-0	Buckley Town
Maesteg Park	0-1	Llandudno
Holyhead Hotspur	2-0 (aet)	Presteigne St Andrews
Neath Athletic	3-2	Brymbo
Newtown AFC	2-0	Dinas Powys
Newport YMCA	1-3	Connah's Quay Nomads
Penrhyncoch	0-2	Llanelli AFC
Porthmadog FC	2-0	Bangor City
Port Talbot Town	3-0	Bala Town
Pwllheli	1-2	The New Saints
Ton Pentre	1-0	Rhyl FC
Welshpool Town	2-1 (aet)	Pontypridd Town

Fourth Round

Carmarthen Town	0-0 (aet)	Caersws FC

Carmarthen Town won 5-4 on penalties.

Connah's Quay Nomads	3-1	Llandudno
Ely Rangers	1-2	Afan Lido
Llanelli AFC	7-0	Newtown AFC
Holyhead Hotspur	2-1 (aet)	Bridgend Town
Porthmadog FC	2-2 (aet)	The New Saints

Porthmadog FC won 3-2 on penalties.

Port Talbot Town	3-1 (aet)	Ton Pentre
Welshpool Town	3-0	Neath Athletic

Quarter-finals

Carmarthen Town	1-1 (aet)	Porthmadog FC
Carmarthen Town won 4-3 on penalties.		
Holyhead Hotspur	1-5	Holyhead Hotspur
Llanelli AFC	6-2	Connah's Quay Nomads
Port Talbot Town	0-1	Afan Lido

Semi-finals

Afan Lido	1-1 (aet)	Welshpool Town
Afan Lido won 7-6 on penalties.		
Played at Park Avenue, Aberystwyth		
Carmarthen Town	1-0	Llanelli AFC
Played at New Bridge Meadow, Haverfordwest		

2007 WELSH CUP FINAL

Played at Stebonheath Park, Llanelli

Afan Lido	2-3	Carmarthen Town
Ian Jones 16' 76'		Kaid Mohamed 13' 47', Sasha Walters 26'

Afan Lido: N.Thomas, Evans, Brace (Keddle 46'), Walters (Loss 83'), Dodds, K.Thomas, D.Thomas, Ramasut, Fowler, Mohamed, Cotterrall.
Sub not used: Hancock.

Carmarthen Town: B.Thomas, C.Jones, Lewis, Williams, Felton (Latham 85'), Martin, McCreesh, P.Evans (C.Evans 68'), I.Jones, O'Leary, Hurley (Piper 68').

Referee: Lee Evans (Llanllechid)

Attendance: 946

2007/08 Welsh Cup

First Round

Bala Town	6-3	Denbigh Town
Bodedern	0-2	Llanfairpwll
Brickfield Rangers	0-12	Brymbo
Bridgend Town	3-1	Garden Village
Bryntirion Athletic	6-1	Pontypridd Town
Caerau Ely	7-0	Garw Athletic
Caerleon	4-0	Treharris Athletic
Carno	1-4	Penrhyncoch
Coedpoeth United	0-1	Mold Alexandra
Conwy United	4-0	Glynceiriog
Corwen	3-1	Lex XI
Cwmaman Institiue	4-2 (aet)	Llangeinor
Cwmamman United	3-0	AFC Llwydcoed
Dinas Powys	3-0	Penrhiwceiber
Ely Rangers	1-4	Llantwit Fadre
Glan Conwy	4-3	Llanrug United
Goytre United	3-0	Pontardawe Town
Guilsfield	2-1	Presteigne St Andrews
Halkyn United	2-1	Ruthin Town
Hawarden Rangers	3-0	Buckley Town
Holyhead Hotspur	3-2 (aet)	Cefn United
Llanberis	4-3 (aet)	Llanrwst United
Llandyrnog United	3-1	Penycae
Llanrhaeadr	3-2 (aet)	Berriew
Llansawel	2-5 (aet)	ENTO Aberaman
Llanwern	4-2 (aet)	Barry Town
Maesteg Park	2-1 (aet)	Seven Sisters
Merthyr Saints	2-0	Cwmbran Town
Montgomery Town	2-1 (aet)	Llanfyllin Town
Mynydd Isa	3-1	Glantraeth
Nantlle Vale	0-2	Chirk AAA
Nefyn United	2-0	Gresford Athletic
Newcastle Emlyn	4-1	Knighton Town
Newport YMCA	2-0	Goytre FC
Pentwyn Dynamos	3-1	Cwmbran Celtic
Pontyclun	1-2	Cambrian & Clydach
Prestatyn Town	1-2	Llandudno
Pwllheli	3-4	GAP Queens Park
Taff's Well	3-2	Caldicot Town
Ton Pentre	3-0	Aberbardoged Buds
Tredegar Town	1-1 (aet)	Cardiff Corinthians
Cardiff Corinthians won 4-3 on penalties.		
Troedyrhiw	3-7	Croesyceiliog
Tywyn & Bryncrug	6-6 (aet)	Rhydymwyn
Tywyn & Bryncrug won 5-4 on penalties.		
West End	2-1	Bettws

Second Round

Aberystwyth Town	3-0	Newcastle Emlyn
Afan Lido	3-1	Croesyceiliog
Bangor City	3-0	Llandyrnog United
Bridgend Town	1-2	Bryntirion Athletic
Brymbo	4-0	Halkyn United
Caerau Ely	3-2	Goytre United
Caerleon	2-1	Taff's Well
Caernarfon Town	2-1	Llanfairpwll
Caersws FC	9-0	Mold Alexandra
Cardiff Corinthians	2-3 (aet)	Ton Pentre
Connah's Quay Nomads	3-1 (aet)	The New Saints
Corwen	1-3	Mynydd Isa
Cwmaman Institute	0-3	ENTO Aberaman Athletic
Cwmamman United	0-5	Dinas Powys
GAP Queens Park	3-1	Penrhyncoch
Guilsfield	3-2 (aet)	Airbus UK Broughton
Haverfordwest County	1-0	Llantwit Fadre
Holyhead Hotspur	2-1 (aet)	Bala Town
Llanberis	1-5	Newtown AFC
Llandudno Town	1-2 (aet)	NEWI Cefn Druids
Llangefni Town	5-0	Hawarden Rangers
Llanrug	5-1	Llanrhaeadr
Maesteg Park	2-0	Briton Ferry
Merthyr Saints	1-2	Carmarthen Town
Neath Athletic	6-0	Llanwern
Nefyn United	2-0	Chirk AAA
Newport YMCA	4-1	Cambrian & Clydach
Pentwyn Dynamos	3-7	Llanelli AFC
Porthmadog FC	0-2	Welshpool Town
Rhyl FC	10-0	Montgomery Town
Tywyn & Bryncrug	3-2	Conwy United
West End	1-2	Port Talbot Town

Third Round

Aberystwyth Town	3-1	Neath Athletic
Bryntirion Athletic	4-2	Dinas Powys
Caerleon	2-0	Brymbo

Caersws FC	2-3 (aet)	Bangor City
Connah's Quay Nomads	0-2	Guilsfield
ENTO Aberaman	3-1	Caerau Ely
GAP Queens Park	3-1	Afan Lido
Haverfordwest County	3-0	Ton Pentre
Llangefni Town	3-0	Mynydd Isa
Llanrug	3-5	Llanelli AFC
Nefyn United	1-3	Caernarfon Town
NEWI Cefn Druids	3-0	Holyhead Hotspur
Newport YMCA	2-1	Carmarthen Town
Newtown AFC	2-1 (aet)	Maesteg Park
Rhyl FC	1-0	Port Talbot Town
Tywyn & Bryncrug	1-3	Welshpool Town

Fourth Round

Aberystwyth Town	0-0 (aet)	Bangor City
Bangor City won 3-2 on penalties.		
Bryntirion Athletic	1-2	Welshpool Town
GAP Queens Park	2-0	Caerleon
Guilsfield	1-0	Caernarfon Town
Haverfordwest County	1-2	Rhyl FC
NEWI Cefn Druids	0-0 (aet)	ENTO Aberaman
NEWI Cefn Druids won 5-3 on penalties.		
Newport YMCA	0-0 (aet)	Llangefni Town
Newport YMCA won 4-3 on penalties.		
Newtown AFC	1-2	Llanelli AFC

Quarter-finals

Guilsfield	0-6	Bangor City
NEWI Cefn Druids	3-6	Llanelli AFC
Newport YMCA	3-2	Welshpool Town
Rhyl FC	3-2	GAP Queens Park

Semi-finals

Bangor City	3-1	Newport YMCA
Played in Newtown		
Llanelli AFC	5-2	Rhyl FC
Played in Aberystwyth Town		

2008 WELSH CUP FINAL

Played at Latham Park, Newtown

Bangor City	4-2 (aet)	Llanelli AFC

A. Stott 20', C. Seargeant 90', D. Swanick 48' (o.g.),
M. Limbert 97' (pen), K. Noon 99'   R. Griffiths 56'

Bangor City: Paul Smith, Dave Swanick, Peter Hoy, Michael Johnston, Lee Webber (Karl Noon 73'), Christian Seargeant, Marc Limbert, Mike Walsh (Keiran Killackey 73'), Les Davies, Ashley Stott, Sion Edwards (Martin Beattie 57')

Llanelli: Duncan Roberts, Lee Phillips, Andrew Mumford, Wyn Thomas, Antonio Corbisiero (Stephen Evans 46'), Rhys Griffiths, Chris Holloway, Mark Pritchard, Craig Jones (Mark Jones 62'), Andy Legg, Matthew Jones (Paul Wanless 97')

Referee: Phil Southall

Attendance: 1,510

2008/09 Welsh Cup

First Round

Afan Lido	3-0	Cwmamman United
AFC Llwydcoed	3-0	Porthcawl Town
Berriew	0-1	Llangollen Town
Bettws	1-1 (aet)	Taff's Well
Taff's Well won 4-3 on penalties.		
Brickfield Rangers	4-3	Nefyn United
Briton Ferry	3-1	AFC Porth
Brymbo	0-8	Mold Alexandra
Buckley Town	6-3	Penycae
Caerau Ely	1-2 (aet)	Pentwyn Dynamos
Caerleon	1-4	Goytre United
Caldicot Town	0-1	Ammanford
Cambrian & Clydach	4-1	Newcastle Emlyn
Cardiff Corinthians	3-0	Ely Rangers
Castell Alun	1-0	Llandyrnog United
Cefn United (withdrew)	v	Rhydymwyn (w/o)
Conwy United	2-3 (aet)	Penrhyncoch
Croesyceiliog	0-3	Maesteg Park
Cwmbran Celtic	3-1	Garw
Denbigh Town	4-1	Llanllyfni
ENTO Aberaman Athletic	2-1	Barry Town
Flint Town United	4-3	Rhos Aelwyd
Glan Conwy	2-1 (aet)	Llanrwst United
Glantraeth	1-6	Bala Town
Halkyn United	4-2 (aet)	Coedpoeth United
Hawarden Rangers	0-2	Llanfairpwll
Llanberis	2-3	Bow Street
Llandudno Junction	4-2	Penparcau
Llangefni Town	3-1	Llandudno Town
Llangeinor	0-2	Dinas Powys
Llanrug	0-2	Pwllheli
Llanwern	3-0	Ton Pentre
Llay Welfare	7-1	Amlwch Town
Mynydd Isa	3-3 (aet)	Holyhead Hotspur
Holyhead Hotspur won 6-5 on penalties.		
Nantlle Vale	1-4	Chirk AAA
Newport YMCA	3-2	Cwmaman Institute
Penrhiwceiber Rangers	3-4 (aet)	Pontypridd Town
Pontyclun	1-3 (aet)	Bridgend Town
Bridgend Town won 3-1 on penalties.		
Risca United	2-0	Pontardawe Town
Tredegar Town	0-1	Gresford Athletic
Treharris Athletic	1-9	Bryntirion Athletic
Tywyn & Bryncrug	4-1	Bethesda Athletic
UWIC	1-3	Cwmbran Town
Venture	1-2	Lex XI
West End	2-3	Garden Village

Second Round

Aberystwyth Town	2-2 (aet)	Afan Lido
Aberystwyth Town won 3-2 on penalties.		
Airbus UK Broughton	2-1	Technogroup Welshpool
Bala Town	3-3 (aet)	Prestatyn Town
Prestatyn Town won 5-4 on penalties.		
Bangor City	1-0	Gap Connah's Quay
Brickfield Rangers	3-4	Buckley Town
Bridgend Town	3-1	Cwmbran Town
Bryntirion Athletic	1-2	Cardiff Corries
Cambrian & Clydach	0-1	Newtown AFC

Carmarthen Town	6-1	Bow Street
Denbigh Town	4-1	Chirk AAA
Dinas Powys	0-1 (aet)	Briton Ferry
Flint Town United	4-1	Mold Alexandra
Garden Village	2-0	Risca United
Gresford Athletic	4-1	Rhydymwyn
Holyhead Hotspur	2-1	Llay Welfare
Lex XI	2-1	Glan Conwy
Llandudno Junction	0-2	Pwllheli
Llanelli AFC	4-0	Neath FC
Llangefni Town	3-0	Llanfairpwll
Llangollen Town	2-1	Tywyn & Bryncrug
Llanwern	1-6	AFC Llwydcoed
NEWI Cefn Druids	4-2	Halkyn United
Newport Civil Service	0-1	Caersws FC
Newport YMCA	3-0	Cwmbran Celtic
Penrhyncoch	3-2 (aet)	Maesteg Park
Pentwyn Dynamos	1-0	Ammanford Town
Pontypridd Town	1-4	Haverfordwest County
Port Talbot Town	1-0	ENTO Aberaman
Porthmadog FC	5-3	Caernarfon Town
Rhyl FC	8-0	Castell Alun Colts
Taff's Well	0-2	Goytre United
The New Saints	4-2	Guilsfield

Third Round

AFC Llwydcoed	1-0	Flint Town Utd
Bangor City	4-0	Garden Village
Bridgend Town	1-0	Llangefni Town
Buckley Town	1-5	Airbus UK Broughton
Caersws FC	0-3	Aberystwyth Town
Cardiff Corries	0-6	Goytre United
Gresford Athletic	2-3	Prestatyn Town
Holyhead Hotspur	2-1	Pentwyn Dynamoes
Lex XI	2-0	Porthmadog FC
NEWI Cefn Druids	1-0	Newtown AFC
Newport YMCA	1-0	Briton Ferry
Port Talbot Town	7-0	Denbigh Town
Pwllheli	0-6	Carmarthen Town
Rhyl FC	4-0	Haverfordwest County
The New Saints	7-1	Penrhyncoch
Tywyn & Bryncrug	0-3	Llanelli AFC

Fourth Round

AFC Llwydcoed	0-3	Aberystwyth Town
Airbus UK Broughton	2-1	NEWI Cefn Druids
Bangor City	1-1 (aet)	Rhyl FC
Bangor City won 4-2 on penalties.		
Bridgend Town	4-0	Lex XI
Holyhead Hotspur	1-1 (aet)	Newport YMCA
Newport YMCA won 6-5 on penalties.		
Port Talbot Town	2-1	Llanelli AFC
Prestatyn Town	5-3	Goytre United
The New Saints	2-3	Carmarthen Town

Quarter-finals

Aberystwyth Town	5-1	Prestatyn Town
Airbus UK Broughton	0-5	Bangor City
Carmarthen Town	1-1 (aet)	Port Talbot Town
The scoreline after 90 minutes was 0-0.		
Carmarthen Town won 4-1 on penalties.		
Newport YMCA	0-1	Bridgend Town

Semi-finals

Aberystwyth Town	3-2 (aet)	Carmarthen Town

Played at Bridge Meadow Stadium, Haverfordwest

Bangor City	2-1	Bridgend Town

Played at Park Avenue, Aberystwyth

2009 WELSH CUP FINAL

Played at Parc Y Scarlets, Llanelli

Aberystwyth Town	0-2	Bangor City

Les Davies 43', Chris Seargeant 49'

Aberystwyth Town: Dave Roberts, Sion James, Kristian James (Colin Reynolds 86'), Aneurin Thomas, Christian Edwards, Robert Evans (Andy Evans 79'), Chris Venables, Bari Morgan, Graham Evans (Tom Bradshaw 54'), Gareth Hughes, Geoff Kellaway.

Bangor City: Paul Smith, Dave Swanick, Peter Hoy, Mike Johnston, Jamie Brewerton, Kieran Killackey (Paul McManus 88'), Marc Limbert, Mike Walsh, Les Davies (Clive Williams 81'), Chris Seargeant, Sion Edwards (Martin Beattie 72')

Referee: Huw Jones

Attendance: 1,044

2009/10 Welsh Cup

First Round

Amlwch Town	2-3	Penrhyncoch
Barmouth and Dyffryn Utd	3-2	Buckley Town
Barry Town	1-5	Ely Rangers
Berriew	3-1	Mold Alexandra
Brymbo	1-6	Llangefni Town
Bryntirion Athletic	4-2	Cardiff Corinthians
Caerau Ely	2-0	Bettws
Cambrian & Clydach	4-0	Ammanford
Carno	2-3	Conwy United
Chirk AAA	1-3	Gresford Athletic
Coedpoeth United	2-0	Penparcau
Corus Steel	0-1	Garden Village
Croesyceiliog	1-0	Risca United
Cwmaman Institute	1-7	Cwmbran Celtic
Glan Conwy	2-1	Denbigh Town
Goytre United	3-1	Pentwyn Dynamos
Guilsfield	1-3	Llangollen Town
Hawarden Rangers	0-2	Ruthin Town
Hay St Marys	2-1 (aet)	Dinas Powys
Lex XI	5-3	Dolgellau Athletic Amateurs
Llanberis	1-2	Flint Town United
Llandudno Junction	3-1	Llanrhaeadr Ym Mochnant
Llandudno Town	1-0	Bethesda Athletic
Llanfairpwll	2-1	Penycae
Llanrug United	4-3	Nefyn United
Llanrwst United	0-2	Llangeinor
Llansantffraid Village	3-1	Llay Welfare

Llantwit Fardre	0-1	Aberbargoed Buds
Newcastle Emlyn	1-2	AFC Llwydcoed
Overton Recreational	1-2 (aet)	Holyhead Hotspur
Penrhiwceiber	3-1	Caerleon
Pontardawe Town	4-1	Presteigne St Andrews
Pontyclun	7-2	Goytre
Pontypridd Town	3-0	Newport Civil Service
Porthcawl Town	2-4	Ton Pentre
Pwllheli	2-0 (aet)	Tywyn & Bryncrug
Rhydymwyn	2-0	Llandyrnog United
Seven Sisters	0-7	Afan Lido
South Gower	0-5	Caldicot Town
Treharris Western Athletic	3-4	Cardiff Bay Harlequins
Troedyrhiw	2-1	Abertillery Bluebirds
Venture Community	3-4 (aet)	Borras Park Albion
West End	6-6 (aet)	Taff's Well

Taff's Well won 4-2 on penalties.

Second Round

Aberaman Athletic	3-2	Penrhiwceiber
Afan Lido	5-1	Croesyceiliog
Bangor City	4-1	Elements Cefn Druids
Borras Park Albion	1-8	Bala Town (at Bala)
Bridgend Town	2-0	Ton Pentre
Bryntirion Athletic	0-3	Aberystwyth Town
Caerau Ely	5-1	Hay St Marys
Cambrian and Clydach	3-1	Troedyrhiw
Cardiff Bay Harlequins	3-2	Aberbargoed Buds
Carmarthen Town	4-1	Pontypridd Town
Conwy United	0-2 (aet)	The New Saints
Ely Rangers	3-2	AFC Llwydcoed
Flint Town United	7-1	Barmouth and Dyffryn Utd
Gap Connah's Quay	2-0	Pwllheli FC
Garden Village	2-6 (aet)	Caldicot Town
Goytre United	0-3	Pontardawe Town
Gresford Athletic	2-3	Llanrug United
Holyhead Hotspur	1-1 (aet)	Newtown AFC

Holyhead Hotspur won 4-3 on penalties.

Lex XI	1-3	Airbus UK Broughton
Llandudno Town	3-0 (aet)	Berriew
Llanfairpwll	1-3	Rhyl FC
Llangefni Town	1-2	Llandudno Junction
Llangeinor	2-1 (aet)	Pontyclun
Llangollen Town	1-0	Glan Conwy
Llansantffraid Village	1-2	Coedpoeth United
Neath FC	2-2 (aet)	Llanelli AFC

Llanelli AFC won 3-2 on penalties.

Penrhyncoch	0-1	Porthmadog FC
Port Talbot Town	5-0	Cwmbran Celtic
Rhydymwyn	1-0	Caernarfon Town
Ruthin United	1-2	Caersws FC
Taff's Well	0-2	Haverfordwest County
Technogroup Welshpool	2-3	Prestatyn Town

Third Round

Aberaman Athletic	2-0	Ely Rangers
Bala Town	1-0	Llanrug United
Caerau Ely	1-2	Afan Lido
Caersws FC	4-1	Coedpoeth United
Caldicot Town	0-3	Port Talbot Town
Cambrian & Clydach	0-2	The New Saints
Flint Town United	0-1	Bangor City
Gap Connah's Quay	3-2 (aet)	Airbus UK Broughton
Haverfordwest County	1-2	Aberystwyth Town
Llanelli AFC	3-1	Carmarthen Town
Llangeinor	1-6	Holyhead Hotspur
Llangollen Town	0-1	Llandudno Junction
Pontardawe Town	2-0	Llandudno
Porthmadog FC	3-1	Rhydymwyn
Prestatyn Town	3-0	Cardiff Bay Harlequins
Rhyl FC	4-2	Bridgend Town

Fourth Round

Aberystwyth Town	0-2	Port Talbot Town
Afan Lido	2-1 (aet)	Gap Connah's Quay
Bala Town	2-0	Caersws FC
Bangor City	3-1	Aberaman Athletic
Llandudno Junction	0-6	The New Saints
Llanelli AFC	4-0	Holyhead Hotspur
Prestatyn Town	1-0	Porthmadog FC
Rhyl FC	7-0	Pontardawe Town

Quarter-finals

Bala Town	2-0 (aet)	Afan Lido
Bangor City	2-0	Llanelli AFC
Prestatyn Town	4-4 (aet)	Rhyl FC

Prestatyn Town won 5-3 on penalties.

The New Saints	2-2 (aet)	Port Talbot Town

Port Talbot Town won 4-3 on penalties.

Semi-finals

Bala Town	0-1	Port Talbot Town

Played at Park Avenue, Aberystwyth

Bangor City	2-0	Prestatyn Town

Played at Latham Park, Newtown

2010 WELSH CUP FINAL

Played at Parc Y Scarlets, Llanelli

Bangor City	3-2	Port Talbot Town

Lee Hunt 6', Jamie Reed 15', Dave Morley 90'+1   *Drew Fahiya 57', Liam McCreesh 85'*

Bangor City: Paul Smith, Peter Hoy, Chris Roberts, Dave Morley, Jamie Brewerton, Craig Garside, Jamie Reed (Les Davies 90'), Michael Johnston, Eddie Jebb, Mark Smyth (Marc Limbert 80'), Lee Hunt (Sion Edwards 69').
Subs not used: Matty Hurdman, Clive Williams

Port Talbot Town: Lee Kendall, Leigh De-Vulgt (Nicky Holland 63'), Scott Barrow, Gareth Phillips, Matthew Rees, Lee Surman, Drew Fahiya (Lee John 66'), Lloyd Grist, Martin Rose, Liam McCreesh, Danny Thomas (Karl Lewis 66').
Subs not used: Matt Thompson, Gary Bansor

Referee: Dean John

Attendance: 1,303

2010/11 Welsh Cup

First Round

Barry Town	3-0	STM Sports
Bettws	0-3	Aberaman Athletic
Borras Park Albion	0-8	Rhos Aelwyd
Bow Street	2-1	Lex XI
Brickfield Rangers	3-4 (aet)	Bethesda Athletic
Bridgend Town	5-3 (aet)	Monmouth Town
Bryntirion Athletic	4-2 (aet)	Cwmbran Celtic
Caerau	1-3	Afan Lido
Caersws FC	4-0 (aet)	Rhayader Town
Cardiff Grange Quins	4-2 (aet)	Bridgend Street
Carno	1-5	Porthmadog FC
Cefn Druids	6-4 (aet)	Penycae
Coedpoeth United	4-3	Greenfield FC
Connah's Quay Town	6-1	Johnstown Youth
Conwy United	4-1	Waterloo Rovers
Corus Steel	5-2	Cardiff Corries
Croesyceiliog	0-2	Garden Village
Cwmaman Institute	1-2	Taff's Well
Dolgellau Amateurs	1-2	Llandudno
Fleur de Lys	1-0	Ely Rangers
Goytre	3-1	Caerau (Ely)
Goytre United	5-3	Ammanford
Gwalchmai	4-0	Barmouth & Dyffryn Utd
Holyhead Hotspur	4-0	Technogroup Welshpool
Llandyrnog United	1-5	Flint Town United
Llangefni Town	3-2	Llanfairpwll
Llanidloes Town	1-0	Ruthin Town
Llanrhaeadr	0-5	Rhyl FC
Nefyn United	3-2	Tywyn & Bryncrug
Newcastle Emlyn	4-0	South Gower
Penmaenmawr Phoenix	3-5	Caernarfon Town
Penrhiwceiber Rangers	0-2	Cambrian & Clydach
Penrhyncoch	2-2 (aet)	Guilsfield
Guilsfield won 6-4 on penalties.		
Pontypridd Town	2-0	Pontardawe Town
Pwllheli	1-6	GAP Connah's Quay
Rhydymwyn	1-4	Buckley Town
Treaddur Bay United	7-3	Penparcau
Treharris Western Athletic	2-1	Pontyclun
UWIC	2-0	Caldicot Town
West End	2-1 (aet)	AFC Porth

Second Round

Afan Lido	1-2	Cambrian & Clydach
AFC Porth	2-0	Goytre
Barry Town	1-2 (aet)	Corus Steel
Caernarfon Town	1-2	Guilsfield
Cardiff Grange Quins	3-0	Treharris Athletic
Connah's Quay Town	1-2	Bow Street
Conwy United	1-4	Porthmadog FC
Flint Town United	3-4	Llanidloes Town
Gap Connah's Quay	6-1	Bethesda Athletic
Garden Village	1-6	Aberaman Athletic
Goytre United	3-1	Fleur de Lys
Gwalchmai	2-2 (aet)	Buckley Town
Gwalchmai won 4-2 on penalties.		
Holyhead Hotspur	1-0	Llangefni Town
Nefyn United	1-3	Caersws FC
Newcastle Emlyn	1-4	UWIC
Pontypridd Town	1-2	Bryntirion Athletic
Rhos Aelwyd	2-1 (aet)	Coedpoeth United
Rhyl FC	2-1	Llandudno
Taff's Well	2-4	Bridgend Town
Trearddur Bay United	0-7	Cefn Druids

Third Round

Aberaman Athletic	0-4	Cefn Druids
Airbus UK Broughton	2-3	The New Saints
Bangor City	2-1	Bryntirion Athletic
Bow Street	2-2 (aet)	UWIC
UWIC Cardiff won 6-5 on penalties.		
Caersws FC	4-2 (aet)	Llanidloes Town
Cambrian & Clydach	2-3	Prestatyn Town
Corus Steel	0-2	Grange Quins
Gap Connah's Quay	5-3 (aet)	AFC Porth
Goytre United	2-3	Carmarthen Town
Guilsfield	1-2	Rhos Aelwyd
Gwalchmai	1-4	Port Talbot Town
Haverfordwest County	3-2	Holyhead Hotspur
Llanelli AFC	1-0 (aet)	Aberystwyth Town
Neath FC	1-1 (aet)	Rhyl FC
Rhyl FC won 7-6 on penalties.		
Newtown AFC	1-2	Bridgend Town
Porthmadog FC	0-1	Bala Town

Fourth Round

Bangor City	5-3	Haverfordwest County
Carmarthen Town	2-3 (aet)	Gap Connah's Quay
Cefn Druids	1-4	Llanelli AFC
Grange Quins	1-0	Bridgend Town
Port Talbot Town	3-0	Caersws FC
Rhos Aelwyd	1-6	Prestatyn Town
Rhyl FC	1-2	The New Saints
UWIC	4-1	Bala Town

Quarter-finals

Gap Connah's Quay	4-0	UWIC
Llanelli AFC	1-0	Prestatyn Town
Port Talbot Town	0-3	Bangor City
The New Saints	2-0 (aet)	Cardiff Grange Quins

Semi-finals

Bangor City	1-0	GAP Connah's Quay
Played at Rhyl		
The New Saints	0-1	Llanelli AFC
Played at Aberystwyth		

2011 WELSH CUP FINAL

Played at Parc Y Scarlets

Bangor City	1-4	Llanelli AFC
Alan Bull 51'		Rhys Griffiths 15' 60',
		Craig Moses 20' Chris Venables 64'

Bangor City: Paul Smith, Peter Hoy, Chris Roberts, David Morley, Darren Moss, Michael Johnston, Chris Jones (Sion Edwards 75'), Clive Williams (Mark Smyth 62'), Les Davies, Nicky Ward, Alan Bull (Eddie Jebb 75'). Subs not used: Michael Jukes, Chris Oldfield (gk).

Llanelli: Ashley Morris, Kris Thomas, Stuart Jones, Chris Venables, Wyn Thomas, Jason Bowen (Jordan Follows 74'), Antonio Corbisiero, Rhys Griffiths, Chris Holloway, Craig Moses, Ashley Evans. Subs not used: Andy Legg, Craig Richards (gk), Adam Orme, Martin Giles

Referee: Mark Petch
Attendance: 1,719

2011/12 Welsh Cup

First Round

Abertillery Bluebirds	0-2	Caerau Ely
AFC Porth	2-0	Aberbargoed Buds
Barmouth & Dyffryn Utd	4-1	Ruthin Town
Bridgend Town	2-0	Splott Albion
Bryntirion Athletic	3-1	Cwmbran Town
Buckley Town	4-0	Penrhyncoch
Caersws FC	1-1 (aet)	Conwy United
Caersws FC won 4-2 on penalties		
Caldicot Town	2-4	Newport Civil Service
Cambrian & Clydach	5-1	Monmouth Town
Cardiff Corinthians	2-0	Cwmaman Institute
Carno	0-2	Coedpoeth United
Cefn Druids	6-1	Caernarfon Town
Dinas Powys	0-2	Builth Wells
Flint Town United	5-1	Chirk AAA
Gap Connah's Quay	7-2	Gwalchmai
Goytre	3-1	Aberaeron
Goytre United	1-0	Ton Pentre
Llandrindod Wells	3-3 (aet)	Llanrug United
Llandrindod Wells won 4-1 on penalties.		
Llangefni Town	2-3 (aet)	Denbigh Town
Llanidloes Town	4-3	Glantraeth
Llanrhaeadr Ym Mochnant	1-6	Holyhead Hotspur
Merthyr Town	0-3	Barry Town
Montgomery Town	4-0	Connah's Quay Town
Penycae	1-2	FC Cefn
Pontardawe Town	3-0	Treowen Stars
Porthmadog FC	3-1	Bethesda Athletic
Rhos Aelwyd	0-1	Guilsfield
Rhosgoch Rangers	2-6	Merthyr Saints
Rhyl FC	5-0	Gresford Athletic
Risca United	0-4	Newbridge on Wye
Taff's Well	5-4 (aet)	Undy Athletic
Tata Steel	3-1	Newcastle Emlyn
UWIC	0-2	Haverfordwest County
Venture Community	1-3	Llandudno
West End	2-0	Cwmbran Celtic

Second Round

AFC Porth	3-0	Pontardawe Town
Barmouth & Dyffryn Utd	0-3	Caersws FC
Bridgend Town	5-3	Tata Steel
Bryntirion Athletic	5-2	Goytre
Buckley Town	5-2	Holyhead Hotspur
Builth Wells	0-5	Taff's Well
Caerau (Ely)	1-8	Goytre United
Caerleon	3-4	Merthyr Saints
Cambrian & Clydach	2-0	Llandrindod Wells
Cefn Druids	8-0	Coedpoeth United
Denbigh Town	1-2 (aet)	Flint Town United
Guilsfield FC	1-3	Llandudno'
Haverfordwest County	1-2 (aet)	Barry Town
Llanidloes Town	0-2	Gap Connah's Quay
Montgomery Town	3-7	FC Cefn
Newport Civil Service	2-0	Newbridge on Wye
Porthmadog FC	2-3	Rhyl FC
West End	2-1	Cardiff Corinthians

Third Round

AFC Porth	0-0 (aet)	Cambrian & Clydach
AFC Porth won 4-3 on penalties.		
Bangor City	2-4	Llanelli AFC
Buckley Town	4-3	Taff's Well
Caersws FC	0-1	Llandudno
Carmarthen Town	2-1	Bridgend Town
FC Cefn	1-6	Aberystwyth Town
Flint Town United	4-0	Newport Civil Service
Gap Connah's Quay	1-2	Cefn Druids
Merthyr Saints	0-6	Bala Town
Neath FC	4-0	West End
Newport County	3-2	Barry Town
Newtown AFC	1-2 (aet)	Rhyl FC
Port Talbot Town	0-1	Afan Lido
Prestatyn Town	6-2	Goytre United
The New Saints	6-0	Bryntirion Athletic
Wrexham FC	1-2 (aet)	Airbus UK Broughton

Fourth Round

Aberystwyth Town	1-1 (aet)	Llandudno
Aberystwyth Town won 5-3 on penalties.		
Afan Lido	2-2 (aet)	Airbus UK Broughton
Airbus UK Broughton won 5-4 on penalties.		
Buckley Town	2-4 (aet)	Bala Town
Carmarthen Town	3-1 (aet)	AFC Porth
Flint Town United	1-3	Neath FC
Prestatyn Town	0-2	Cefn Druids
Rhyl FC	3-3 (aet)	Llanelli AFC
Llanelli AFC won 5-4 on penalties.		
The New Saints	4-0	Newport County

Quarter-finals

Aberystwyth Town	0-1	Cefn Druids
Airbus UK Broughton	3-1	Carmarthen Town
Bala Town	1-1 (aet)	Llanelli AFC
Bala Town won 5-4 on penalties.		
The New Saints	1-0	Neath FC

Semi-finals

Bala Town	0-4	The New Saints
Played at Maes Tegid, Bala		
Cefn Druids	4-1	Airbus UK Broughton
Played at Belle Vue, Rhyl		

2012 WELSH CUP FINAL

Played at Nantporth, Bangor

Cefn Druids	0-2	The New Saints

Greg Draper 13' Alex Darlington 15'

Cefn Druids: Chris Mullock, Mark Harris, Joe Price, Adam Hesp, Tom McElmeel, George Hughes, Marc Griffiths, Kieron Quinn (Jack Edwards 88'), Tony Cann, Andrew Swarbrick (Paul Speed 90'), Warren Duckett. Subs not used: John Keegan, Ian Hughes, Lewis Jones.

The New Saints: Paul Harrison, Simon Spender, Chris Marriott, Phil Baker, Steve Evans, Christian Seargeant, Aeron Edwards (Scott Ruscoe 84'), Greg Draper (Nicky Ward 77'), Alex Darlington, Craig Jones, Ryan Fraughan (Tom Roberts 68'). Subs not used: Sam Finley, Connell Rawlinson.

Referee: Mark Petch

Attendance: 731

2012/13 Welsh Cup

First Round

Aberbargoed Buds	2-1	Treforest
AFC Porth	0-0 (aet)	Monmouth Town
Monmouth Town won 6-5 on penalties.		
Ammanford	1-2	Chepstow Town
Brecon Corinthians	2-5	Haverfordwest County
Brickfield Rangers	2-5	Pwllheli
Bridgend Town	0-1	Pontardawe Town
Brymbo	1-1 (aet)	Penycae
Brymbo won 3-0 on penalties.		
Caerau	8-0	Llantwit Fardre
Caerleon	2-5	Barry Town
Caernarfon Town	0-0 (aet)	Conwy Borough
Conwy Borough won 4-3 on penalties.		
Cardiff Grange Quins	4-3	Llanwern
Cefn Druids	7-1	Llanberis
Coedpoeth United	1-2	Caersws FC
Corwen	2-1	Ruthin Town
Croesyceiliog	3-7	Caerau Ely
Cwmamman United	1-5	Newbridge on Wye
Cwmbran Celtic	0-1	Cambrian & Clydach
Dinas Powys	1-3	Ton Pentre
Ely Rangers	3-1	Bryntirion Athletic
Flint Town United	3-2	Guilsfield
Four Crosses	1-2	Llanrug United
Goytre	3-0	AFC Llwydcoed
Goytre United	6-0	Pontyclun
Gwalchmai	4-1	Carno
Halkyn United	1-6	Llanidloes Town
Holyhead Hotspur	6-2	Llansantffraid Village
Holywell Town	3-1	Denbigh Town
Llandudno Junction	4-1	Mold Alexandra
Llanllyfni	0-4	Greenfield
Llanrhaeadr Ym Mochnant	2-1	Glan Conwy
Llanuwchllyn	3-6	Buckley Town
Pontypridd Town	0-0 (aet)	Aberdare Town
Aberdare Town won 3-0 on penalties.		
Porthmadog FC	2-3	Llandudno
Presteigne St Andrews	0-2	Penrhyncoch
Rhayader Town	2-0	Risca United
Rhyl FC	7-0	Bodedern Athletic
Tata Steel	7-4	Bridgend Street
Venture Community	2-5	Montgomery Town
Waterloo Rovers	5-1	Rhydymwyn
West End	4-0	Taff's Well

Second Round

Aberdare Town	2-1	Tata Steel
Brymbo	1-3	Cefn Druids
Caerau	1-3	Goytre
Cambrian & Clydach	0-1	Haverfordwest County
Chepstow Town	4-1	Grange Quins
Conwy Borough	1-1 (aet)	Buckley Town
Conwy Borough won 4-3 on penalties.		
Corwen	1-2	Gwalchmai
Ely Rangers	6-1	Aberbargoed Buds
Flint Town United	3-0	Greenfield
Goytre United	2-4	Caerau Ely
Holyhead Hotspur	5-2	Pwllheli
Holywell Town	5-3	Llandudno'
Llanhaeadr	2-3	Llanrug United
Llanidloes Town	3-2	Caersws FC
Montgomery Town	1-3	Llandudno Junction
Newbridge	1-5	Monmouth Town
Penrhyncoch	1-2	Barry Town
Pontardawe Town	2-0	Ton Pentre
Waterloo Rovers	0-5	Rhyl FC
West End	2-0	Rhayader Town

Third Round

Aberystwyth Town	2-5	Rhyl FC
Afan Lido	3-4	Prestatyn Town
Airbus UK Broughton	3-0	Port Talbot Town
Bangor City	4-1	Aberdare Town
Barry Town	3-1	Ely Rangers
Flint Town United	1-0	Llanidloes Town
gap Connah's Quay	4-2	Llanelli AFC
Gwalchmai	0-2	Chepstow Town
Holyhead Hotspur	1-2	Carmarthen Town

2013/14 Welsh Cup

First Round

AFC Porth	1-2	Monmouth Town
Barry Town United	1-0	Taff's Well
Bridgend Street	1-3	Tata Steel
Briton Ferry Llansawel	3-1	Aberbargoed Buds
Caerau Ely	4-0	Cardiff Hibernian
Caernarfon Town	4-1	Llanrug United
Caersws FC	2-0	Denbigh Town
Caldicot Town	2-1	Splott Albion
Cambrian & Clydach	4-0	Butetown FC
Cardiff Metropolitan	4-1	Aberaeron
Coedpoeth United	2-6	Barmouth & Dyffryn Utd
Cwmbran Celtic	0-1	Penybont FC
FC Nomads of Connah's Quay	3-0	Pwllheli
Flint Town United	3-1	Llanberis
Garden Village	1-2	Rhoose FC
Glan Conwy	1-3	Llanidloes Town
Goytre FC	1-2	Pontardawe Town
Goytre United	3-1	Trefelin
Guilsfield	6-1	Machynlleth
Holyhead Hotspur	0-3	Cefn Druids
Holywell Town	3-0	Penrhyncoch
Llandrindod Wells	3-0	Newport Civil Service
Llandudno	5-1	Llanrhaeadr
Llanfair United	3-2	Gwalchmai
Llangollen Town	0-2	Buckley Town
Llanrwst United	3-4	Conwy Borough
Llantwit Major	2-3	Treharris Athletic Western
Nefyn United	2-1	Penrhyndeudraeth
Newcastle Emlyn	1-2	Chepstow Town
Penycae	7-4	Brickfield Rangers
Porthmadog	1-0	Mold Alexandra
Rhayader Town	1-0	Chirk AAA
Rhydymwyn	2-1	Caerwys
Sully Sports	3-1	AFC Llwydcoed
Ton Pentre	3-0	Fairfield United
Treowen Stars	2-4	Aberdare Town
Tywyn & Bryncrug	2-2 (aet)	Berriew

Tywyn & Bryncrug won 5-4 on penalties.

Undy Athletic	5-2	Presteigne St. Andrews
West End	2-3	Haverfordwest County

Second Round

Barmouth & Dyffryn Utd	1-3	Cefn Druids
Barry Town United	4-3 (aet)	Undy Athletic
Bodedern Athletic	5-1	Tywyn & Bryncrug
Briton Ferry Llansawel	2-3	Aberdare Town
Buckley Town	1-0	Rhayader Town
Caernarfon Town	1-2	Porthmadog FC
Caldicot Town	3-0	Penybont

Caldicot Town were subsequently dismissed from the competition for fielding an ineligible player. Penybont progressed to the next round.

Cambrian & Clydach	2-0	Pontardawe Town
Cardiff Metropolitan	6-1	Haverfordwest County
Conwy Borough	3-2	Flint Town United
Goytre United	0-1	Chepstow Town
Holywell Town	3-0	Penycae
Holywell Town	0-2	Caerau Ely
Llandudno Junction	2-3	Haverfordwest County
Llanrug United	0-5	West End
Monmouth Town	2-3	Bala Town
Newtown AFC	2-0	Cefn Druids
Pontardawe Town	2-0	Goytre
The New Saints	3-1 (aet)	Conwy Borough

Fourth Round

Barry Town	2-1	Pontardawe Town
Carmarthen Town	3-2 (aet)	Bala Town
Chepstow Town	3-4	Haverfordwest County
Flint Town United	3-1	Caerau Ely
Gap Connah's Quay	0-2	Bangor City
Newtown AFC	1-1 (aet)	Airbus UK Broughton

Airbus UK Broughton won 5-4 on penalties.

Prestatyn Town	2-0	West End
The New Saints	5-1	Rhyl FC

Quarter-finals

Bangor City	1-0	Airbus UK Broughton
Carmarthen Town	2-3 (aet)	Prestatyn Town
Flint Town United	0-2	Barry Town
Haverfordwest County	0-1	The New Saints

Semi-finals

Bangor City	1-0	The New Saints

Played at Belle Vue, Rhyl

Barry Town	1-2	Prestatyn Town

Played at Latham Park, Newtown

2013 WELSH CUP FINAL

Played at The Racecourse Ground, Wrexham

Bangor City	1-3 (aet)	Prestatyn Town
Chris Davies 60' (o.g.)		Jason Price 2', 111', Andy Parkinson 103'

Bangor City: Lee Idzi, Liam Brownhill (Peter Hoy 105'), Chris Roberts, Jamie Brewerton, Michael Johnston, Dave Morley (Robbie Booth 65'), Chris Jones (Sion Edwards 59'), Damien Allen, Les Davies, Chris Simm, Ryan Edwards. Subs not used: Corey Jones, John Owen.

Prestatyn Town: Jon Hill-Dunt, Chris Davies, Greg Stones, Dave Hayes, Anthony Stephens, Gareth Wilson (Rhys Owen 106'), Michael Parker, Neil Gibson, Jason Price (Carl Murray 119'), Andy Parkinson, Ross Stephens. Subs not used: Adam France, Dan Evans, Rhys Lewis.

Referee: Kevin Morgan

Attendance: 1,732

Llandrindod Wells	3-3	Caerau Ely

Llandrindod Wells won 4-3 on penalties.

Llanfair United	2-1	Guilsfield
Llanidloes Town	2-0	Llandudno Junction
Nefyn United	1-3 (aet)	Caersws
Rhoose FC	1-0	Tata Steel
Rhydymwyn	4-1	FC Nomads of Connah's Quay
Ton Pentre	0-1	Sully Sports
Treharris Athletic Western	1-7	Monmouth Town

Third Round

Aberdare Town	4-2	Prestatyn Town
Afan Lido	2-0	Rhydymwyn
Airbus UK Broughton	2-0	Penybont FC
Bodedern Athletic	2-0	Buckley Town
Caersws FC	2-1	gap Connah's Quay
Cambrian & Clydach	3-1	Chepstow Town
Carmarthen Town	2-1	Port Talbot Town
Cefn Druids	5-2	Barry Town United
Conwy Borough	1-2	The New Saints
Llandrindod Wells	1-3	Holywell Town
Llanfair United	2-4	Aberystwyth Town
Monmouth Town	2-1	Llanidloes Town
Newtown AFC	2-1	Cardiff Metropolitan
Porthmadog FC	2-1	Sully Sports
Rhoose	1-6	Bala Town
Rhyl FC	1-2	Bangor City

Fourth Round

Aberdare Town	4-1	Bodedern Athletic
Aberystwyth Town	5-1	Afan Lido
Airbus UK Broughton	2-0	Bangor City

Played at Bangor

Bala Town	5-0	Cefn Druids

Played at Cefn

Caersws FC	4-3 (aet)	Cambrian & Clydach
Carmarthen Town	0-2	The New Saints

Played at The New Saints Ground

Monmouth Town	2-3 (aet)	Porthmadog FC

Played at Porthmadog

Newtown AFC	2-3	Holywell Town

Quarter-finals

Aberdare Town	1-2	Bala Town
Aberystwyth Town	2-1	Caersws FC
Holywell Town	2-1	Porthmadog FC
The New Saints	2-0	Airbus UK Broughton

Semi-finals

Aberystwyth Town	3-1	Holywell Town

Played at Latham Park, Newtown

The New Saints	2-1	Bala Town

Played at The Airfield, Broughton

2014 WELSH CUP FINAL

Played at the Racecourse Ground, Wrexham

Aberystwyth Town	2-3	The New Saints

Chris Venables 10', 12' (pen)   Greg Draper 73' (pen), 78', Michael Wilde 87'

Aberystwyth Town: Mike Lewis, Antonio Corbisiero, Peter Hoy, Stuart Jones, Chris Venables, Mark Jones, Geoff Kellaway, Cledan Davies, Luke Sherbon, Craig Williams (Krzysztof Nalborski 82'), Wyn Thomas. Subs not used: Sion James, Tom Shaw, Rhydian Davies, Jamie Butler.

The New Saints: Paul Harrison, Aeron Edwards, Chris Marriott, Phil Baker, Kai Edwards, Christian Seargeant, Sam Finley (Simon Spender 68'), Chris Jones (Jamie Mullan 46'), Michael Wilde, Matty Williams (Greg Draper 60'), Ryan Fraughan. Subs not used: Lee Fowler, Connell Rawlinson.

Referee: Brian James

Attendance: 1,273

2014/15 Welsh Cup

First Round

Aberdare Town	4-2	Barry Town Utd
Afan Lido	4-0	Chepstow Town
Albion Rovers	3-1	Cardiff Corinthians
Ammanford	5-2	Sully Sports
Briton Ferry Llansawel	4-1	Aberbargoed Buds
Caernarfon Town	4-0	Porthmadog
Caersws FC	1-0	Llandudno
Cambrian & Clydach	0-2	Undy Athletic
Canton Liberal	1-2	Risca United
Cardiff Metropolitan	9-0	AFC Llwydcoed
Carno	0-1	Rhayader Town
Coedpoeth United	0-3	Denbigh Town
Cornelly United	1-0	Pontardawe Town
Cwmbran Celtic	2-1	Llanelli Town
Dinas Powys	0-1	Penybont
Dyffryn Nantlle Vale	5-5 (aet)	Llanberis

Llanberis won 4-2 on penalties.

Dynamo Aber	4-2	AFC Butetown
FC Nomads of Connah's Quay	1-0	AFC Brynford
Garden Village	9-0	AFC Porth
Goytre FC	0-4	Goytre United
Guilsfield	3-1	Penycae
Holyhead Hotspur	0-2	Conwy Borough
Holywell Town	4-2	Hay St Mary
Kerry	1-2	Brickfield Rangers
Llandrindod Wells	2-3	Llangollen Town
Llangefni Town	3-6	St Asaph City
Llanidloes Town	4-0	Gaerwen
Llanrhaeadr Ym Mochnant	4-2	Glan Conwy
Llay Miners Welfare	1-3	Gresford Athletic

Mold Alexandra	4-0	Welshpool Town
Monmouth Town	3-0	Ton Pentre
Penrhyncoch	2-1	Flint Town United
Penrhyndeudraeth	2-3	Llanfair United
Rhydymwyn	0-3	Meliden
Ruthin Town	2-3	Buckley Town
STM Sports	0-2	Haverfordwest County
Taff's Well	0-3	Caerau Ely
Tata Steel	1-1 (aet)	Marshfield
Marshfield won 3-1 on penalties.		
Tiger Bay	3-2	Trefelin
Waterloo Rovers	2-1	Llanuwchllyn

Second Round

Afan Lido	4-1	Marshfield
Albion Rovers	0-2	Undy Athletic
Played at Undy.		
Ammanford	2-3	Cardiff Metropolitan
Brickfield Rangers	1-2	Llanrhaeadr
Briton Ferry Llansawel	5-1	Aberdare Town
Buckley Town	6-0	Waterloo Rovers
Caernarfon Town	1-0	Guilsfield
Conwy Borough	5-0	Denbigh Town
Cornelly United	1-5	Goytre United
Cwmbran Celtic	0-2	Caerau Ely
Dynamo Aber	2-3	Tiger Bay
FC Nomads of Connah's Quay	5-2	Llangollen Town
Gresford Athletic	2-1	Llanfair United
Haverfordwest County	2-1	Rhayader Town
Llanberis	0-3	Caersws FC
Llanidloes Town	0-2	Penrhyncoch
Mold Alexandra	0-1	Holywell Town
Monmouth Town	3-1	Penybont
Risca United	1-2	Garden Village
St Asaph City	1-0	Meliden

Third Round

Afan Lido	0-3	Llanrhaeadr
Airbus UK Broughton	5-0	Haverfordwest County
Bala Town	2-1	Port Talbot Town
Bangor City	1-0	Garden Village
Buckley Town	0-1	Holywell Town
Caernarfon Town	2-3	The New Saints
Cardiff Met University	4-1	Prestatyn Town
Cefn Druids	1-5	Aberystwyth Town
Conwy Borough	4-3	Briton Ferry Llansawel
Gap Connah's Quay	5-3	Monmouth Town
Gresford Athletic	5-0	St Asaph City
Newtown AFC	2-0	FC Nomads of Connah's Quay
Penrhyncoch	0-3	Caerau Ely
Rhyl FC	2-1	Goytre United
Tiger Bay	0-4	Caersws FC
Undy Athletic	2-4	Carmarthen Town

Fourth Round

Bangor City	3-0	Conwy Borough
Caerau Ely	0-4 (aet)	Carmarthen Town
Caersws FC	2-3	Newtown AFC
Cardiff Met University	1-4	Airbus UK Broughton
Gap Connah's Quay	2-2 (aet)	Bala Town
Gap Connah's Quay won 3-2 on penalties.		

Holywell Town	0-0 (aet)	Aberystwyth Town
Aberystwyth Town won 4-2 on penalties.		
Llanrhaeadr Ym Mochnant	2-4	Rhyl FC
TNS	3-0	Gresford Athletic

Quarter-finals

Aberystwyth Town	1-1 (aet)	Airbus UK Broughton
Airbus UK Broughton won 4-2 on penalties.		
Bangor City	1-2	Newtown AFC
Carmarthen Town	1-2	Rhyl FC
Gap Connah's Quay	0-1	The New Saints

Semi-finals

Airbus UK Broughton	2-4	The New Saints
Played at Latham Park, Newtown		
Newtown AFC	2-1	Rhyl FC
Played at The Rock Stadium, Rhosymedre		

2015 WELSH CUP FINAL

Played at Latham Park, Newtown

Newtown AFC	0-2	The New Saints
		Matty Williams 53', 84' (pen)

Newtown: Dave Jones, Craig Williams, Steff Edwards, Matty Owen, Kieran Mills-Evans, Shane Sutton, Tom Goodwin, Matthew Cook (Matthew Hearsey 89') Luke Boundford, Jason Oswell, Neil Mitchell (Sean Evans 78'). Subs not used: Max Penk, Jack Perry, Jamie Price

The New Saints: Paul Harrison, Simon Spender, Chris Marriott, Phil Baker, Connell Rawlinson (Chris Seargeant 10'), Kai Edwards, Matty Williams, Jamie Mullan, Aeron Edwards, Mike Wilde (Greg Draper 87'), Adrian Cieslewicz (Scott Quigley 71'). Subs not used: Jamie Reed, Chris Mullock

Referee: Dean John

Attendance: 1,579

2015/16 Welsh Cup

First Round

Aberaeron	0-1	Brecon Corries
Aberffraw	0-5	Penrhyncoch
Afan Lido	5-1	AFC Butetown
Briton Ferry Llansawel	2-3	Barry Town United
Caerau Ely	4-0	Undy Athletic
Caerleon	2-1 (aet)	Treharris Athletic Western
Caersws FC	1-6	Llandudno Junction
Cambrian & Clydach	3-0	AFC Llwydcoed
Carno	0-4	Flint Town United
Cefn Druids	4-0	Gresford Athletic

Chirk AAA	5-0	Prestatyn Sports
Conwy Borough	5-3	Cefn Albion
Corwen	2-3	Prestatyn Town
Cwmamman United	2-1	Taff's Well
Cwmbach Royal Stars	0-3	Aberdare Town
Dinas Powys	4-1	Cwmbran Town
Dyffryn Nanttle Vale	1-2	Knighton Town
FC Nomads of Connah's Quay	1-3	Denbigh Town
Garden Village	2-1	Rhayader Town
Goytre	2-0	Llantwit Major
Goytre United	4-2 (aet)	Monmouth Town
Guilsfield Athletic	4-2 (aet)	Glantraeth
Gwalchmai	0-3	Mold Alexandra
Hawarden Rangers	0-4	Llanfair United
Holyhead Hotspur	8-0	Pentraeth
Llandrindod Wells	0-3	Cwmbran Celtic
Llanelli Town	6-3	Panteg
Llanrug United	2-3 (aet)	Caernarfon Town
Llantwit Fardre	0-1	Cardiff Metropolitan University
Penmaenmawr Phoenix	0-1	Buckley Town
Penrhyndeudraeth	2-0	FC Queens Park
Pontypridd Town	0-2	Penybont
Porthmadog FC	3-1	Bow Street
Rhostyllen	2-1	Berriew
Risca United	2-3	Aberbargoed Buds
RTB Ebbw Vale	1-1 (aet)	Caldicot Town
Caldicot Town won 5-4 on penalties.		
Ruthin Town	0-1	Holywell Town
Ton Pentre	0-4	STM Sports
Treowen Stars	2-3	West End
Waterloo Rovers	1-7	Trearddur Bay United

Second Round

Afan Lido	2-0	Caerleon
Barry Town	7-2	Aberdare Town
Brecon Corries	3-0	Aberbargoed Buds
Caernarfon Town	4-0	Llandudno Junction
Cardiff Met University	4-2	Penybont
Cefn Druids	2-0	Porthmadog
Cwmamman United	4-2	Caldicot Town
Denbigh Town	4-1	Conwy Borough
Garden Village	1-4	STM Sports
Goytre	4-1	Dinas Powys
Goytre United	1-4	Caerau Ely
Guilsfield	3-2	Penrhyndeudraeth
Holyhead Hotspur	4-0	Chirk AAA
Holywell Town	6-3	Knighton Town
Llanelli Town	0-2	Cambrian & Clydach
Llanfair United	3-5	Prestatyn Town
Mold Alexandra	0-1	Buckley Town
Penrhyncoch	4-0	Trearddur Bay United
Rhostyllen	0-2	Flint Town United
West End	2-3	Cwmbran Celtic

Third Round

Afan Lido	1-0	Holywell Town
Barry Town United	6-1	Denbigh Town
Caerau Ely	4-0	Brecon Corries
Cardiff Met University	2-0	STM Sports
Carmarthen Town	1-3	Bala Town
Cefn Druids	1-0 (aet)	Rhyl FC
Flint Town United	0-2	Newtown AFC
Goytre FC	4-2	Caernarfon Town
Guilsfield	3-0	Cwmamman United
Haverfordwest County	0-2	Airbus UK Broughton
Holyhead Hotspur	2-1	Bangor City
Llandudno FC	0-0 (aet)	Buckley Town
Buckley Town won 4-3 on penalties.		
Penrhyncoch	2-3	Cwmbran Celtic
Port Talbot Town	2-1 (aet)	Cambrian & Clydach
Prestatyn Town	0-3	Gap Connah's Quay
The New Saints	3-0	Aberystwyth Town

Fourth Round

Afan Lido	0-2	Cardiff Met University
Airbus UK Broughton	3-0	Guilsfield
Barry Town United	2-5	The New Saints
Cwmbran Celtic	5-3	Goytre FC
Gap Connah's Quay	4-1	Buckley Town
Holyhead Hotspur	1-3	Bala Town
Newtown AFC	6-0	Cefn Druids
Port Talbot Town	3-0	Caerau Ely

Quarter-finals

Airbus UK Broughton	3-0	Bala Town
Cardiff Met University	0-2	Gap Connah's Quay
Cwmbran Celtic	1-2	Port Talbot Town
The New Saints	1-0	Newtown AFC

Semi-finals

Port Talbot Town	0-7	Airbus UK Broughton
Played at Latham Park, Newtown		
The New Saints	5-0	Gap Connah's Quay
Played at Latham Park, Newtown		

2016 WELSH CUP FINAL

Played at the Racecourse Ground, Wrexham

The New Saints   2-0   Airbus UK Broughton

Ryan Brobbel 33', Scott Quigley 51'

The New Saints: Paul Harrison, Simon Spender, Chris Marriott, Kai Edwards, Chris Seargeant (Phil Baker 66'), Ryan Brobbel, Matty Williams (Mike Wilde 46'), Connell Rawlinson, Adrian Cieslewicz, Scott Quigley, Aeron Edwards. Subs not used: Chris Mullock, Greg Draper, Ryan Price.

Airbus UK: James Coates, Mike Pearson, Ian Kearney, Chris Budrys, Tony Gray, Ryan Wignall, Ashley Williams, James Owen (Jordan Barrow 61'), Matty McGinn (Bailey Jackson 60'), Lee Owens, James Murphy (Ryan Fraughan 81'). Subs not used: Liam Blake, Kevin Monteiro.

Referee: Bryn Markham-Jones

Attendance: 1,402

2016/17 Welsh Cup

First Round

Aberaeron	1-4	Caldicot Town
Aberbargoed Buds	0-5	Barry Town United
Abergele	0-2	Llanrug United
Afan Lido	4-1	Pontyclun
Barmouth & Dyffryn	0-2	Buckley Town
Bridgend Street	2-2 (aet)	Goytre FC

Goytre FC won 5-4 on penalties.

Cambrian & Clydach	1-3	Trefelin BGC
Coedpoeth United	0-8	Holywell Town
Conwy Borough	1-5	Caernarfon Town
Croesyceiliog	1-1 (aet)	Goytre United

Goytre United won 4-2 on penalties.

Cwmamman United	2-0	Caerau
Dyffryn Nantlle Vale	0-3	Holyhead Hotspur
Flint Town United	6-0	Penycae
Glantraeth	3-5	Mynydd Llandegai
Greenfield	3-2	Llandudno Albion
Gresford Athletic	3-0	Denbigh Town
Guilsfield	6-3	Welshpool Town
Hawarden Rangers	2-1	Carno
Lex Glyndwr	1-2	Corwen
Llangefni Town	4-0	Brymbo
Llanidloes Town	0-2	Llanfair United
Llanrhaeadr Ym Mochnant	5-3	Prestatyn Sports
Llanuwchllyn	0-3	Ruthin Town
Merthyr Saints	2-3	Llandrindod Wells
Mold Alexandra	4-0	Llanberis
Monmouth Town	1-0	Brecon Corries
Newport YMCA	1-2	Haverfordwest County
Penrhyncoch	2-0	FC Nomads of Connah's Quay
Penybont	3-1	AFC Porth
Pontardawe Town	1-0	Cwmbran Celtic
Porthmadog	4-0	Caersws
Rhayader Town	4-3	Caerau Ely
RTB Ebbw Vale	1-2	Ynysygerwn
St Asaph City	0-8	Prestatyn Town
Sully Sports	2-6	Llantwit Major
Taff's Well	0-0 (aet)	Port Talbot Town

Taff's Well won 5-3 on penalties.

Ton Pentre	4-2	Abergavenny Town
Treowen Stars	4-1	Risca United
Trethomas Bluebirds	0-6	Llanelli Town
Undy Athletic	3-0	Blaenrhondda

Second Round

Afan Lido	1-0	Pontardawe Town
Barry Town United	0-3	Penybont
Buckley Town	1-6	Corwen
Caldicot Town	2-0	Cwmamman United
Flint Town United	3-4	Llanfair United
Haverfordwest County	3-2	Undy Athletic
Hawarden Rangers	1-4	Prestatyn Town
Holyhead Hotspur	2-1 (aet)	Llanrug United
Holywell Town	6-0	Llanrhaeadr Ym Mochnant
Llangefni Town	4-4 (aet)	Caernarfon Town

Caernarfon Town won 4-3 on penalties.

Llantwit Major	1-0	Llandrindod Wells
Mold Alexandra	2-4 (aet)	Guilsfield
Mynydd Llandegai	0-3	Greenfield
Penrhyncoch	3-0	Ruthin Town
Porthmadog	2-2 (aet)	Gresford Athletic

Porthmadog won 3-1 on penalties.

Rhayader Town	1-2	Goytre
Taff's Well	2-3	Llanelli Town
Trefelin	0-1	Goytre United
Treowen Stars	1-2	Ton Pentre
Ynysygerwn	7-3	Monmouth Town

Third Round

Aberystwyth Town	2-0	Holywell Town
Bala Town	6-1	Caldicot Town
Caernarfon Town	3-1	Carmarthen Town
Cardiff Met	4-0	Porthmadog
Cefn Druids	2-0	Llantwit Major
Gap Connah's Quay	3-2	Goytre United
Greenfield	0-3	Guilsfield
Haverfordwest County	1-0	Afan Lido
Llandudno FC	0-2	Goytre FC
Llanelli Town	5-1	Ynysygerwn
Llanfair United	1-0	Corwen
Newtown AFC	0-3	The New Saints
Penybont FC	4-1	Airbus UK Broughton
Prestatyn Town	2-1 (aet)	Holyhead Hotspur
Rhyl FC	6-0	Penrhyncoch
Ton Pentre	0-2	Bangor City

Goytre FC were removed from the competition for a breach of the rules.

Fourth Round

Aberystwyth Town	1-5	Prestatyn Town
Bala Town	4-1 (aet)	Penybont
Bangor City	4-0	Llandudno FC
Caernarfon Town	3-2 (aet)	Rhyl FC
Guilsfield FC	4-2	Cardiff Met
Haverfordwest County	1-5	Gap Connah's Quay
Llanfair United	4-1	Cefn Druids
The New Saints	7-0	Llanelli Town

Quarter-finals

Guilsfield	0-3	Bala Town
Llanfair United	0-7	Caernarfon Town
Prestatyn Town	2-2 (aet)	Gap Connah's Quay

Gap Connah's Quay won 4-3 on penalties.

The New Saints	2-1 (aet)	Bangor City

Semi-finals

Caernarfon Town	1-3	Bala Town

Played at Corbett Sports Stadium, Rhyl

Gap Connah's Quay	0-3	The New Saints

Played at Bangor University Stadium

2017 WELSH CUP FINAL

Played at Nantporth, Bangor

Bala Town	2-1	The New Saints
Jordan Evans 77', Kieran Smith 85'		*Greg Draper 56'*

Bala Town: Ashley Morris, Anthony Stephens, Stuart Jones, Stuart J.Jones, Ian Sheridan (Ryan Wade 71'), Kieran Smith, Lee Hunt (Jordan Evans 65'), Chris Venables, John Irving, David Thompson, Nathan Burke. Subs not used: Ryan Valentine, Mark Connolly, Ryan Goldston.

The New Saints: Paul Harrison, Simon Spender, Chris Marriott, Jon Routledge, Ryan Brobbel (Alex Darlington 88'), Greg Draper (Scott Quigley 74'), Jamie Mullan (Chris Seargeant 88'), Steve Saunders, Connell Rawlinson, Adrian Cieslewicz, Aeron Edwards. Subs not used: Ryan Pryce, Andrew Wycherley.

Referee: Huw Jones

Attendance: 1,110

2017/18 Welsh Cup

First Round

Aberdare Town	0-0 (aet)	Ammanford
Ammanford won 3-2 on penalties.		
Caersws walkover to the next round		
Conwy Borough	5-1	Bodedern Athletic
Aberbargoed Buds	2-0	Port Talbot Town
STM Sports	5-2	Afan Lido
Caldicot Town	2-3	Goytre
Porthmadog	3-0	Penyffordd
Garden Village	3-4	Penrhyncoch
Brickfield Rangers	1-0	Chirk AAA
Mochdre Sports	1-1 (aet)	FC Penley
FC Penley won 5-3 on penalties.		
Pontypridd Town	2-1 (aet)	Cambrian & Clydach
Llay Welfare	1-0	Llanrug United
Buckley Town	2-1	Llanidloes Town
Gaerwen	1-3	Llandudno Junction
Haverfordwest County	2-1	Croesyceiliog
Guilsfield	4-0	Mold Alexandra
Llandudno Albion	3-2	Rhyl
Cwmamman United	3-1	Rhayader Town
Carno	0-4	Gresford Athletic
Bridgend Street	4-3	Machen
Cardiff Draconians	1-2	Ton Pentre
Llanrhaeadr	3-0	FC Queens Park
Caerau (Ely)	0-1	Cwmbran Celtic
Briton Ferry Llansawel	3-1	Goytre United
Abergavenny Town	1-3	Panteg
Denbigh Town	4-3	Holyhead Hotspur
Aberaeron	1-6	Llanelli Town
Flint Town United	3-0	Llanfair United
Cardiff Corinthians	0-4	Penydarren
Monmouth Town	4-1	Ynysygerwn
Abermule	0-4	Berriew
Saltney Town	6-0	Llanrwst United
Caerphilly Athletic	4-1 (aet)	Carmarthen Stars
Caernarfon Town	5-1	Lex XI
Llantwit Major	3-2	Taff's Well
Meliden	0-4	Ruthin Town
Pontyclun	0-0 (aet)	Pencoed Athletic
Pencoed Athletic won 8-7 on penalties.		
Holywell Town	3-0	Corwen
Pen-y-Bont	1-0 (aet)	Undy Athletic
Airbus UK Broughton	3-0	Bow Street

Second Round

Goytre	2-1	Briton Ferry Llansawel
Haverfordwest County	2-0	Aberbargoed Buds
Airbus UK Broughton	4-0	Saltney Town
Pen-y-Bont	2-1	Monmouth Town
Brickfield Rangers	2-3 (aet)	Ruthin Town
Buckley Town	2-1	Llandudno Albion
Ton Pentre	1-2	Panteg
Caernarfon Town	4-1	Berriew
Caersws	1-2	Llanrhaeadr
Porthmadog	10-0	F.C. Penley
Gresford Athletic	5-1	Conwy Borough
Holywell Town	2-3	Guilsfield
Llay Welfare	1-3	Flint Town United
Ammanford	1-1 (aet)	Llantwit Major
Ammanford won 3-2 on penalties.		
Caerphilly Athletic	2-4	Penrhyncoch
Cwmamman United	3-0	Bridgend Street
Cwmbran Celtic	2-1	Llanelli Town
Pencoed Athletic	1-3	Pontypridd Town
Penydarren	2-1	STM Sports
Llandudno Junction	3-2 (aet)	Denbigh Town

Third Round

The New Saints	6-0	Penrhyncoch
Llandudno	4-0	Gresford Athletic
Newtown	2-0	Guilsfield
Llandudno Junction	0-4	Penydarren
Pontypridd Town	3-1	Haverfordwest County
Ammanford	2-3	Carmarthen Town
Buckley Town	0-1	Flint Town United
Pen-y-Bont	1-3	Cardiff Met University
Bangor City	4-3	Cwmamman United
Aberystwyth Town	4-0	Bala Town
Prestatyn Town	0-3	Ruthin Town
Llanrhaeadr	3-2	Cefn Druids
Connah's Quay Nomads	3-0	Cwmbran Celtic
Porthmadog	7-2	Panteg
Airbus UK Broughton	3-2 (aet)	Goytre
Caernarfon Town	2-0	Barry Town United

Fourth Round

Caernarfon Town	1-3	The New Saints
Llanrhaeadr	2-3	Bangor City
Pontypridd Town	1-2	Penydarren
Flint Town United	2-2 (aet)	Newtown

Newtown won 4-3 on penalties.

Connah's Quay Nomads	3-1	Porthmadog
Cardiff Met University	0-1	Aberystwyth Town
Llandudno	4-3 (aet)	Ruthin Town
Airbus UK Broughton	1-4	Carmarthen Town

Quarter-finals

Bangor City	7-0	Penydarren
Connah's Quay Nomads	2-1	The New Saints
Carmarthen Town	1-3	Aberystwyth Town
Llandudno	0-2	Newtown

Semi-finals

Connah's Quay Nomads	6-1	Bangor City
Newtown	1-2	Aberystwyth Town

2018 WELSH CUP FINAL

Played at Latham Park, Newtown

Aberystwyth Town	1-4	Connah's Quay Nomads

Ryan Wade 45'
Michael Bakare 23',
Michael Wilde 26', 40',
Andy Owens 90'

Aberystwyth Town: John Owen, Ashley Young, Tom Owens (Craig Hobson 57'), Malcolm Melvin, Ryan Wollacott, Ryan Wade (Kurt Sherlock 70'), Matthew Jones, Declan Walker, Damien Allen, Chris Mullock, Joe Phillips (Geoff Kellaway 78'). Subs not used: Samuel Kersch, Jack Rimmer.

Connah's Quay Nomads: Danny Harrison, James Owen, John Danby, Ryan Wignall (Nathan Woolfe 78'), Michael Wilde (Andy Owens 73'), George Horan, Michael Bakare, Kai Edwards, Declan Poole (Rob Hughes 90'), Mike Pearson, Sean Smith. Subs not used: John Rushton, Jonny Spittle.

Referee: Iwan Griffith

Attendance: 1,455

2018/19 Welsh Cup

First Round

Llandudno Amateurs	2-4 (aet)	Dyffryn Nantlle Vale
Cwmamman United FC	4-0	Dinas Powys
Penycae FC	0-4	Airbus UK Broughton
West End FC	0-6	Caldicot Town FC
Bangor City	4-2	Mold Alexandra
Garden Village	1-2	Blaenrhondda FC
Panteg FC	1-3	Penybont FC
Conwy Borough	1-2	Rhyl FC
Cwmbran Celtic FC	3-0	Ammanford AFC
Gresford Athletic FC	4-3 (aet)	Brickfield Rangers FC
Llangefni Town FC	2-0	Borth United
STM Sports	1-2	Haverfordwest County
Llandrindod Wells	1-1 (aet)	Aberbargoed Buds FC
Llanidloes Town	1-2	Pontypridd Town
Prestatyn Town	5-1	New Brighton Villa
Cambrian & Clydach BGC	5-0	Port Talbot Town FC
Treharris Western Athletic	3-2	Cornelly United FC
Guilsfield FC	2-0	Rhostyllen FC
Radnor Valley	1-2	Goytre FC
Undy Athletic	3-4	Monmouth Town FC
Llanrhaeadr Ym Mochnant	1-2	Flint Town United
Cwmbran Town	3-2	Afan Lido
Buckley Town	3-1	Brymbo FC
Coedpoeth United	2-3	Ruthin Town FC
Ton Pentre AFC	3-1	Pencoed Ath. Amateur
Berriew FC	2-2	Penrhyncoch

Berriew won 5-4 on penalties.

Pwllheli	0-3	Porthmadog
Pontyclun FC	3-1	Llantwit Major
Caersws FC	3-2 (aet)	Holywell Town FC
Hawarden Rangers FC	2-3	Llanfair United
Trefelin BGC	1-2	Swansea University FC
Llay Welfare FC	2-0	Rhydymwyn FC
Denbigh Town FC	9-3	Holyhead Town FC
Ynysddu Welfare	2-1	Taffs Well FC
Sully Sports FC	3-1	Brecon Corries
Holyhead Hotspurs FC	4-2	Corwen
Briton Ferry Llansawel	1-0	Caerau Ely FC
Llandudno Albion	3-4 (aet)	St. Asaph City FC
Cefn Albion Amateur FC	7-1	Dolgellau Athletic
Penlan FC	0-1	Goytre United

Second Round

Aberbargoed Buds	0-2	Pen-y-Bont
Cwmmamman United	2-1	Blaenrhondda
Buckley Town	1-3	Denbigh Town
Flint Town United	3-2	Gresford Athletic
Guilsfield	4-3	Nantlle Vale
Holyhead Hotspur	3-1	Ruthin Town
Llangefni Town	5-1	St. Asaph City
Prestatyn Town	6-3	Berriew
Rhyl	3-1	Caersws
Goytre United	1-0	Pontyclun
Haverfordwest County	4-3	Swansea University
Airbus UK Broughton	9-1	Llay Welfare
Bangor City	6-1	Cefn Albion

Pontypridd Town	6-3	Goytre United
Treharris Athletic Western	3-4	Briton Ferry Llansawel
Sully Sports	1-3	Cwmbran Celtic
Llanfair United	1-4	Porthmadog
Cwmbrân Town	1-2	Ton Pentre
Monmouth Town	1-3	Ynysddu Welfare
Caldicot Town	2-3	Cambrian & Clydach

Third Round

Prestatyn Town	0-3	Caernarfon Town
Barry Town	4-1	Pen-y-Bont
Bangor City	4-1	Holyhead
Cwmbran Celtic	0-3	The New Saints
Cwmamman United	3-4	Aberystwyth Town
Newtown	1-2	Rhyl
Llangefni Town	1-0	Llanelli Town
Ynysddu Welfare	1-3	Cefn Druids
Goytre United	0-3	Carmarthen Town
Ton Pentre	1-4	Cardiff Met University
Haverfordwest County	3-0	Pontypridd Town
Airbus UK Broughton	1-1 (aet)	Porthmadog
Airbus UK Broughton won 4-2 on penalties.		
Denbigh Town	1-2	Cambrian & Clydach
Guilsfield	2-4	Connah's Quay Nomads
Briton Ferry	2-3	Llandudno Town
Flint Town United	0-3	Bala Town

Fourth round

Carmarthen Town	1-3	Connah's Quay Nomads
Haverfordwest County	0-4 (aet)	Bala Town
Bangor City	1-2	Caernarfon Town
Barry Town United	3-2	Cefn Druids
Airbus UK Broughton	2-5	The New Saints
Cambrian & Clydach Vale	1-1 (aet)	Rhyl
Cambrian & Clydach Vale won 5-4 on penalties.		
Aberystwyth Town	1-3	Cardiff Met University
Llangefni Town	1-3	Llandudno

Quarter-finals

Caernarfon Town	1-2	Connah's Quay Nomads
Barry Town United	3-2	Cambrian & Clydach Vale
Bala Town	0-1	Cardiff Metropolitan University
Llandudno	1-8	The New Saints

Semi-finals

The New Saints	2-0	Barry Town United
Cardiff Met University	0-3	Connah's Quay Nomads

2019 WELSH CUP FINAL

Played at The Rock, Rhosymedre

Connah's Quay Nomads 0-3 The New Saints

Greg Draper 7',
Ryan Brobbel 33', 61'

Connah's Quay Nomads: John Danby, John Disney, George Horan, Danny Harrison, Callum Morris, Michael Wilde, Declan Poole, Danny Holmes, Jay Owen (Adam Barton 87'), Michael Bakare (Ryan Wignall 46'), Jamie Insall (Andy Owens 69'). Subs not used: Lewis Brass, Rob Hughes

The New Saints: Paul Harrison, Chris Marriott (Joash Nembhard 60'), Blaine Hudson, Jack Bodenham, Jon Routledge, Ryan Brobbel, Greg Draper (Dean Ebbe 81'), Danny Redmond, Adrian Cieslewicz, Jamie Mullan, Kane Lewis (Simon Spender 74'). Subs not used: Connor Roberts, Kurtis Byrne

Referee: David Morgan

Attendance: 1,256